Kim

TABLE OF CONTENTS

8 Preface

Chapter 1
10 Early Life

Chapter 2
36 Cars and Planes – Learning the Trade

Chapter 3
58 The Man Behind the Name – William Morris

Chapter 4
76 Making a Marque

Chapter 5
108 Becoming Established

Chapter 6
126 Building a Range – and Discovering Devon

Chapter 7
146 The Move to Abingdon

Chapter 8
170 Sailing, Racing and a New Six-cylinder Car

Chapter 9
188 Technical Advances but a Marriage in Retreat

Chapter 10
208 Success in the Mille Miglia

Chapter 11
232 Cowley takes Charge

Chapter 12
254 Goodbye to Motor Racing

Chapter 13
274 Reconstruction and Disintegration

Chapter 14
296 A Marriage Ends, a New Car Arrives

Chapter 15
324 Record-breaking in Germany – and a Life Renewed

Chapter 16	**Appendix 2**
352 Sunshine Before the Storm	**438** 'The Trend of Aesthetic Design in Motor Cars'
Chapter 17	**Appendix 3**
372 War on Two Fronts	**460** Cecil Kimber on Sports Cars
Chapter 18	**Appendix 4**
386 Victim of the Snakepit	**472** 'Making Modest Production Pay in Motor-Car Manufacture'
Chapter 19	**Appendix 5**
396 Starting Out Again	**478** Cecil Kimber on Motor Racing
Chapter 20	**Appendix 6**
410 Conversations with the Tractor King	**496** M.G. after Kimber
Chapter 21	**Postscript**
420 The Death of Cecil Kimber	**520** When should the M.G. Centenary be Celebrated?
428 In Closing	
	524 Acknowledgements
Epilogue	**525** Bibliography
430 The Kimber Family after 1945	**526** Index – and a Selection of Memorabilia
Appendix 1	
436 M.G. Car Company Accounts, 1930-35	

CECIL KIMBER, 1888-1945

'Kimber organised himself very well; he was very unflappable – he really was. He was a wonderful chap with people, a wonderful outgoing man. He was quite an enigma; he wasn't an engineer; he wasn't a salesman; he wasn't an accountant; but he was a great personality with a great ability of picking out schemes that were put to him – and he knew what to chuck out and what to use.'

George Tuck, former M.G. publicity man

'Kim built a great team and I was privileged to carry on more or less where he left off. None of those he picked could be said to be overburdened with formal education, but they succeeded by the application of innate common sense and an ability, stimulated by love of motor sport and the challenge of the times, to learn as they went along.'

John Thornley, Motor *13 December 1969*

'My stepmother once said, quite vehemently for her, "Of course he was ruthless. M.G.s were his baby." However, his secretary, Miss Wakelin, who was with him for years, told me he was certainly not a tyrant, but that he never thought about anything else than M.G.s.'

Jean Kimber Cook, The Other Tack

'You are quite right in thinking that he had a very complex personality. In some ways he was quite ruthless and uncompromising, but in others there was a very kindly streak. Above all, he had an enormous enthusiasm, and this, I think, produced the uncompromising ruthlessness which could make him a distinctly prickly personality at times. We on *The Light Car* used to regard him with an odd mixture of affection and respect, coupled with a measure of apprehension as to what he would find to grumble at next!'

Journalist Harold Hastings, quoted by Wilson McComb

'I admired Kimber for what he did. He had the imagination and drive to start it all. He was a visionary, and he had the ability to instil his enthusiasm into others – take those things together and that's enough, really.'

John Thornley, quoted by Wilson McComb

'At any rate I have the satisfaction of having created a car that has given lots of fun and pleasure to thousands and of leaving behind me a factory operating more efficiently and more profitably than ever before.'

Cecil Kimber, after his dismissal, to M.G. specialist Edward Lund

PREFACE

In the year in which the centenary of M.G. is celebrated, it seems appropriate to look at the history of the marque through a fresh optic, and explore the life of the man who was behind its creation. There would have been no M.G. without Cecil Kimber. But in common with many industrialists and businessmen, the story of the person has tended to take second place to recounting the history of the enterprise he ran: there are many books about M.G. and its cars, but little is written about the man who initiated the world's best-known make of sports car.

To redress the balance has been a challenge. In the inter-war years the motor industry, the motoring press and the world of motor sport formed a tightly-knitted coterie. Everyone knew everyone else, and wrote about their friends in glowing terms that did not always reflect the real nature of the person so casually placed on a pedestal. At the same time family life, with its emotional ups and downs, was treated with more reticence than is the case today. Penetrating this twinfold opacity is made more difficult when the subject of the biography is so long dead that virtually everyone who might have known him is also no longer alive, and thus not able to provide testimony. To have been say 15 years old and to have known Cecil Kimber in 1945, the year of his death, would make one 93 years old today.

Happily, Cecil Kimber's younger daughter Jean devoted considerable effort to trying to reconstruct her father's life. She carried out much research, collated albums of family photos, and ultimately wrote a detailed memoir. What she left behind is a precious resource. To a degree, alas, this work is compromised by the extent to which she clearly worshipped Kimber. Further to this, she was a child during the crucial pre-war years, and cannot have had fully-formed first-hand experience of much of what she recounts.

In contrast, her sister Betty – later known as Lisa – fell out with her father and handed down to her children stories that were largely negative. It has not been possible to run to earth the interview with the two daughters that M.G. historian Wilson McComb carried out, or a tape-recording of Lisa's memories, along with an annotated photo album. This is regrettable, but thanks in particular to the recollections of her daughter Sara it has been possible to build up an alternative narrative that is as balanced and complete as possible.

Jean Kimber Cook's memoir, entitled *The Other Tack*, is a key element of *The Cecil Kimber Centenary Book*, edited by Dick Knudson and published in 1988 in the United States by the New England M.G. T Register. The book also contains the memories of Kimber's step-daughter Bobbie Walkinton, a chapter by journalist John Dugdale, and another on Kimber and advertising by M.G. Car Club stalwart Norman Ewing. With the accord of the late Dick Knudson I have drawn extensively on *The Cecil Kimber Centenary Book*, and gladly acknowledge it as an important source, along with a chapter Jean contributed to the 1993 book *The MG Log*, edited by Peter Haining. In recognition of the work Dick Knudson carried out, it feels fitting to dedicate this biography to his memory, with thanks for his support and that of the Register.

Jon Pressnell
Lherm, France
May 2023

SOURCES

The principal written source for this work has been *The Kimber Centenary Book*, edited by Richard Knudson and published by the New England M.G. T Register. I am grateful to the late Dick Knudson for his permission to use this material. Unless stated otherwise, all quotes from Jean Kimber Cook are taken from here, as are the memories of Bobbie Walkinton and John Dugdale.

Quotations from various Morris managers are from the unpublished transcripts of interviews carried out by Philip Andrews and Elizabeth Brunner for their 1955 biography of Lord Nuffield, as held in the London School of Economics archives. The testimony of various former M.G. employees given the attribution 'Cousins/Jarman reminiscences' was collated by Morris author Lytton Jarman with the assistance of Cecil Cousins; previously published by P.L. Jennings in *Early M.G.*, it is not clear whether these memories were originally in oral or written form.

The 1930-35 accounts of the M.G. Car Company were examined when in the custodianship of the Modern Records Centre of the University of Warwick. Other writers have analysed these papers but the conclusions drawn in this book are the author's own.

Books that have been consulted are listed in the bibliography. The author particularly signals his use of Wilson McComb's *M.G. by McComb* and *Oxford to Abingdon* by Robin Barraclough and Phil Jennings, as well as his own book *Morris – The Cars and the Company*.

The greater part of the illustrations for this book are drawn from the collections of the Kimber family, and many were taken by Cecil Kimber himself. Some of the same photos are held by different branches of the family. If an image is not credited, it comes from one or other of the McGavin, Kirkland or Delamont collections. Finally, a large number of photos, including press images in the public domain, have been acquired by the author in the course of 40 years as a journalist and writer.

A WORD ABOUT THOSE DOTS

Throughout this book the initials 'M.G.' are rendered thus. Nomenclature is an important issue in the early history of the marque and during Cecil Kimber's life the two full points were invariably used. After the war their use in corporate advertising was inconsistent. It was only during the 1960s that the full points were definitively excised, at a date the author has not determined; certainly in 1964 they were still in use in advertising and in 1966 *Motor* was still minded to use them in its road test of the MGB GT. Cecil Kimber, asked by his daughter Jean why he insisted on the dots, said "They looked more visually attractive". This is debatable, but in the pages that follow we have voted – through gritted teeth – for pedantry and consistency over typographical elegance and ease of punctuation.

EARLY LIFE

It is thought that the Kimber family originated in Brittany and arrived in England – possibly Cornwall – in the wake of William the Conqueror. The antecedents of Cecil Kimber have been traced back to the early 17th century, and are recorded in *The Descendants*

Edward Kimber (1820-93) was Cecil Kimber's paternal grandfather and was a significant figure in the British printing industry.

OPPOSITE: *The Kimber family, around 1908 to 1909.*

The Kimber family crest, featuring three Cornish choughs – a member of the crow family also known as the red-billed chough. The motto Frangas non flectes *translates as 'Thou mayest break but shall not bend me' and was also used by the recently-disbanded No.5 squadron of the Royal Air Force.*

of Richard Kimber, a small family-published book dating from 1894. Richard Kimber, born 'about 1610', was a modest landowner from Grove, near Wantage, who fought for Cromwell in the English Civil War. His grandson Isaac became a Baptist minister and moved to London in around 1717, where he wrote a life of Oliver Cromwell and a four-volume history of England. Working as a journalist, he edited *The London Magazine* for 23 years. His son Edward, also a journalist, took over the editorship on Isaac's death in 1755, and in

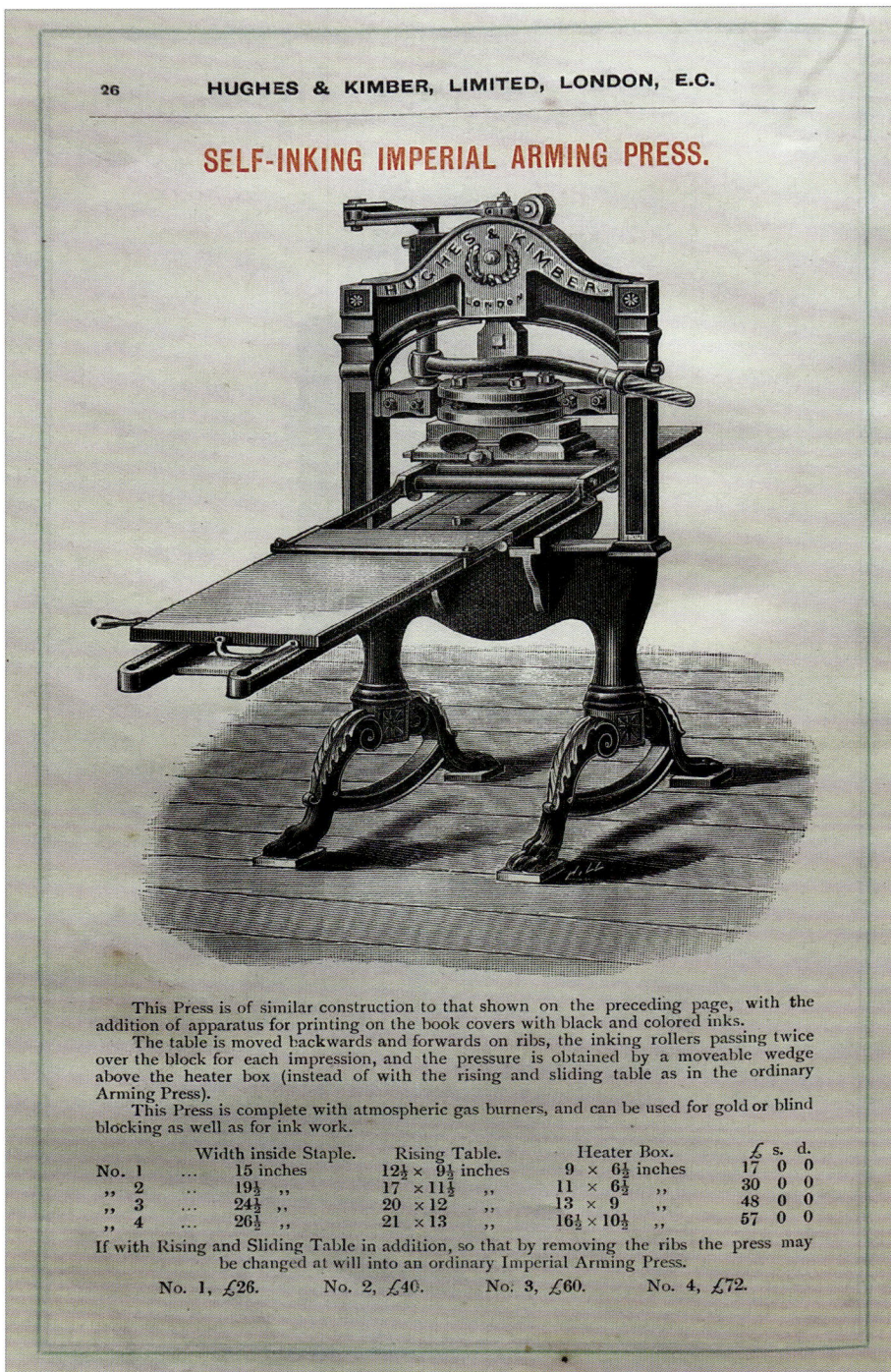

An image from an 1880s Hughes & Kimber catalogue of machinery and materials for bookbinders, showing one of the company's presses. (Trevor Lloyd)

addition helped edit *The Gentleman's Magazine*, as well as producing a guide to the peerage.

The ancestor who set Cecil Kimber's branch of the family on its way as members of the British printing industry is his paternal grandfather Edward, a great-grandson of Isaac Kimber's son Edward. Born in 1820, this third Edward Kimber began his professional life as a clerk for a bookseller[1]. In 1844 he married Sarah Hughes, whose father Richard had pioneered the use of steel plates for engraving, manufacturing these at his printing works in Shoe Lane, off London's Fleet Street. A year after the marriage, Richard Hughes died, and Sarah inherited his business, which Edward Kimber ultimately took over and by 1850 had renamed Hughes & Kimber. He went on to introduce the first machines to print from lithographic stone using steam[2], and acquired the sole rights to import lithographic printing into China. Becoming a Fellow of the Royal Geographical Society and the holder of an honorary doctorate from Rostock University, Edward Kimber is described in *The Descendants of Richard Kimber* as 'an agreeable and intelligent companion, having acquired much knowledge by very considerable reading and travelling, and retaining it by an unusual memory'.

Alas, Edward Kimber's erudition does not seem to have been matched by his commercial acumen, and in 1874 he was subject to liquidation proceedings. A year later Richard Godsell Kimber, the second-born of his ten children, paid £12,750 for most of the business's assets. The newly-constituted Hughes & Kimber Ltd took on directors from outside the family and carried on as manufacturers of machinery and materials for printers. Edward Kimber, who had remained as manager, died in 1893, leaving an estate worth only £55. In a memoir for Wilson McComb, Cecil

---

[1] In the book *The Descendants of Richard Kimber* the bookseller is given as 'W. Smith'. Wilson McComb writes of 'W. H. Smith' – the well-known British chain of booksellers and stationers. This may be correct, or it may be a misunderstanding.

[2] Lithography, a Bavarian invention from the end of the 18th century, originally used a smooth tablet of limestone. In Britain from the mid 19th century the process was commonly employed for the production of maps.

Kimber's brother Vernon would remark that his grandfather Edward had 'made and lost two fortunes'.

Notwithstanding the vicissitudes of the business, the Kimber family gradually increased its shareholding until by 1901 the family held the majority of the shares. Thereafter the ride was a bumpy one. In 1909 the company went into liquidation. It was re-established in 1910, survived the war, and then in 1930 notice was given that the firm would be wound up. However, a successor business, Hughes & Kimber, continued to operate in London until 1940 as a supplier of printer's materials, in premises at 9 Gough Square previously occupied by T. I. Lawrence & Co, whom Hughes & Kimber had acquired in the 1880s.

Working alongside Richard Godsell Kimber in the Hughes & Kimber business was his brother Henry, Cecil Kimber's father. Henry Kimber had been educated at Iver Grammar School in Buckinghamshire[3] and at Heidelberg and Dresden universities

ABOVE: *Henry Kimber was apparently not the most cheerful of men, possibly as a result of suffering continual headaches. 'He had been unable to bear noise all his life, and required absolute tranquillity,' writes his grand-daughter Jean.*

TOP RIGHT: *Fanny Matthewman at the time of her 1887 marriage to Henry Kimber.*

---

[3] This is again according to *The Descendants of Richard Kimber* – McComb says that Henry Kimber was educated at Dulwich College, which is not correct.

in Germany, and had married Fanny Matthewman in 1887, in Huddersfield. Fanny's father Sidney was an accountant at the time of her birth in 1858, and later worked as a representative for United Alkalis, a forerunner of ICI. Cecil Kimber's younger daughter Jean was told by a great-aunt that the family lived at Brooke Hall, in Derbyshire, and that the young Fanny had once ridden her hunter up the steps of the Hall, much to her father's shock. She later came to discount this story, when documentation emerged that in 1890 Sidney and Elizabeth Matthewman were living in Manningham, Bradford, having moved there from Huddersfield.

ART AND THE BICYCLE: KIMBER'S PARENTS

Fanny went to London to study art, conceivably at the Slade[4]. Family legend has it that whilst in London she fell in love with popular novelist Morley Roberts but was pushed by her parents to marry Henry Kimber[5]. Again, this might not be true. Certainly it is difficult to square with the movements of Roberts, an adventurer who spent the years of 1876-79 in Australia working on railways and sheep stations and from 1884 to 1887 was in the United States and Canada. Perhaps, though, the two met in 1887, in which year Roberts had returned to London. If so, it is easy to understand that his travelling life, which included working on a ranch in Texas and at a sawmill in British Columbia, might have made him rather too unconventional a choice to win the approval of Mr and Mrs Matthewman.

---

[4] The Slade School of Fine Art had only recently been established, opening its doors in 1871. It would go on to become Britain's pre-eminent art and design educational institution, with an extensive list of world-famous alumni.

[5] 'None of us would have existed if great-grandmother Frances had not been forced to marry dreary Henry Kimber, but had managed to elope with the love of her life, the novelist Morley Roberts,' comments Jonathan, son of Cecil Kimber's elder daughter Betty.

RIGHT: *Fanny Kimber as a young woman (top)...and a portrait of her a few years later (bottom).*

Whether Henry Kimber was the best husband for their daughter is another matter. Fanny was a talented watercolourist, and according to Jean 'she spent most of her time after her marriage painting' – some of her landscapes surviving in the family. The suggestion is that she painted to escape from a marriage that was far from joyous, and a family life that she did not find fulfilling. Such, at any rate, is the impression of his mother that Cecil Kimber handed down. 'He did... once confess to my stepmother that he felt she was too absorbed with her painting to have much time for her family,' writes Jean, who carried with her for a long while an image of Henry Kimber as 'a disagreeable and gloomy man who did little for his children, apart from providing for them.'

By the time she was contributing to the book *The MG Log*, Jean had arrived at a different view of her grandfather. '[From] odd remarks, and stories told by our mother, we – my older sister, Betty, and I – grew up with the impression that my father had suffered a miserable childhood. His father, Henry Kimber, always referred to as "HK", was tyrannical, gloomy, demanded that children should be seen and not heard, and, most heinous crime of all, would not buy [my father] any rails for his model steam train. Most writers have copied this version from Wilson McComb, who talked to us in the 1960s.'

But this view changed after Jean visited Kimber relatives in New England and was able to see some papers kept by the family of Cecil Kimber's uncle Sydney. 'I learned... that Henry, my grandfather, could not help his gloom and his longing for quiet. As an adventurous young man, he had marketed, with his brother-in-law, ingenious, wheel-mounted luggage carriers for penny-farthing bicycles, but careering along the rough tracks of the New Forest in the 1860s, he crashed. There were no helmets in those days to save him from concussion and a lifetime of blinding headaches.'

Corroboration of this story came from Jean's discovery of a childhood drawing by her father: it was on the back of an advertisement from an 1880 issue of *Bicycling News* for a luggage

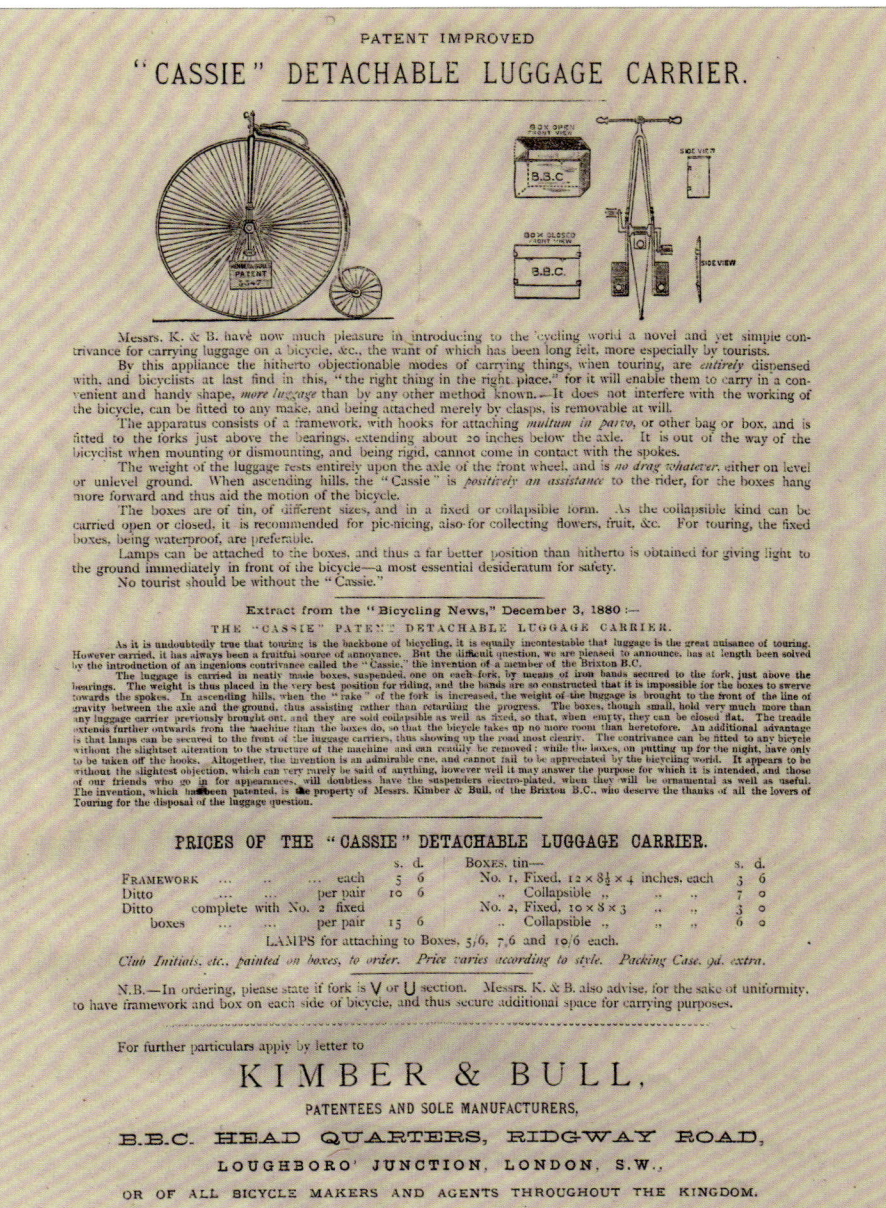

The Cassie carrier for penny-farthing bicycles was marketed by Henry Kimber and his brother-in-law; one imagines that it did not add to the stability of the bicycle.

View of the Interior of the principal Work Shop at the Britannia Iron Works, Bury, Hunts.

carrier patented by Messrs Kimber & Bull, who were members of the Brixton Bicycling Club. 'My father's Aunt Margaret married Wallace Bull, so it looks as if my grandfather helped him invent the "Cassie" luggage carrier.'

A CHESHIRE CHILDHOOD

Cecil Kimber was born on 12 April 1888 in London, his parents then living at 51 Park Road, West Dulwich, where they had started married life. Subsequently the family would move to Merton, near Wimbledon, and then to south London suburb Streatham. Henry Kimber had responsibility for the Hughes & Kimber varnish factory in New Church Road, Mitcham, and may also have been involved with the making of copper and steel printing plates at the company's Britannia Iron Works in Bury, Huntingdonshire. Every year he went to Germany to buy lithographic stone, as his father had done. Meanwhile two of his brothers, Walter and Edward, were running a Manchester-based printing and lithography business under the Kimber Brothers name.

In about 1896, Henry Kimber moved north and opened a printing-ink business with Walter, living first in Oak Avenue, Romiley, a village-turned-suburb just outside Stockport, and then in a large house called Moorfields, in Shaw Road in the Stockport suburb of Heaton Moor.

Cecil Kimber was educated at the old-established Stockport Grammar and Free School. Records show that he entered the school on 17 January 1898, when he was nine years old. As a schoolboy he showed an early interest in drawing and painting and in photography. His first photographs, the negatives of which he carefully stored, labelled and dated, in an adapted school exercise book, are studies of his parents, his brother and sister, Mary the maid, views of historical buildings, and shots of outings to Lytham St Annes – unremarkable childhood photographic fare. In adult life Kimber would remain a keen photographer, with occasional flashes of talent.

Another pastime which he would continue to pursue all his life was

ABOVE: *The house Moorfields, in the Stockport suburb of Heaton Moor, was the second family home of the Kimbers after Henry and Fanny had moved to the Manchester area.*

OPPOSITE: *A view from the 1880s Hughes & Kimber catalogue of the Britannia Iron Works, where Henry Kimber possibly had some managerial role; this cannot be confirmed. (Trevor Lloyd)*

ABOVE: *A copy of the birth certificate of Cecil Kimber, dating from 1925.*

RIGHT: *Cecil Kimber at the age of two or three.*

FAR RIGHT: *Cecil and his sister Phyllis photographed in 1894 or thereabouts.*

sailing. This passion took root during one of the family holidays at Runswick Bay, a fishing village on the Yorkshire coast. An aunt and uncle had given Kimber a German-made toy sailing yacht so badly designed that it would not even float upright. 'Fortunately for me, in the party was a bachelor uncle who did some yachting in the Thames estuary. I have an idea he was rather frowned on by the rest of the family for having such wild tastes,' he would later recount in *The Evolution of a Yachtsman*, a hand-written memoir of his love of sailing. 'How my boyish soul went out to him when he took that boat in hand and we fixed on a lead keel. Then the little ship was re-rigged and the elementary principles of sailing explained. The thrill, after we had toiled up Runswick's one and only precipitous main street, when we launched the little craft on a claypit way back from the cliff top! And the fashioning of a swinging lead rudder when the necessity of some weather helm became apparent, and I came to understand what a rudder really meant in a sailing vessel. That holiday the family rarely saw me. Every available hour I spent sailing that boat across and across that pond. All by myself and perfectly happy. Little did that uncle of mine realise what joy he had brought me.'

It was at Runswick, Kimber relates, that he took the next step in learning about boats, when a local fisherman called Ned Clark

Two photographs showing Cecil (left) and Vernon Kimber as young boys; Vernon was born in 1894, so was six years Cecil's junior.

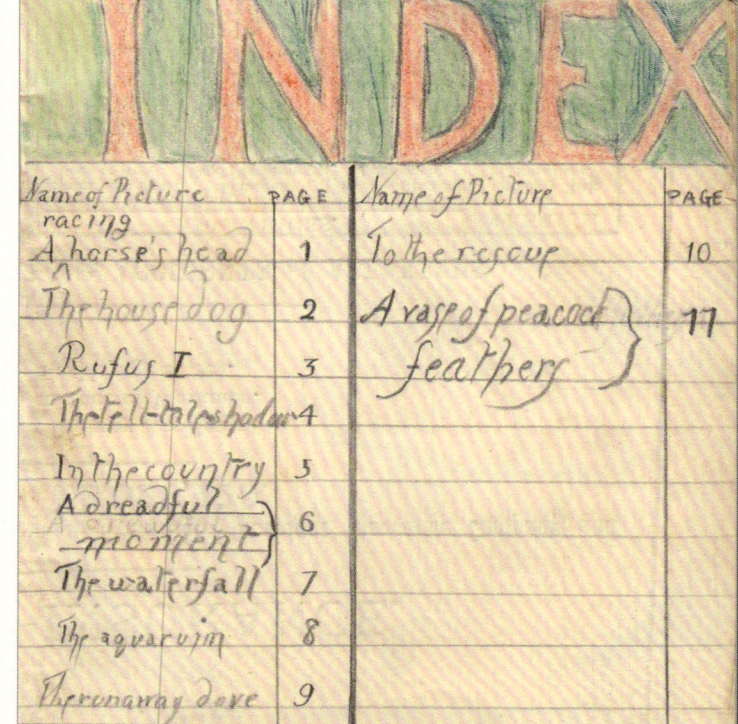

Chapter One: Early Life

THESE TWO PAGES: *Some images and the cover and index from a book of sketches offered to his parents. As a child Cecil Kimber was already cultivating an elegant and precise style of handwriting.*

A pencil sketch by Cecil Kimber of the house and garden at Grappenhall.

taught him to row. 'Through him I learned how to manage those hefty rowing boats they use, with heavy flat-shafted oars carried on stout iron thole pins, and how to beach a boat in a heavy sea. I was too young to be allowed out in a cobble with the fishing fleet but what a marvellous apprenticeship it was.'

When the family holidays shifted to Bridlington, to suit the tastes of his aunts, now young ladies, Kimber was disappointed, he writes. 'How I hated its promenades and no Ned Clark with whom to spend hours out on the sea. At Runswick, I knew everyone, including the many famous artists who were so fond of it.' The change of holiday venue was a brief one, to Kimber's relief, later summer holidays being spent in Wales near Pwllheli, his parents having a cottage in the nearby village of Abererch.

Kimber went out with the Welsh fishermen sometimes for two to three days in a row.

'How well I remember the getting underway at dusk and the cramped quarters with a red-hot stove going and no ventilation, an atmosphere composed of many smells, the predominating ones being defunct fish, tar, thick twist[6] and the human body, all intermingled with an indefinable one that must have been the bilge. How happily I'd roll up an overcoat and sleep on a hard board, waking up in the morning to wolf huge slices of fried fat ham between enormous slices of bread. Then perhaps we would be close to St Tudwal Isle and over the side would go the dinghy;

[6] Traditional full-bodied pipe tobacco hand-spun into a rope form.

loaded until there were only a few inches of freeboard, we would ride against a sluicing tide and troll for pollack,' he recounts in *The Evolution of a Yachtsman*.

At about the time Kimber left school, the family moved to a spacious house in the Cheshire village of Grappenhall. From here the teenaged Cecil – motivated by what he called 'an overpowering attraction towards motorcycles and motor cars in general' – sallied forth on his bicycle. 'During those early years, 1900 onwards, before I even owned a motorcycle, let alone a car, I would cycle miles, and go to any amount of trouble just for the opportunity of seeing a solitary example of the early efforts of the automobile industry, which was then very much in its infancy,'

ABOVE: *A self-assured young Cecil Kimber photographed at Heaton Moor, dressed as many a middle-class English boy of the late Victorian era.*

TOP & MIDDLE RIGHT: *A watercolour for his mother, dated August 1900, and another painting from around the same time.*

RIGHT (BOTH): *Fanny (left) and Phyllis at Sandhills in 1903; the photos were most likely taken by Cecil Kimber.*

ABOVE: *A photograph, kept by Kimber in an annotated album, of a street in the North Yorkshire village of Runswick Bay.*

TOP RIGHT: *Another image from the same album of photos dating from the early 1900s.*

RIGHT: *Here the subject is a threshing machine – or a 'thrashing machine', to use an alternative spelling.*

ABOVE: *Cecil Kimber's sister Phyllis.*

LEFT & INSET: *These two photos show Ned Clark, the Runswick fisherman who befriended Cecil Kimber and taught him to row.*

LEFT: *Fanny Kimber painting – an activity that seemingly provided her with a welcome escape from family life.*

BELOW: *One of Fanny Kimber's paintings. The family still has examples of her work, her paintbox, and a brush clipped for painting trees.*

OPPOSITE: *The Cheshire village of Grappenhall at the turn of the century. Kimber's mother is buried in the churchyard.*

S 2516 GRAPPENHALL VILLAGE, WARRINGTON.

he would tell the Derby Branch of the Institution of Automobile Engineers in an October 1944 talk (see Appendix 3). 'I used to cycle to Dunham Hill, Altrincham – a gentle slope you wouldn't notice on a modern 8hp car – to watch the few motorcycles and cars coming back to Manchester after their Sunday afternoon run. This fearsome acclivity used to test the cooling systems to the utmost, and if in the course of a couple of hours I saw half a dozen I thought my 14-mile pushbike ride well worthwhile.'

Records at Kimber's school say that he left in 'approximately 1903 to go into business'. This tallies with Kimber saying in later life that he joined the family firm, Kimber Brothers, 'just before I turned 15'. Quite how he received a prize for the Cambridge Local Examinations in April 1904 is open to question, as this would seem to suggest that he in fact left the school at a time when he was 16 years old.

Possibly with an eye to the future he enrolled in evening classes in

Cecil Kimber's first motorbike was this single-speed Rex, which he soon dismantled to study its mechanicals.

Manchester. This gave him a useful grounding for his subsequent career, as he told the same audience. 'Compared with many of you here, my early engineering training was of the most sketchy nature. It must be remembered that in the early 1900s the opportunities for technical training in automobile engineering were very scant as compared with the facilities provided today. Evening classes at the Manchester Technical School – taking quite the wrong subjects – helped a bit,' he related. 'Actually, the subject that stood me in the best stead in my later business life was accountancy, and to those of you with your eyes on high administrative posts in the years to come, I would strongly recommend a study of this subject... after all, if you go into business you do it with one object and that is to make money. If you don't make money you won't be in business very long...'

MOTORCYCLING – AND A GRIM ACCIDENT

After two years working for his father, Cecil had saved the £18 he needed to buy his first motorcycle, a 1906 3⅜hp single-speed belt-drive Rex. Within three weeks, according to his brother Vernon, Kimber had the bike in bits to see how it worked, and he discovered that he could save money by doing minor repairs himself. Joining the Warrington and District Motor Cycle Club, he went on runs into Wales with fellow members, gaining the confidence to cover longer distances on the bike – for example a run of 70 miles non-stop from Warrington to Colwyn Bay, as part of a day in which he covered 120 miles. He also made his first foray into journalism when in 1908 he wrote an article for *The Motor Cycle* on his experiences.

In August 1909 Kimber traded up to a 1907 twin-cylinder Rex. He was soon tinkering with his new acquisition, improving its performance by such standard tricks as opening out the ports. His work proved its worth when he won a dawn race against a Warrington enthusiast's Triumph. There is no evidence that he ever raced either motorcycle in formal competitions.

It was in 1910, when he was riding his future brother-in-law Billy Sutton's Rex, that he had a serious accident. Sent on an errand by

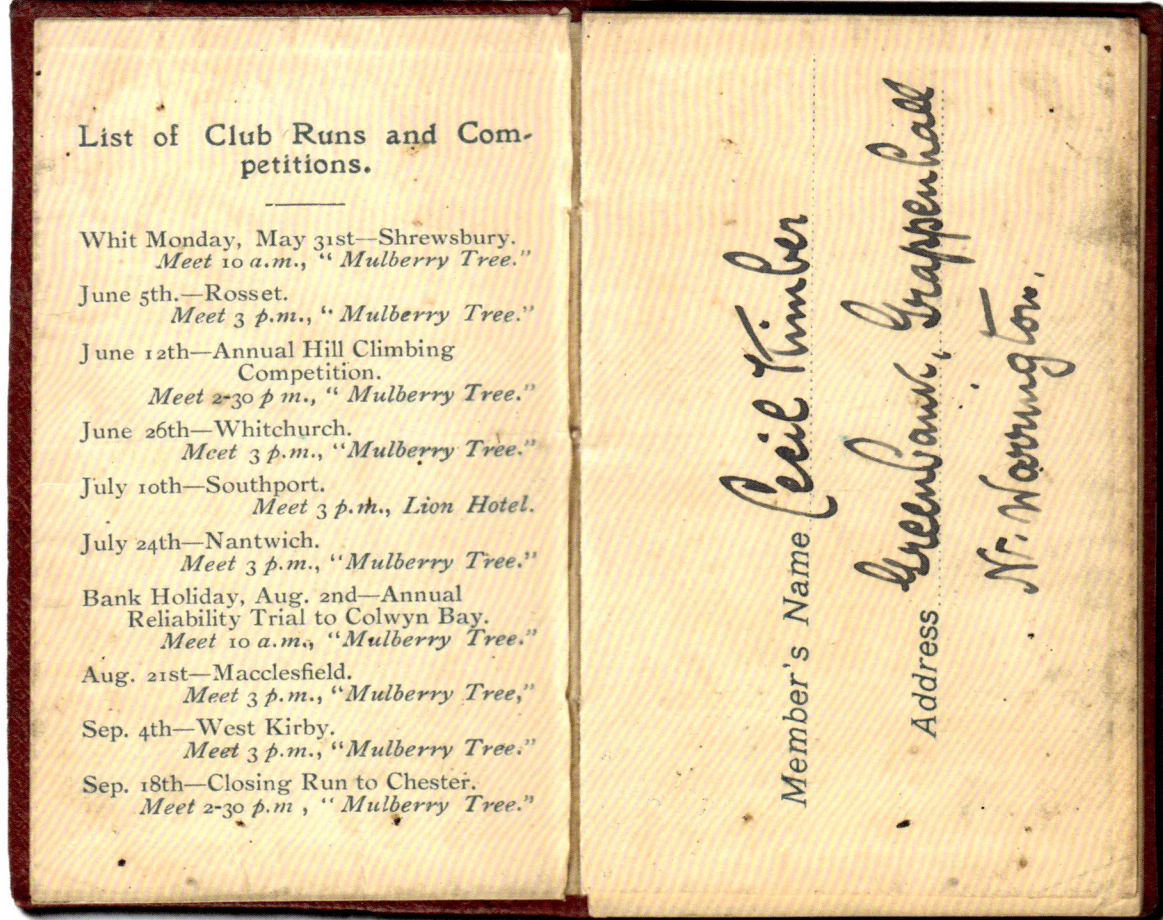

Kimber's membership card for the Warrington and District Motor Cycle Club; the group's outings were an important part of his social life at the time.

ABOVE: *An unknown friend on his bike, photographed around 1910. The impressive-looking device may have been home-built.*

RIGHT & OPPOSITE: *Kimber's second motorcycle, a 1908 twin-cylinder 3½hp Rex, which he describes on the reverse of the photo as being the most comfortable machine he had ever ridden.*

his mother, as a way of avoiding the chore of mowing the lawn, he was hit by an elderly solicitor in a car at Grappenhall crossroads. Kimber's injuries included a broken kneecap and a badly smashed right thigh. For the next couple of years he was on crutches, and in and out of the Manchester Royal Infirmary. The thigh-bone was plated but did not mend. In a second operation the bone was cut back and bound with wire. This didn't work, and there was a third operation to remove the wire binding. At this stage the surgeons despaired of making good the damage, and decided to amputate the entire right leg. This was to be done three weeks later, but a final X-ray revealed that the bones had at last begun to knit. The leg was not setting straight but the surgeons dared not touch it. Kimber ended up with a right leg some two inches shorter than before, necessitating a built-up shoe and leaving

him with a limp for the rest of his life. But at least he still had two legs – and could drive a car. The other party involved in the accident was held responsible, so Kimber was awarded reasonably substantial damages of £700; as compensation for destroying Sutton's motorcycle he gave him his own Rex.

'I never had any sense that my father was crippled,' Jean would later write. 'He took us for country walks, danced and… even learned to skate, but I think he chose fishing and sailing as his chief hobbies very wisely. Golf or tennis were too difficult.

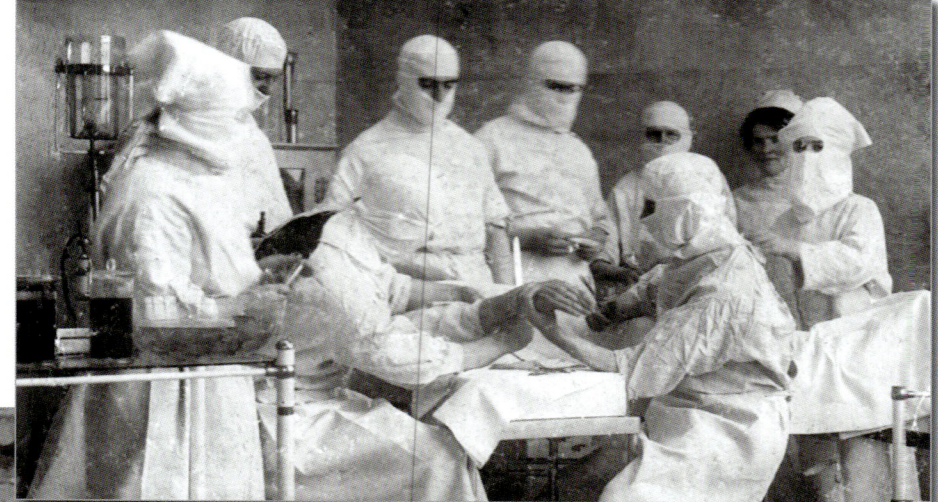

ABOVE: *Not a gathering of the Ku Klux Klan, but an extraordinary photo of Cecil Kimber undergoing surgery after the accident that nearly cost him a leg.*

LEFT: *Future brother-in-law Billy Sutton's crashed Rex; Sutton would marry Phyllis Kimber in 1916.*

He wore a built-up shoe, and limped, but all he would ever say about his leg was that he could foretell rain because then the old wound ached. I believe it ached more than we knew.'

During the two years that Kimber was on crutches, his mother Fanny died of cancer, at the age of 42. By this stage the ink business was faltering, and the family had moved to a more modest house in Parsonage Road, in the Manchester suburb of Withington, and it was here that Kimber's sister Phyllis and aunt Nance nursed his mother. Kimber 'missed her all his life and often talked to me about her,' Jean wrote in one of the photo albums she went on to compile in her later life.

Billy Sutton on Cecil Kimber's 3½hp Rex, which he was given by Kimber in around July 1910.

Kimber outside his father's cottage in Wales in 1912.

ABOVE: *A friend by the name of Gilbert, visiting from Warrington in 1912 or thereabouts, on his JAP-powered vee-twin Norton.*

TOP LEFT: *Ready for a night out on the town? Kimber and friend, 1912/1913, dapper in their boaters.*

LEFT: *Kimber in about 1912, in which year he would have been 24 years old.*

CARS AND PLANES – LEARNING THE TRADE

Having some time previously learnt to drive in North Wales on a 10hp Wolseley – which he later recalled 'driving in reverse and in the rain from Beddgelert to the Pen-y-Gwryd Hotel, to see the competitors in the Six-Day Trial attack the Llanberis Pass' – in February 1913 Cecil Kimber made the transition to four wheels. His first car was a 1912 Singer, a 10hp model on which he spent £185 of his £700 compensation money. 'It was... a very early one[1], and after some initial trouble in the engine, it gave good service for over 20,000 miles,' he would relate in a 1944 talk to the Institution of Automobile Engineers. Kimber purchased the Singer primarily for business, within a 40-mile radius of Manchester – where, he reported, its diminutive size often caused amusement.

---

[1] Kimber variously gives it as being car number 51 and car number 53.

Kimber by his first car, a Singer Ten – he said that he sold it 'for a scandalous profit'. Note the built-up heel of his right shoe.

OPPOSITE: *Rene during the Kimber honeymoon, at the wheel of Cecil Kimber's second Singer.*

Writing about the car in a detailed article in *The Light Car and Cycle Car* magazine, for its 28 December 1914 issue, he says that during his first year with the Singer he increased the turnover of the firm by 45 per cent, claiming that the use of a car allowed him to do the work of at least three men: he said that he averaged 60 to 70 miles per day and managed an astonishing 30 to 40 calls, depending on the district. In the end the Singer had more leisure use than anticipated, running up just 5,856 miles on behalf of the printing-ink business, out of the total of 17,172 miles he covered between purchase and August 1914. With running costs calculated to three decimal places of a penny, in this article Kimber was already demonstrating, as Wilson McComb observes, a 'remarkable enthusiasm for detailed cost analysis' – something on which he would expound in future papers and articles.

Despite the pleasures of being out on the road in his little Singer, Kimber felt frustrated by working for his father's company, on a wage of £1 a week, according to his brother Vernon. 'It was a very

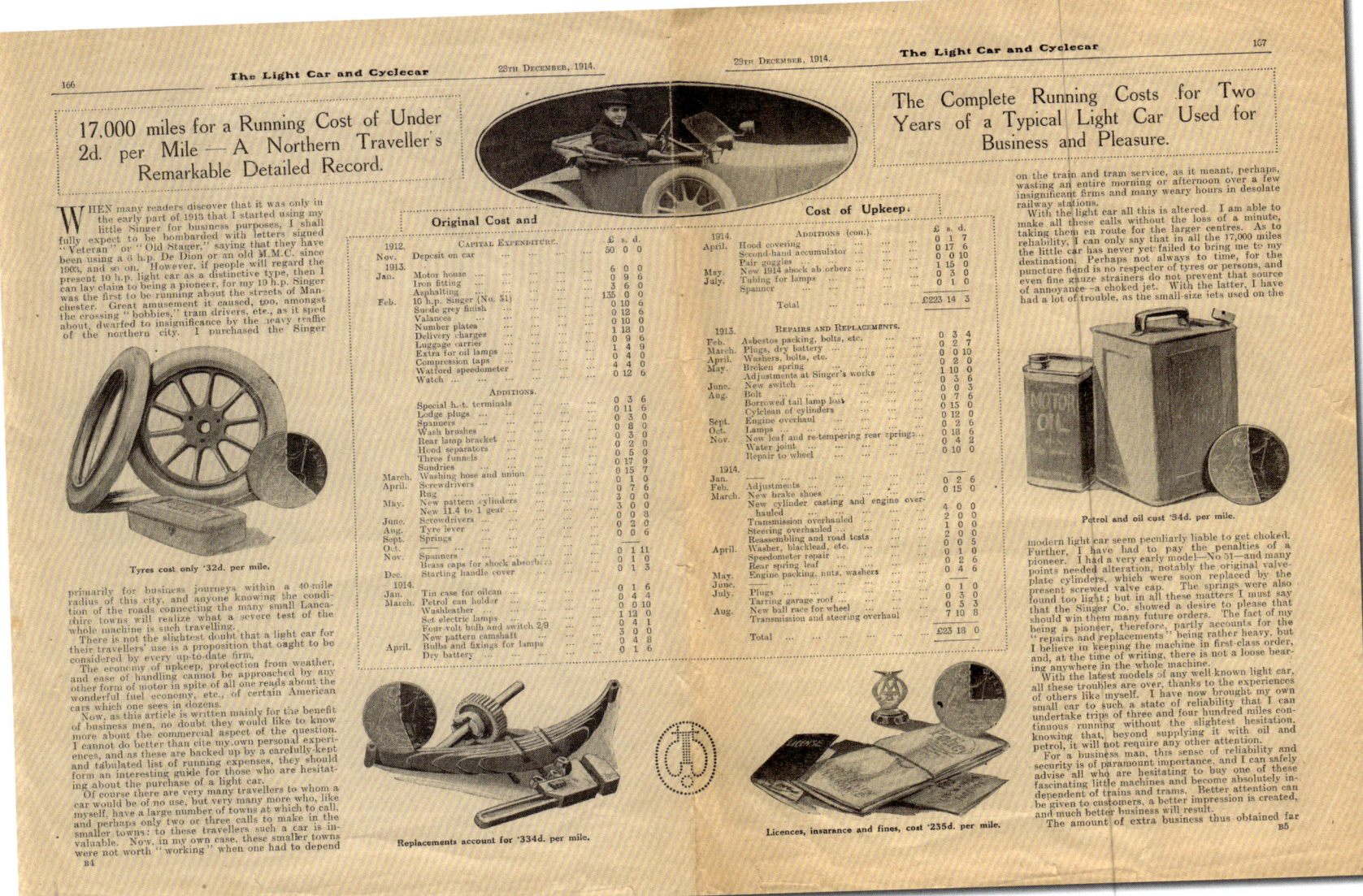

In an article for The Light Car and Cycle Car, *Kimber recounted his experiences running the 10hp Singer.*

poor little business. He wanted to enlarge, and [our] father hadn't got the money. [He] had bad luck. He wasn't a good businessman. But he worked hard.' Perhaps things would have been different had Kimber put his compensation money into the business. This was not to be.

'When he asked for a rise, in order to get married, pointing out his contribution, his father refused on the grounds that the business was none too secure[2] and asked my father instead to hand over the rest of his compensation money,' relates Jean. 'They had a furious quarrel, and my grandfather refused to have any more to do with his elder son and, in fact, never spoke to him again.' Henry Kimber retired to a cottage near Towyn[3], with a housekeeper, and all attempts by Cecil to heal the breach came to naught[4].

Vernon Kimber, meanwhile, was left carrying the can. 'I had to keep my father when he retired, out of the firm's profits,' he told Wilson McComb. 'Cecil kept all his money. It wasn't long before I realised I had to wind up the firm. Printing ink was becoming very technical, it needed a laboratory, and I couldn't afford that.'

MARRIAGE – AND A SPECIAL SINGER

On 4 August 1914, Britain had declared war on Germany, following the German invasion of Belgium. In light of his injured leg, Kimber was not called up, and continued working for the family business. By the end of the year he had met his future wife, Irene Hunt, at what he termed a 'diddy dance' in Withington, to where his father had moved after the death of his wife in 1911.

A portrait from 1914 of Cecil Kimber.

---

[2] According to Vernon Kimber his father was forced to leave £10,000 behind in the London business, which subsequently failed in 1910; then on the death of his brother Walter he was obliged to buy out his widow's share of the Manchester business. 'He worked hard, but fate was against him,' commented Vernon to Wilson McComb.

[3] Today known as Tywyn.

[4] 'He tried to heal the breach with his father,' Vernon Kimber told Wilson McComb. 'When my father was dying, I asked him "Do you want to see Cecil?"… "No", he said. My father's fault, I'm afraid.'

TOP LEFT: *Cecil Kimber's future father-in-law, Charles Hunt, c.1896, in Ireland, with eldest daughters Irene (left) and Maud.*

ABOVE: *The Hunt family in 1906: a plentiful supply of aunts would be on hand for Kimber's daughters.*

LEFT: *Irene Hunt, again in 1906.*

ABOVE: *Irene Hunt in 1909, when she was a pupil at Manchester High School.*

TOP RIGHT: *Charles and Aimée Hunt in a photograph thought to date from 1910.*

RIGHT: *Charles and Aimée Hunt on Charles's motorcycle combination.*

Chapter Two: Cars and Planes – Learning the Trade

Irene was one of six daughters and one son born to Charles and Aimée Hunt. Charles, born in 1866, was an engineer for Selson Ltd, who made agricultural machinery, and Aimée, née Milnes, born in 1865 and the daughter of a gentleman-farmer, taught at Leeds High School for Girls. All Aimée's brothers and sisters were teachers, and unmarried sisters Ethel and Blanche, who ended up living together in Ilkley, were in the 1950s still fondly remembered by locals in the West Yorkshire town.

Charles Hunt grew up in Beeston, Leeds, not far from the Milnes farm, and Irene was born on 5 August 1891 in the Leeds suburb of Headingley, also the birthplace of her sisters Maud, Blanche and Ethel and her brother Herbert. Madeleine and Kathleen, however, were born in Ireland, where Charles Hunt worked for a while, before returning to Britain in 1906 and settling in the Manchester area. It was a prosperous family, well-anchored in Victorian-cum-Edwardian middle-class 'county' values. Tradesmen delivered to the home in the Manchester suburb of Fallowfield rather than Aimée going shopping, for instance, and her mother rode to hounds until she was 80 years old.

The household was a cheerful one, writes Jean, and one which the

Wedding transport, the Hispano-bodied Singer: 'it made a very nice motor car to drive and for those days had quite a satisfying performance,' Kimber would later write.

Rene and Cecil Kimber at Cwmystradllyn Lake, 8 September 1915, in the course of their honeymoon.

two Kimber sons found congenial. 'My aunts Bannie and Effie have described to me the happy social life into which my father and Uncle Vern were drawn, with a crowd of friends always in and out, and singsongs around the piano. Vern could play brilliantly, and there were endless practical jokes and much teasing.'

The six sisters were educated at Manchester High School for Girls and according to Jean 'they all had strong characters and spoke their mind'. Irene went on to be trained as a secretary, and was working as a translator for a Manchester cotton firm when she met Cecil Kimber. "She was bright enough to have gone to Manchester University. She had a place to read modern languages, but her father wouldn't let her go," says Kimber's grand-daughter Sara Delamont.

According to Jean there was evidently some competition among the Hunt sisters for the hand of Cecil Kimber, something to which Irene unsurprisingly took exception. 'My aunts told me that she shook her sister, Maud, until her teeth rattled, saying "Leave him alone! He's mine!" She suspected Maud of trying to poach her

TOP & RIGHT (BOTH): *Rene in the Singer. Kimber gave the car, a one-time Brooklands racer, the nickname 'Gladys Emily'.*

ABOVE: *Kimber behind the Singer's wheel, at Rhyddybeulig.*

OPPOSITE: *On their honeymoon, the couple visited the Kimber family's cottage at Abererch, where Fanny had painted many pictures.*

property.' It seems Charles Hunt warned Kimber of his eldest daughter's temper and the lack of compatibility of the couple, but his future son-in-law was not swayed, and on 4 September 1915 Irene Hunt and Cecil Kimber were married.

'One could wonder what qualities my much admired mother was perceptive enough to value in a lame, penniless salesman of printing ink who was not as tall as she might have wished[5],' writes Jean. 'I now think that she succumbed, as my sister, my stepsister and I all did later on, to my father's sense of adventure. He could make the simplest picnic into a memorable event. My mother would have responded to this, as she once told me that her father went off to skate and row on his own, never considering that his children might have enjoyed sharing his outdoor pursuits.'

After their marriage in Chester, Cecil and Rene Kimber – as Irene was usually known – spent their honeymoon touring Wales in Kimber's new acquisition, a former racing Singer he nicknamed 'Gladys Emily' or 'The Bus'. From Chester they motored to Pentre Vuelas, and thence to Criccieth, Towyn and Montgomery. Stops on the way included Rhyddybeulig, Cwmystradllyn, where the pair tried some fishing, and Aberdovey, where they went sailing: right at the start of the marriage, Rene was being initiated into two of her husband's greatest passions. Then it was to their married home, 52 Linden Avenue in Norton Woodseats, outside Sheffield.

As for the somewhat fearsome-looking Singer, it had an interesting history – and an even more interesting previous owner. A 15.9hp model with a T-head engine[6], it had competed at Brooklands in the July 1909 Junior Private Competitors Handicap, carrying the name 'Jabberwock'. It was unplaced, and recorded a maximum lap speed of 43.8mph, which is somewhat short of the 80mph at which Kimber told his family it had lapped the famous banked circuit. The car was entered in two further races during 1909 but started in neither, after which it does not appear to have raced again.

The Singer had previously belonged to pioneer aviator Vivian Hewitt, who ran the car with a very tight-fitting pointed-tail body – complete with an exaggerated bird-like beak over the radiator – before having it rebuilt with the bodywork from an Hispano-Suiza. In its earlier form it was sampled by Cecil Kimber when a friend of his by the name of Gilbert brought the car to Abererch, where Henry Kimber had a holiday cottage; a photo dated by Jean to 1912 captures her father in the car. This suggests that Kimber and Hewitt were acquainted before Kimber bought the car, which by the time he acquired it had been further modified with a square-cut rear in place of the Hispano body's original bolster-tank arrangement.

---

5 Kimber was 5ft 5in tall.

6 A T-head engine is an early type of side-valve unit with the inlet valves on one side of the block and the exhaust valves on the other, as opposed to the more conventional side-valve arrangement which has all the valves on the same side.

exhibition flights in his Blériot – 'fancy flying' as it was called – and for his first flight with a passenger he carried a black lamb. In 1912, at the age of 24, he was the first aviator to fly across the Irish Sea.

After war service as a test pilot and as an inspector for the British government at the Curtiss aircraft factory in the United States, Hewitt returned to Rhyl and developed a passion for ornithology and the collection of eggs. Inheriting a massive fortune at the beginning of the 1930s, he created a walled bird sanctuary on Anglesey, living there without running water, indoor sanitation or electricity, amidst half a million eggs, three stuffed Great Auks,

The ex-Hewitt Singer in its earlier guise, with a beak-like nose; Kimber is at the wheel, and the photo is dated to 1912.

If the two knew each other, Hewitt has to count as one of Kimber's more colourful acquaintances. The grandson of the founder of the Hewitt Brothers brewery in Grimsby, Harrow-educated Hewitt grew up in the Flintshire village of Bodfari. After working in Portsmouth Dockyard and as a railway apprentice in Crewe, in 1909 he rented a flying shed at Brooklands and set up as a specialist in repairs to Blériot monoplanes and the construction of aircraft wings. He also dealt in second-hand cars, buying them at the London used-car mecca of Great Portland Street and modifying them for racing.

He returned to Wales in 1911 and settled in the seaside town of Rhyl, through which he sped in a variety of racing cars, including no doubt the Singer, with which he sometimes towed his aeroplane. An exuberant young man with a keen sense of publicity, he gave

Vivian Hewitt, the previous owner of the racing Singer, in later life, contemplating two stuffed Great Auks. (Author's collection)

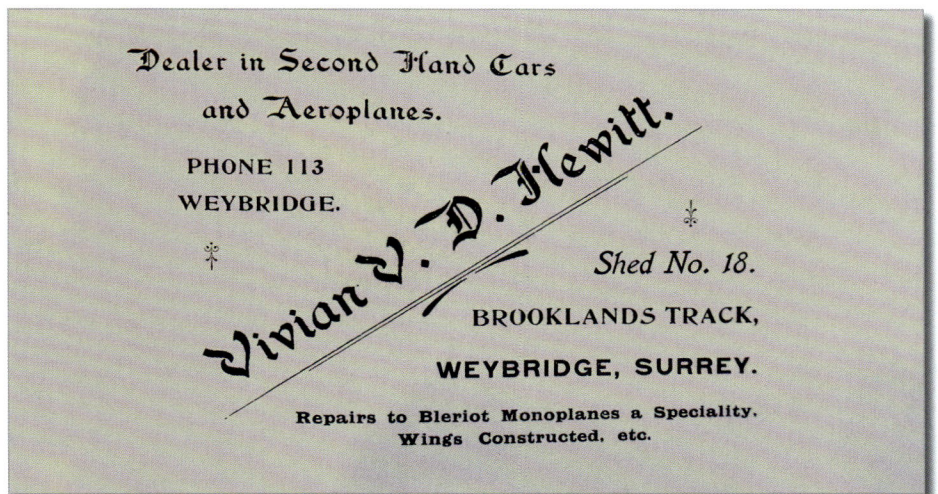

Hewitt, an early resident of the aircraft sheds at the Brooklands circuit, was a pioneer aviator. (Author's collection)

a collection of miniature and full-sized traction engines, and a roomful of African Grey Parrots. Maintaining his interest in fast cars, he kept one of his two 8-litre Bentleys in the middle of the house's hall. By contrast, when in London he stayed in a suite at the Savoy, whilst his home in Nassau, to where he moved after the Second World War, had all modern conveniences.

Given that both Kimber and Hewitt had a passion for cars and shared ties to Wales, in the closed little world of pre-WWI motorists it is highly likely that the paths of the two men crossed. Certainly they both had Chester in common: the town in which Kimber was married was also that in which Hewitt was fined in October 1913 'for driving a motor-car to the danger of the public' – the car, reported *The Manchester Guardian*, being 'of the racing type'. Perhaps the vehicle in which Hewitt was caught at 40mph downhill, in the village of Barrow, was the Singer that Cecil Kimber would later buy…

FIRST STEPS IN THE MOTOR INDUSTRY

In the course of 1915 – the exact date is not known, but has to have been before the marriage – Kimber, encouraged by Rene, had abandoned the family business and entered the motor industry.

His employer was Sheffield-Simplex. Based, as the name suggests, in Sheffield, in the suburb of Tinsley, the company, backed by coal magnate Earl Fitzwilliam, produced a high-quality six-cylinder car. Its work during the First World War included making shells, mines, armoured-car chassis and ABC aero-engines.

The post was as personal assistant to the chief engineer, according to Jean; however, Kimber's entry in *Who's Who in the Motor Trade* says he was a buyer, so one cannot be sure. His daughter writes that the job came about through Kimber having come to know A. W. Reeves, then one of the two senior engineers at Manchester motor company Crossley. The suggestion is that the two men might have met through attending events of the Manchester Motor Club and the Lancashire Automobile Club.

According to Frank Dewhurst, who in 1916 was working as a junior in the drawing office of Sheffield-Simplex, the young Cecil Kimber was full of innovative ideas. At about this time, indeed, he contributed to a paper on works organisation that was read before the Institution of Automobile Engineers in London by its co-author, Crossley engineer Reeves. In the preamble to his 1934 Institution of Automobile Engineers paper *Making Modest Production Pay in Motor-Car Manufacture*, Kimber mentions standing 'with stage fright and diffidence' before an IAE audience 'nearly 20 years ago, being then the joint author of a paper on works organisation, which my co-author read before the Society'.

In 1917, as far as can be ascertained, Kimber left Sheffield-Simplex. Where he went after that is not totally clear: it was either to Martinsyde Aircraft or to AC Cars[7], both of which were based in Surrey. 'Information about his working life before he went to

---

[7] Established in 1904 by John Weller, as Autocars & Accessories Ltd, AC had made its name with the Auto-Carrier delivery tricycle and derived AC Sociable. In 1913 it had introduced a 10hp light car, followed by a 12hp model on the same chassis. After the First World War, Weller developed the long-lived six-cylinder AC engine, to remain in use until 1962. In business with three of his brothers, Weller was backed by John Portwine, a partner in London and Suburban Meat Stores who had gone on to establish a chain of butcher's shops under his own name. In 1922 the company would pass into the hands of pioneer racing motorist S. F. Edge.

ABOVE: *Cecil and Rene Kimber had as their first home 52 Linden Avenue in Norton Woodseats, outside Sheffield.*

TOP RIGHT: *The sitting room of the Linden Avenue house.*

LEFT: *Cecil Kimber in the garden of the house in Norton Woodseats.*

THIS PAGE: *Kimber and Rene in a sequence of images taken during a visit from a lady by the name of Mary – whether friend or family is not known.*

Chapter Two: Cars and Planes – Learning the Trade

The Morris Garages as Sales Manager in 1921 is practically nil, other than the barest outline. He practically never talked about the past, preferring always to think about the newest M.G.,' admitted Jean in a 1993 letter to Martinsyde historian J. M. Bruce.

Who's Who in the Motor Trade has Kimber moving in 1917 from Sheffield-Simplex to Martinsyde Aircraft, as Stores Organiser, and thence in 1918 to Birmingham-based axle manufacturer E. G. Wrigley. The date 1918 is likely to be incorrect – 1919 is more probable – but more to the point there is no mention of AC Cars.

In contrast, Jean, writing in *The Other Tack*, has her father going from Sheffield-Simplex to AC and then to Wrigley, with no mention of Martinsyde. But in the later *The MG Log* she revises this, having Kimber going from Sheffield-Simplex to AC and thence to Martinsyde, before joining Wrigley in 1919. This is logical, in that Kimber in joining AC would have been sticking to what interested him, in moving from one car firm to another. Having uprooted himself from the North of England to relocate to AC, he may then have preferred to stay in the Surrey area, even if it meant straying from the motor industry. This sequence does not accord, however, with Kimber's entry in the 1939 edition of Grace's *Who's Who in the Motor Industry*, which gives his pre-M.G. history, in order, as Sheffield-Simplex, Martinsyde, AC Cars, and finally Wrigley.

Whatever the sequence, it is not known what post Kimber occupied at AC, which was then making fuses and shells; only that, according to Jean, his wife Rene worked alongside him as his secretary. Why did he spend what was evidently such a short time at AC? According to Jean, her father told her that he left an unspecified employer when he had a falling-out with the company's stuffy management, after he had suggested ways to improve the factory's functioning. His note had been returned with 'What is this? See me' scribbled across it, and Kimber had resigned on the spot, he related to his daughter.

Assuming this dispute did not take place at Sheffield-Simplex, it has to have been at either AC or Martinsyde[8]. Jean variously describes the people with whom Kimber fell out as being 'two elderly owners' and 'two elderly brothers'. It seems unlikely, therefore, that the company was Martinsyde, as neither partner was elderly: in 1918 one would have been 37 and the other 41.

'Me and my Jigger!' is the caption for this image, date unknown, of Kimber on what is probably a Sun motorcycle; surprisingly, he had gone back to a motorbike despite his earlier accident.

---

[8] Helmuth Paul Martin and George Harris Handasyde had made something between 15 and 40 Martin-Handasyde aircraft before the First World War; the exact figure is not known. In 1910 the pair were the first permanent tenants at Brooklands – initially in the first aero shed. There they must have come to know Vivian Hewitt, the previous owner of Cecil Kimber's ex-Brooklands Singer; indeed it is possible that Kimber's employment by Martinsyde, as the business became in 1915, might have been a result of just such a connection. After the war, aircraft production wound down, and in 1920 Martinsyde began making motorcycles. The company fell into receivership and closed down in 1923.

A Sheffield-Simplex open tourer at Hendon aerodrome, c.1913. (Nostalgic Picture Library)

Over at AC, John Weller would also have been 41 but his backer John Portwine, however, would have been a rather older 52 and might have seemed an old man to the 30-year-old Kimber; further to this, the talk of brothers may refer to some combination or other of the various Weller brothers. Jean told J. M. Bruce that she was inclined to put her money on AC Cars, but her hunch cannot be confirmed.

Kimber's spell at Martinsyde – spanning the two years 1917 and 1918 according to his entry in *Who's Who in the Motor Trade* – would have seen him working at either the company's Brooklands factory or its large facility in nearby Woking. Said to be Britain's third-largest aircraft manufacturer in the First World War, Martinsyde made several different planes, but was best-known for its G100 and related G102. A big and lumbering bi-plane,

The chassis of a 30hp Sheffield-Simplex. Kimber approved of the car's power-to-weight ratio, but said that the gearchange was poor.

The 10hp light car marked AC's move into four-wheelers. Kimber would no doubt have sampled one when he was at AC. (Wikipedia)

Martinsyde's best-known aircraft was the G100/G102 'Elephant' shown here – but the SE5a it built under licence was a rather better machine. (Imperial War Museum)

the design was given the 'Elephant' nickname; it was described by J. M. Bruce as 'an aircraft that had an undistinguished performance, was inadequately armed and gave its pilot a restricted view in all directions vital for bombing.' Martinsyde also made 600 – some sources give 500 – of the rather more well-regarded SE5a, on behalf of Royal Aircraft Factory, and by 1918 had over 3,000 employees. In contrast to the much more modestly-sized AC, this bustling enterprise would certainly have furnished a challenging environment for the still-young Kimber.

By 1919 Cecil Kimber was employed by E. G. Wrigley & Co Ltd, apparently as a works organiser. According to his brother Vernon, Kimber secured the job through his friendship with Frank Woollard, who would become an important figure at Morris, but who was then Wrigley's Chief Engineer. Kimber would remain with the company until 1921: 'You could have eaten your dinner under the machines when he had finished with the place,' Vernon Kimber told Wilson McComb.

During this period the Kimbers lived at Wayside, 10 Eastern Road, in the Birmingham suburb of Selly Park. A typical suburban semi-detached house, it soon became a family home, with the arrival on 11 October 1919 of Betty, the couple's first child. According to Jean, Rene Kimber was 'quite seriously ill' after the birth, so Betty's early upbringing devolved more to her father.

Before the war Wrigley had supplied William Morris with front and rear axles and steering gear, drawn up for him by Woollard, but the relationship with the company was not a happy one on the personal level. The directors had a condescending attitude to Morris, whom they referred to as 'Woollard's little garage friend from Oxford'. Further to this, according to Woollard the Managing

The suburban house in the Selly Oak district of Birmingham where the Kimbers lived between 1919 and 1921.

An Angus-Sanderson, wearing the ripple-pattern disc wheels that were a characteristic of the model. (Alamy)

Director was very proud of being descended from ancient Scottish kings – "and was going to let everyone know it". On a visit to Cowley, Woollard told Morris biographers Andrews and Brunner, "Morris... had about an hour of this Scots kings business, and was absolutely furious. When the war was over, instead of coming back to Wrigley's, he went elsewhere for his axles..."

Having in this manner lost its contract to supply the British motor industry's rising star, Wrigley looked for replacement business, and became a member of the consortium behind the ill-fated Angus-Sanderson car. This was to have unfortunate consequences for Cecil Kimber.

As with the first Morrises, the 2.3-litre Angus-Sanderson was conceived as an 'assembled' car, one built from outside-sourced components, and it was subsequently advertised as 'The result of combined energy' and as the first all-British demonstration of what its makers termed 'Massed Production'. Sir William Angus-Sanderson & Co Ltd were long-established Newcastle coachbuilders, and would oversee the project, provide bodies, and be responsible for assembly. Wrigley would design and build the axles, gearboxes and steering gear, and intended to commit the whole of its production to the Angus-Sanderson. Chassis were to come from Mechins of Glasgow. Finally J. Tylor & Sons Ltd were to build the engine. Although Tylor built engines for the London General Omnibus Company and other commercial-vehicle manufacturers, the London-based iron founders were also well-known – to the delight of generations of writers – as a leading maker of lavatory cisterns.

The Angus-Sanderson went into production during 1919 in a large former shell-making factory in Birtley, Co Durham. With long supply chains, an untrained workforce and the inevitable teething troubles of a hastily-conceived design that had been rushed into production, commercial disaster was just around the corner for the undercapitalised business. With the extensive factory not running anywhere near capacity, cashflow problems were then compounded by a moulders' strike at the end of 1919 and the beginning of 1920. Output ground to a halt as the result of a lack of engines, gearboxes and back axles. Orders were cancelled. Production re-started, and reached its peak in May 1920. Then came the 1920 slump that put paid to many an over-ambitious motor manufacturer. By February the following year the Angus-Sanderson business was in receivership. The company was reconstructed via a dealer consortium, the cars in process completed, and the factory in Birtley returned to the Ministry of Munitions. Assembly of cars moved to London, and staggered on until 1927, with a further company restructuring along the way.

The Wrigley business, meanwhile, had been mortally wounded. "Wrigley's had an inner cabinet which did not discuss with the whole board, and they ran themselves into a difficult position, and were on the rocks," Frank Woollard later observed to Andrews and Brunner. Cecil Kimber was one of those who suffered collateral damage in this industrial shipwreck, as he had invested the remaining compensation money from his motorcycle accident – or at least a significant proportion of it – in the Wrigley participation in the Angus-Sanderson project. This money was lost when the venture collapsed[9].

Kimber's involvement is said to have gone beyond his financial contribution: according to his brother Vernon he designed the radiator shell of the car. Kimber seems never to have mentioned this when referring to his time at Wrigley, so Vernon Kimber's statement should be treated with a degree of caution. It should however be noted that in the 'You'll be interested to know' column of the 10 September 1929 issue of *The Motor* it was said that Kimber had 'assisted in the production of the first tank gearbox and later in the design of the Angus-Sanderson car.' The reference to a tank gearbox might in fact relate to Frank Woollard's work on the design and manufacture of tank gearboxes during the war, for which he was awarded the OBE in 1918. The mention of Angus-

---

[9] As Kimber recounts in his 1934 IAE paper *Making Modest Production Pay in Motor-Car Manufacture;* see Appendix 4. He also says that one of the problems with E.G. Wrigley was that the MD was unable to read an ordinary trading account.

Sanderson is frustratingly vague, but may well suggest that there is something in Vernon Kimber's story.

Whatever the truth, during 1921 Cecil Kimber left the sinking E. G. Wrigley – at about the same time as did Frank Woollard, who had risen to be Assistant Managing Director. 'I was broke to the world, having lost all my savings in the shares of the company I was with who in turn had put all their eggs in the ill-fated Angus-Sanderson car basket,' Kimber told the Motor Enthusiasts Club of Birmingham in a 1944 talk. His next appointment, taken up in the course of 1921, was as Sales Manager of The Morris Garages in Oxford, as will be discussed more fully.

Wrigley, meanwhile, survived until December 1923, when it in turn called in the receiver. Frank Woollard, by this stage General Manager of Morris Engines Ltd, had tipped off Morris that a grouping was being constituted to buy the company, and Morris swiftly stepped in to purchase it out of receivership as a going concern. Its well-equipped works in Soho, Birmingham, were immediately put to use to manufacture Morris's new one-ton Morris-Commercial lorries. It is important to be clear about this chronology, as there are some writers who have said that William Morris had his eye on Kimber, and plucked him out of Wrigley on its collapse. This is manifestly not the case, as Kimber's appointment pre-dates the failure of Wrigley by a good two years; given that Morris had ceased doing business with the company during the war, it is not even sure that the two men knew each other before Kimber joined The Morris Garages.

THESE TWO PAGES: *Rene Kimber and Betty, born in October 1919, photographed at Wayside. Rene suffered health problems after the birth of Betty.*

Chapter Two: Cars and Planes – Learning the Trade

THE MAN BEHIND THE NAME – WILLIAM MORRIS

That William Morris – later Lord Nuffield – was the most important person in Cecil Kimber's professional life is beyond contest. Without Morris, without the Morris cars he created, without the existence of The Morris Garages, there would have been no M.G. motor cars. Had there not been the personal financial support of Morris the M.G. company would not have developed, blossomed – and indeed survived. Without Morris's backing, the record-breaking of the late 1930s and the attendant publicity would not have been possible. So who was Morris, what sort of a man was he, and how did he rise to become Britain's most prominent inter-war industrialist?

At the point when Kimber joined his employ, Morris was a businessman of some significance, running one of the country's more prominent motor manufacturers. But he was not the dominant figure that he would become. Just as Cecil Kimber would progress through the 1920s to the point where at the beginning of the new decade he was running a semi-autonomous concern in its own sizeable factory, so William Morris would advance in the same period, through acquisition and expansion, to achieve market leadership at the head of a multi-interest manufacturing conglomerate. During this period, from 1921 to 1930, both men had yet to achieve their definitive status as captains of industry,

ABOVE: *Morris, aged 18 or thereabouts. (Author's collection)*

OPPOSITE: *William Morris at the wheel of a very early Morris Oxford. His passenger is Frank Barton, one of his partners in he Oxford Automobile & Cycle Agency, and manager of The Morris Garages between 1911 and 1918. (Author's collection)*

RIGHT: *William Morris's initiation to cycling was on an old penny-farthing. (Author's collection)*

and both were engaged on an exciting adventure with an upward trajectory. Kimber was fortunate to have as his employer such a quick-acting and shrewd person as Morris, and Morris was fortunate in having the energetic Kimber running his garage business and creating out of it a manufacturer of sports cars.

LEFT: *Morris was an extremely successful cycle-racer, winning countless championships; it was through cycling that he met his wife. (Author's collection)*

ABOVE: *Morris's first bicycle, built for the Reverend Pilcher, had an usually tall 27in frame, to accommodate the lanky vicar : it was still in excellent order when it turned up at a jumble sale in the late 1930s. (Author's collection)*

TOP: A well-known photo of the Morris showroom at 48 High Street, Oxford; next door is the tobacconist's shop of sometime partner George Cooke. (Author's collection)

ABOVE: The Morris motorcycle had several unusual features, not least its frame. (Author's collection)

Morris (far right) and his workers with the frames of some Morris motorcycles. (Author's collection)

In 1903 Morris (centre, with cigarette) was looking after the workshops of The Oxford Automobile & Cycle Agency, of which he was a partner; he still sometimes wore a cap, but this came to be replaced by a felt hat to reflect his status. (Author's collection)

For brave passengers, the Morris motorcycle was also available with a fore-carriage. (Author's collection)

FROM BICYCLES TO MOTOR CARS

So many times have Morris's early days been recounted that the story has entered into myth – and myth into the story. The essentials are briefly told. William Richard Morris was born on 10 October 1877 in Worcester, and grew up in Oxford. His father Frederick worked as a bailiff – what we would today call a farm manager – running his father-in-law's farm at Headington Quarry. He came from a long line of Oxfordshire yeoman farmers, self-employed tenant farmers who ran their farms with their own capital. At a time when farming was a key part of the economy, such people were the backbone of the rural middle classes. Both his parents were well-educated, and Morris was not born into a disadvantaged or poverty-stricken family, something he was keen to stress in later life.

An enterprising and able young man, in 1893 William Morris started out repairing and building bicycles in Oxford. He worked at first from the back of the family home in James Street, in the Oxford suburb of Cowley St John, operating from a brick outbuilding – not a tumbledown shed, as some romanticising biographers have it – and exhibiting his bicycles in the front window of the house. He was a meticulous craftsman, and in later life even those who had ambivalent feelings about him admitted that his brazing work was beautiful. From the start he was prudent in his business practices: stock and expenses were kept to a minimum, and sometimes he would cycle to Birmingham to get parts.

He moved on to make motorcycles, and by 1905 was co-running a business looking after the garaging and care of undergraduates' cars. In 1905 he began hiring out vehicles with drivers. This was followed by a taxi service – a new thing at the time – and the provision of driving lessons. Morris's reputation built up, and he took on agencies for Arrol-Johnston, Belsize, Humber, Hupmobile, Singer, Standard, and Wolseley cars, plus Douglas, Royal Enfield, Sunbeam and Triumph motorcycles. As for the bicycle side of operations, this was sold in 1907 to another Oxford cycle dealer; that same year the business partnership he had been in was dissolved and Morris continued on his own.

By 1910 he was running The Oxford Garage, a thriving enterprise servicing and selling motorcycles and cars from newly-built premises on the corner of Longwall Street. Advertised as 'The Oxford Motor Palace' and described as 'The Rendezvous of Varsity & County Motorists' in its early days, this would become The Morris Garages, and the business would remain the personal property of Morris until shortly before his death in 1963, when he passed ownership to his charitable trust, the Nuffield Foundation[1].

As so many who had begun as cycle-makers, William Morris sought to make the transition to being a manufacturer of motor cars. But unlike so many such people, he was not a trained

---

[1] In 1932 The Morris Garages centralised its operations in a large tailor-made building in St Aldates, the frontage of which survives today as part of the Oxford Crown Court. The business – latterly with branches in Newbury, Reading, Aylesbury and High Wycombe – moved to a commercial estate on the outskirts of Oxford in 1976, in which year it also vacated its Longwall Street premises, retained for the hire-car business. In 1980 it would cease trading.

The Longwall Street garage in c.1907. As well as servicing and selling cars, Morris had a small hire fleet. This photo is from before the re-development of the site to create his 'Oxford Motor Palace' – the frontage of which still exists. (Author's collection)

engineer, versed in the theories – arcane or otherwise – of the discipline. Nor was he, despite occasional early-days dabblings, an enthusiastic participant in motor-sport. Rather differently, Morris approached car design via the garage trade. As opposed to an exercise in engineering vanity, the car he conceived was one based on his practical experience of what worked and what did not work, borrowing as appropriate from existing designs.

THE FIRST MORRIS – A LIGHT CAR WITH A DIFFERENCE

Morris did not need to be hugely perspicacious to work out where the market was going. The motor industry was developing in same way as had the cycle industry, with a progressive democratisation of what had started out as a plaything for the aristocracy. The future lay in producing a car at an accessible price – not a

for the cars revived, and by the end of the year production was up by over half on the 1920 figures.

Having made it through the slump and seen off less fortunate or less astute competitors, Morris started to buy up his suppliers, putting in place competent managers who raised output. Standardised parts prices and service charges were introduced, along with a hire-purchase scheme. Sales moved upwards in bounds, on the back of steadily improved Oxfords and Cowleys, and in 1924 Morris was market leader, with a production of 32,910 cars, or 28 per cent of national output. The following year he claimed over 40 per cent of the British market.

Unlike many of his peers who were engineers, he did not feel an endless need to tinker with the design of his car, to the detriment of production efficiency and business profitability. The Bullnose – as the Morris came to be nicknamed – was improved only in detail for most of its long career, thereby assuring reliability and low prices. The downside was that the emphatically conservative Morris did not want to move on, and his managers had a struggle to convince

An example of a later Oxford, this is the folding-head variant of what was called the Three-Quarter Coupé. (Author's collection)

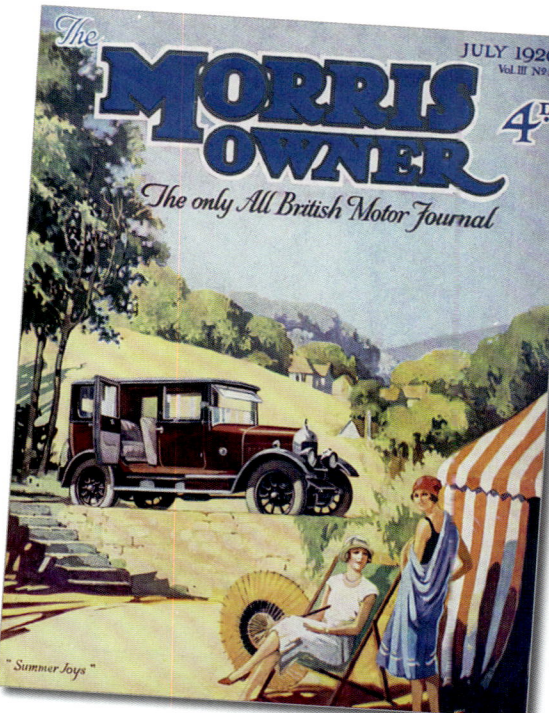

him that he should replace it with the more modern-looking Flatnose – again an informal appellation – that would arrive in September 1926. That same year Morris restructured his business interests for the second time, creating Morris Motors (1926) Ltd to bring under one umbrella all the subsidiaries he had acquired earlier in the 1920s; floating the new company on the Stock Exchange enabled him to raise the funds necessary to enter into a joint-venture to create the Pressed Steel Company for the production of all-steel bodies to Budd patents[2].

In the final years of the decade William Morris updated and expanded the range of cars he offered. Not all the newcomers were successful: he remained in mentality an assembler, and was unwilling to build up a design team that could engineer a vehicle as a whole. He entered the 1930s with too many different models, a falling market share and a business making diminishing profits.

ABOVE: *William Morris in 1925 with the 100,000th engine made by Morris Engines Branch. This was formerly a British offshoot of French company Hotchkiss, and had been making engines for Morris since 1919. Morris acquired the company in 1923, after commissioning a report from Frank Woollard, whom he immediately installed as General Manager. (Author's collection)*

TOP RIGHT: *In 1924 Morris established* The Morris Owner. *It was initially edited by journalist Miles Thomas, who had been recruited by Morris in January that year, to look after sales and promotion. (Ken Martin collection)*

[2] This was followed, in 1927, by the establishment of a new holdings company for all Morris's interests, called Morris Industries Limited. Coming to realise that his participation in Pressed Steel deterred competitors from using the company, in 1930 Morris withdrew from the tripartite ownership consortium. The business returned to the fold in 1965, when it was acquired by the British Motor Corporation and merged with fellow body manufacturer Fisher and Ludlow, which BMC had bought in 1953.

OPPOSITE: *Views of the factory at Cowley, dating from 1925. Wood-framed bodies were labour-intensive to build, which was why Morris started to make the transition to Pressed Steel bodies for 1927. In this he was a pioneer, but there were dreadful problems with the quality of the pressings of the early all-steel bodies. (Peter Seymour collection)*

Chapter Three: The Man behind the Name – William Morris

Morris himself, confronted with a business that had grown too large for him to control personally, became increasingly an absentee proprietor, with consequences that will be recounted in Chapter 18.

The ship was turned around when in 1933 Sir William Morris – he had been knighted in 1929 – appointed Leonard Lord as Managing Director at Cowley. Lord had risen to prominence as Assistant Chief Engineer at Morris Engines Branch and had gone on to become Managing Director at Wolseley, which Morris had acquired in 1927. He was a brilliant production engineer, and a brusquely decisive manager. His new broom was soon sweeping vigorously.

The model range was rationalised, production facilities improved, Wolseley design commonised with that of Morrises, and the

OPPOSITE: *Morris in his office in the early 1930s. In his lapel is the badge of the League of Industry, a pressure group he set up in 1931 to promote industrial protection, 'patriotic' Empire-centric values, and a national or coalition government that sat above petty inter-party bickering. The cigar in the ashtray, admittedly unsmoked, seems out of character: Morris was a voracious cigarette smoker. (Morris Register)*

ABOVE: *The Morris Six, the revised version of the Light Six that would donate its engine and gearbox to the M.G. 18/80. Not a huge success, the Six was replaced for 1930 by the Isis, which at first shared its Pressed Steel body with the Dodge Victory Six. (Ken Martin collection)*

best-selling Eight introduced to replace the commercially disappointing Minor. At the same time the Morris combine was re-structured and a flotation resulted in Lord Nuffield, as Sir William Morris had become in 1934, becoming stratospherically rich. All this had consequences for Cecil Kimber and the M.G. business, as will be discussed in later chapters.

Lord left Morris in 1936[3], and at least some of his work was undone: by 1939 the combine was again making too many different and unrelated models. Not content with that, in late 1938 Nuffield had

---

[3] See Chapter 14 and Chapter 18.

The drift and lack of focus at Cowley in these later pre-war years was perhaps thankfully not apparent to the outside world. What people observed instead was that Lord Nuffield was now a national figure of considerable stature. He commentated on industrial policy, dabbled in politics, hob-nobbed with royalty, dipped in and out of aero-engine manufacture, and above all was a high-profile philanthropist supporting many worthy causes, even sponsoring the creation of his own college at Oxford University[4].

THE LEGACY OF A MODEST MAN

After war years that involved – at least initially – a tense relationship with the government, he would steer the Nuffield Organization towards a merger with major rival Austin, to create the British Motor Corporation[5]. It is tempting to condemn this as an act of resignation by a tired old man who had lost interest in the increasingly arduous struggle to run a complex company in complex times. But there is another argument, namely that Lord

---

[4] People can today profit from his benefactions at every step in their life. As a child one can be cared for in the paediatric ward of a Nuffield Hospital. One can study a Nuffield syllabus at school, be supported in one's research by the Nuffield Foundation, and carry out post-graduate work at Nuffield College, Oxford. One can have one's wisdom teeth extracted in the Nuffield House wing of Guy's Hospital (as did the author), and be looked after in later life through a BUPA scheme that owes its existence to a Nuffield gift, before spending one's last days in a Nuffield Care Home.

[5] The alliance was announced in November 1951 and formalised early in 1952. During the Second World War the Morris conglomerate had been re-named the Nuffield Organization.

---

purchased Riley, which had fallen into receivership thanks to the usual cocktail of poor management, too many models, and the distractions of a motor-sport programme. Why he should have spent £143,000 to acquire the respected Coventry maker of sports cars and sporting saloons, when he already had M.G. in exactly that sector of the market, was a question that perplexed Abingdon management, who were reported to be less than pleased with the acquisition.

LEFT: *This photo of Sir William Morris – or Lord Nuffield as he became in 1934 – was seen in early 1930s advertising, including some M.G. publicity. (Author's collection)*

OPPOSITE: *Early Eights on the remodelled Cowley production line, with behind it, at the body-drop stage, a Fifteen-Six, one of the cheaper six-cylinder models. (Peter Seymour collection)*

Nuffield was ahead of the curve, with a visionary appreciation of the new industrial realities.

In global terms, Austin and Morris were relatively small affairs, and they were devoting a lot of energy to fighting each other. Nuffield, with his mentality of a buyer rather than a creator, could see that to compete with the US firms that were now expanding rapidly in Europe, and with state-supported companies such as Renault and Volkswagen, it was necessary to drive costs down by sharing components, so that they could be bought or produced in greater numbers, and thus more cheaply. Creating the world's fourth-largest motor-manufacturing business could be judged as the crowning achievement in a dazzling career, and one calculated to ensure the survival and continued development of the enterprise he had created.

The story of the British Motor Corporation – in which, of course, that of M.G. in the 1950s and 1960s was interwoven – was not to prove a happy one. It is legitimate to ask whether the business might have had a more robust future had at least some of the money disbursed to charitable causes by Lord Nuffield been ploughed back into improved production facilities, engineering research and the like. On the other hand, the history of the British motor industry suggests that however healthy a company he might have bequeathed to the newly-formed BMC, his legacy would inevitably have been squandered by the manifest incompetents who ran the combine and its successor companies.

'A BRIGHT-EYED TIGHT LITTLE MAN'

What sort of a man was Morris? Perhaps his essence is summed up in a terse description by his penultimate Vice-Chairman, Miles Thomas: Morris was, he wrote, a 'bright-eyed tight little man'. Speaking more of the younger Morris, Thomas more expansively portrayed him in his conversations with official biographers Andrews and Brunner. "There was something about him which gave people more than normal confidence. He was small in stature, wiry, friendly and yet remote…he combined a working knowledge of engineering and tremendous attack as a mechanic with a magnetic personality which attracted people, made people anxious to serve him, proud to work for him and with him. But at the same time they never got to know him because he was so brittle, so exclusive and unpredictable in his likes and dislikes".

Retaining an Oxfordshire burr to his voice, he remained an undemonstrative man, despite his wealth. Reginald Rootes, used to the flamboyance of his larger-than-life cigar-chomping brother Billy, found Morris dull company when he accompanied him on a boat to Argentina. "Morris was a more popular man in the trade than Austin, but a man of not much personality. He couldn't talk much, but he was very honest, very straightforward. He was admired by his dealers. He never left the boat. He just sat on it, and didn't mix with other people at all. I had dinner with him; he had nothing to talk about except the motor business."

Always prudent with his money, Morris had ordinary tastes, as will be appreciated by anyone visiting his former home, Nuffield Place. He was not a man of culture, had no real hobbies, read little, and had unrefined music-hall preferences in entertainment. But if he was no intellectual, he was mentally very sharp, as Thomas impressed on Andrews and Brunner. "Whereas the college professor could talk and impress by rarified logic, Nuffield had not got that ability. But he would make a devastatingly simple remark which went right to the root of the matter. That was one reason for his success."

His great skill, when he set out in business, was in being an ambitiously forward-looking buyer, demanding from his suppliers higher quantities of parts than was thought prudent, and thereby driving the cost of those parts downwards, enabling him in turn to sell his cars at ever-lower prices and thus in increasing numbers. He was a challenging man with whom to do business, but was always regarded as honest and true to his word.

Although no accountant, he was a natural and meticulous man with figures, as his painstakingly-kept personal ledger books testify; he had that gift of seeing the general implications of financial problems and of acting decisively once these had been assessed. Rigorous weekly budgeting was a cornerstone of the Morris empire, and was based on long contracts with suppliers and prompt and regular payment of their bills. In the formative years of the company, profits were ploughed back into the company and cash reserves were kept low; more crucially, Morris did not borrow extensively from the banks, and when he did have loan facilities in place they were always for more than he knew he might need.

The Morris Garages became very much a shop-window for Morris. It was never regarded as a tiresome appendage, and he kept a keen watching brief on the business. He made sure it was generous with its customers, even if this meant not making money on a transaction. In his early days as a manufacturer it continued to be an agent for other marques, notably Humber, Sunbeam, Hillman, Daimler and American makes Dodge and Hudson. It also handled various makes of motorcycle, and vigorously advertised this side of the organisation. By 1925 or thereabouts it had abandoned all non-Morris agencies, but at the time of Cecil Kimber's arrival it still had a richly varied range of activities. Being Sales Manager of such an enterprise was no sinecure.

OPPOSITE: *Lord Nuffield at the 1956 Henley Regatta. By this time he was Honorary President of the British Motor Corporation, which was run by Leonard Lord, who in 1938 had taken up the top job at then-rival Austin. The merger created much bitterness amongst senior Morris management and Vice-Chairman Reggie Hanks was furious that the deal had been done behind his back. (Author's collection)*

RIGHT: *The entrance to the Queen Street showrooms of The Morris Garages, at around the time that Cecil Kimber joined the company. Agencies for Scott and Douglas motorcycles are advertised on the windows; employees recalled Kimber lighting up with enthusiasm when conversation turned to motorbikes. (Magna Press Library)*

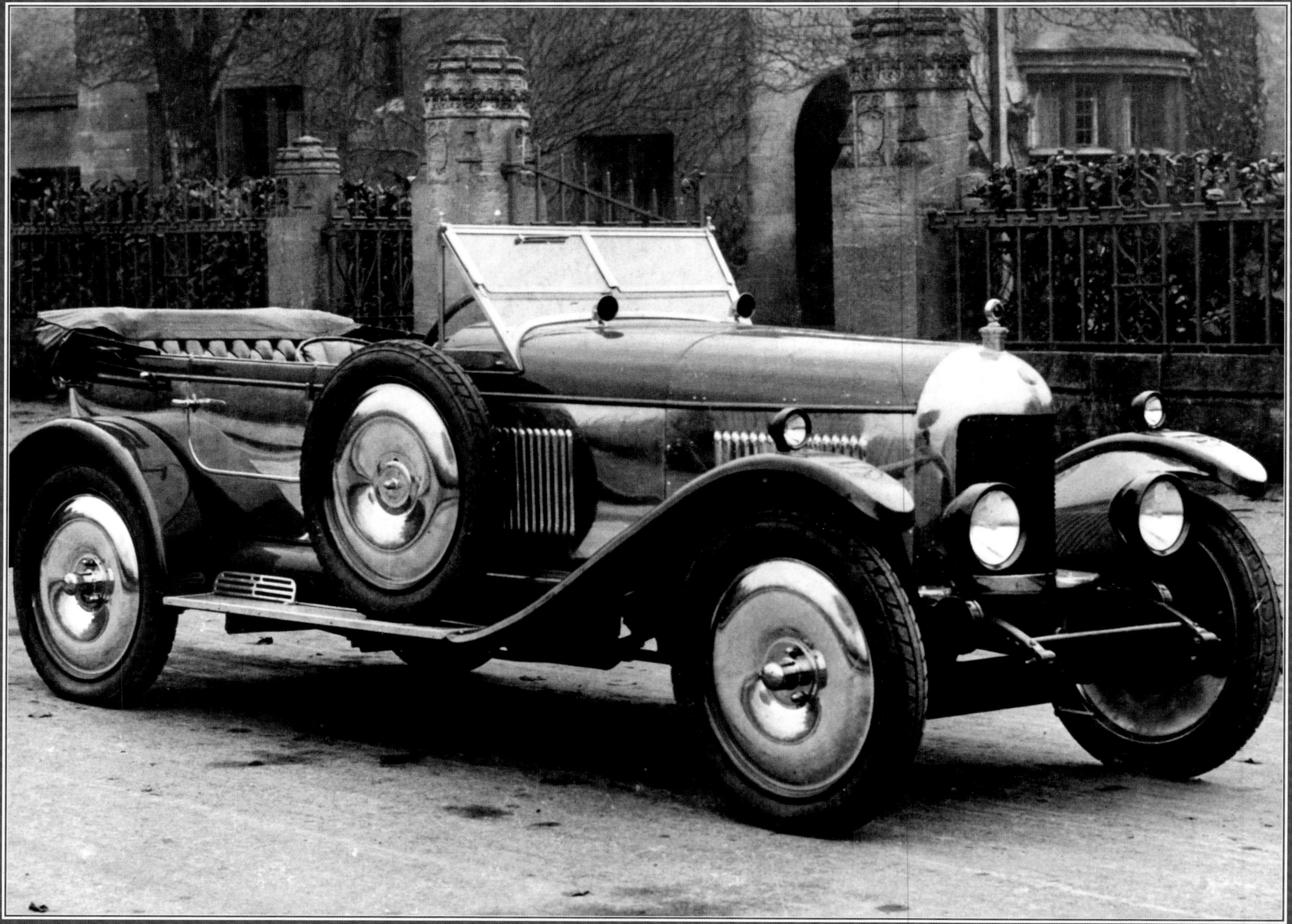

MAKING A MARQUE

Cecil Kimber's tenure as Sales Manager of The Morris Garages did not last long: in February 1922, two months short of his 34th birthday, he became General Manager. According to Wilson McComb this swift and unexpected promotion came about because the previous incumbent, Edward Armstead, had resigned. This is not the case. During 1921 a boardroom row between brothers-in-law Carl Breeden and Oliver Lucas had seen Breeden's departure from car electrics company Joseph Lucas. Breeden had promptly been recruited by William Morris as General Manager of The Morris Garages – apparently with Armstead being pushed to one side.

Quite what happened, and in what time frame, is not fully clear, but Cecil Kimber fills in some detail in a letter of 16 February 1922 to Frank Woollard. 'Since I last wrote you Breeden has come – and gone! Something rather more attractive engaged his attention in B'ham from which city he seemed very loath to part. I immediately tackled W.R.M. with the result I am now General Manager at 500 per with a decent percentage of profits – if any. Old Armstead says goodbye to us at the end of the month thank goodness…'

Armstead, who had been suffering from depression, committed suicide a few weeks later, gassing himself. As for Breeden, his short stay with The Morris Garages was due to his acquisition of the Wilmot Manufacturing Company of Birmingham, in 1927 to become Wilmot-Breeden Ltd. A leading supplier of brightwork to the motor industry, it was financially supported by William Morris, who was of course a major customer[1].

---

[1] The author is grateful to Peter Seymour for his research on Edward Armstead and Carl Breeden.

OPPOSITE: *A later long-wheelbase four-seater M.G. Super Sports. Harry Charnock, an owner of both a Bullnose and a Flatnose Super Sports, described the former as 'a scaled-down 3-litre Bentley at one-third the price'. (Author's collection)*

The Queen Street showroom of The Morris Garages during 1928, with a straight-eight Wolseley 21/60 saloon to the fore. Just visible on the sides of the mezzanine is a frieze depicting various M.G. models. (Magna Press Library)

THE MORRIS GARAGES CHUMMY

It was common practice at the time for larger dealers and distributors to offer their own coachwork on the chassis of the cars they sold. Sometimes these special bodies were in-house creations and sometimes they were designed and made – or perhaps just made – by outside coachbuilders. In his new post, Kimber decided to market a special Morris Garages version of the Bullnose Morris.

The car he came up with had close-coupled 'occasional four-seater' open bodywork. This followed the lines of a similar vehicle built on an early Morris Oxford chassis, images of which survive amongst photos belonging to the Kimber family. As far as can be judged the car is a one-off built in 1914 by Hollick and Pratt for company co-founder and close Morris associate Lancelot Pratt, and it has the unusual feature of two additional inward-facing folding occasional seats. This arrangement was duly copied by Kimber. Advertised as seating one adult or up to three children on the fold-down rear seats, the new creation was given the 'Chummy' name – as also used to refer to the first Austin Seven open tourers. Launched in time for the 1922 Motor Show, it had coachwork by

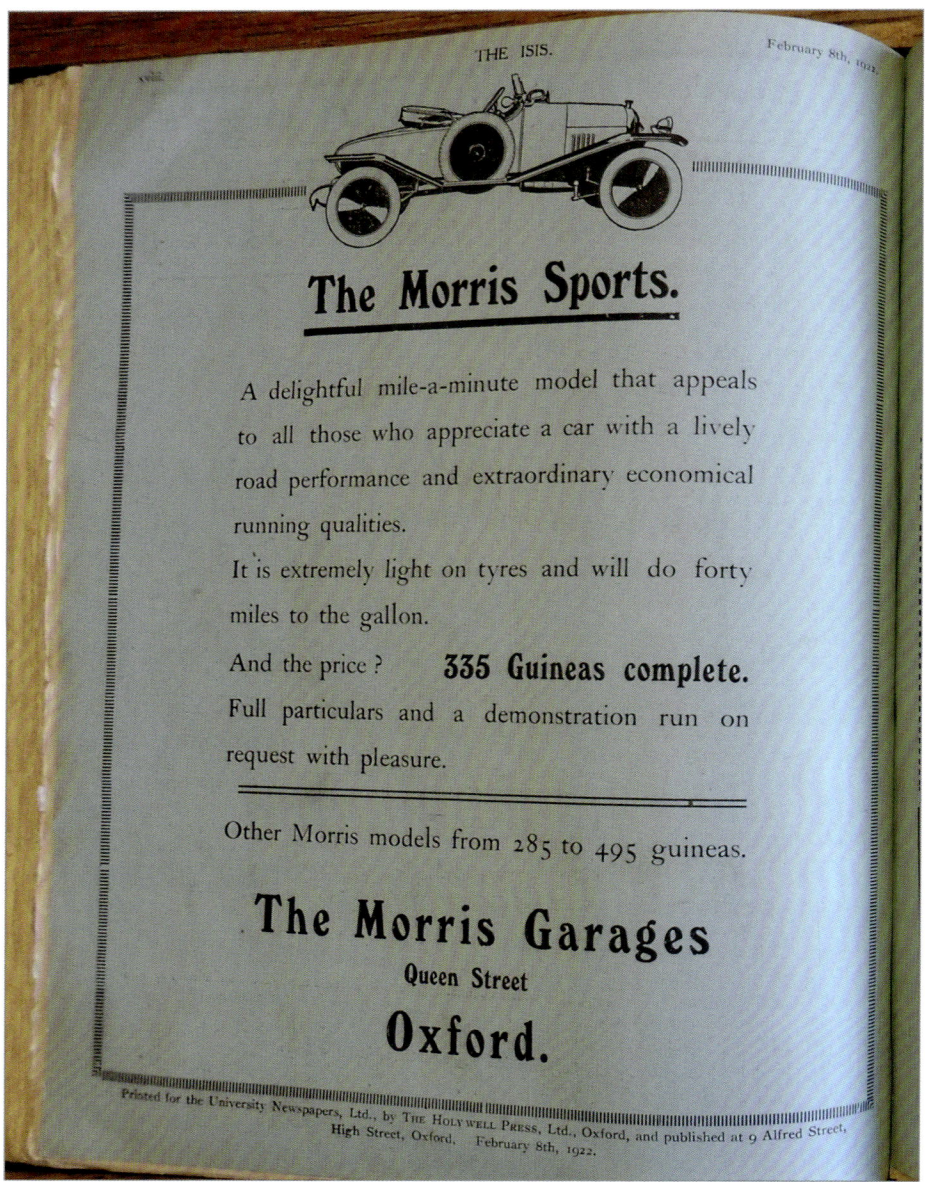

ABOVE: *The Morris Garages took prominent advertising in the Oxford student magazine* The Isis; *this back cover from February 1922 depicts the Sports Cowley, which would no longer be a catalogued model after the 1923 season. (Author's collection)*

RIGHT: *Cecil Kimber in a formal portrait from 1921 or 1922, after he had taken up his position with The Morris Garages; at this stage he and Rene were living in Clifton Hampden, a village near Abingdon.*

Coventry firm Carbodies[2], and was also sold by Morris dealers Parkside Garage of Coventry and Buist of Newcastle-on-Tyne.

According to future M.G. Works Manager Cecil Cousins, who had joined The Morris Garages in 1920, the cars were at first completed at the Longwall Street premises, but when demand for the Chummy gathered pace, it became necessary to take on mews premises in what was then called Alfred Lane but was later to be re-named Pusey Lane. Chassis were collected from Cowley, fitted with accessories such as dampers – using nothing more sophisticated than a hand-operated belly-brace drill – and then delivered to Coventry for the body to be mounted. The cars then returned to Alfred Lane where the instruments, dashboard controls, wiring and so on were installed – 'in our spare time, which started as a rule about 6 o'clock at night.'

The move to Alfred Lane in 1922 is described in colourful tones by Barré Lyndon in *Combat*, his romanticised account of the early M.G. years. 'In the heart of Oxford, down a narrow turning now known as Pusey Lane, he found some stables. They were dark and dilapidated, with rusted hay-racks in the stalls and roofing which dribbled water at every shower of rain. But the stalls had the floor space that he needed, and a shed at the end promised possibilities as a machine-shop. He began to build his cars where horses had once stamped, while in the machine-shop he installed drills and tools from his garage at home.

'The reek of oil replaced the scent of hay, and the jingle of harness was succeeded by the blare of exhaust and the thunder of engines. This evoked complaints from the tenants of neighbouring buildings, but the noise was pleasant to the enthusiastic motorists who found their way to the stables, seeking the man who was building cars solely for them,' writes Lyndon, whose real name was Alfred Edgar, and who was better known as a playwright and film scriptwriter.

During the 1923 Easter weekend Cecil Kimber took a Chummy on the Land's End Trial with Russel Chiesman[3], and won a gold medal – in place of which he chose to accept a pair of cufflinks. Reliability trials were at the time a popular and well-publicised form of competition motoring, involving covering long distances over often challenging terrain, against the clock. For manufacturers whose cars were not suitable for racing on the track at Brooklands, they were an excellent shop-window for the company's products, and for many years Kimber would use them as a promotional tool. More to the point, his gold medal was the start of a long history of competition successes for what would become the M.G. marque.

Medals from 1921, when Cecil Kimber took part in various speed trials and hillclimbs. Whether this was on a motorcycle or with a car has not been confirmed. (Author)

---

[2] Cecil Cousins said that the cars were bodied in Coventry, and Jack Gardiner (Cousins/Jarman reminiscences) that the coachwork was by Carbodies; this seems reasonable confirmation of whom was responsible.

[3] Russel Chiesman, whose family ran Chiesman's Department Store in Lewisham and who would help build the business into a thriving nine-store concern, was a long-term friend and a regular competitor in Kimber's early cars; his first name is indeed spelt with a single 'l'.

CLOCKWISE, STARTING WITH TOP LEFT: *Betty Kimber at the age of two and a half; Rene Kimber with Betty; and Betty (front row, second from left) in an early school photograph, dating from October 1924.*

Whether or not the Land's End 'gold' boosted sales, the jaunty Chummy, finished as standard in Pastel Blue, proved a winning formula. From February 1923 until the end of September that year Morris supplied a total of 109 chassis to Chummy specification – 85 being Cowleys and 24 being in higher-priced Oxford guise[4]. Alas, over at Cowley the Chummy's commercial success was noted, and for the 1924 season Morris decided to market its own near-identical version of the car, cutting the ground out from under Kimber's feet.

SECOND THOUGHTS: THE RAWORTH TWO-SEATERS

As a result of Morris's ungentlemanly appropriation of the Chummy design, Kimber decided to go off on a different tack. Quite possibly prompted by the gap in the Morris range left by the discontinuing for 1924 of the factory Sports version of the Cowley, he decided to offer a two-seat open Morris with a more sporting flavour. Rene's sister Kathy, staying in 1923 with the Kimbers[5], had memories of the pair sketching the outline of the car – with Rene 'very much involved and very happy,' according to the story handed down to daughter Jean.

Based on the lower-priced 11.9hp Cowley with its 1545cc engine, Kimber's new car had a body line that descended towards the tail, a five-pane windscreen, nautical-style scuttle vents, and a slightly modified chassis using components fabricated or machined in the Longwall Street workshops. As for the body, this was sub-contracted to Charles Raworth, an Oxford coachbuilder with workshops in St Aldates. Advertised variously as the M.G. Super Sports Morris, the M.G. Morris Sports and the Super Sports Morris, it retailed at £350, when the standard two-seater Cowley cost £198; what is most probably the first example[6] was registered towards the end of the summer of 1923.

---

[4] There are no records of any Chummy-specification chassis before February 1923, but this does not preclude a small number being supplied earlier but not identified as such.

[5] By 1923 Cecil and Rene Kimber had moved to an old Georgian house in Oxford, at the point where St Giles merges into Banbury Road.

[6] Barraclough and Jennings incline to the first car being that of Oliver Arkell of the Arkell brewery family, registered on 16 August 1923 and delivered on 5 September. The example supplied to Russel Chiesman, carrying registration FC 4908, shows signs of being a later car, built on a 1924-season chassis.

LEFT: *Under Kimber's management The Morris Garages were local agents for the motorcycles briefly produced by his former employer Martinsyde. (Author's collection)*

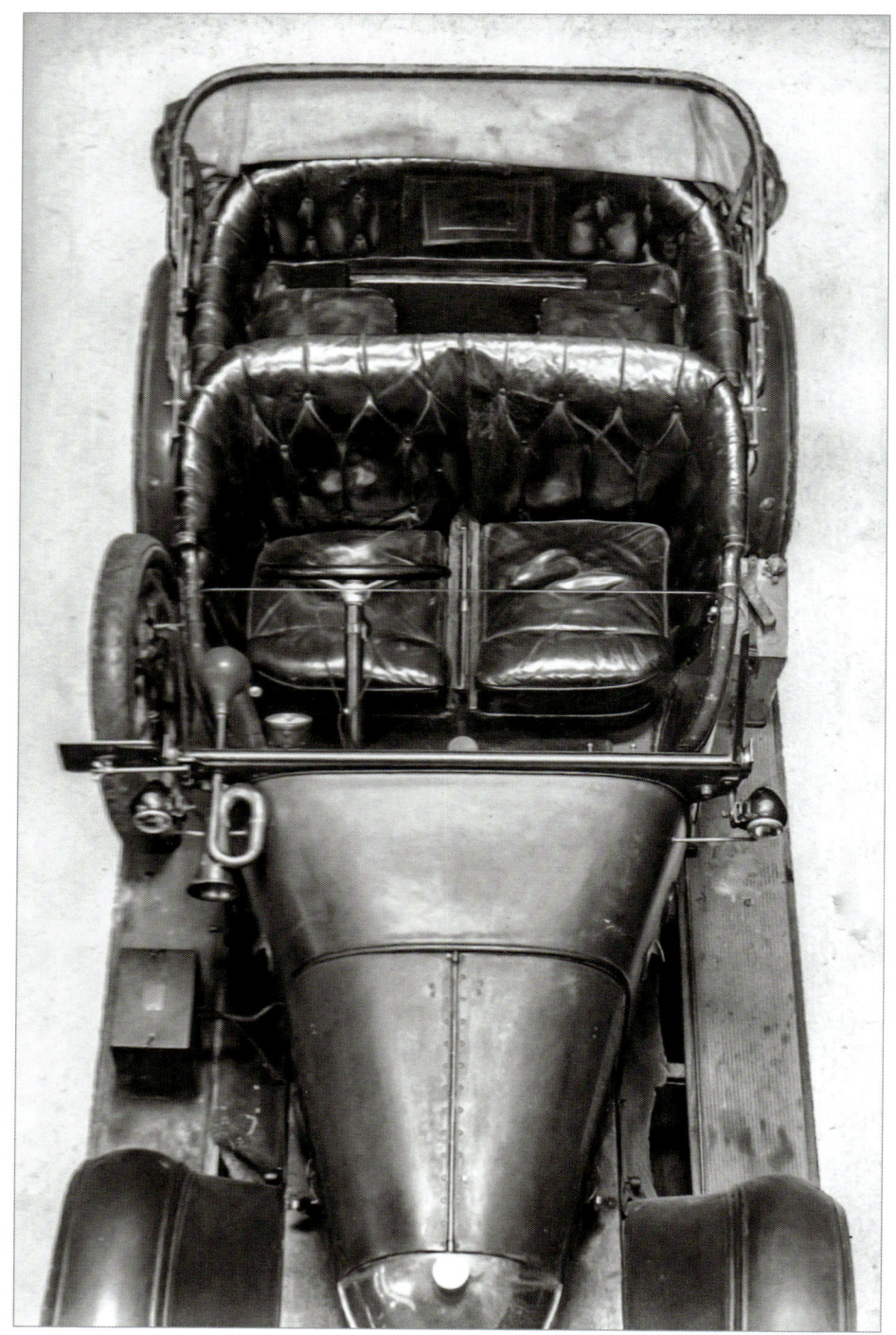

ABOVE: *Not just an old Morris Oxford: this is the car built with occasional four-seater bodywork for Lancelot Pratt of Hollick and Pratt.*

LEFT: *This photograph shows the fold-down jump seats in the rear, imitated by Kimber for his Chummy.*

OPPOSITE TOP: *The Chummy created by The Morris Garages can be recognised by its railway-carriage door handles. The occasional rear seating offered more comfortable accommodation than the dickey of a standard two-seater Morris.*

OPPOSITE BOTTOM: *Another view of the same car. "Whenever Kimber and I went out in one he used to drive like the devil and frighten me to death," accountant Ted Lee told Jonathan Wood. "I used to criticise him because the Chummy's proportions were a bit on the small side. You see Kimber was rather short himself and I suggested that if he altered the seating arrangement he could sell to taller people!"*

Chapter Four: Making a Marque

Chapter Four: Making a Marque

This Chummy is a factory car, and as such it does not have external door handles, access to the internal catches being by lifting the triangular rear section of the front sidescreens. (Author's collection)

The announced deletion of the Sports Cowley – which was in fact supplied into 1924 – might have prompted Kimber to come up with his own sporting version of the Cowley. (Author's collection)

The new model was, said the advertisements, 'an exceptionally fast touring motor car, capable of 60 miles an hour on the flat, and wonderful acceleration' – and with the modified steering and springing giving 'a glued-to-the-road effect producing finger-light steering at high road speeds'. Notwithstanding such seductive claims, just six of the cars would be made: customers were evidently thin on the ground, as the model was still being advertised in the summer of 1924.

Despite their lack of commercial success, the sporting character of the cars has led to an acceptance that, at least in genealogical terms, these sports Morrises can be considered the starting point for the M.G. marque. 'These were really the first M.G. Sports,' Cecil Cousins related to Lytton Jarman, emphasising the chassis upgrades. 'We did considerably more alterations to the chassis, i.e. specially-cambered springs, a special carb, and a special rake

Chapter Four: Making a Marque

The Alfred Street mews: the entire space was 20ft wide and 100ft long. The buildings were demolished in 1976 – some of the bricks being salvaged by Dick Knudson of the New England M.G. T Register. (Magna Press Library)

to the steering. To obtain this the steering box was mounted on a special bracket with an extra long drop arm.' In reality these were pretty minor changes, but they did give more sporting handling, and were carried through to later models that more clearly wore an M.G. identity; all the same, the issue of what car can be judged the first M.G. is a continuing subject of debate.

Used from the start in advertising the cars was the octagonal M.G. badge. In fact this pre-dates the Raworth two-seaters, being seen in Morris Garages advertisements as early as March 1923. The badge was the creation of the business's accountant, Ted Lee, and sprang from a conversation with Kimber, as Lee related to Jonathan Wood. "He then cleared off to his office and I stopped

ABOVE (BOTH): *Two views of the Raworth-bodied two-seater supplied to Oliver Arkell; it was finished in yellow and black. The long tail contains a dickey seat. (Early M.G. Society)*

TOP RIGHT: *Another of the six Raworth (pronounced 'Rayworth') two-seater M.G. Super Sports. This is Russel Chiesman's car, which won a gold medal on the 1924 Land's End Trial, making it arguably the first M.G. to be used in motor sport. (Phil Jennings)*

in mine. Then I drew out this badge with a little ruler I'd brought from High School. I was good at art and had painted for years. Kimber saw it and said 'That's just the thing'..." The badge was duly shown to William Morris[7] and Lee remembered him saying that it was "the best thing that has come into the company" – adding "and it will never go out of it".

It is apparent that Kimber was casting around for a formula that would give him a product to be made in decent numbers to replace the Chummy. In early 1924 he advertised a smart vee-fronted saloon, but with Morris offering its own perfectly presentable D-back Oxford saloon for £395 there was never going to be much of a market for the £460 Morris Garages version. Various other bodies were mounted on Bullnose chassis in the course of the year, not least two landaulettes.

---

[7] Lee recalled how Morris wanted to see how Kimber's M.G. experiment was progressing, writes Jonathan Wood. 'So every month Lee took his M.G. accounts to him at Cowley and although he remembers that Morris was not very interested in sports cars himself, he had great confidence in Kimber.'

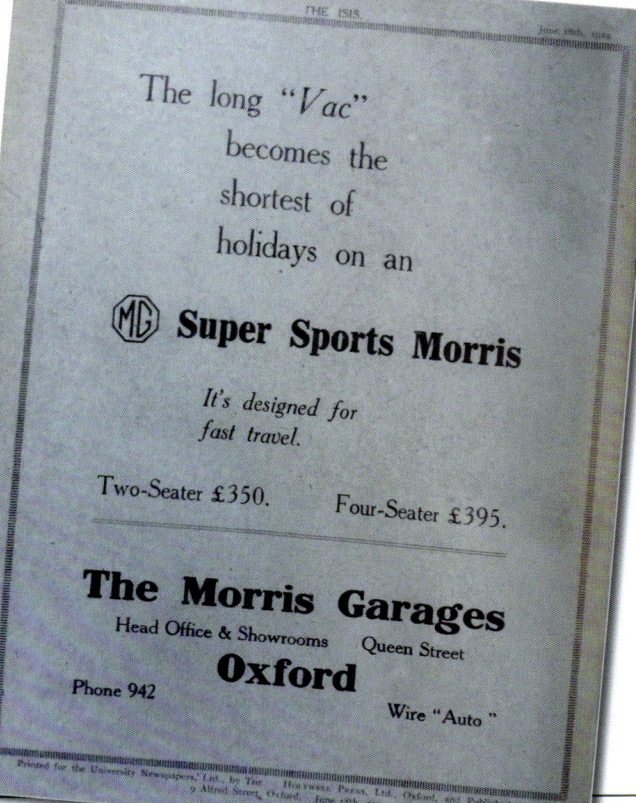

FAR LEFT, TOP: *This advertisement for what was called the M.G. Super Sports Morris appeared in* The Isis *for 5 December 1923, following one in the 21 November issue with the same wording. (Author's collection)*

LEFT: *Here, in a March 1924 issue, there is no use of the M.G. appellation – indicating that this was merely seen as an alternative tag for a product of The Morris Garages, rather than signifying a marque in its own right. 'Imshi' was a Morris used by the* Daily Mail *motoring correspondent for a six-month journey through France, Italy, Morocco, Algeria, Tunisia and Spain in 1920-21. (Author's collection)*

FAR LEFT, BOTTOM: *This time the car is called the M.G. Morris Sports rather than the Super Sports. (Author's collection)*

LEFT: *The company was still selling the old two-seater model in June 1924. (Author's collection)*

FINDING THE RIGHT FORMULA

Wilson McComb gives the most detailed account of what happened next, one that is corroborated in its essentials by the reminiscences of Cecil Cousins. It seems that Kimber was visited

LEFT: *'For a car of such distinction the price, £350, is surprisingly modest,' claimed the advertisements, this when the Sports Cowley's last quoted price had been 335 guineas or £352. (Early M.G. Society)*

BELOW: *The polished aluminium body of this 1924 four-seater is matched to claret wings; the open cars were initially all in this finish, with wings in smoke blue, claret or to choice, with matching upholstery and trim. Ace wheel discs were normal wear. (Early M.G. Society)*

THE 1924-1926 BULLNOSE SUPER SPORTS

The modifications to make a 13.9hp Morris Oxford into an M.G. Super Sports were subtle. There was a bracket to rake the steering, allowing a lower line to the scuttle. The springs were flattened, which meant that at the rear the Gabriel Snubbers – dampers using spring-tensioned webbing – were replaced by Hartford friction dampers; at the front the Gabriels remained. In addition the engine was lightly modified, an SU 'sloper' carburettor generally replacing the Smiths unit and the ports being polished, while the back axle ratio was raised to allow more relaxed cruising. A special exhaust system was also fitted, and the looks were sharpened by the fitment of Ace wheel discs. The revised steering, which brought with it a longer drop arm, meant that there was no room for the central throttle still retained by the Morris, so the pedal was moved to the right; additionally the central handbrake was soon displaced to a position beside the driver, who had to avoid entangling it with his trousers.

Naturally enough, the four-wheel brakes of 1925 Oxfords were standardised on the Morris Garages productions, although a few cars may have been supplied with two-wheel braking. For 1926 the Super Sports gained a Dewandre brake servo and Barker dipping headlamps that physically dipped on their mounting bar; further to this, the long-wheelbase chassis was standardised for all models. Wire wheels came in, too, for the open Super Sports, with the option of Ace wheel discs, and still in conjunction with narrow beaded-edge tyres. On the engine side, a Solex carburettor was henceforth used, along with a special magneto, and power units were now dismantled and inspected and the reciprocating parts balanced and the ports polished. Bodies, meanwhile, were two inches wider, and had steel wings.

One distinguished owner was the heir to the Spanish throne, the Prince of the Asturias, who while up at Oxford had a four-seater finished in the Spanish royal colours. The combination was certainly striking: purple wings and upper body, a red-and-gold coachline, and a red-painted chassis with gold pinstripes. Capitalising on this royal patronage, the Morris distributor in Madrid advertised the M.G. Super Sports Morris Oxford tourer as the 'Prince of the Asturias' model.

Excluding the six 1923 Raworth-bodied two-seaters, 327 Bullnose M.G. Super Sports Morris Oxfords are thought to have been made, the accepted tally being 101 two-seaters, 220 four-seaters and six Salonettes; in addition 15 standard-specification Salonettes are recorded.

This four-seater is a long-wheelbase model dating from 1925. The Ace wheel discs this example wears were a popular accessory in the 1920s and 1930s. (Author)

by Reg Brown, a salesman for Sunbeam motorcycles – for whom The Morris Garages was an agent – and was shown a special Morris Oxford he was running. It had a polished aluminium sports body, and sat on a chassis with flattened springs, raked steering and wire wheels. The body was the work of Clarey Hughes, a sidecar-maker in Birmingham, and was supposedly modelled on that of a 30/98 Vauxhall; Kimber was impressed.

At around the same time, a salesman for The Morris Garages called Jack Gardiner[8] had bought a 13.9hp Oxford chassis with the 1805cc engine standardised for 1924. In preparation for fitting a sporting body, he started modifying the chassis, lowering the springs and in addition raking the steering column. Gardiner showed Kimber sketches of what he had in mind for the body, and Kimber ended up taking him up to Birmingham and Coventry. It is not known whether Gardiner saw the Brown car or not, but he said that he did visit Carbodies, where according to his

---

[8] Jack Gardiner would eventually become Personnel Manager at the Abingdon factory, retiring in 1966 or thereabouts.

Kimber in a 1925-season car with the longer (by 6in) wheelbase and painted upper body. Short-wheelbase four-seaters can be recognised by the bevelled rear edge of the single door on the driver's side.

account Kimber showed him a four-seater aluminium body and said that this was the type of body that would be used on his chassis. Gardiner's car was duly built with polished-aluminium coachwork exactly in this style, and was registered on 13 March 1924 as FC 6333.

McComb is unsure whether Hughes or Carbodies was responsible for the body, but as it is largely identical to that of subsequent M.G. Super Sports Morris Oxfords, which were definitely bodied by Carbodies, it is reasonable to suppose that they can claim paternity of the car. A fly in the ointment, however, is the version of events recounted by Carbodies historian Bill Munro. This has the car being built by Hughes, and Kimber asking the company to build more like it. But Hughes apparently was not in a position to take the order, said to be for six cars, states Munro, and so Kimber commissioned Carbodies, thereby setting in motion a lucrative collaboration that would last into the following decade.

ABOVE: *The cars were said to be aimed at the motorist with 'sporting proclivities and cultivated taste'. This advertisement from 1925 was placed in* The Brooklands Gazette, *the original name for what became* Motor Sport *magazine. (Author's collection)*

RIGHT: *The 1925-1926 two-seater was a more elegant piece of work than the preceding Raworth cars; the body, as that of the four-seaters and Salonettes, came from Carbodies in Coventry. (Ken Martin collection)*

The head of Carbodies, Bobby Jones, had briefly been general manager at Hollick and Pratt, the company that made most of the first Morris bodies and ultimately became Morris Bodies Branch, so there was already a link, albeit a tenuous one, with William Morris. Jones's cleverness was in extrapolating the same body style across different chassis, and the bodies for the cars for The Morris Garages were essentially the same as those provided to Alvis for its 12/50 model. Talk of the coachwork as being designed by Cecil Kimber is therefore fanciful, although there is no reason to doubt that he would have sought at least some modest input into the look of the cars.

To return to the Gardiner tourer, this sat on undisguised artillery wheels and did not have the scuttle ventilators of the earlier two-seaters; nor was the steering column raked to anything like the same degree as later cars. In all other respects, though, it was the clear starting point for the first generation of M.G.-badged Morris Oxfords built by The Morris Garages. As such, M.G. in-house magazine *The Sports Car*, in its February 1938 issue, described it as 'the first M.G.' – but, as will be discussed in the Postscript on pages 520-523, the company was woefully inconsistent, and even blatantly inaccurate, in such matters.

Bullnose M.G. authorities Robin Barraclough and Phil Jennings estimate that perhaps six further four-seat tourers were built as 1924-season models. When for 1925 the wheelbase of the Oxford tourer, saloon and cabriolet was extended to 9ft, the Super Sports four-seater followed suit, while two new Super Sports models, an open two-seater and a closed Salonette, retained the 8ft 6in chassis for the 1925 model year. The extra six inches in the wheelbase enhanced the lean look of the four-seater, as did the introduction of a painted top half to the body, applicable equally to the two-seater; Kimber would claim that he pioneered this

The shapely rear deck housed a dickey seat. In all, 101 Carbodies two-seater Bullnose Super Sports were made, against an estimated 220 four-seaters. (Ken Martin collection)

Chapter Four: Making a Marque

ABOVE: *Betty and Rene Kimber pose with an F-type landaulette presumably with what would have been described as M.G. bodywork. In October 1924 The Morris Garages supplied an F-type for the pre-London run at Oxford's New Theatre of 'Six-Cylinder Love' by William Anthony McGuire – 'One of those rather naive things that occasionally slip through from the other side of the Atlantic,' according to the somewhat acidic review that appeared in* Punch *magazine.*

OPPOSITE: *Three six-cylinder F-type Morris chassis were acquired by The Morris Garages in February 1924; the model suffered engine problems and it was abandoned after just 49 had been made. This example has Super Sports tourer coachwork. Rene Kimber is seated at the rear, furthest from the camera, with her sister Kathy, whose husband John Stevenson is in the front passenger seat.*

DALTON WATSON FINE BOOKS

NEWEST RELEASES

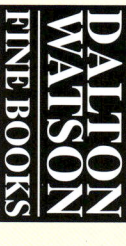

IMAGINE TOO!
Patrick G. Kelley

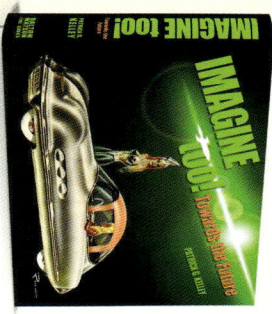

A companion book to Patrick Kelley's previous book, IMAGINE!, which featured vivid illustrations of a wide range of concept cars from the 1930s onwards, IMAGINE too! showcases a new crop of images and artists, along with some familiar favorites. The three hundred incredible designs in this book have been untouched and unseen since they were first drawn and provide a singular look into the imagined future with visions of flying cars and other marvels. The majority of the drawings spotlighted in IMAGINE too! are concepts that never made it off the drawing board to the factory floor or showroom, but their imaginative designs can nevertheless inspire us today.

456 pages | 710 illustrations $150

BUGATTI THE ITALIAN DECADE
Gautam Sen

When, in 1987, Romano Artioli and his high-profile associates – Ferruccio Lamborghini, Paolo Stanzani and Jean-Marc Borel – decided to reincarnate Bugatti, one of the most famous automotive marques of all time, they had in Ferruccio Lamborghini, Paolo Stanzani and design legend Marcello Gandini, three of the most prominent names in the Italian supercar firmament, suggesting a bright future for the marque. Eight years later, Artioli's dream was over. Bankruptcy was declared, the factory was closed, and the beautiful campus reduced to a ghost building. Not even a decade had passed between the first germs of an idea and the end in 1995, yet there are enough ingredients for an exciting action-filled story: discord, rivalry, pride, power, money, prestige, stars, crises and a dramatic end. What happened? Why did it happen? *Bugatti: The Italian Decade* answers all that and more.

400 pages | 790 photographs $150

RAYMOND HENRI DIETRICH:
Automotive Architect of the Classic Era & Beyond
Necah Stewart Furman

Originally written in 1961, this revised, comprehensive, and entertaining biography of famous classic car designer Raymond Henri Dietrich—known as "the automotive architect of the classic era"—is an accurate record of his life and times based upon records and interviews unavailable to others. Featuring more than six hundred photographs and documents, many never previously published, this entertaining and well-researched societal history traces the eight decades of the designer's life, revealing little known aspects of his career and his triumphs over tragedy. Historians and auto enthusiasts alike will appreciate how this handsomely illustrated book skillfully transports the reader from one era to another in the life of an extraordinary man who left an impressive legacy of classic car design.

616 pages | 615 illustrations $150

FORTY SIX
THE BIRTH OF PORSCHE MOTORSPORT
Multiple authors

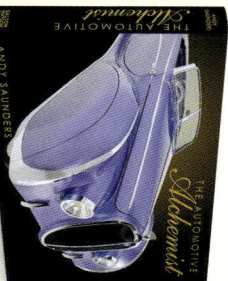

Forty Six tells the unlikely underdog story of the car that scored Porsche's first racing victories and helped establish their commercial success: 356/2 SL 063. Beginning at the company's post-World War II nadir, the authors illuminate how Porsche rose from the ashes to overcome multiple trials and near disasters to compete with this vehicle at Le Mans, the Liège-Rome-Liège Rally, and Montlhéry, where they set new racing records in the 1950s. The tale continues into the twenty-first century, making clear how 356/2 SL 063 helped set Porsche Motorsport on its way to becoming the juggernaut that we know today. Including a wealth of archival photographs and documents that have never been previously published, along with a look at the car's US history.

336 pages | 500 photographs $150
PUBLISHER'S ED: 250 signed/numbered, plus 20-pg supplement $285

RECENT RELEASES

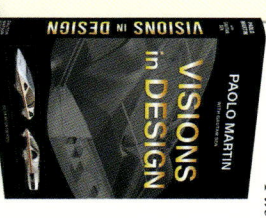

THE AUTOMOTIVE ALCHEMIST
Andy Saunders

464 pages | 1,055 photographs
$115

VISIONS in DESIGN
Paolo Martin

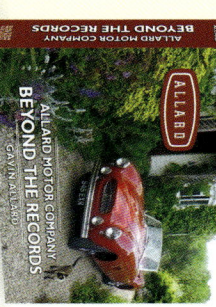

304 pages
1,167 illustrations
$125

BEYOND THE RECORDS
Allard Motor Company
Gavin Allard

2 volumes
736 pages
1,313 illustrations
$175

Dalton Watson Fine Books
Glyn and Jean Morris
www.daltonwatson.com
+1 847 274 5874
info@daltonwatson.com

Dalton Watson MyRewards When you buy a book from daltonwatson.com, you will receive points for the product(s) you purchase. Not all items accrue points. Each product indicates how many points you will earn below the price in the description. It's a great way to save on your next purchase, whether it's for you or someone special and is our way of saying "thank you" to our returning customers.

COACHBUILDING/DESIGN

Berlinetta '60s: Exceptional Italian Coupés of the Sixties	Xavier de Nombel and Christian Descombes	$95
Gaston Grümmer: The Art of Carrosserie *(2-Volume Set)*	Philippe-Gaston Grümmer and Laurent Friry	Regular: $295
Marcel Pourtout: Carrossier	Jon Pressnell	$150
Paolo Martin: Visions in Design	Paolo Martin with Gautam Sen	$125
Park Ward: The Innovative Coachbuilder 1919-1939 *(3-Volume Set)*	Malcolm Tucker	Regular: $375; Custom Leather: $1600
Raymond Henri Dietrich: Automotive Architect of the Classic Era & Beyond	Necah S. Furman	$150
The Bertone Collection	Gautam Sen and Michael Robinson	$95
The Kellner Affair: Matters of Life and Death *(3-Volume Set)*	Peter Larsen with Ben Erickson	Regular: $445
Tom Tjaarda: Master of Proportions	Gautam Sen	$150
V. Morel and AJ Grümmer: Builders of Exceptional Carriages	Philippe-Gaston Grümmer	$195

GENERAL AUTOMOTIVE/RACING

Audi RS: History • Models • Technology	Constantin Bergander	$79
Augie Pabst: Behind the Wheel	Robert Birmingham	Regular: $79; Signed/Numbered: $99
The Automotive Alchemist	Andy Saunders	$115
Bahamas Speed Weeks	Terry O'Neil	$155
Bugatti: The Italian Decade	Gautam Sen	$150
Cobra Pilote: The Ed Hugus Story	Robert D. Walker	$89
Concours d'Elegance: Dream Cars and Lovely Ladies	Patrick Lesueur, Translated by David Burgess-Wise	$69
Cunningham: The Passion, The Cars, The Legacy *(2-Volume Set)*	Richard Harman	Regular: $350; Leather: $1200
Ferrari 333 SP: A Pictorial History 1993-2003	Terry O'Neil	$150
Fit for a King: The Royal Garage of the Shahs of Iran	Borzou Sepasi	$150
Formula 1	Peter Nygaard	$89
Imagine too!	Patrick Kelley	Regular: $150; Signed/Numbered: $200
Lime Rock Park: The Early Years 1955-1975	Terry O'Neil	$225
Meister Bräuser: Harry Heuer's Championship Racing Team	Tom Schultz	Regular: $95; Signed/Numbered: $125
Mid-Atlantic Sports Car Races 1953-1962	Terry O'Neil	Signed/Numbered: $155
Pebble Beach Concours d'Elegance: The Art of the Poster	Robert Devlin, Kandace Hawkinson	Regular: $69; Silk: $295
QPRS: F1 Grand Prix Racing by the Numbers, 1950-2019	Clyde P. Berryman	$95
Shelby Cobras: CSX 2001 - CSX 2125 *(2-Volume Set)*	Robert D. Walker	$250
Sports Car Racing in the South: Vol. I 1957-1958, Vol. II 1959-1960, Vol. III 1961-1962	Willem Oosthoek	Vol I: $125; Vol II: $155; Vol III (Signed/Numbered): $155
The Golden Days of Thompson Speedway and Raceway 1945-1977	Terry O'Neil	Signed/Numbered: $195
The Straight Eight Engine: Powering Premium Automobiles	Keith Ray	$95
Watkins Glen: The Street Years 1948-1952	Philippe Defechereux	$49

BRITISH CARS

Allard Motor Company: Beyond the Records *(2-Volume Set)*	Gavin Allard	$175
Bentley Motors: On the Road	Bernard L. King	$165
Bentley: Fifty Years of the Marque	Johnnie Green/Hageman, King, Bennett	$92
Making a Marque: Rolls-Royce Motor Car Promotion 1904-1940	Peter Moss and Richard Roberts	$125
Rolls-Royce: Silver Wraith	Martin Bennett	$125
Rolls-Royce: The Classic Elegance	Lawrence Dalton/Bernard L. King	$85
The Rolls-Royce Phantom II Continental	André Blaize	Regular: $395; Leather: $1750
The Silver Ghost: A Supernatural Car	Jonathan Harley	$69
Why Not? The Story of The Honourable Charles Stuart Rolls	David Baines	$89
Jaguar E-Type Six-Cylinder Originality Guide	Dr. Thomas F. Haddock & Dr. Michael C. Mueller	$125
Vintage Jaguar Keyrings, 1955-1980	Morrill 'Bud' Marston	Regular: $95; Signed/Numbered: $135

FRENCH CARS

Title	Author	Price
Crossing the Sands: The Sahara Desert Trek to Timbuktu	Ariane Audouin-Debreuil/Ingrid MacGill	$65
Eighty Years of Citroën in the UK	John Reynolds	Regular: $70; Special Edition: $450

GERMAN CARS

Forty Six: The Birth of Porsche Motorsport Forty Six – Publisher's Edition *(250 signed/numbered, includes 20-pg supplement)*	Multiple	Regular: $150 Publishers Edition: $285
Gulf 917	Jay Gillotti	Regular: $150; Leather (2-vol): $1500
Porsche by Mailander	Karl Ludvigsen	$150
Rudolf Uhlenhaut: Engineer and Gentleman	Wolfgang Scheller and Thomas Pollak	$89

ITALIAN CARS

Lamborghini: At the Cutting Edge of Design *(2-Volume Set)*	Gautam Sen	$250
Maserati 300S *(Revised, 2-volume set)*	Walter Bäumer	Regular: $270
Maserati A6GCS	Walter Bäumer and Jean-François Blachette	$175
Maserati A6G 2000 Frua • Pininfarina • Vignale • Allemano	Walter Bäumer	$125
Maserati Tipo 63, 64, 65: Birdcage to Supercage	Willem Oosthoek	Regular: $140; Special Edition: $550

ICON / GENERAL INTEREST

Steve McQueen: A Tribute to the King of Cool	Marshall Terrill	Special Edition: $95
Steve McQueen: *Le Mans* in the Rearview Mirror	Don Nunley with Marshall Terrill	$79
Steve McQueen: In His Own Words	Marshall Terrill	$95
Steve McQueen: The Last Mile Revisited	Barbara McQueen and Marshall Terrill	$49

ORDER FROM: Dalton Watson Fine Books / **www.daltonwatson.com** / info@daltonwatson.com / +1 847 274 5874

treatment. This upper portion of the body was now in steel, but the lower panelling remained in polished aluminium.

These were appealing cars, combining trusted Morris mechanicals with racy looks and a dose of extra performance. All this came at a reasonable price: £350 for a two-seater and £375 for a four-seater, against £260 and £285 for the respective mainstream Oxford models. Kimber had found the way forward, and in 1925 a full 142 two-seater and four-seater Super Sports would be made, as well as six Super Sports Salonettes and – apparently – three ordinary-chassised Salonettes.

Not all Kimber's eggs were put in this basket, all the same: The Morris Garages continued to offer resolutely non-sporting coachwork on the Morris chassis through until 1927, predominantly saloons, landaulettes and the rather gothic six-light Weymann fabric saloon. Additionally it furnished bodies on the odd chassis for marques it did not handle: Barraclough and Jennings show photographs of a Daimler fixed-head coupé and a Voisin open tourer, the latter with coachwork very similar to that used on the M.G. Super Sports.

Although this new activity was largely one of final assembly and finishing, its scale was not insignificant. Cecil Cousins recounts how 'a large re-organisation of the plant' occurred with the arrival of two electric drills. 'The strength of the depot had now risen to about half a dozen. So also had the sales of the standard Morris

product, and so we continued to collect and deliver the standard cars during the daytime, and build the saloons and sports models on overtime. Our average week usually ran into round about 80 hours,' he relates. 'In the summertime we commenced at six o'clock in the morning and usually worked till ten or twelve at night, but a difficulty arose owing to a neighbour complaining that our hammering and singing was causing her to lose her beauty sleep. A note was then sent round by Mr Kimber saying that we were not to make a noise before seven in the morning. After that I don't think anyone in the neighbourhood had any doubt in their mind as to when it was 7am, because at that time everyone made as much noise as they possibly could.'

It was quite a circus operating within the tight confines of the mews, even after a neighbouring stable had been annexed. With up to 25 cars packed in overnight like sardines, the first job in the morning was to put most of them outside to allow room to work. At night, the reverse had to happen. Eventually a lock-up shed in St Ebbes was rented to store cars and chassis, which were then ferried from one end of Oxford to the other according to requirements.

the experiment failed dismally. Too wild.

Modern man has discovered a new form of this pastime. He makes a pet of a car.

Wisely he chooses a car of 11 to 14 horse power : tractable : swift : sweet in motion : economical in food : beautiful to the eye. For preference he chooses a MORRIS.

The very act of choosing

(4)

the pet is a delight. There are varieties for every taste. Shall it be a sober grey 4-seater MORRIS COWLEY, an M.G. Super-Sports in glittering aluminium painted to your taste, or a MORRIS OXFORD Saloon in rich maroon?

Every home should have a pet of this description. Call in right away and choose yours.

(5)

In the early days in particular Kimber often displayed a sense of whimsy in the advertisements he sanctioned. This 1926 booklet suggests adopting an M.G. Super Sports as a family pet. (Early M.G. Society)

Rene and a vee-front Morris Garages saloon, photographed at Blenheim Palace in Woodstock. Although having none of the features of the Super Sports, these cars were sold under the M.G. name, as the M.G. Four-door Saloon Morris Oxford.

THESE TWO PAGES: *By 1926 the Salonette was called the Sporting Salonette. The alloy coachwork was by Carbodies. Two-seat Salonettes – with the bustle back – had a folding rear seat and were generally in duo-tones. The Motor hailed their 'harmonious yet racy lines'. (Magna Press)*

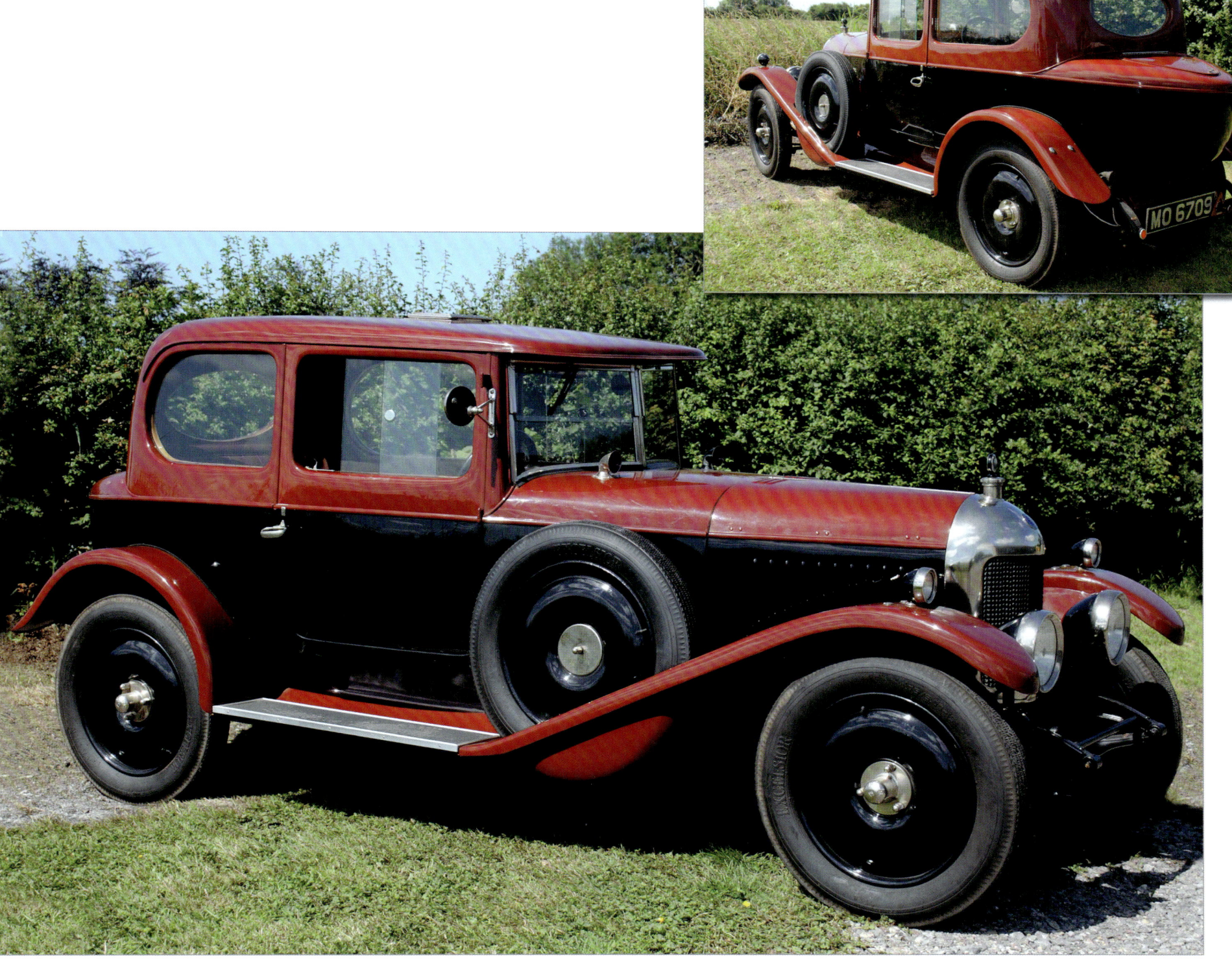

Chapter Four: Making a Marque

LEFT: *The fabric-bodied Morris Garages Weymann saloon; despite its gothic looks it was latterly available as a Super Sports. (Phil Jennings)*

BELOW: *Merry japes after a 1924 event, possibly an Oxford Motor Club trial. Perched on the bonnet of the Oxfordshire-registered Morris – it is not an M.G. Super Sports – is Wilfrid Mathews, who would be navigator to Cecil Kimber (seen second left) on the 1925 Land's End Trial.*

The memories of Jack Lowndes[9], another early employee, confirm the challenging working conditions. 'Our workshop was at the back of the premises in Alfred Lane, and when we wanted to get another M.G. sports car to work on, we had to push about 15 standard cars out into the lane, to get ours in. That was the place to teach one to drive: the cars were packed wing to wing, until we could not get another car into the yard. One morning when we arrived at work, we found every car covered with snow [and] the open cars full right up with frozen snow…We had to boil water on our oil stove to thaw the snow…'

---

[9] Cousins/Jarman reminiscences.

'OLD NUMBER ONE' – AND A SECOND DAUGHTER

It was in early 1925 that the most famous car created by Cecil Kimber saw the light of day. This is the car that has become known as 'Old Number One' and is regularly described as being the first M.G. – a claim that is most certainly contestable. First registered in March 1925, in Cecil Kimber's name, the car was a one-off built for him to use in the Motor Cycle Club's Land's End Trial, to be held over the Easter of 1925.

The basis of the car was a Morris chassis with the rear rebuilt to incorporate semi-elliptic springing, for better axle location. The

Kimber in his 1925 special. When, after the Land's End Trial, he called in on Devon Morris agent Frank Barton, William Morris's former business partner and general manager of The Morris Garages from 1911 to 1918, he ill-advisedly invited his wife for a spin in the car, took a bend on two wheels and nearly turned it over. Mrs Barton was not impressed, her son related to the author.

engine was an 11.9hp unit acquired from Morris Engines Branch, but was not the regular 'Hotchkiss' side-valve type used by Morris: instead it was an overhead-valve variant that had been made in small numbers for a Scottish would-be motor manufacturer by the name of Gilchrist who had ceased trading with a mere 20 or so cars built. The quoted power was 28bhp at 2,500rpm, but the overhead-valve configuration made it more amenable to tuning, and Kimber had the engine duly modified for greater power; he also – so he said – had the capacity reduced to fit into the under-1500cc class. The mechanicals were topped by a tightly-drawn doorless two-seater body of undeniable sports-car looks, albeit with rather crude folded mudguards.

Kimber took the car out on test and recorded an indicated 82mph – a profoundly impressive figure when a regular Morris Oxford, with the bigger 13.9hp engine, was good for no more than 55mph. Alas, he returned from his testing of the car with its chassis having developed a fracture. This was on the Thursday before Easter. The chassis was repaired overnight and into Good Friday, with welded-on plates, and Kimber made it to the start of the trial in time. Despite plug and carburettor problems and a puncture, he and his passenger, insurance broker Wilfrid Mathews, successfully completed the event and were awarded a gold medal.

Soon after the trial the car was sold to Stockport Morris agent Harry Turner, for £300 – a modest profit on the sum of 'about £285' that Kimber would later say[10] that the car had cost him. In November 1930 it passed to a Ronald Davidson, for £50, and in

---

[10] In *The Motor*, 5 October 1937 issue.

TOP: *This rear shot clearly shows the upswept chassis with its semi-elliptic springs.*

LEFT: *The Kimber trials special outside the family home in Woodstock Road, with Betty.*

OPPOSITE: *A famous image of Kimber tackling Blue Hill Mines on the 1925 Land's End Trial. (Author's collection)*

A 1926 tourer on wire wheels; these were new for 1926-season open Super Sports models. (Early M.G. Society)

This 1926 advertisement, as others in the same series, carries the wording 'They are W.R. Morris productions' – but the M.G. name is now to the fore. (Author's collection)

February 1932 Kimber wrote to Davidson – saying that the car was 'virtually the first M.G. ever produced' – and asking if it had its original body and might be for sale. Kimber was too late, as the car had been sold at auction for 11 guineas. Seen towing a trailer of pig food in Birmingham, it finished up in a Manchester scrapyard where it was spotted by an M.G. employee and purchased at the end of 1932 by the company. Refurbished and put on show in the Abingdon factory, the car survives to this day, surrounded by a fog of misinformation about its origins that seems never fully to dissipate[11].

Returning to 1925, on 27 May a second daughter, Jean, was born to Cecil and Rene Kimber, by this time living at 339 Woodstock Road on the outskirts of Oxford. Having already suffered from gallbladder troubles, again the birth brought complications for Rene, as Jean recounts in *The Other Tack*. 'I have been told that she was not very pleased to be pregnant again – understandably, as she was ill for quite a while: the first signs of colitis appeared, which is now thought by some doctors to be related to stress. I think my mother, not alone in her generation, had problems with the sexual side of marriage. My sister told me that my mother was an admirer of the writings of Elinor Glyn, who advised women to remain on pedestals, wrapped in mystery, whereas my father longed for friendship, natural warmth and affection,' she writes[12].

'Though my mother apparently thought my arrival was forced on her, I was never made to feel unwanted, as so many unlucky children that I have worked with in family therapy have told me. My parents may not have been great lovers, but they were excellent parents. My sister and I certainly felt special. Wherever we lived the gardens were designed primarily for us to play in. The sandpit

---

[11] That this misinformation has frequently emanated from Abingdon itself, and dates back to pre-war times when memories would have been fresher, is piquantly comic: the whole question of 'Old Number One' and what car can be judged to be the first M.G. is discussed on pages 520-523.

[12] This is an interesting interpretation of the values and writings of romantic novelist and screenwriter Glyn (1864-1943), whose books were considered daring and even erotic, and who had affairs with various British aristocrats.

Jean Kimber was born in 1925; here she is just one year old.

at 339 Woodstock Road was a central, brick-built feature that was covered with boards in wet weather; we also had a large ex-Army hut as our outdoor playroom, and in the winter we were allowed to turn the dining room table upside down to make a pirate ship or a robber's stronghold for the games suggested by my sister's fertile imagination. On the weekends, when I was too small to travel far, my father took us on expeditions to Shotover Common, or to walk in Blenheim Park where he would pretend to fall off the bridge over the lake. He was also a marvellous storyteller. The adventures of Henrietta, her dog Woozie, and her friend the mermaid, who took them under the sea in Tunny the Taxi, went on for years[13].'

BAINTON ROAD: KIMBER'S FIRST FACTORY

In September 1925 Cecil Kimber moved his manufacturing operations – if that is not too grandiose a term – to a part of the Morris Radiators Branch factory that was in the process of being constructed on derelict ground overlooking a former brickfield situated off Oxford's Woodstock Road. 'Kim had discovered the derelict ground near Bainton Road, and had suggested that it held possibilities, as a result of which the radiator works were erected there and, as some sort of return for discovering the site, he was given space in the new factory," writes Barré Lyndon in *Combat*. 'Workmen were still extending it when he moved in, and as fast as one bay was completed another was begun, partly to accommodate the growing output of Morris Radiators and partly to make room for Kim and his cars. At first he had half a bay, with his machine-shop in one corner. Presently he took over a whole bay, wresting a newly-built extension from the radiator works.'

With 50-odd employees and their own premises, the car-building arm of Morris Garages was on its way to becoming the M.G. Car

---

[13] Typical of Kimber's playful inventiveness was his distribution of Christmas presents. 'At Woodstock Road they had two rooms with a shutter in between. At Christmas he insisted on a ritual. There were parcels at one side of the room, and strings through, and you pulled a string to get a parcel,' Vernon Kimber told Wilson McComb.

Company. 'When we went to Bainton Road... considerably more men were engaged, [and] an extra operation was put into being in the shape of running-in the chassis with their rear wheels jacked up in a lean-to shed attached to the main building. Some pretence was then made to operate...on a line principle, with separate staff working on the chassis, [and] others working on the cars when they were returned from the coachbuilders,' recounts Cecil Cousins.

The 1926 season was even more successful, with 167 two-seater and four-seater Super Sports made, plus 12 Salonettes. All these cars were registered as Morrises, and advertising generally but not invariably mentioned that the cars were built on a Morris chassis, even if it was the M.G. Super Sports name that was most prominent in the advertisement. The radiator badging, meanwhile, always read 'Morris Oxford' – albeit with a surrounding ring on the badge reading 'The M.G. Super Sports'.

With their smart coachwork and sensibly-honed mechanicals, the sporting Bullnoses made by Kimber and his team were a perfect complement to the regular Cowley products. Perhaps the last word should go to Bullnose author and Super Sports owner Lytton Jarman. 'On the road...the 14/28 M.G. and the contemporary Morris Oxford seem two entirely different cars, in spite of the similarity of the chassis specification, and the only features common to both which are immediately recognisable are the delightfully sweet clutch and the gearbox,' he wrote in a 1960 issue of *Safety Fast*, at the time the Abingdon house magazine. 'The M.G. has a much higher and more effortless performance than one would anticipate, but the very real charm of the 14/28 M.G. cannot be measured in terms of performance alone. I think Kimber's real genius lay in the way he could completely transform a car with the minimum of modification, and consequently offer such excellent value for money.'

Cecil Kimber in 1925: at this stage he was administering premises at Longwall Street, Clarendon Street, Alfred Lane, Queen Street and George Street, as well as the Bainton Road works.

5

BECOMING ESTABLISHED

In September 1926 William Morris announced a replacement for the car on which he had built his empire. It is not too dramatic to say that on the success or otherwise of this new model would hang the future of the enterprise. With the Bullnose, he had been a one-hit wonder, successfully offering one design in various forms rather than building up a diverse range of models. Although there was a world of difference between the spindly Morris light car of 1913 and the big-tyred longer-wheelbase four-wheel-braked Oxford of later times, there had also been an essential continuity in design over the 13 years in question. Equally, though, beyond the walls of Cowley there had been an evolution in technology and in fashion since Edwardian times, and the charming bullet-nosed prow of the Morris was by 1926 as outdated as its three-quarter-elliptic rear springing.

The risk, though, was that in modernising the Morris car it would lose its character – and at the same time its customer base. Such fears were misplaced. The evidence shows that the new 'Flatnose' Cowleys and Oxfords with their tombstone-shaped radiators not only arrived at just the right time, but also gave a major boost to company fortunes. In 1926, total sales – mainly of the Bullnose – fell from their peak in 1925 of 53,582 cars to a mildly less impressive 48,330 units. In 1927, however, dispatches from Cowley would accelerate to 61,632 cars. At the first AGM of Morris Motors (1926) Ltd, in May 1927, William Morris was able to announce that home-market sales had increased by a third during the first four weeks of 1927.

OPPOSITE: *This 1928-season two-seater – thus a 14/40 MkIV in Cecil Kimber's new marketing language – is thought to have at the wheel Florence, wife of Kimber's friend Wilfrid Mathews.*

EMBRACING THE NEW MORRIS LOOK

Penetrate beyond the brouhaha about the 'Astounding Morris Programme for 1927' and the would-be buyer would discover that the new cars were basically a repackaging of the old mechanicals in a fresh body and chassis. The engine, clutch and gearbox were largely unchanged, as were the front and rear axles. The new and more rigid chassis had deeper side-members and better cross-bracing and incorporated semi-elliptic rear springing, and the flat radiator, claimed to have a 60 per cent greater cooling surface, eliminated the Bullnose's tendency to boil. The new radiator and the accompanying higher scuttle resulted, however, in less elegant lines for the cars.

All this was a challenge for Kimber and his small team, as they needed to create a satisfactory amalgam of their special coachwork and the new chassis. The latter 'necessitated a lot of alteration and experimental work,' according to Albert Eustace[1], at the time a storeman at the Bainton Road factory. 'Production was held up for about six weeks, the lads playing cricket up the shop, waiting for someone to make up their minds. Then there was a sudden rush to get the job through, [with] everybody working.'

The cars that emerged in late 1926 as the flat-radiator 14/28 Super Sports and Sporting Salonette looked superficially similar to the Bullnose cars, and were still built by Carbodies, with the exception of a few examples with coachwork by Raworth. But the body, which in open form now had an engine-turned finish to the aluminium panelling, was in fact of revised and lighter construction; to hide the height of the radiator, meanwhile, a blanking plate was soldered to the bottom of the shell. As on later Bullnose Super Sports, the engines were dismantled, balanced, and their ports enlarged and polished. Turning to the chassis, flattened springs aided handling, and the Morris worm-and-wheel steering was replaced by a more precise Marles box, bolted rigidly to the chassis rather than attached to the engine as on the Morris.

---

[1] Cousins/Jarman reminiscences.

TOP: *The four-seater Salonette is what some would call a D-back saloon; a near-identical body was used by Carbodies on Alvis chassis. (Phil Jennings)*

MIDDLE & BOTTOM: *The Sporting Salonette with its distinctive duck-tail rear was billed as a two-seater but had small folding rear seats. From the front the rather nautical vee'd windscreen is just visible. (Early M.G. Society)*

In 1927 the four-seater Super Sports retailed at £350 – or £110 more than an Oxford tourer. The engine-turned lower sides are a feature of Flatnose cars. (RM Sotheby's)

Even with the M.G. Special Sports being produced in significant numbers, Kimber still accepted bodying some other chassis. This Morris-Léon-Bollée, probably dating from 1927, and captioned as having an 'M.G. Saloon de Luxe' body, was at least an in-house vehicle – a product of William Morris's ill-fated venture to manufacture cars in France. (Robin Barraclough)

THIS PAGE: *Further illustrating the fluidity of the M.G. name, this is a 1927 Morris with an eight-cylinder Wolseley engine, used by William Morris, and quite possibly a Morris-Léon-Bollée try-out; according to well-known racer and journalist John Bolster it was involved in a hushed-up accident in which Morris's wife was injured. It is described in the same catalogue as that featuring the photo on the left as being an 'M.G. Weymann saloon-coupé'. (Robin Barraclough)*

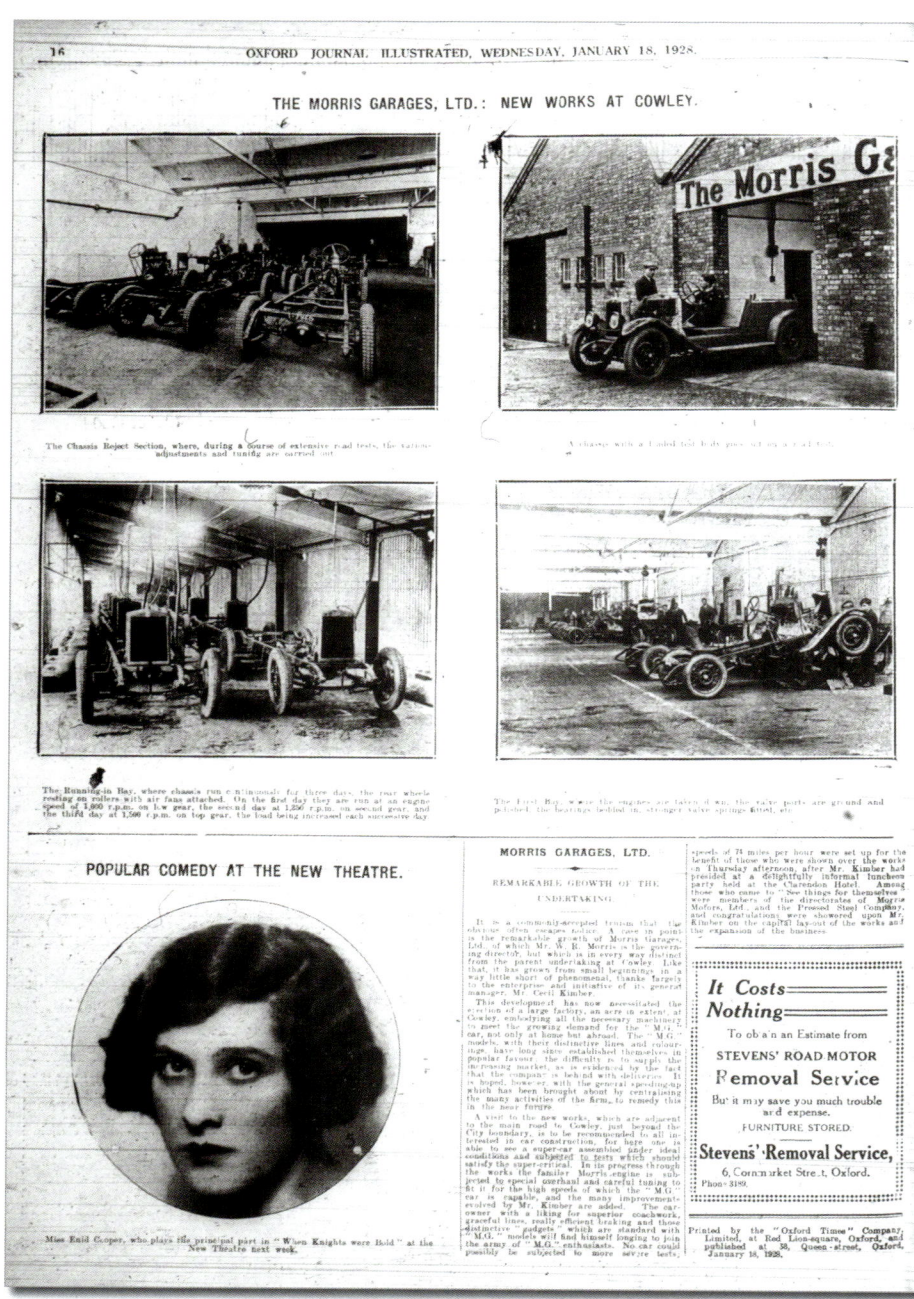

Kimber made sure that the new Edmund Road factory received maximum publicity. The reporter from the Oxford Journal Illustrated was clearly impressed by a visit to the works, writing in January 1928 of how one was 'able to see a super-car assembled' and subjected to tests 'which should satisfy the super-critical'. (Oxfordshire History Centre)

Overseeing these changes was a Cowley engineer by the name of Hubert Noel ('H. N.') Charles, a high-powered London University graduate then working as a technical assistant in the production department, and whom Kimber had persuaded to help in his spare time. 'He came along on Saturday afternoons and Sundays, and did various drawings and made endless suggestions as to the right way of doing things,' Cecil Cousins recalled.

Wilson McComb writes of how Charles became a regular visitor at the Kimber home in Woodstock Road – and of Rene Kimber's continuing input: 'Hubert Charles, then unmarried, had little hope of escaping the Kimber charm, and soon found his evenings and weekends taken up with design work on the new cars. He, too, recalled the important part played by Mrs Kimber: "Kimber and Irene together amounted to far more than any one person ever could. She was a most cultured, charming, wonderful person."...'

ANOTHER FACTORY: THE MOVE TO EDMUND ROAD

After a short while, Morris Radiators decided it needed the shop in which the M.G. operations had been installed. This necessitated a wholesale move over one weekend to a new unit within the works. This was to prove only a temporary home, as once production of the new cars had gathered pace it became apparent that more space would be required. Kimber found some suitable land in Edmund Road, off the main Cowley Road into Oxford, and approached William Morris for the estimated £10,000 cost of building a new factory.

Morris was wealthy enough not to have to hesitate, following the creation the previous year of Morris Motors (1926) Ltd and its floating on the Stock Exchange – and as the sole ordinary shareholder he retained full control of the business and could decide for himself where to invest his money. 'I can get things done while a Board would be brooding over them,' he wrote in an article in System magazine.

This speed of reaction didn't mean that setting up the factory went without a hitch. 'The interview lasted less than five minutes

Chapter Five: Becoming Established

THE FLATNOSE M.G. SUPER SPORTS

With the arrival of the Flatnose – never, of course, a formal appellation – The Morris Garages M.G. Super Sports now had a more rigid and better-suspended chassis, even if this added to the car's weight. Brakes were initially the standard Oxford set-up, only boosted by a servo. All in all, the revised cars managed to be an improvement on their predecessors, even if the looks were not to everyone's taste.

The new radiator was certainly accepted by Kimber's team only through gritted teeth – "They had to change to the flat radiator and that nearly broke their hearts, for the bull-nose was streamlined for speed," Edward Tobin, future manager of The Morris Garages, sighed to Andrews and Brunner. A palliative for the open cars was to use the smaller Cowley radiator, albeit with a thicker core, to give a lower bonnet and improve appearance; the closed cars had the taller full-sized Oxford radiator.

The models offered were initially as before, with two-seater and four-seater open cars (now with engine-turned lower body sides) and a Salonette with or without bustle tail. For 1928, a Featherweight Fabric Saloon and coupé and drophead variants joined the range – although very few of the latter two would be made – whilst the two-seater Salonette was deleted.

The 1928 season's cars, built in the new factory in Edmund Road, Cowley, were only superficially different, despite their re-naming as the 14/40 MkIV; the previous 14/28 tag, borrowed from Morris and in fact rarely used, was admittedly not an accurate reflection of the output of the modified M.G. engine, which was indeed around the 40bhp mark. The only mechanical changes were the fitment of shrunk-on bands on the brake drums to rigidify them and the removal of the servo, part of a simplified braking system described as 'M.G. high-efficiency brake gear' that had in fact been introduced on the last 50 cars of the 1927 model year.

Manufacture continued for one more season, but sales slowed right off with the arrival of the M-type and 18/80. The last ten chassis were collected from Morris Motors in April 1929, and cars were still available in October that year, at which juncture prices were cut and the stock sold as 'shop-soiled'. In all, 776 Flatnose cars had been made, 290 in the first season, 328 in the second, and 158 in the final short 1929 model year. Production amounted to 295 two-seaters, 374 four-seaters, 71 Salonettes, 32 Featherweight Fabric Saloons, and just two each of the dropheads and coupés.

An M.G. Super Sports two-seater from the 1927 season, recognisable as such by the lack of a front apron and the presence of a large M.G. octagon fixed to the radiator honeycomb. (Author's collection)

The flecked finish on this Gordon England Fabric Saloon led to the car being nick-named 'Old Speckled Hen' – although one school of thought says this should in fact be 'Old Speckled 'Un'. (Author's collection)

With the arrival of the re-branded 14/40 – sometimes rendered 14-40, as here – the two-seat Salonette was discontinued. (Author's collection)

The main clocks, all octagonal, were surrounded by a pressing of oxidised metal reminiscent of the worst kind of fireside fittings found in third-rate hardware stores. It was horrible, and, although I plastered it with extras, I never got used to it nor understood how Kim allowed it in the first place.'

Thankfully Charnock found the driving experience rather better, praising the ride and handling and the performance. He also appreciated Kimber's personal touch. 'During my many visits to Morris Garages I had become tremendously impressed by the personality of the late Cecil Kimber; he was always there to welcome you, to show you the latest mod, and, above all, to encourage you to talk about your own car while he made little notes. I think he did this to everyone, thus amassing a quantity of data which was to help towards improving the breed. By spring 1928 I fell for the current M.G. and travelled westward to collect it… and there, sitting in my new car, was Kim ready to hand over.'

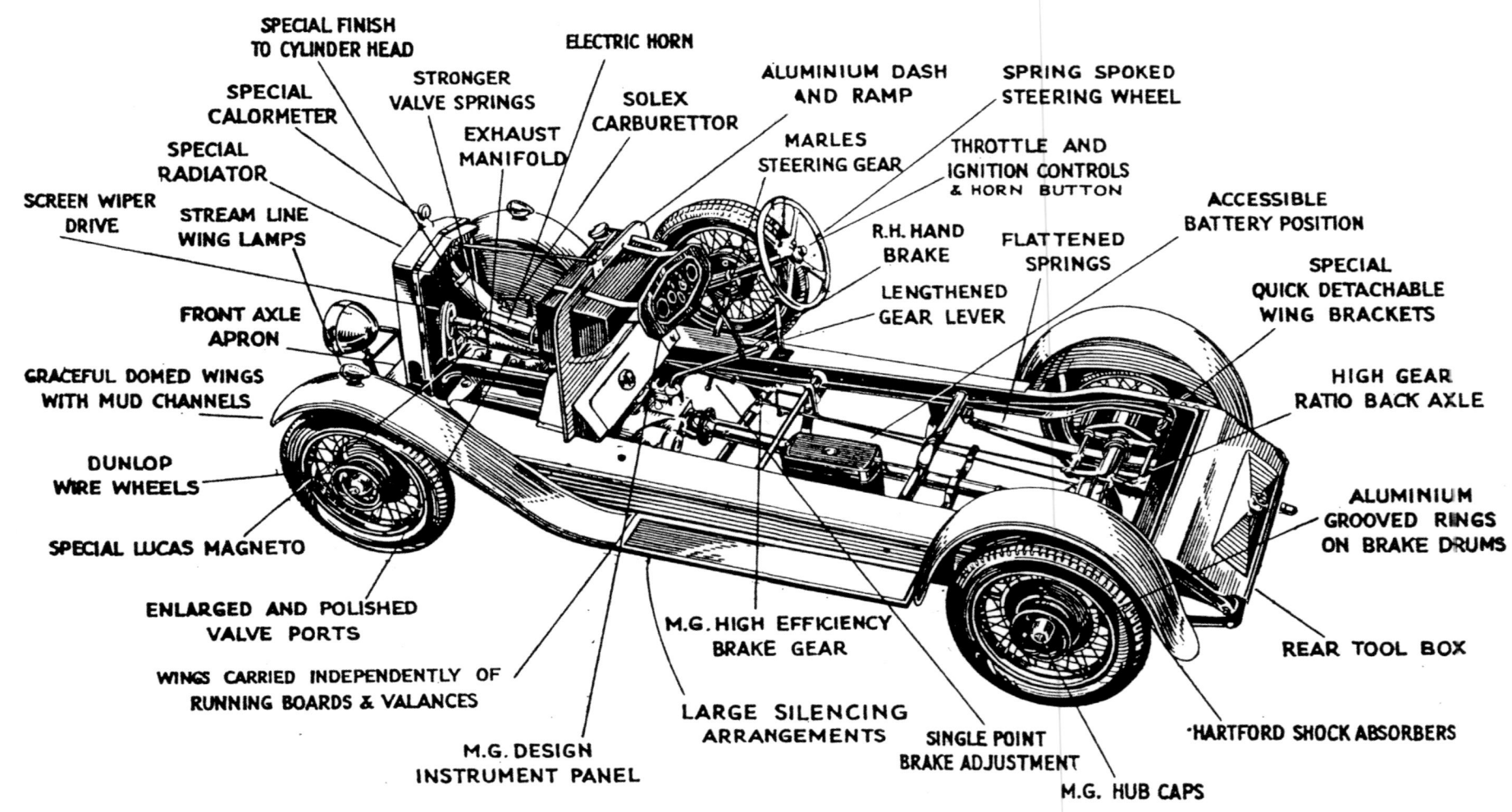

This view of the chassis stresses how the 14/40 specification deviates from that of a humble Morris. The changes were often minor, but as a whole they transformed the car – although the advertisement that vaunted 'the effortless smoothness of a straight-eight' was one hopes taken with a pinch of salt. (Early M.G. Society)

In the course of the trip Kimber managed to fit in some fishing, but his day at a trout stream on Skye – with Rene joining in – was not blessed, he wrote, with much luck.

A jokey moment during the holiday: Kimber's short stature and characteristic slight lifting of his right foot are evident.

the market. But despite the failure of the F-type Bullnose, his first real attempt at a six-cylinder model, he did indeed launch a new 'six' for the 1928 model year. It has been suggested this was less out of a burning personal commitment than because his arm was twisted – indirectly by Cecil Kimber.

This story, flagged up by Miles Thomas in his autobiography *Out on a Wing* and engagingly retailed by Wilson McComb in his history of M.G., has it that the starting point for what became

By Loch Slapin on Skye during the Highlands trip. This is a further image from Kimber's annotated photo album of the 1928 journey to Scotland with Rene, in the prototype 18/80 Salonette.

unsporting of raw material and were manifestly derived from a standard Morris product. To further his ambitions as a maker of sports cars what Cecil Kimber coveted was a more modern power unit than the workhorse ex-Hotchkiss American-designed sidevalve. With this, he could move up-market, and away from any association with run-of-the-mill Morrises. Unfortunately he was tied to the corporate parts bin. But then came an opportunity – or did Kimber himself make that opportunity?

'THE FIRST REAL M.G. CAR'

It might be thought that with the 1927 purchase of the Wolseley company William Morris would have been prepared to give up on the idea of a six-cylinder car under his own name, and leave this field to his new acquisition, better positioned in this part of

the Morris Six was an engine project cooked up by Cecil Kimber and Frank Woollard, Kimber's old colleague from E.G. Wrigley. Woollard was now running Morris Engines, apparently at Kimber's recommendation, and it is said that Kimber intimated to him that he might like to look into a new six-cylinder engine, and Woollard and his chief designer, Arthur George Pendrell (commonly called George), duly obliged.

Ahead of the 1927 Motor Show a 2468cc 'six' with a single chain-driven overhead camshaft did indeed emerge, installed in a new Morris model called the Light Six. Developing 52bhp at 3,200rpm, the 'JA' engine of the Light Six was just the potentially sporting power unit Kimber desired. Whether he had influenced its creation is another matter. As Barraclough and Jennings point out, the timings do not add up: design work on the engine started in 1925, when the M.G. operation was in its infancy and Kimber was only just coming to grips with series production of his Bullnose-based Super Sports. There is no reason to doubt that he would have followed the development of the engine with interest, and – why not? – have schemed it into his future plans. But it does not seem likely that he initiated the project.

Any new Morris model obviously had potential as the basis for a new M.G. – especially if it had an up-market six-cylinder engine. Unfortunately the Light Six was worryingly under-developed, not least in having a narrow and whippy chassis derived from that of the four-cylinder Flatnose cars. Steps were taken, however, to improve the new model before letting it loose on the public, and with a redesigned and lower-slung chassis with a wider track it was relaunched in March 1928 as the Morris Six. Meanwhile, a fabric-bodied narrow-track Light Six saloon had been passed to The Morris Garages. Kimber's men soon discarded the frame in favour of a new design and thoroughly revised the rest of the mechanicals; the result would be announced in August 1928 as the M.G. Sports Six, also known as the 18/80.

How the car came about is recounted by Cecil Cousins in his memoir for Lytton Jarman. 'Mr Kimber came to me one morning and asked me if I could draw. I told him that I had not done any, other than that I had learnt at school. He said he had a blueprint with him of a suggested chassis frame for a new six-cylinder model and, as this was the only one he had, and he did not like some of the details, would I trace it for him. I said in the spirit in which we had always carried on, that I would have a go. I succeeded in tracing this frame in a rough and ready manner, and when he came up the following morning, he said did I think that the MkIV axles could be made to fit, and also what sort of springs could be fitted in, so I commenced to draw in some axles from the blueprints we had obtained from Morris Motors. All this was done without any elaborate equipment, as the drawing board was only a sheet of plywood.' When the essentials had been drawn up, the project looked feasible, writes Cousins, and a draughtsman was employed to draw all the details in a professional manner, suitable for production.

In fact this seems to be a telescoping of events. Research by Barraclough and Jennings makes it clear that initially the Morris Light Six components, flimsy chassis included, were built into a prototype open tourer which was extensively tested by Kimber. When it was found wanting, a revised and stronger chassis was adopted and a new prototype was duly built.

Photographs in Kimber's albums tie in with this, showing both the initial prototype and what can only be the first car on the new chassis, a two-door Salonette; the same WL 4440 registration was used on both cars. Cecil and Rene Kimber, accompanied by Russel Chiesman, took the open tourer to the West Country during Easter 1928, to coincide with the Land's End Trial. Then with the Salonette the pair, this time without Chiesman, toured Wales and the Highlands. Kimber recorded the trip by compiling a photo album entitled 'The book of our first journey to the Western Highlands on the first M.G. Six, September 1928' – the wording being a clear indication that the Salonette was indeed the first definitive example of the future six-cylinder model.

The reminiscences of Cousins provide corroboration, when he

THE M.G. 18/80 SIX

The 2468cc Six can claim the distinction of being the first 'true' M.G. – as opposed to being a modified Morris with a special body, as was the case with the earlier Bullnose-derived and Flatnose-derived models and the M-type Midget. That said, the 18/80 – as it is commonly called – was very much of Morris parentage, right down to its cork-in-oil clutch and three-speed gearbox.

The 18/80 was available as an open tourer, a two-seater with dickey, a two-door closed Salonette and a four-door saloon; for 1930 and 1931 the last two were offered in addition with a fabric-covered body. Later a drophead arrived, with coachwork by Carbodies, the source for all the catalogued 18/80 body styles. Sales of closed models constituted a clear majority.

There was also (see next chapter) the MkIII competition variant. Its full catalogued name was the M.G. Six Sports Mark III Road

Racing Model, but it was sometimes referred to as the 18/100 and was also known as the Tiger or Tigress, and sometimes as the Tigresse. Ready to go racing off the showroom floor, the MkIII was priced at a substantial £895, so its lack of commercial success, with just five made, is perhaps understandable.

The principal evolution in the 18/80's specification was constituted by the arrival in September 1929 of the slightly larger four-speed MkII, series production of which began in April 1930 after the company's move to Abingdon, as recounted in the next chapter. There was an overlap with the original MkI type, which carried on being assembled until July 1931, including an open tourer Speed Model introduced in September 1930; some of these had fabric-covered bodies left over from those commissioned for the ill-fated MkIII. Additionally a handful of MkII chassis were sold as a Speed Model, with a similar but wider open tourer body. In Speed Model form a MkI was capable of just shy of 80mph, a more than respectable performance given the relatively modest 60bhp

or so (no definite figures are available) delivered by the overhead-cam 'six'. With good looks, sound engineering and a delightfully smooth engine, the 18/80 apologised to nobody, and was fast enough to keep up with such thoroughbred machinery as the 3-litre Lagonda.

The first six-cylinder M.G. was however destined to remain a minority interest; perhaps it would have sold better had it benefited from a halo effect created by competition successes. In all, 500 of the MkIs were assembled and 236 of the MkIIs. The final chassis number was issued in October 1932, but cars continued to be sold until 1934.

THESE TWO PAGES: *Some catalogue images of the 18/80 by Harold Connolly, who regularly illustrated publicity material for Kimber.*

recounts how the project was given the go-ahead by Morris at a time when just a saloon and a chassis were in existence. 'A great moment in our history had now arrived – would Sir William Morris, as he was then, allow us to build this motor car of our own creation, or must we continue to put pretty bodies on modified chassis? An appointment was made one morning for Sir William to view the car and the chassis at the Morris works. Mr Kimber drove up the saloon, I sat on a chassis which was not driveable, and was towed up to Cowley by [Works Manager] Mr Propert. Mr Kimber then took Sir William for a ride, not in the American fashion of course, and Mr Propert and I were left standing by the chassis wondering what the outcome would be. When they returned we found Sir William had a large grin on his face, and we made a guess that we had won the first round. This, it proved afterwards, was the case and we started to get into production on this model, which was the first real M.G. car.'

With the crossflow Morris engine given a new block and twin carbs, and the sturdier chassis now sitting on Rudge-Whitworth centre-lock wire wheels, at its launch in August 1928 the new M.G. looked an attractive proposition, even if the retention of the Morris Light Six's 4ft track, to accommodate the MkIV axles, made it seem a little narrow. Details included a fly-off handbrake, a full set of up-market Jaeger dials, and an elegant new radiator design with a central rib that was destined to be used on all M.G. models through to the TD.

FROM MINOR TO MIDGET

But events were in the process of overtaking Kimber. In Britain the success of the Austin Seven was causing a realignment of the market away from the 11-14hp sector dominated by the Morris Cowley and Oxford. It took Morris until 1928 to react, and come up with his riposte. With running gear laid down by Morris Commercial Cars and an engine designed by Wolseley, the 8hp Morris Minor was announced in June 1928, ahead of its introduction for the 1929 model year. It was built around a straightforward channel-section ladder frame and was a large car in miniature to an even greater degree than the Seven, in that it featured longitudinal leaf springs front and rear, a damper at each wheel, and fully coupled four-wheel braking[1].

If the Morris's chassis specification was well-considered, the engine, mated to a single-plate dry clutch and a three-speed 'crash' gearbox, was too ambitious for its own good. Possibly out of a wish to impress those at Cowley with its superior engineering skills, Wolseley followed the practice of its larger cars, and drawing on its First World War experience building Hispano-Suiza aero-engines it came up with a dainty overhead-cam power unit of 847cc capacity.

Looked at in general terms, this was hardly a sensible choice for a low-cost car, such an engine inevitably costing more to produce than a simple side-valve design. But there was a more specific failing: the overhead camshaft was driven by shaft and bevel with a shaft that went through the centre of a vertically-mounted dynamo, serving at the same time as the armature of the generator. This was conceptually neat, but left the dynamo prey to being drowned in oil, whilst also – initially at least – restricting its size and thus output. Quite why William Morris, a man of conservative mechanical tastes, allowed himself to be talked into such misguided sophistication is something of an imponderable. Was he sufficiently happy with the overhead-cam Morris Six engine to casually endorse a similar configuration for the Minor? Was he simply too remote by now from the conception of the cars being his name to have any serious influence over their engineering?

Whatever the reasons, the result would play a major part in forging the destiny of the M.G. marque. Whilst working on the 18/80, during a visit to the Cowley drawing office mechanic Reg Jackson had come across the Minor, and could see its potential

---

[1] In contrast the Austin had transverse-leaf front suspension incorporating a single damper, and a rear axle hung on two quarter-elliptics – a combination that could give rise to somewhat eccentric cornering behaviour – whilst it was only for 1931 that it forsook separate front and rear braking.

Chapter Six: Building a Range – and Discovering Devon

as the basis for a smaller M.G. model. He reported back to Cecil Cousins, who was soon equally enthusiastic, and the two took the idea to Kimber, who was not convinced. Such, at any rate, is the story retailed by author and former M.G. engineer Mike Allison[2]. 'Kimber felt he had enough on his plate with the new Six. Cousins and Jackson together talked over their ideas with H. N. Charles, who also became keen, and it was he who talked Kimber round, and accompanied Kimber to see Morris with their ideas,' writes Allison. 'Morris could see sense in the idea of an M.G. sports car based on the Minor, and so allowed Kimber to have one of the development chassis frames[3] to put their ideas into action.'

Jackson and Cousins then drew up some schemes for a body. "We cobbled together a body with a pointed tail. Harry Herring[4] made the framework and we stretched Rexine over it as a covering. I made up a smaller version of the 18/80 radiator shell in German silver, and polished it and fitted it over the Morris radiator," Jackson recounted to Allison. "It looked OK but a bit amateurish, so Kimber got Carbodies to make a couple of proper bodies in a few days, which looked a lot better. When Kimber tried it, he was pleased."

In September 1928, barely days after full details of the Minor had been released, came news of the new small M.G., called the Midget. In its initial report *The Autocar* described the car as the 'Morris Midget'. This becomes more understandable when one considers that the M.G. 14/28, which was based on the Flatnose Morris, was still being described in 1927 as the 'M.G. Super Sports Morris Oxford' and still carried Morris badging. Additionally the Carbodies order book for the two prototype bodies records them as 'Morris Minor 2-seater (Midget)'. A year into the new identity of M.G. as a marque in its own right, not everyone had assimilated Kimber's marketing 'spin'.

As for the car itself, it was nothing more involved than a Morris Minor rolling chassis with the springs re-set, a higher compression ratio, and that jaunty body, made of fabric-covered plywood, popped on top – this form of construction cutting out the need for painting, thereby bringing manufacturing costs down.

SUCCESS FOR A NEW BREED OF SPORTS CAR

Displayed at the Motor Show that October, the Midget attracted much attention, and according to legend at least 200 orders were placed, against substantially fewer for the 18/80. A sanction for 498 bodies – the biggest single order M.G. had ever placed – was commissioned from Carbodies, who set up a special 'Midget Shop' and were soon shipping bodies three to a crate to the M.G. works, at an invoiced price of £6.10s each. This was a new way of operating for both companies, involving quantity production and with bodies crated and shipped rather than chassis being driven or transported to the Coventry-based coachbuilder.

Production began in the spring of 1929, at a price of £175, rising to the same £185 as the unblown Austin Seven Ulster by the time of the 1930 show. The chassis were assembled at Edmund Road from kits of parts obtained from the Morris factory and the cars driven to the Morris Garages bodyshop in Oxford's Leopold Street to have their painted wings and bonnets fitted, before returning to Edmund Road for final finishing. In the autumn of 1929 a chic Sportsman's Coupé would join the range. Initially this had fabric-covered coachwork but it became metal-panelled from late 1930; the body of the open Midget would in turn became steel-panelled for 1932, although a fabric body would continue to be listed.

The Midget was as good-natured as its looks suggested, with safe handling, quick steering and acceptable (and latterly improved) cable-operated braking; with a weight of 10cwt, it could turn in over 60mph on its 20bhp – or 27bhp on later cars – while returning

---

[2] 'I was told this story of the M-type's coming-about independently by each of the M.G. people named, when I worked at the factory. It was corroborated by Frank Stevens, who was also around when I first went to Abingdon,' says Allison.

[3] Not according to Cecil Cousins, who in his memoir for Lytton Jarman says a fully-built Minor was passed to M.G. and its body then removed.

[4] Harry Herring, at the time one of the M.G. bodyshop men, would go on to be a talented modelmaker, producing a large number of beautiful scale models over the years, as part of the process of developing the lines of future M.G. cars.

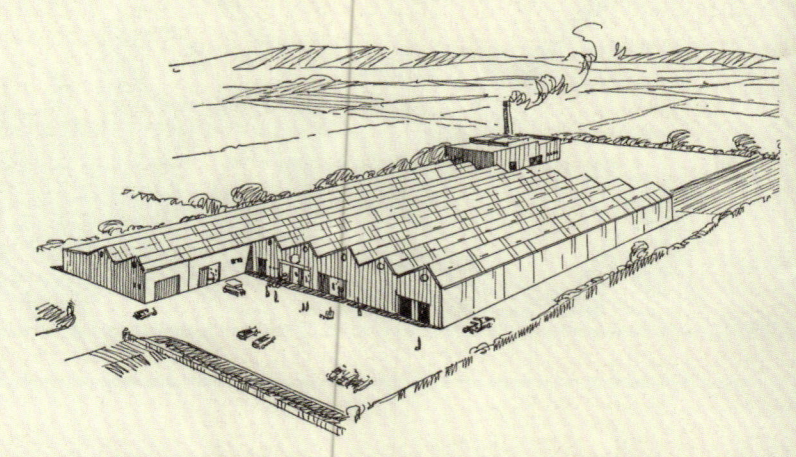

This page from a 1929 range catalogue shows the initial four catalogued styles for M.G. Six Sports. The tourer had a small boot with a drop-down lid to provide a luggage platform while the two-seater had a dickey seat in the rear deck. Initially in aluminium, for 1930 and 1931 the four-door saloon and Sportsman's Salonette would also be available with a fabric finish. (Author's collection)

The opening page of the catalogue continues to promote the notion of M.G. cars being completely unrelated to Morrises. The press retailed the same line, The Motor writing in its 10 September 1929 of the M.G. Six 'in which every component part is special and exclusive to this car'. It also suggested that, at 41, Kimber 'must surely be our youngest motor car manufacturer'. (Author's collection)

THIS PAGE: *The starting point for Kimber's genre-defining Midget was the chassis and running gear of the Morris Minor. 'The Minor is a blithe little car; happiness made manifest in metal,' cooed The Autocar, going on to describe the engine as 'full of fire and life'. (Author's collection)*

Chapter Six: Building a Range – and Discovering Devon

LEFT: *The Sportsman's Coupé was formally announced with the 1930 range in October 1929. The Autocar had published a 'scoop' photograph in August, depicting five Coupés in a line, each with slightly different styling – proof, said the magazine, of the lengths M.G. would go to in order to evolve the most attractive body style.*

BELOW: *The M-type Midget had a fabric-covered plywood body, as here, for most of its life. Given that a fabric-bodied Morris Minor Semi-Sports two-seater retailed at £125 and was basically mechanically identical, Kimber had a nice business model in offering the Midget at £185 in 1931. (Author's collection)*

TOP LEFT: *Russel Chiesman (centre) competed in the 1929 Land's End Trial in this pre-production 18/80 – the bolt-on wheels are a clue. Kimber makes sure the car is presentable.*

LEFT: *One of the party that went to the West Country was journalist Rodney Walkerley, on the left.*

ABOVE: *A pause for tea. Kimber, taking this photo of Chiesman, has left his mug on the running-board.*

close to 40mpg. What soon became clear in addition was that it had potential in motor sport. For the MCC Land's End Trial of March 1929 Kimber arranged for four Midgets to be entered; two won gold medals and the other two won silver medals. He then cooked up with Harold Parker of oil company Shell-Mex the idea of three early owners entering their cars in the Junior Car Club High-speed Trial at Brooklands that June – Parker himself, the Earl of March, and a friend by the name of Leslie Callingham. Accompanied by three mechanics from the M.G. factory, the trio were joined by two privately-entered cars. The Midgets finished in first, third, fourth and sixth places, and generated welcome publicity. 'They appeared to hold the track in a remarkably steady fashion and did the job without any fuss,' observed *The Motor* in its report.

Retrospectively known as the M-type and sometimes given the 8/33 tag[5], the first Midget effectively brought into being the small British sports car and set M.G. on its way as a manufacturer in its own right. It would spawn a whole generation of four-cylinder and six-cylinder overhead-cam models that would see M.G. become the world's premier maker of sports cars, and its engine would provide the building block for specialised power units that would end up developing more bhp per litre than a V16 Auto Union racer. On a more prosaic level the M-type would be a commercial success, with 3,235 in all being made, more than any other overhead-cam M.G. model.

As far as family life was concerned, Kimber needed to cater for his two growing daughters: in 1929 Betty would be ten and Jean four. After a few summers when the family had visited Cornish resort Looe[6], that year they began a series of holidays in Instow, on the North Devon coast between Bideford and Barnstaple. This was the base of the Taw and Torridge Sailing Club, of which Kimber became a seasonal member, meaning that he could borrow club boats for outings with the children or with friends. As a result, Betty and Jean had an early training in how to sail.

With the family staying at the family-run Marine Hotel, these summer holidays were convivial affairs shared with personal friends and colleagues of Cecil and Rene Kimber and local friends and acquaintances. Carl Kingerlee and Reggie Hanks[7] came down to sail, Bentley driver Bill Gibbs, an old friend of Kimber's – described by Jean as 'an insurance manager and professional bachelor' – brought along his latest lady-friend and added jollity to the proceedings, and people such as the local doctor and his family drifted in and out of the social scene.

The welcome pause constituted by a summer messing around in and about boats would no doubt have re-energised Kimber for the challenges ahead. It might not have been quite how he had originally intended things, but with the Midget he had now launched the fledging company on an extraordinary trajectory. September 1929 would see the next – and most important – step in the development of the M.G. business.

---

[5] The '33' may have signified a vastly optimistic rendering of the Midget's brake-horsepower. Another story has the figure being adopted simply because there was a certain ring to it. According to a 1943 item in *The Motor* it represented the car's maximum oil pressure, whereas others have said that it was a Kimber private joke, the 8.33 being a train from Oxford to London. Readers may take their pick..

[6] Kimber mentions this in his handwritten sailing memoir *The Evolution of a Yachtsman*. Mistakenly situating Looe in Devon, he says the family visited 'a few years in succession' and hired dinghies to go out sailing and fishing; strangely there are no known photos of these summer holidays in Cornwall.

[7] Carl Kingerlee worked for Morris-Léon-Bollée and M.G. and ultimately became Lord Nuffield's personal secretary. Hanks had joined Morris in 1922 to work in the Service Department and would rise to become Vice-Chairman in 1947 of what was then known as the Nuffield Organization.

OPPOSITE: *Rene relaxing on the beach below Instow's Marine Hotel, where the Kimbers would always stay during these seaside holidays.*

Chapter Six: Building a Range – and Discovering Devon

THE M-TYPE M.G. MIDGET

Following its September 1928 announcement, the M-type entered production in March 1929. The mechanicals being barely modified from those of the Morris, the 847cc engine retained a single SU carburettor, the gearbox was a three-speeder with a willowy direct change, and the brakes (as on all ohc M.G. models) were by cable. Later cars had the revised valve timing first tried on the 'Double-Twelve' racing Midgets (see below), this pushing output up from 20bhp to 27bhp, and for the final year a four-speed gearbox with a remote change became available at extra cost.

Manufacture ceased in August 1932, by which time 2,705 two-seaters and 530 Sportsman's Coupés had been made, and 82 chassis dispatched to outside coachbuilders. Special-bodied M-types included an open-backed two-seater by Jarvis (looking like a four-seater, it in fact had an open luggage area behind the seats, enclosed by the hood) and a drophead 'University Foursome' offered by University Motors.

In addition, Abingdon assembled 21 examples of the 'Double-Twelve' racing model. As well as the modified valve timing the specification included a larger fuel tank, a Brooklands-compliant fishtail exhaust and a revised fabric body with cutaway doors.

A late metal-panelled Sportsman's Coupé. 'Coachwork of the M.G. Midget Coupé is admittedly high in price,' said one catalogue, 'but it is intended to appeal to the connoisseur, to those who want the very best in miniature cars'. The model was deleted at the end of the 1931 season, replaced by the more spacious D-type Foursome Coupé. (Classic & Sports Car)

RIGHT: *Jean with cousin Wendy Edwards, daughter of her Auntie Maudie, one of Rene's numerous sisters, in 1928 or 1929.*

BELOW: *Cecil Kimber with Rene (left) and another of her sisters, Kathleen or Kathy, sometimes called Kattney. Kimber's snazzy socks look almost as colourful as Rene's cloche hat.*

Chapter Six: Building a Range – and Discovering Devon

THIS PAGE: *Three further images taken in the garden at Woodstock Road at the same time.*

Chapter Six: Building a Range – and Discovering Devon

THE MOVE TO ABINGDON

M.G. FINDS ITS HOME

Thanks to the success of the M-type, it soon became clear that the Edmund Road factory was not large enough for Kimber's needs. With three models in production, output was set to rise from roughly 300 cars in 1928 to 900 in 1929 and with the space taken up by the storage of cars from the retail business in Queen Street, some finishing operations were having to be carried out off-site, as mentioned earlier. So it was that in September 1929 the M.G. Car Company and most of its workforce moved to a disused factory in Abingdon belonging to the Pavlova Leather Company.

The First World War had brought a rapid expansion of Pavlova's business and a second facility had been built to the south of its main works, to manufacture leather coats and jerkins for the British armed forces, alongside other leather products such as gloves, belts, flying helmets and saddles. All of this had made Pavlova the largest employer in Abingdon. But bad business decisions and a shrinking post-WWI market led the company to retrench to its original factory. The new building was gradually

THESE TWO PAGES: *Opposite, a re-touched view of the new M.G. factory at Abingdon, from Cecil Kimber's photo album devoted to the inaugural lunch. Another view (above), showing more clearly the Pavlova Leather Company's works – the buildings set in a slight vee in the upper left-hand corner of the photo. (Magna Press Library)*

emptied of a huge stock of skins, and ended up being unused for some years. The Morris Garages had come to rent space there, in order to store second-hand cars, and it is said that future M.G. chief engineer Syd Enever, then a mechanic at The Morris Garages, pointed out its potential as a suitable site for the M.G. company.

William Morris agreed to bankroll the move, at a reputed cost of £100,000, and the disaffected Pavlova premises were leased for a period of five years, the acquisition being announced in July 1929. The lease would be renewed in 1934 – but not in 1939, as by then Morris had entered into negotiations to buy the factory, still often referred to as the Pavlova Works. The sale would be duly completed in February 1940, in the early days of the Second World War.

Plenty of work was needed to make the premises usable as a manufacturing plant, not least demolishing the brick vats that had been used for tanning and laying fresh concrete floors. 'The first time I was taken over it I thought what a mess it was, and it was expected to be ready in about six weeks…There was not a light in the whole 5½ acres. No part of the steel work had been painted, and there were large holes in the roof and floors,' Jack Lowndes recalled[1]. 'However, we set about it with a small army of electricians, fitters, carpenters, builders, etc, and got it something like ready by the time the crowd wanted to come over. The big rush started on a Friday morning, and continued through the night. We finished, really tired, at 12 midday on Saturday.'

The move to Abingdon was accompanied by an administrative tidying-up that saw ownership of The M.G. Car Company passing from Morris Garages Ltd to the M.G. Car Co Ltd at the end of 1929, for £18,995. In fact the agreement was only signed on 21 July 1930 but it was back-dated to 31 December 1929. The first directors of the M.G. Car Company Ltd were Sir William Morris as Governing Director and Cecil Kimber as Managing Director, plus Morris company secretary Wilfred Hobbs and company lawyer Andrew Walsh, who was also secretary of The M.G. Car Company Ltd. At this stage Cecil Kimber resigned as General Manager of The Morris Garages Ltd: M.G. with its move to Abingdon had come of age, and the last apron string had been cut.

Even at this juncture, just seven or so years from the appearance of the first car to use the M.G. badge, Cecil Kimber was a figure in the motoring world. 'Usually managing directors do not particularly interest the people who use the cars produced by the companies the said directors direct. But with Kimber it is different; M.G. owners who have met him – and there must be hundreds – regard him as a friend, and henceforth look upon the welfare of the M.G. organisation as a personal matter,' wrote *The Autocar* in its 8 August 1930 'Disconnected Jottings' column.

A FACTORY WITH A UNIQUE ATMOSPHERE

In the new premises – fêted in January with an inaugural lunch laid out in the works – were for the first time all the facilities of a proper motor factory, from a spares store for the service department to sales and accounts departments and a well-equipped machine shop. There was also a modest drawing office, presided over by Hubert Charles, who formally joined the M.G. Car Company at the beginning of 1930 as chief designer.

"Charles and I got on well. He was really my tutor – he taught me how to draw accurately, consistently and fast. We had to be fast, because there was only Charles, Gibson, a new man called George Cooper and myself on drawing boards at Abingdon," remembered Jack Daniels[2], who went on to scheme the chassis for future roadgoing and racing M.G. models.

Some found Charles an impossible character, but there is no doubt that he added to the Abingdon atmosphere. 'Charles was a jolly man. However serious the subject under discussion, however grim the prospect, laughter was never far away. And when he laughed, the whole of him laughed from tip to toe, and we laughed with him,' recalled John Thornley in his 1982 *Safety Fast!* obituary of Charles. 'Naturally, in the course of the years, there were many crises. The boys would work long hours, days,

---

[1] Cousins/Jarman reminiscences.

[2] Interview with Graham Robson.

The Abingdon works seen from the window of Cecil Kimber's office. It was, claimed The Morris Owner, *'the largest factory in this country, possibly in the whole world, confined to the manufacture of sports cars'.*

weeks, but on test – bang! Morale would be shattered...and then the door would open, and "Papa" would come in – we called him "Papa" among ourselves, albeit he was only 40 years of age at the time – a rotund figure with a beaming smile and twinkling blue eyes, and he would clap his hands together, saying "Oh well. We'll get it right next time, chaps, won't we?"'

In those days the M.G. factory was a very happy-go-lucky place, operating in a somewhat improvised fashion, despite the improvement in facilities at the new works. "In retrospect it was almost farcical. For instance we did a thing called a chassis test, which we did indoors, round and round the assembly line where everybody was working. And those testers drove like crazy! The place ought never to have worked at all – but it did," John Thornley told the author.

"M.G. was a fascinating place then: rough, even primitive in some ways, but a marvellous place to work," confirmed Jim Simpson[3], who joined M.G. in 1930 as a messenger boy. Simpson was another to recall the in-factory testing routine. "In those days Midget chassis were tested by being driven round a course INSIDE the factory: down one side of the Rectification Department, a left-hand hairpin along the other side to a second hairpin to complete the circuit – a bit daunting for newcomers. It was an advantage to have good hearing and nifty footwork when in this part of the building!"

Sam Bennett, who joined M.G. in 1932 to work on rectification and later moved to the racing department, remembered the testing of the completed cars[4]. "At this time every complete

---

[3] Interview published in the MGCC *Triple-M Yearbook* for 1997.

[4] Interview published in the newsletter of the North American MMM Register and subsequently in the MGCC *Triple-M Yearbook* for 2001.

M.G. was road-tested. When the testers left the workshops they would make a racing change almost before they had reached the door. Wheelspin used to make tyre marks and sometimes you could count the number of changes by the rubber stripes on the floor. I never tried this myself in case I chewed up the gearbox, but the testers were all expert drivers, even if they were a little adventurous sometimes!

"On the works noticeboard there was a map of the area around the factory, and on this map were marked the various points where complaints had been made to the police about test drivers taking bends on narrow roads at great speeds. This was brought to the attention of the testers but it seemed to make very little difference."

When he moved to the racing shop he was surprised at how primitive it was: "[There] were no such things as pits to get beneath the cars. We used to jack up the rear wheels and put them on wooden 'shoes' before lifting up the front with block and chains. These 'shoes' ensured that the tailpipes etc didn't catch the floor."

Above all, though, there was what Bennett called "a tremendous atmosphere" at the factory. "Everybody was willing to help each other and we had no aggravation whatsoever. It was not uncommon for one of the worker's wives to walk into the factory to see her husband and perhaps say 'Your dinner is in the oven' or 'Your mother-in-law has come to stay'. Most of the workers at Abingdon came from the surrounding countryside and had never worked in heavy industry before…They were grateful to be employed at M.G. and this contributed to the family atmosphere. Incidentally, we always kept our swimming costumes in our lockers. On warm days, before we had lunch, we used to hop across the road and swim in the River Ock, which runs parallel with Marcham Road opposite the works."

Over the years the specialist press would pick up on this more informal side to the works. 'I was very much taken with the M.G. works. I should say they are very efficiently run, while the camaraderie among the staff is particularly noticeable,' wrote The Scribe – Kimber's friend Ernest Appleby – in the 'Disconnected Jottings' column of *The Autocar* for 13 July 1934. 'I think life would be easier if one's business were always situated in country surroundings, and Abingdon, like the people who run the M.G. business, is a friendly place,' commented *The Motor* in the 'You'll be interested to know' column in its 21 June 1938 issue. At the same time the writer commented on the order imparted to the factory by Kimber. 'I could not help likening it to those gleaming steel buildings which have been put up in recent years in Germany. The aluminium-painted steel work, relieved by piping in red and blue, heightens the similitude. And, in the German manner, they keep the works spick and span.'

As a relaxation from the stresses of running the new works, Kimber was able to profit from the nearby Berkshire countryside, as Jean recalls in *The Other Tack*. 'Most weekends from when I was about three we went over to Eastleach, between Lechlade and Fairford, where my father rented some fly-fishing. The local farming family, the Monks, let us picnic in their cottage, help on the farm, and roam at will over their stone-walled, hilly fields. I don't know who taught my father to fish, but he could cast a fly with a marvellous deftness and precision. My mother explored the Cotswold villages in her car and became very fond of Mrs Monk Senior, an old countrywoman of remarkable wisdom, who, quite unusually for a farmer's wife, had a marvellous garden. Her living conditions were almost medieval in their simplicity, but she was a character we were all privileged to know. Her son, Bill, a builder, and his wife, Ethel, of Bridge Farm Cottage, were endlessly kind to me, and I kept in touch and visited them to the end of their lives. My father had a gift for finding special places inhabited by special people.'

OPPOSITE: *Kimber (middle) with William Morris (right) and Morris company secretary Wilfred Hobbs; a former articled clerk with Price Waterhouse, Hobbs also served as accountant for Morris Commercial Cars and personal secretary to Morris, for whom he was a trusted right-hand man.*

Chapter Seven: The Move to Abingdon

OPPOSITE: *Four scenes from the reception at the factory's official inauguration. Kimber knew how to work a room, according to former Abingdon PR man George Tuck: "Kim could charm the birds out of the trees if he wanted to, and he built up great friendships with people who in time became wonderful ambassadors for M.G."*

ABOVE: *Sitting down to table: after just nine or so years Kimber had very much arrived as a respected industrialist.*

Chapter Seven: The Move to Abingdon

Sir Francis Samuelson (to Morris's left) at the inauguration with the 18/80 saloon he was to take on the 1930 Monte Carlo Rally, following his participation in the previous year's event in the prototype 18/80 Salonette. The Samuelson family operated blast-furnaces and had local connections, with a factory in Banbury – to close in 1933 – that manufactured agricultural machinery.

ABOVE: *Kimber and Morris with the Samuelson car and a few gentlemen of the press. Samuelson had a life marked by tragedy, his mother dying when he was an infant from burns suffered after her waist-length hair caught fire whilst she was receiving a petroleum hair wash at a London hairdressing salon.*

RIGHT: *Cecil Kimber shows Sir William Morris around the Abingdon chassis shop, where an 18/80 frame is being assembled. The bulkhead featured the letters 'MG' cast into the aluminium uprights; this charming detail was however not visible once the chassis was bodied.*

TAKING TO THE TRACK

The move to the new factory brought with it the full production of a revised 18/80. Called the MkII, it had been announced in September 1929 and a handful are thought to have been assembled at Edmund Road. Before manufacture began, pre-production examples were tested over 14 days and nights of continual running on a 100-mile circuit, via Benson and Ewelme, across country to High Wycombe, across country again to Bicester, through to Banbury, and from there back to Cowley, recalled test-driver George Morris[5]. The new model had a track wider by 4in, a stiffer chassis and a four-speed gearbox, along with uprated running gear. Better-braked and with better roadholding, as well as more spacious bodywork, the MkII was a further step forward. The original narrow-track car – which continued in production – was a more sporting machine, however, three-speed gearbox notwithstanding, as it weighed roughly 3cwt less than the substantially-constructed MkII.

There was also a racing version of the 18/80, announced in May 1930. Called the MkIII, this had a dry-sump version of the ex-Morris engine with all new internals and twin-spark ignition, and was intended to deploy a healthy 100bhp. At launch, however, the output was 83bhp, with 96bhp only being achieved after a period of further development.

---

[5] Cousins/Jarman reminiscences.

An 18/80 MkII with the catalogued drophead body; just 18 would be made, out of a total of 236 MkII 18/80s. (Magna Press Library)

More seriously, on its Brooklands debut the MkIII ran its crankshaft bearings in the early stages of 1930's Double-Twelve race, and reliability remained a problem. This Kimber attributed to Morris Engines Branch, who developed the MkIII engine, and who had refused to follow the M.G. recommendation that the crankshaft be fully balanced[6]. With its deep-valanced tourer bodywork, built in conformity with international racing regulations, the MkIII looked the business, but in fact it proved something of a dud, and manufacture was stopped after only five of the intended first batch of 25 had been made.

---

[6] See Appendix 5.

The small M.G. was meanwhile starting to earn its competition spurs, not least in trials, with 30 Midgets being entered in the 1930 Land's End Trial. But the race track was where lay the glamour. Early in 1930 Kimber was persuaded by two Midget owners to enter a team of three M-types in the JCC Double-Twelve Race, for the specific purpose of trying to win the team prize. In the end five cars were prepared, to a more evolved racing specification, and M.G. duly carried off the team award. This led to a limited run of 'Double-Twelve' Midgets – constituting the marque's first series of 'off-the-peg' racing models.

Perhaps more surprising was the entry of two Midgets in that year's Le Mans 24-hour race. This was the first M.G. participation in

An 18/80 MkI Speed Model with one of the fabric bodies left over from the aborted run of MkIIIs. The car was pronounced 'an enthusiast's delight' by The Autocar *in its road test. (Magna Press Library)*

OPPOSITE: *Given the preponderance of jackets rather than overalls, it is a reasonable assumption that this image of the production lines in 1930 was carefully posed; the 18/80s would be driven to Carbodies in Coventry for their coachwork, whereas the Midgets behind were given their much simpler body at Abingdon. (Mike Allison)*

ABOVE: *Brake-testing of an 18/80 chassis. In the background, beyond the Midget, can be seen an 18/80 saloon. 'The whole atmosphere at Abingdon is keen, alert and enthusiastic. It is the sports car atmosphere. I noticed just the same air at Molsheim,' wrote Maurice Sampson of The Autocar in 1932, making a flattering comparison with the Bugatti factory. (Magna Press Library)*

LEFT: *Dropping the engine into an M-type Midget chassis; the vertical dynamo, source of much grief, is clearly visible at the front of the engine. (Magna Press Library)*

the legendary French event, and Cecil and Rene Kimber travelled to Le Mans in an 18/80 to support the private venture, leaving the children in the care of the latest in a succession of nannies. Alas the cars, one driven by Sir Francis Samuelson and M.G. mechanic Fred Kindell and the other by Robert Murton-Neale and Jack Hicks, both suffered engine problems and failed to finish.

SUPPORTING THE M.G. OWNER – THE M.G. CAR CLUB

The year 1930 brought with it another development: the creation of a factory-supported M.G. club. This came about after a letter in the 5 September issue of *The Light Car and Cyclecar* magazine, proposing the establishment of an organisation for Midget enthusiasts. After an inaugural rally in October the M.G. Car Club came into being, with a young John Thornley, at the time a Midget owner, becoming secretary.

TOP LEFT: *Connolly artwork of the 18/80 M.G. Six Sports MkII saloon. With a kerb weight of 29cwt for the metal-panelled version, the MkII saloon was far less sprightly than the MkI Speed Model, which weighed 22.75cwt.*

ABOVE: *The fabric-covered plywood bodies for the Midget were sent in crates containing three tubs. Their invoiced cost was £6.10s a unit. The final M-types would have an all-steel body that was slightly wider. (Magna Press Library)*

OPPOSITE TOP: *A completed Midget: all but 300 or so of the 3,235 M-types would be assembled at Abingdon, the first in March 1930. (Magna Press Library)*

OPPOSITE BOTTOM: *A Midget on one of the 'Comparator' rolling roads devised by H. N. Charles: the original output of the 847cc engine was a modest 20bhp. (Magna Press Library)*

ABOVE & OPPOSITE TOP: *The MkIII was a special racing model with a body designed to comply with international road-racing regulations. (Magna Press Library)*

The club had the keen backing of Cecil Kimber. Recognising its potential as a marketing tool, he regularly participated in club events, supported the publication of an M.G. magazine, and launched initiatives such as the annual dinner-dance at Motor Show time[7]. "He was from the very start very enthusiastic, and gave us a lot of encouragement. I had in the meantime designed a badge, which was a funny thing with 'M.G.C.C.' in an octagon. Kimber didn't like it at all, so he got Gordon Crosby to design a badge. And that's the one we still use today," Thornley told the author in 1989.

The club grew rapidly, and Thornley was soon devoting a lot of time to it, including spending most Saturdays at the factory. As well as holding down his position as a trainee at London accountants Peat Marwick he was studying in the evening at the London School of Economics, so he felt something had to give. He succeeded in persuading Kimber to take him on as a full-time staffer, and in November 1931 became assistant to the Service Manager, whilst remaining, at this stage, secretary of the M.G. Car Club – with some ambiguity over which post had priority. "Kimber was a genial man, with this very pronounced limp, of course. I suppose I was automatically a little wary of him to begin with, as so often cripples are of uncertain temper, but I was swept along by his enthusiasm, as most other people were…"

---

[7] This always received a mention in the motoring weeklies. In 1934, in which year 315 people attended, including club patron Lord Nuffield, it was described in the 'Disconnected Jottings' column of *The Autocar* as 'one of *the* affairs of the Motor Show season'.

LEFT: *This MkIII Tigress was supplied new to Victor Rothschild, of the banking family, when a student at Cambridge. (Author)*

BOTTOM: *Two of the Midgets on the banking at Brooklands during the 1930 Double-Twelve race; M.G. won the team prize.*

OPPOSITE: *Kimber, Morris and M.G. staff, photographed at the time of the January 1930 inaugural lunch. In the back row with cigarette is H. N. Charles, with next to him Cecil Cousins and then Works Manager George Propert, shortly to become General Manager. To Kimber's right, in glasses, is Ted Colegrove, who later in 1930 would move from being in charge of publicity to the post of Sales Manager.*

Chapter Seven: The Move to Abingdon

THE PAVLOVA LEATHER COMPANY

The Pavlova Leather Company Ltd was established in Abingdon in 1912. Leather had been a local industry since at least the 17th century, there being an abundance of sheep in the Cotswolds and the Berkshire woods providing plenty of the oak trees used in the tanning process. Indeed, there is archaeological evidence that leatherworking had existed in Abingdon since the 14th century. Whilst nearby Woodstock became the region's principal centre for glovemaking, Abingdon was not far behind.

It was in 1835 that W.B. Bailey opened a business as a woolstapler (a dealer in wool) and fellmonger (a dealer in hides and skins), and a maker of parchment. Requiring a plentiful supply of water, by the 1860s he was operating from Spring Grove Works, located at Larkhill Stream, close to what would become Cemetery Road. He lived in what is today Kimber House, the current home of the M.G. Car Club.

In 1911 the Spring Grove Works were acquired by Thomas Tate and Son and in 1912 Tate's son John formed the Pavlova Leather Syndicate with Robert Atkin Fraser. A lover of ballet, London-based Fraser was apparently a friend of Russian ballerina Anna Pavlova, a key performer with the Imperial Russian Ballet and in the Ballets Russes of Sergei Diaghilev, and a dancer best known for her interpretation of solo performance 'The Dying Swan'. Fraser, evidently smitten by Pavlova, decided to name the company in her honour. The enterprise, still run by Bailey, specialised in supplying leather to clothing, shoe and glove manufacturers.

After the commercial success of its wartime activities, the Pavlova Leather Company – as it had become after a 1918 restructuring – hoped for a post-war boom. Bailey gambled on the price of sheepskins rising and packed his new factory with thousands of them. But prices tumbled, and in 1921 Fraser was forced to sell out to one of its shareholders. This was Albert Booth and Company, a major merchant-shipping company that had come to specialise in the purchase and transport of hides and treated leather and had ended up owning tanneries in a number of different countries including Britain.

After reverting to its original factory, and subsequently leasing to M.G. the newer buildings, Pavlova concentrated on tanning, glovemaking and the production of chamois leather and skivers – the upper half of sheepskin after the chamois has been removed and which is used to line handbags,

THESE TWO PAGES: *Two views inside the Pavlova tannery, taken in 1916 or thereabouts. (Abingdon County Hall Museum)*

shoes, hats and the like. Drawing on Booth's expertise, skins of different types were sourced from all over the world – including, it is said, a small number of penguin skins for making into gloves and shoes. Subsidiaries of Pavlova Leather Company were the Savernake Glove Company and the Boniface Sheepskin Company, and there was a tannery in Abingdon's Radley Road.

Following the Second World War the Booth empire divested itself of its shipping interests in 1946 to concentrate on the leather trade and the building industry. In the early 1960s a family split led to the leather operations being hived off as Booth International. In 1981 this merged with Garnar-Scotblair to form a more broadly-based business under the Garnar Booth name. Various closures followed, as the UK leather industry contracted in the face of the massive increase in imported footwear and a collapse in the price of hides. In 1987 Somerset-based Pittard bought the diminished remains of the business to create what was briefly known as Pittard Garnar.

The Abingdon tannery became one of the combine's four operating divisions, responsible for leather for clothing and the production of chamois leather. Some 80 per cent of output was exported but the world recession of the early 1990s resulted in the business recording a £600,000 loss in 1993. That year the factory's closure was announced, with the loss of 290 jobs, and the buildings were demolished in 1998; Pittard still exists, as a producer of specialist leathers and leather products, and has operations in Yeovil and in Ethiopia – but not in Abingdon.

With acknowledgement to Jonathan Wood.

THESE TWO PAGES: *Four 1929 Cecil Kimber photos of the family at Eastleach. In the photograph above, Rene and the girls are with maid Ethel, whilst in the one to the right, they are with Sir Henry Lytton, the singer and actor famous for his roles in the Gilbert and Sullivan operas Kimber so enjoyed – and also the owner of an 18/80 tourer.*

8

SAILING, RACING AND A NEW SIX-CYLINDER CAR

Despite the move to Abingdon, the Kimber family home remained in Oxford – which was, after all, under ten miles from the new M.G. factory. There was, however, a move to a larger house, still rented, at 1 Hernes Road, just off Banbury Road. The old Army hut made the move, cut in two with a door and windows added to the back half, so that each of the girls had their own playhouse, furnished with child-sized chairs and tables. 'My sister and the boys from the big family next door were allowed to build a platform in a tree, and my father got the gardener to rip out a row of laurels on a high bank, which hid the vegetable garden, and designed a pond there with a waterfall. I can only look back in amazement that time was found in his busy life to plan all this,' writes Jean in *The Other Tack*.

'There were electric trains running around the nursery indoors, and at last my father could use his beloved steam train...It was at this time that we use to see a lot of Lord March, the future Duke of Richmond and Gordon, who not only came to play with the trains but also to go fishing...I also remember H. N. Charles, who lived near us and followed the fashionable craze for playing roulette at home with mother-of-pearl counters – at least when we were there. Gambling was not one of my parents' interests as far as I know, except for small flutters.'

Speaking to Wilson McComb, Betty recalled one visit by March. "The Earl of March...met my father when he was up at Oxford, and they were really friends all his life; he used to come and stay with us. One night Mother and I went to the theatre. We got back about eleven, and couldn't make anyone hear. Eventually we found the nursery windows all lit-up, so we went and threw stones at them. Daddy and Uncle Freddie, as we called him, were playing with my trains, and completely absorbed in them[1]."

OPPOSITE: *Queen's Wharf, Bideford, on the Torridge Estuary, photographed in 1930 by Cecil Kimber.*

RIGHT: *The Kimber family home at 1 Hernes Road, Oxford; it no longer stands.*

THE DELIGHTS OF DEVON – BUT TENSIONS AT HOME?

Summers continued to be spent at Instow, described by Kimber in *The Evolution of a Yachtsman* as 'the impecunious yachtsman's paradise'. He clearly thoroughly enjoyed himself in the North Devon sailing resort. 'I know of no other place where there is such a genuine one-design class, where there is such a cheery little club, where the club own six of the boats, where during the holiday season there is a race every day, and where as a temporary member for a mere subscription of about 30 shillings you can draw lots for these six boats with the certainty of getting some racing with yourself at the helm. Even when you are unlucky and do not draw a boat, crews are always in demand,' he continues.

'The racing is interesting and varied in its results because tides, eddies, river currents, channels and sandbanks are all factors with which to be reckoned. The boats are very stiff 18ft semi-

---

[1] "Theoretically it was Betty's train set. The track ran all around the room at shoulder height, with a flap over the door. Kim used to take men up there and play trains and talk business," recounts Sara Delamont.

decked Bermudian C.B. sloops with the foresail on a permanent spinnaker boom, so that it can be used as such when running[2]…

'The one disadvantage, if it truly is one, is that racing can only take place two hours each side of high water, as the estuary dries out, but if you are content to stay out until the tide floods again there is always water nearer the mouth. The best thing is to keep a sailing dinghy in commission for picnicking, prawning and bathing.'

These holidays may equally have seemed a tonic to Rene Kimber: if the impressions gleaned by Betty's daughter Sara Delamont are any guide, she had ended up being excluded from any direct involvement with M.G. and life in Oxford had descended into an empty tedium. "My mother talked quite a lot about Cecil Kimber getting richer and moving to bigger and bigger houses. When she talked about Rene, she described her life in Oxford as entirely vacuous – bridge and more bridge. The way she told it, Rene led a parasitic, vapid life."

Jean saw things differently, suggesting in *The Other Tack* that Kimber suffered the brunt of his wife's feelings of being cut loose from a business life the two had once shared. 'I cannot help wondering if my mother encouraged him fatally. Why else should he say long afterwards that her interest was welcome, but not when it became "a whip to drive me"? The only clue I have is that my mother once took me with her when she went to talk to H. N. Charles, the M.G. chief designer, when we lived in Oxford. We walked round to his house, and I played with his roulette wheel – a fashionable pastime at parties then – during the discussion. By the tone, it was clearly "business" talk…My mother could no longer play any role in M.G. design, and she was keeping up with developments through old friends.'

---

[2] In other words, a small racing dinghy with a half deck, a centreboard, a tall triangular mainsail and a forward sail attached to a horizontal boom projecting forward from the bow, for use when the wind is behind one.

This portrait of Kimber dates from the beginning of the 1930s. As with William Morris, a pipe provides a suitable prop: up until at least the end of the 1950s pipe-smoking was seen as a symbol of reflective masculine wisdom, as examination of period advertising will confirm.

Rene (left) with the Earl of March, the future Duke of Richmond, and the Countess of March. Kimber and Freddie Richmond, as he was informally known, were good friends. The M.G. closest to the camera is an M-type Sportsman's Coupé. Rene Kimber later used a D-type Salonette; statistics suggest that over 20 per cent of these smart sliding-head coupés were bought by women.

THIS PAGE: *A series of photos from an early 1930s Kimber family holiday in Instow. That in the middle shows Rene (left) with her sister Kathy. Elder daughter Betty (top right) would have been nearly 13 years old in the summer of 1932 and Jean (above) seven years old; given the physique of the girls, this is a more feasible date for the images than that of 1931 conferred on them by Jean.*

Kimber with regular holiday companion Bill Gibbs, on the beach at Braunton, in the 1929-31 period.

Carl Kingerlee, a family friend, seen in 1930 on one of the club boats Kimber used to borrow when staying at Instow.

ABOVE (BOTH): *Betty with a mouse, at Instow in 1930, and a shot of Jean taken at the same time.*

Chapter Eight: Sailing, Racing and a New Six-cylinder Car

'OFF-THE-PEG' RACING AND THE START OF RECORD-BREAKING

It was in 1931 that Kimber made the first step in a defining expansion of the company's activities: the construction of specialist racing models in small numbers, for sale to the general public. It was an innovation to be able to buy at a relatively modest price an 'off-the-peg' competition car, and this would make a major contribution to establishing the marque's reputation. An experimental department would be set up at Abingdon to develop and prepare the cars, but Kimber showed proof of his astuteness in that these special M.G.s and the services of the racing department, as it soon became, would be financed by those who bought and raced the cars.

The first of these special models, the C-type or Montlhéry Midget, was announced in March 1931, at a starting price of £490, all nuts and bolts split-pinned and wired and with the car ready to hit the track. Available in both supercharged and unsupercharged form, the C-type had a more highly tuned engine, reduced in capacity to 746cc to fit into the under-750cc racing class, and an all-new chassis. When tested by *The Autocar* a supercharged example (price £575) recorded 87.8mph over the half-mile, an impressive figure for a road-equipped sports car of such small capacity.

The first 14 customer cars were hurriedly built for the 1931 Double-Twelve race, and in a masterful publicity coup were handed over en masse to their owners at the Brooklands track in time for practice, having been driven down in convoy from Abingdon. Kimber personally delivered one of the cars, and when one of the batch had to be fitted with a new engine he himself did the running-in by driving the car for 400 miles during the night[3].

---

[3] As recounted by Mike Allison in *The Works MGs*.

The C-types all aligned for the May 1931 Double-Twelve race at Brooklands. 'These little cars formed one of the most remarkable teams ever put into a race of this sort,' commented The Autocar. *The cars ran unsupercharged. (Goldie Gardner courtesy Mike Jones)*

Chapter Eight: Sailing, Racing and a New Six-cylinder Car

LEFT: *The March/Staniland C-type that was victorious in the Double-Twelve, with the Earl of March at the wheel. The cowled radiator was later abandoned by M.G. as it was found to restrict cooling. (Magna Press Library)*

BELOW: *Kimber with the C-type that had come home first in the Double-Twelve. During the celebration at the Savoy, reported* The Autocar *in its 'Disconnected Jottings' column, William Morris 'maintained his reputation as a non-racing enthusiast by wagging his finger at Mr Cecil Kimber, the M.G. managing director, and forbidding him to race "as a concern" – this after offering the heartiest congratulations to all who took part in the recent success.' (Author's collection)*

Eddie Hall (right) with his C-type at Shelsley Walsh in 1931. Later C-types abandoned the pointed tail, thereby establishing the M.G. design vocabulary: cutaway doors, a dual-flared scuttle and a slab tank. (National Motor Museum)

Chapter Eight: Sailing, Racing and a New Six-cylinder Car

ABOVE: *George Eyston's EX120 after catching alight at Montlhéry. Inspecting the damage are (left to right) George Propert, Eyston, Reg Jackson, Kimber, Jimmy Palmes. (Author's collection)*

OPPOSITE: *In the Ulster TT of August 1931 the entry included 12 supercharged C-types and one unblown version. Three of the former were in first seven cars home, victory going to the C-type of Norman Black. (National Motor Museum)*

Almost the entire Abingdon workforce came down to Brooklands to cheer on the cars, and were rewarded by M.G. taking the first five places and scooping the team and class prizes, in what *Motor Sport* sourly headlined as an 'uninteresting' race. A little bit of perspective is indeed desirable. As *The Autocar* observed, only half the M.G. entry was still running on the second day, whereas of the ten Austin Sevens entered a full eight finished the course.

The Double-Twelve was followed by victories in the Irish Grand Prix and the Ulster Tourist Trophy, thereby firmly establishing MG's sporting credentials. '[The] Double-Twelve, the Irish Grand Prix and the Ulster TT…were regarded as the three most important races held in the British Isles. Moreover, the two Irish races were held on circuits that – unlike Brooklands – tested every aspect of a car's behaviour to the full. M.G. could scarcely have given the motor-racing world a more convincing demonstration of their virtues,' writes Wilson McComb.

Kimber was present at both Irish races. Indeed, as he recounts in the booklet *The Luck of the Game* that he wrote after the Ulster TT, he himself drove the C-type practice car over to Northern Ireland and then participated in the Craigantlet hillclimb – an event held on the outskirts of Belfast on the Saturday before the TT. The C-type, shared with Elsie Wisdom, managed second-fastest time of the day, and three first places and four second places, in what would seem to be Kimber's last appearance in competition outside M.G. Car Club events.

Accompanying the race-track successes, four Midgets were amongst the finishers in the 1931 Monte Carlo Rally, and picked up a couple of minor awards. More significantly, George Eyston had started to attack the speed records for up-to-750cc cars with EX120, a streamlined and supercharged single-seater Midget with its engine reduced in capacity to under 750cc. In February 1931 he achieved the first 100mph average for cars in this class – 'A Milestone in the History of Records' according to *The Autocar*. At Montlhéry in September he added some long-distance records to his tally, despite EX120 bursting into flames after clocking 101.1 miles in the hour, having thrown a con-rod. Eyston managed to jump out of the speeding car, a drama recounted in crisp detail in his book *Flat Out*.

When he had recovered from his burns, in December he pushed his speed up to 114.77mph, again at Montlhéry – this time with the protection of a pair of asbestos overalls. The car he used was a new streamlined single-seater with a diagonally-offset transmission line to allow the driver to sit lower; coded EX127, the car became known as the 'Magic Midget' and would in the future garner more laurels for Abingdon.

Although fully supported by M.G., who built both cars, these ventures were financed by George Eyston, with further backing coming from Jimmy Palmes of dealers Jarvis of Wimbledon. Eyston would remain a loyal sponsor of M.G. competition activities and would continue to be involved with the company in post-war years, as an advisor on Abingdon's return to record-breaking with its EX179 and EX181 streamliners.

MAGNA – ARRIVAL OF THE SMALL SIX-CYLINDER M.G.

By late 1931 it was apparent that sales of the 18/80 had been totally eclipsed by those of the M-type. In the summer the last of the narrow-chassis model had been assembled, total production amounting to 500 cars. The MkII would continue to be offered until 1934, presumably until stocks of parts had been exhausted, but only 236 would be made – against 3,235 M-types in the March 1929 to August 1932 period.

The move so far up-market with the 18/80 had evidently not borne fruit, and there was a sizeable factory to keep humming in a time of economic recession that would see Abingdon's output for 1931 fall by 25 per cent[4]. Given the proven success of the chirpy little Midget, why not profit from the fashion for small six-cylinder engines and offer an attractively-priced model derived from the

---

[4] Already Kimber had been obliged to trim the workforce: from 387 employees in April 1930 the figure had dropped to 256 by the end of 1930, with the tally in March 1931 being 270 people.

An advertisement from early 1931, by which time M.G. was offering a four-car range. The famous M.G. slogan 'Safety Fast!' arrived in 1929, inspired by Publicity Manager Ted Colegrove seeing a bus with a triangle carrying the wording 'Safety First!' painted on its rear. He reported back to Kimber, who was sitting at his desk with an advertisement which featured the then current slogan 'Faster than most' – to which some wag had added the word 'bicycles'. He immediately seized on Colegrove's 'Safety Fast!' as being ideal for his cars.

Midget but with two extra cylinders? The template already existed: in April 1930 the Morris Minor had gained a six-cylinder Wolseley sister, the Hornet, that was nothing more than an extended Minor chassis fitted with a 1271cc 'six' based on the overhead-cam four-cylinder Minor engine.

Kimber and Charles repeated the same trick, but using the Wolseley engine not in a modified M-type chassis but in an adaptation of the superior C-type frame. Making the operation even sweeter, or so the story has it, because Wolseley was moving over to a chain-driven camshaft it was happy to agree a low invoiced price for a final run of now obsolete shaft-drive engines. Having proudly announced four years earlier that M.G. cars were not related to more humble cars from the Morris organisation, Kimber craftily had the engine disguised a little, by having two steel side-covers fitted to the block.

The resultant 12/70hp F-type Magna was announced in September 1931, ahead of that year's Motor Show, at which a further novelty was the D-type four-seater, which used a longer-wheelbase adaptation of the C-type's underslung chassis along with the later 27bhp M-type engine. Kimber's friends on *The Autocar* greeted the F-type with rhapsodic prose. 'It is a design which must inevitably fascinate those enthusiasts to whom a sporting performance is the true zest of motoring, in whom there is an aesthetic ability to appreciate beauty of line, and by whom refinement of running is admired and enjoyed,' began the magazine's description of the car. 'To look first at the low-built and utterly workmanlike chassis of the Magna, and then at the finished clean-cut car, is to experience a feeling of insular gratification that this job is British. Emanating as it does from a firm whose 750cc Montlhéry Midgets have handsomely won this year the three most important international races held on British and Irish soil, the Magna is definitely something more than a mere new model: it is a car of latent possibilities.'

Casting aside notions of 'insular gratification', the apparently attractive recipe was in reality compromised by some of the

The F-type Salonette shown here has the same Carbodies coachwork as the D-type Foursome Coupé. (Richard Monk)

ingredients. "It was a car of length but no breadth, I used to say – and it had directional qualities roughly what you'd expect from that, too," John Thornley commented to the author. "I thought it a very poor thing. Of course it was a Wolseley Hornet engine. It had these extraordinary main bearings which bolted round the crank and then you fed the whole outfit in from one end, and the intermediate mains were held in dural castings. Well, they distorted all over the shop as soon as the crank started to wander about a bit. So the life of the bearings was minimal. And some of the noises the crank made! You'd rev it up, and on the way down, at around 3,000rpm, it would go WEEOWWW…The extraordinary torsional oscillation of that crank was quite something."

Whatever the technical shortcomings of the F-type, it would prove a commercial success, with 1,250 being made in little over a year, on the back of a recovering economy. Indeed, as early as April 1932 *The Motor* was able to report that in the first three months of the year M.G. turnover was up 130 per cent on 1931. This was in fact hardly a surprise after the grim results of the previous year: the only way things could go was upwards. All the same, the company was riding a wave, and would finish the year with its highest-ever net and gross profits for the 1930-35 period. Helping along this performance, an attractive replacement for the M-type Midget – by then getting on for four years old – would arrive in the course of August 1932.

Kimber at his desk, around 1931. 'Mr Cecil Kimber has one of the most attractive offices I know,' wrote the author of the 'You'll be interested to Know' column in the 19 March 1935 issue of The Motor. 'It is upstairs, built in Tudor style, and radiates calm and dignity. Below, the windows look down on to an apple orchard which, in springtime, is a sea of blossom. A contrast from factory roofs and chimneys.'

THREE SISTERS – THE C-TYPE, D-TYPE AND F-TYPE

The 746cc C-type Montlhéry or MkII Midget, announced in March 1931 was a racing version of the M-type. To reduce capacity to under 750cc it had an engine with a shorter-throw crankshaft, this being counterbalanced. Optionally supercharged, the comprehensively revised power unit ultimately delivered 41.1bhp unblown and 52.5bhp blown, and was mated to a remote-change four-speed gearbox. Supposedly inspired by the frame of the French-made Rally cyclecar, the chassis had an underslung rear and tubular crossmembers; an unusual feature was a more rigid arrangement for the rear shackles, using trunnions in which the spring leaves slid. The aluminium body was a unique design, and the first 14 cars had a cowled radiator. In all, 44 C-types were built, the last in mid-1932; the final cars had a crossflow head and were given the MkIII appellation.

An F-type Magna tourer: the body, shared with the D-type, is basically identical to that used on the front-wheel-drive Alvis 12/75. The new six-cylinder M.G. 'opens up an entirely new field in fast sports cars with abundant touring comfort,' The Morris Owner *proclaimed. (Magna Press Library)*

Chapter Eight: Sailing, Racing and a New Six-cylinder Car

In some ways the style of the Salonette made it a pocket-sized version of the SSI of William Lyons.

Current from September 1931 to August 1932, the D-type was available as an Occasional Four four-seat tourer or a Foursome Coupé. The use of the C-type design of underslung chassis improved roadholding and the option of a four-speed gearbox helped extract the best from the 847cc engine. There was a remote control for the gearchange, centre-lock wire wheels, and a 12-volt electrical system; later cars had the wheelbase extended by two inches to 7ft 2in. Somewhat heavier than the M-type, the D-type suffered from a leisurely performance, something remedied if one specified the optional supercharger. Total production was 250 cars, split between 208 open tourers, 37 Salonettes, and five cars bodied by outside coachbuilders.

Also announced in September 1931, the first of the small six-cylinder M.G. models had its Wolseley Hornet engine installed in a D-type chassis lengthened by 10 inches. For M.G. use the overhead-cam 1271cc 'six' had twin SU carbs, different inlet and exhaust manifolds, a large aluminium-alloy sump and an alloy valve cover, and developed 37.2bhp; the gearbox was a four-speed manual, with remote change, and was sourced from specialist gearbox manufacturer ENV. The F-type's bodies were essentially as the D-type and J-type, later Salonettes having a side-mounted spare and an opening boot with a lid that could form a luggage platform. In September 1932 an open two-seater F2 was introduced, and larger brakes (of 12in rather than 8in diameter) and a modified cylinder head were standardised, at which stage the F1 tourer and Salonette were given the F3 tag.

Replaced in March 1933 by the L-type Magna, the 1,250 F-types that were sold in little over a year made it the most successful of the ohc six-cylinder models. Substantially the most popular variant was the tourer, with 532 made, against a nonetheless impressive 390 Salonettes and just 40 F2 two-seaters. As with the sister Wolseley Hornet, a large number of F-type chassis were supplied to outside coachbuilders – 188 in all, more than for any other pre-1936 M.G. model.

9

TECHNICAL ADVANCES BUT A MARRIAGE IN RETREAT

The M.G. company's third year in its Abingdon factory marked a key point in the swift-paced evolution of the marque. Having arguably created the genre of low-priced British sports car with the M-type, Cecil Kimber's replacement for the original Midget significantly advanced the game, and opened up new potential in motor sport for the four-cylinder M.G. models. At the same time the F-type's technically uninspiring mechanicals were re-thought, leading to a revised engine that would be used in new six-cylinder models that would prove more competent as road cars but also singularly effective in competition form.

THE NEW MIDGET: SWEET AND SPEEDY...BUT NOT THAT SPEEDY

Announced in August 1932, the new J-type Midget had an uprated 847cc engine with a more efficient crossflow cylinder head, and used the C-type/D-type chassis. What gave the J-type its edge was the sparse elegance of its lines – at least in classic two-seat J2 form. To perfect proportions were added a dual-cowl scuttle and an abbreviated tail with a slab tank and exposed spare wheel. When a set of swept wings replaced the original cycle wings for 1934 the result was an aesthetic rightness that has probably never been bettered in a traditionally-styled sports car and which could still be seen in the last M.G. TF of 1955.

Any relationship to a humble mass-produced Morris Minor was now tenuous at best. For this, Cecil Kimber deserves a measure of the credit. "He had a lovely flair for line, a lovely idea of what the young lad of the village wanted, and that's what he built," Harold Connolly observed to Wilson McComb. "He always said a sports car should look fast even when standing still, and that was the basis of all his designs."

The small M.G. had grown up, and could in addition be marketed

OPPOSITE: *Kimber in an F-type two-seater, most probably at an M.G. Car Club event. Established in 1930, the club was an important tool of promotion for the marque. (Magna Press Library)*

M.G. advertising tried to have it both ways, but here the message is unmistakably aimed at huntin'-fishin'-shootin' men rather than ladies in cloche hats. (Magna Press Library)

on a platform of sporting successes for the marque. 'This M.G. Midget is not a fancy toy, but a man's car. Just as in the past the M.G. Midget has given overwhelming proof of its superiority in all the stiffest trials and most gruelling races, so will this J2 model worthily carry on the tradition,' a guide for M.G. salesmen trumpeted. 'It is designed for the job. As a competition car it is ideal. As a really fast touring mount, a sheer delight. Lavishly equipped, upholstery in real leather, with a coachwork finish above criticism, this trim little road craft will appeal, instantaneously, to every true motor lover.'

Armed with such arguments, Abingdon's salesfolk probably didn't have too much of a struggle convincing would-be buyers of

ABOVE: *The new J-type Midget was marketed on the back of M.G. success in competition – which had also influenced the car's lines, with the abbreviated rear finishing in an exposed slab tank. 'The origin of this type of body was in the Ulster TT the previous year, where it was necessary to have the body of as light construction as possible and also with a large tank capacity,' Cecil Cousins recounted to Lytton Jarman.*

RIGHT: *The salesman's guide gives a flavour of how Cecil Kimber thought the J2 should be promoted.*

FOREWORD

First of all it should be realized that in all the M.G. Models there is offered, each in its class, quite one of the fastest standard sports cars you can buy. Also that M.G. Cars emanate from a factory which has specialized consistently in the production of fast cars, and which have abundantly proved their claim to speed by the large number of successes on road and track.

When it is realized also that the whole of the vast resources controlled by Sir William R. Morris, Bt., including his wonderful engine factory at Coventry—the finest in Europe, probably in the world—are at the disposal of the M.G. Car Company Ltd., of which concern Sir William is Governing Director, then one can appreciate that M.G. design, development and production are not hampered by lack of adequate resources.

It is important to get this angle of view and so judge in true perspective the sometimes fantastic claims and emphereal successes of our competitors, who cannot possibly and by any stretch of the imagination turn out a product that is in any way better.

Another most important point, and one not always appreciated even by the Motor Trade, is that the engines, frames, axles, steering, radiators and coachwork are, except certain proprietary parts, to M.G. design and absolutely exclusive to the M.G. Car.

Turning now to the individual models, the following are the salient points:—

Page Four

the J-type's superiority over its predecessor. Having given birth to what can legitimately be regarded as the definitive representation of the affordable pre-war sports car, Kimber himself pushed just a little too hard, however, when it came to promoting the car through his friends in the motoring press. The incident in question has entered into M.G. mythology, and relates to the road test of the J2 that appeared in *The Autocar* during August 1932, in which the car recorded a maximum speed of 80.35mph over the quarter-mile. As the story's veracity is regularly challenged, the testimony of John Thornley is particularly valuable.

"The biggest excitement was with the introduction of the J2, when Kimber sent a souped-up car out to the press, calling it a standard

The M.G. Midget Sports Two-Seater. Model J.2.

This **M.G. Midget** is not a fancy toy, but a man's car. Just as in the past the M.G. Midget has given overwhelming proof of its superiority in all the stiffest trials and most gruelling races, so will this J.2. Model worthily carry on the tradition. It is designed for the job. As a competition car it is ideal. As a really fast touring mount, a sheer delight. Lavishly equipped, upholstery in real leather, with a coachwork finish above criticism, this trim little road craft will appeal, instantaneously, to every true motor lover.

The hood and side curtains provide most adequate protection against the weather, and when not in use fold neatly away in the space provided behind the seat squab, where there is also room for a suit case. Ample space is provided on the panel for extra instruments. The standard equipment includes a five-inch speedometer and revolution counter, callibrated oil gauge, ammeter, the usual switches and a neat horn and dipper switch.

Selling Points of the M.G. Midget J.2.

Chassis design identical to our racing models.

Chassis underslung at rear with tubular cross members, the finest method of cross bracing, but not the cheapest.

Springs flat and sliding at their rear ends in bronze trunnions totally enclosed.

12-volt lighting and starting.

Rudge Whitworth Racing type wheels.

Very low centre of gravity with 6 inches ground clearance.

Single-piece windscreen that will fold down flat forward.

Page Five

ABOVE: *In* The Morris Owner *the author of this article tried to persuade readers that 80mph was an achievable maximum for the J2 Midget.*

Chapter Nine: Technical Advances but a Marriage in Retreat

THE J-TYPE MIDGET

The 847cc J-type was introduced in August 1932 as a two-seater J2, a four-seater J1 tourer and a J1 closed coupé that was effectively a four-cylinder sister to the F-type Magna coupé. Replacing both the M-type and the D-type, in simple terms it was a better M-type, using the improved chassis of the D-type and a detuned 36bhp version of the C-type crossflow-head engine in conjunction with a four-speed gearbox with a remote change.

The J-type was adequately swift – inflated 80mph claims notwithstanding – and its son-of-C-type chassis gave it good handling. But the two-main-bearing engine was prone to crankshaft breakages and the brakes – by cable, as on all ohc MGs – weren't the best. Manufactured until January 1934, total production was 2,494 cars, of which 2,061 were two-seaters. The next most popular style was the four-seat tourer, with 262 made before its early deletion in September 1933, with the rear being taken up by the Salonette, with just 117 being assembled. The two competition models were a minority interest, and were also discontinued in September 1933, after 22 of the J3 and nine of the J4 had been made. J-type chassis to outside coachbuilders numbered 23, including a coupé by Uhlik of Czechoslovakia and another by Belgian company Van den Plas, not to be confused with London-based British concern Vanden Plas.

The J1 open tourer was a minority interest, accounting for just 262 of the 2,494 J-types made. (Magna Press Library)

Early J2s retained cycle wings. The move to more flowing wings with running-boards came for the 1934 model year, and some of these last J2s had coachwork supplied by Morris Bodies Branch rather than by Carbodies. (Magna Press Library)

one, and got a figure of 80.3mph out of one newspaper," Thornley recalled in his 1989 interview with the author. "We were deluged with complaints from people who couldn't do more than 70mph – and we had to do something about it. So we put the compression ratio up, and this meant changing cylinder heads…I had to get an exchange head system going, so we could begin to cope with the problem. I always say, semi-jocularly, that the whole of my period in the Service Department until the war was spent trying to make the product live up to Kimber's claims for it!"

In December 1932, surely not coincidentally, the same car was the subject of road impressions in *The Morris Owner* under the heading 'An 80mph Midget'. Whether this test took place before or after the introduction of the revisions described above is not known. The writer, most likely Miles Thomas, then Sales Director of Morris Motors, said that he managed only 76mph – presumably on an optimistic speedometer – but that he felt confident that an extra 4mph could have been wrung out of the car. It seems likely that this article in the Morris house journal was an attempt by deft propagandist Thomas to convince readers, in the wake of the *The Autocar* episode, that the M.G. in standard form was well and truly capable of 80mph.

One enthusiast who was not convinced was future racing driver

A catalogue image of the J1 Salonette, in a colour scheme that no doubt had Kimber's approval. "I always went by his choice of colours entirely in designing a catalogue," said Harold Connolly to Wilson McComb.

Reggie Tongue of the Oxford University Automobile Club. "I wrote pieces on cars in *The Isis*. I suppose it was the J2 Midget we tried and I wrote 'This car might achieve 80mph if you got it on a steep hill, with a strong following wind!' Cecil Kimber was annoyed and told me I was dishonourable to write such things, after he had kindly lent me the car," Tongue told John Dugdale.

Leaving aside the J2's contested maximum speed, the new Midget was an appealing buy, but one not without its generally acknowledged weaknesses. 'It was an instant best-seller on looks alone and at £199.10s it deserved to be, while its superb four-speed gearbox with remote control was all the better for having no synchromesh,' veteran racer and journalist John Bolster would later write[1]. 'Though it had only 847cc it was slightly faster than a typical French 1100, but its Achilles heel was its two-bearing crankshaft. If only the owners had realised that, at that price, one

---

[1] 'Wottle she do, mister?' in *Old Motor*, June 1981.

could not expect a car to stand up to continuous hard driving but, instead, they revelled in that glorious gearbox and there was an appalling disaster at 15,000 miles. People tuned J2 Midgets to achieve 80mph, but that entailed handling Mr Laystall a lot of folding money for a special crank.'

RE-THINKING THE 'SMALL SIX'

As well as an open four-seat tourer and a close-coupled fixed-head coupé[2], two racing versions of the J-type were additionally offered. The J3 was a supercharged J2 and the J4, introduced in March 1933, a no-holds-barred blown racer with a high-set Brooklands exhaust and no doors; both had 746cc engines to fit into the up-to-750cc competition class. Cecil Kimber's motor-sporting ambitions didn't stop there. Back in its 8 March 1932

---

[2] Known as the Salonette, this had the same body as the D-type and F-type Salonettes. Rene Kimber used one, and according to Jean she competed in the car in early M.G. Car Club rallies. This may tie in with a story that as a youngster future M.G. racer Dorothy Stanley-Turner navigated for Rene in a trial. Miss Stanley-Turner was the daughter of Abingdon GP and friend of Kimber Dr Henry Stanley-Turner, a one-time RAF wing-commander and the former Principal Medical Officer for the Middle East.

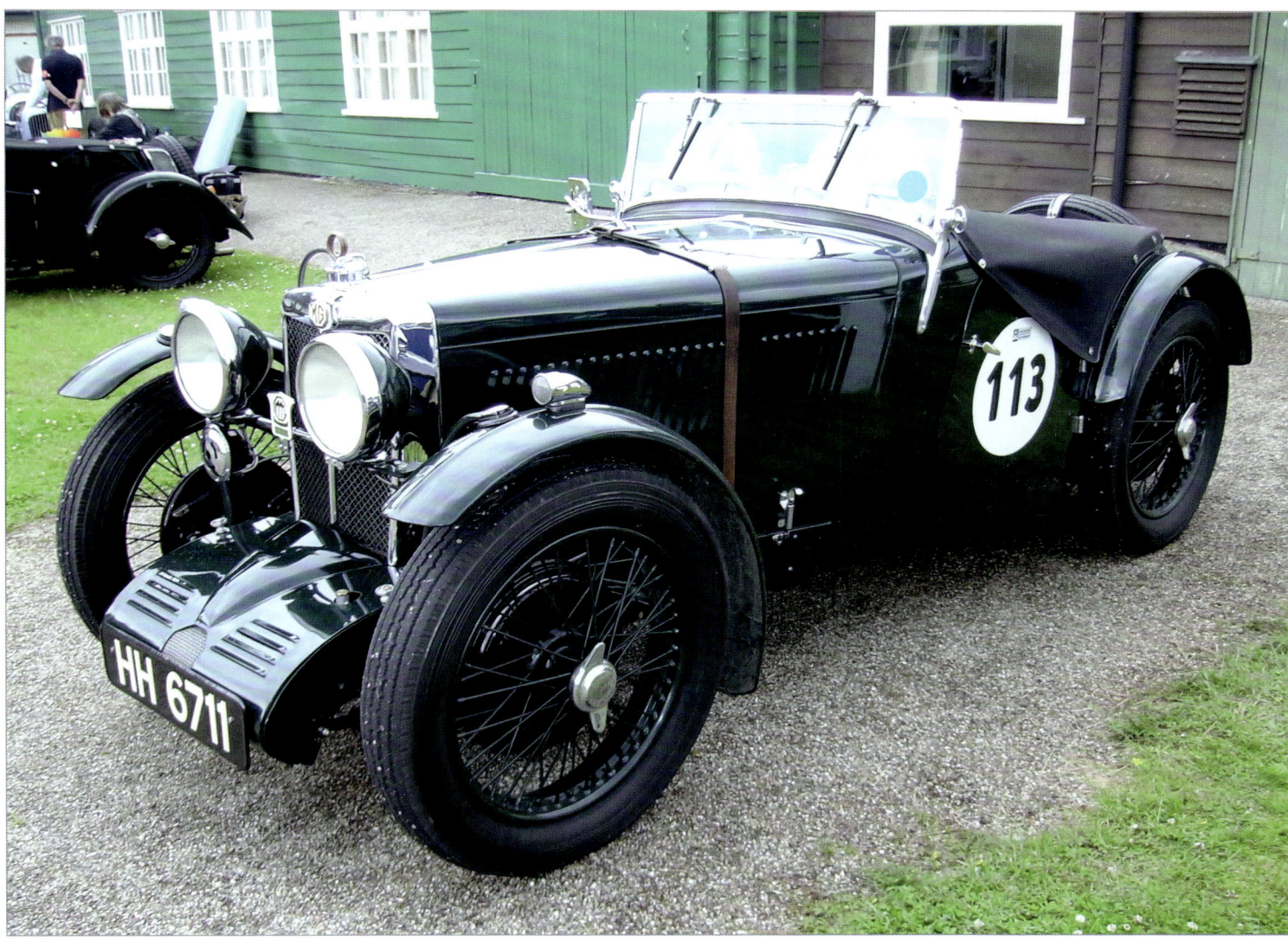

The J3 was a supercharged J2; to cope with the extra performance, bigger brakes from the L-type were fitted. (Author)

issue *The Motor* had related how he had told an MGCC dinner that there was a 2.5-litre supercharged model at the drawing-board stage, to take on Alfa and Maserati, and expected to be ready for 1933. Meanwhile, the experimental department, he said, was working on a racing version of the Magna – 'a supercharged small car that will probably make history,' the magazine reported.

Nothing was to come of the 2.5-litre car; indeed the author is not aware of any evidence that it ever existed as anything more than a twinkle in Kimber's eye. But the smaller supercharged Magna-derived model would come to pass. The starting point was a desire to make a more robust engine out of the Wolseley Hornet 'six'. This saw Hubert Charles working with Wolseley's engineers on what

Kimber in an F-type at an MGCC gymkhana.

Chapter Nine: Technical Advances but a Marriage in Retreat

The business-like rear of the F-type two-seater; note the octagonal surround for the combined speedometer and tachometer and the matching switch panel. (Magna Press Library)

was in effect a new power unit – one which would correspond to the up-to-1100cc class in international competition. The engine made its first appearance in yet another new M.G. model, the K-type Magnette announced in September 1932 ahead of that year's Motor Show.

The block remained essentially unchanged but the shorter-stroke crankshaft had larger main and big-end bearings, there was improved lubrication, and the con-rods were stronger. Allied to a crossflow head and strengthened valvegear, all this made for a design that was robust and would happily take a high level of tune, not least when supercharged. The new engine was mounted in a more rigid chassis with a wider track, and mated to either a conventional unsynchronised four-speed 'crash' gearbox or a pre-selector unit. The latter were starting to become fashionable, as an aid to easier gearchanging, and would also be adopted by Riley; their use by M.G. would however not be without problems.

In what might seem to be a bizarrely misplaced piece of marketing, the headline model was the K1, a four-seater saloon of unusual pillarless design. At launch this was the only Magnette available for illustration in the magazine write-ups, but there would also be a K2 two-seater, a four-seater tourer and a K3 competition model, to be available both supercharged and unsupercharged – neither of these being more than briefly alluded to in the press descriptions of the new car.

THE K-TYPE MAGNETTE

Launched in September 1932, the K-type Magnette, with its improved 1086cc version of the F-type's Wolseley Hornet engine, was intended as a way of getting M.G. into the under-1100cc racing class. As well as the revised and stronger crossflow-head engine there was a more rigid chassis, a wider track, and uprated brakes and steering. For road use the Magnette was available as a pillarless four-door K1 saloon with an ENV pre-selector gearbox and as a four-seater K1 tourer and a short-wheelbase two-seater K2, both open cars generally with a normal 'crash' gearbox.

The K3 was the racing six-cylinder derivative, and although trailed at the September 1932 announcement of the K-type it was only unveiled in early 1933. Based on the K2 Magnette chassis (with an additional crossmember), its supercharged engine, mated to a preselector gearbox, developed up to 120bhp. The body was initially a door-less slab-tank affair, but this soon gave way to one with a pointed tail built around the fuel tank. Only 33 K3s were made, the last being laid down in August 1934; one received a Jensen body and one formed the basis of the EX135 record-breaker.

The K-type saloon in its later KN form. The pillarless M.G. saloon was similar in philosophy to Lancia's Augusta – but somewhat less rigid than the monocoque Italian car. (Magna Press Library)

A K1 tourer – the rear compartment lid could be let down to form a platform. Compared to the F-type, the K-type had deeper chassis side rails and a substantial central crossbrace; an unusual feature was the use of divided track rods for the steering. (Magna Press Library)

Output of the new K-type engine in standard roadgoing form was disappointing, at 39bhp – and this despite the use of three SU carburettors. The Magnette, especially in saloon form, was also heavier than the L-type, which didn't help matters. Accordingly in July 1933 a new 1271cc engine known as the KD-series was introduced, developing 48.5bhp on twin carburettors, and the smaller unit phased out: excluding cars supplied as chassis, all but a handful of these bigger-engined K-types were pillarless saloons with an improved version of the pre-selector gearbox incorporating a clutch.

The larger power unit was frequently described as being of 1286cc. In fact it retained the 1271cc capacity of the original Wolseley Hornet engine. Cecil Kimber however didn't want the new M.G. engine to be confused with the Wolseley 'six', and so arbitrarily added a fictitious extra millimetre to the stroke of the engine.

Production of the K1 and K2 ceased in March 1934, ahead of the arrival of the N-type Magnette in April, but in September 1934 the pillarless saloon reappeared as the KN saloon, with the N-type engine. In this guise it was made up until August 1935. There was also a batch of an estimated 22 K-type tourers with the N-type engine, put together by – or on behalf of – University Motors and sold as the 'University Special' Speed Model. Both these hybrid models almost always used a regular four-speed gearbox rather than the pre-selector unit.

With 97 K1 tourers, 74 K1 pillarless saloons, and just 20 K2 two-seaters made, plus 201 KNs and a total of 35 chassis that went to outside coachbuilders, the K-type was not a huge success. It catered for those wanting a closed four-seater M.G., as the continuing sales of the KN saloon demonstrate, but in open form there was no real reason to buy a K-type rather than a cheaper and physically almost identical L-type Magna (see next chapter). As discussed later on, the K-types did not prove satisfactory in service, and all too many customers of early cars ended up demanding they be fitted with the later KD engine and its matching pre-selector gearbox.

TOP LEFT: *This K-type tourer with its badging and radiator stoneguard seems to have been Cecil Kimber's personal car.*

LEFT: *The hood, when erected, does not flatter the K2 two-seater. (Magna Press Library)*

OPPOSITE: *Goldie Gardner, riding mechanic Oscar Paterson (centre) and Cecil Kimber in the pits at the 1932 TT. 'The drivers were like gods to me in their white overalls, and it is no secret that I worshipped "Hammy" Hamilton,' writes Jean. 'When he was killed, I was heartbroken. His mother sent me his lucky charm, a tiny harlequin on a chain, which he had left behind on that fatal day. I treasured it for years.' (National Motor Museum)*

AN EYE FOR PUBLICITY

The year 1932 had initially been only modestly successful in motor sport. Troubles plagued the C-types and M.G. could boast nothing better than a third place in the Ulster TT and another third in the Brooklands 1,000-mile race; at least the Ulster event proved a congenial break for Cecil and Rene Kimber, who attended the race with Kimber's great friend Bill Gibbs. The only ray of sunshine was a class win for Hugh Hamilton in the German GP. But then in September Ronnie Horton in his special Jensen-bodied supercharged single-seater C-type took the up-to-750cc class record at Brooklands, at 115.29mph, and two weeks later he won the 500-mile race at a remarkable average speed of 96.29mph – with, in addition, M.G. coming home with the team prize.

This was followed in November 1932 by Eddie Hall in a supercharged C-type taking the standing kilometre and mile records for up to 750cc at Brooklands, records previously held by an Austin Seven. In December, finally, George Eyston cracked his 120mph target at Montlhéry with the EX127 'Magic Midget', effacing the disappointment of managing only 118.39mph when setting mile and kilometre records in February at Pendine Sands in Wales[3]. Along with Tommy Wisdom and Bert Denly he also took the 750cc International 24-hour record in a supercharged J3, at an average speed of 70.61mph, pocketing at the same time the 1,000-mile and 2,000-kilometre records. Kimber, who had been an active presence at Pendine, was very much behind Eyston on these ventures, and in particular had been keen to see the two-miles-a-minute barrier broken.

Even ahead of these last two successes, there was thus sufficient cause for celebration at the first Motor Show dinner-dance held by the M.G. Car Club. These events, steered by Kimber and generally

The 'Magic Midget' EX127 at Pendine in January 1932, with an elated Cecil Kimber. The beret and plus-fours strike an interesting sartorial note.

attended by the club's patron, Sir William Morris, would be held up to and including 1938, and brought together industry figures, racing motorists and the specialist press. They provided further media exposure for M.G. and a platform for Kimber to ventilate his opinion on matters of import, or to trail his coat about the future year's activities.

This was a further example of Cecil Kimber's astute grasp of publicity and public relations, something that began with the close eye he kept on M.G. sales material, working much of the time with Harold Connolly. "He generally sent for me about February or March and said we'd better start getting out some ideas for next year's Show," Connolly related to Wilson McComb. "He couldn't stand a shoddy catalogue: 'If the car's good, let's make the literature

---

[3] In its report on 'Eyston's Crowning Achievement at Pendine' *Motor Sport* took the opportunity to stir the cauldron of debate on the value of racing. 'Let us hope that the enterprise of the M.G. Car Company in developing their product by an intensive racing programme will inspire those makers who do not race to take up the sport and reap the benefit which successful entry to the competition world would bring with it,' wrote the monthly in its March 1932 issue.

good.' I don't think he ever counted the cost. I once said to him 'These cost a packet, don't they?' He said 'Price of a couple of door-handles, that's all. If they sell the car it's worth it. Remember, the catalogue is the salesman that goes home with you.'

"He always asked me what I thought, but I don't say I influenced him in any way – if he liked it that way it stayed that way, and you could talk till you were blue in the face; he'd just dig his heels in. He liked to have a pretty girl in his cars, and a touch of the country house or a college background. I couldn't draw girls as pretty as I'd have liked, but I did my best. Kimber said he liked my drawing because the cars looked as if they were made of metal – the airbrush drawings of those days made cars look like silk stockings. He didn't think much of my figure work, but it was getting better, he said; he was frank like that..."

Publicity manager George Tuck recalled to Norman Ewing how Kimber steered operations. "I can tell you he was very particular about those catalogues; he knew what he wanted, both finished product and the colours to be used, and he wanted the cars to look solid and have substance and look from the drawings like they could go. I used to pay Harold Connolly five guineas for his drawings."

Tuck remembered that he had "a very modest budget, which Kim always exceeded on my behalf!" The brief came from Kimber, with an indication of the slant he wanted it to take. "Kim was very interested in all the advertising, and was adamant that any motoring promotional matter had to have some sort of objective..."

Although Kimber was prepared to spend what it took to achieve effective advertising, he didn't allow himself to be swept away by the extravagancies of London's advertising whizz-kids, said Tuck. "I remember one time some people sent these girls down to sit gracefully on the bonnets, but it looked very artificial and Kim never liked those shots; it was Kim who said 'What are you messing about at? I'm sure we should do better if we got George Propert's daughter to come and do a bit of modelling.' We tried it and from that moment on she featured in most of our publicity matter and very successfully, too."

The team of C-type Midgets entered by Goldie Gardner (left, with stick) for the 1932 Ulster TT; to Gardner's left is M.G. mechanic Reg Jackson, reserve driver Cyril Paul (with pipe) is standing by car 31 (for Randolph Jeffress), and far right (by number 30, the Hamilton car) is further reserve driver Stanley Barnes. (Goldie Gardner courtesy Mike Jones)

Goldie Gardner's Ulster TT ended in this accident, in which the car somersaulted three times: the dramatic incident nearly cost him his right leg, which had been badly injured during the war. (Goldie Gardner courtesy Mike Jones)

Cecil Kimber at the 1932 Ulster TT with his twin-lens-reflex Rollei camera. The image was taken by Bill Brunell, who was well-connected with the M.G. factory; his daughter Kitty, whom he obsessively photographed, was briefly a rally driver and at one stage competed in an M.G. Magna. (National Motor Museum)

Rene (fourth from left) and Goldie Gardner (sixth from left) in the pits at the Ards circuit, during the 1932 Ulster Tourist Trophy. Second from left (with pipe) is Kimber's friend Bill Gibbs, with Elsie Wisdom to his left. (National Motor Museum)

TWO SISTERS IN COCKTAIL PYJAMAS

This wasn't just a period of excitement for the Abingdon factory. On the personal front there were also developments. It is difficult to be precise about whether it was in 1931 or 1932 when Cecil Kimber met the lady who would upend his married life and become his second wife. 'It really was love at first sight when my father met my future stepmother, Muriel Dewar,' writes Jean in *The Other Tack*. 'My sister and I were with him in the garden of Cecil Graves-Morris, an Oxfordshire dentist, [in] about 1931, and looking back I realise that I saw it happen – one of those instantaneous attractions so powerful that in time they could override all obstacles.

'My stepmother did, of course, meet my father, but she did this reluctantly, not very often, and nearly always in the company of her elder sister as a chaperone. She told my stepsister, Bobbie, long afterwards, that she resisted the attraction she felt for two or three years, as she did not want to break up a marriage. There was also her own family to consider…Bobbie was settled in a good school, and my stepmother quite rightly feared the damage that a scandal might do both to herself and to my father.'

Muriel Lillias Greenwood, who worked for Cecil Graves-Morris as a dental nurse, was born in 1900 in Headington, Oxford, and had married an Anzac soldier by the name of Dewar towards the end of the First World War, according to Jean. 'They were very young, and he was quite unable to afford to send for her once he was back in New Zealand and demobilized. When all hope had evaporated, her uncle paid for the divorce.'

This is not quite the case. Although it was not realised at the time, Muriel Greenwood – later to be invariably known by the nickname Gillie – had never married Australian-born New Zealander Owen Dewar. Their daughter Pauline, known as Bobbie, and born in 1920 in Chorlton-on-Medlock, Lancashire, was therefore illegitimate. When Dewar returned to New Zealand, contact dried up at about the time Bobbie was seven. Suddenly letters were returned, says Bobbie's daughter Easter Kirkland, who assumes this was because

LEFT: *Muriel Dewar was Oxfordshire-born and when Kimber met her she was working as a dental nurse in Oxford.*

RIGHT: *Gladys Hamilton, Muriel Dewar's sister. The two were close, and shared a home.*

Dewar had found a wife in his home country. It was only on her grandmother's death that she discovered that she and Dewar had never been husband and wife.

Muriel Dewar, as she called herself, brought up Bobbie in the company of her sister Gladys Hamilton, who had also suffered a broken relationship. In 1919, at the age of 22, she had married 29-year-old Claud Reginald Matheson Hamilton, a lieutenant in the Australian armed forces, but the marriage fell apart and in 1922 she and Hamilton divorced; the marriage had been childless.

The image handed down of the sisters is one of uncomplicated good-time girls: not 'fast' or of loose morals but having a sense of fun and an easy and infectious complicity. As such, they were a contrast to the more cerebral Rene Kimber. "They were bobby-dazzlers. My mother said there was a scandal in Oxford because they wore cocktail pyjamas. That might have been OK in London, but evidently Oxford was a bit more backward," says Betty's daughter Sara Delamont.

This exuberant way of dressing may well have caused raised eyebrows. Cocktail pyjamas, comprising a blouse or jacket and loose-fitting trousers, started to become popular in the 1920s, most notably on the French Riviera, where pyjamas worn as a swimsuit cover-up began to be worn away from the beach – and started to use more decorative fabrics. Initially considered shocking, by the start of the 1930s they were more widely accepted, but still had a whiff of bold unconventionality about them. 'A woman may and does wear pyjamas to quite formal dinners in her own house, to other people's dinners in town and country if you know them well and the more iconoclastic members of the female sex even wear them to the theatre,' noted *Vogue* in 1931.

These pyjamas most probably weren't an extravagant item for the sisters, who may well have run them up themselves. "Both of them were able to sew, and often used to get hold of old material," recalled Bobbie's husband, John Walkinton, when the author interviewed him in 2017. The duo remained a warm memory for Walkinton. "When they got together, they'd make Kimber's life hell. They set about him. He loved it. He lapped it up. They were a couple of devils, once they got going. They brightened up our lives. They were always up for a bit of fun."

As mentioned above, an affair did not begin straightaway, but Kimber evidently soon began to figure in the life of the Dewar-Hamilton household, as Bobbie's recollections testify. 'When I was 12 years old I met a girl of the same age at a party. We looked at each other up and down, and she said "You're a tomboy!" "You're another!" I said, and that was my first contact with Cecil Kimber's family – his elder daughter. The year was 1932...Over the next few years, I continued to meet the family from time to time – at home, where Kim ran steam trains all round his younger daughter's nursery[4], and particularly at the ice rink in Oxford, where Kim was a very competent skater in spite of his pronounced limp. And [he was] no mean squash player[5] and dancer, either.'

Bobbie appreciated the effort Kimber put into making activities fun. 'As Kim was a great friend of the adults in my family I saw a good deal of him when I was the only youngster around. He always took such trouble with me, like writing a set of rhyming clues to lead to a birthday bicycle, and thinking up a surprise evening picnic on a beautiful summer evening, on the way to a military tattoo.'

Clearly Bobbie Dewar fell under the spell of her future step-father. 'Kim had such a personality, and was so kind to me, that I literally worshipped the ground he walked on,' she writes. 'Many people one met in Oxford worked at M.G., in fact my uncle did, and they all seemed to feel part of a family with Kim as the head.'

A young Muriel Dewar with her daughter Pauline, who was generally known as Bobbie.

---

[4] As readers will have noticed, stories vary about this famous train set.

[5] This is unlikely to be correct. If tennis and golf were found 'too difficult' (see Chapter 1), then it is hard to see how Kimber would have been able to cope with such an intense high-speed ball game as squash.

SUCCESS IN THE MILLE MIGLIA

In 1933 the Kimber family moved to Abingdon, where they rented Boundary House, a substantial property on the Oxford road. Cecil Kimber had now reached a certain station in life, and he and Rene had the services of a cook, a gardener and a maid to make life more agreeable. He also had the pleasure of his own tailor-made M.G. – a supercharged K-type with drophead coachwork by Corsica. In his hands from 1934 until 1936, it was in effect a K3 with a touring body, and was said by *The M.G. Magazine* to have been built 'with the idea of developing the supercharged car for ordinary every-day use.'

These were happy times for the Kimber daughters. 'We had a wonderful life in that friendly house and large garden that was complete with a miniature wood, a tennis court, a tall elm with the inevitable platform built by my sister, a gravel pit...and a lovely pond with stone herons to guard it,' writes Jean in *The Other Tack*. 'The vegetable garden and fruit trees supplied us with fresh produce, and we also inherited a flock of hens and a handsome cock. We had to help feed them, but it was fun. We always had dogs and cats, and later piebald Lundy Island mice brought back from our holidays at Instow, in North Devon. Down the road lived Carl and Eileen Kingerlee, at The Holt, an equally lovely house full of children...It was a second home. Carl Kingerlee of Morris Motors was a lifelong friend and often went sailing and fishing with my father.'

RIGHT: *The slightly inclined radiator shell of the F-type Magna was carried over to its replacement; this is an L2 two-seater. The L-type had a track narrower by 6in than that of the Magnette. (Magna Press Library)*

OPPOSITE: *The Mille Miglia K3s – K3001, K3002, K3003 – after their arrival in Milan. M.G. would win the team prize, despite the retirement of the Birkin car. (M.G. Car Club)*

INSET: *Eyston and Lurani on the way to their class win. (Author's collection)*

Chapter Ten: Success in the Mille Miglia

ABOVE: *Classic pre-war M.G. lines: just visible at the rear on this L2 are the trunnions in which the rear of the leaf springs slide, an unusual arrangement that makes for more rigid location of the springs than a swinging shackle. (Magna Press Library)*

LEFT: *The L-type Salonette was built by Abbey Coachworks and featured glazed rear quarters; the sliding roof with its long windows remained a feature. (Mike Allison)*

Jean and Betty relayed to Wilson McComb their fond memories of Boundary House. 'It was a full house and a full life. Despite continually recurring pain in his right thigh, Kimber would rise early every morning to do keep-fit exercises, and danced or played tennis[1] with equal enthusiasm,' he writes. 'Every day, friends or favoured M.G. customers would be brought home to lunch, and Rene Kimber's considerable linguistic skill would be put to good use if it were someone like the Luranis or Tazio Nuvolari.' McComb tells how Kimber still found time to entertain his daughters with stories or adventurous outings. "I don't think I brought out sufficiently what a good father 'CK' was in the sense of doing things with us. He was always taking us sailing, fishing, swimming, skating and just exploring generally," recalled Betty.

Kimber's elder daughter had also added riding to her interests, recounts Sara Delamont. "She loved riding. The Oxford University polo team had stables in Oxford. If you went along and mucked them out you could ride the ponies when the undergraduates weren't riding them. She also liked skating – and had her own boots. She also had a really, really good sledge, with metal runners – it came, I believe, from one of Kim's customers or agents in Switzerland or Austria."

Discipline in the Kimber home was firm, as Betty related to Wilson McComb. "We didn't get our pocket-money unless we worked for it – we didn't just get a handout. I had to make a mash for the chickens in the morning and feed them [and] every night it used to take me an hour to boil the dogs' food[2]. I had to chop logs, all sorts of things." This strictness extended to Rene Kimber, who was expected to record all household expenditure in a large account book. "They had an awful row once about her not keeping proper accounts," Betty told McComb. "He was parsimonious about a lot of small things."

DEMANDING BUT DECENT – KIMBER AS BOSS

At the factory, Kimber presented a somewhat different figure, writes McComb. 'He could be and often was a martinet. His terse memoranda, always signed in green ink, were something to be dreaded. When a shop floor employee was summoned to Kimber's mock-Tudor office, it was understood that first one removed greasy overalls and made oneself presentable. He might make unreasonable demands of his men, as he often did when they were working against the clock for some race or record attempt, but his scrupulous fairness made every one of them – it sounds so archaic, nowadays – a loyal servant who would have done anything for him.'

Many stories are told. One, regarding his future boss Tom Viner, was related to the author by Mike Allison. "Tom used to take sandwiches in to work and sit in the back of a car to eat them. One day he saw Kimber walking along, so he kept a low profile. Kimber walked by. Then he returned. Tom ducked down. Kimber got in the car and drove round to Boundary House. When he got out, Tom hot-footed it back to the factory. After he'd returned from lunch Kimber said to Tom 'You had a good lunch, Viner? Well, next time, don't eat it in the back of my car.' Another boss would have sacked him on the spot. Kimber knew everybody in the factory by name – and would know their wife's name as well. I only had to mention Cecil Kimber and people would say 'Oh, he was a good boss!' Once people had been told what to do he left them to get on with it. He didn't sit on their shoulder and tell them what to do. He would take an interest in what was going on, but without interfering."

Cecil Kimber ran a tight ship – as was necessary – and as a result he was regarded with a certain amount of trepidation by the workforce. "He used to frighten everyone to death. Well, he did me. It was my first job, so I was nervous anyway. I was still in short

---

[1] Kimber did indeed dance, but the reference to tennis may not be accurate; see Chapter 1.

[2] Similar stories were passed down by Betty to her daughter: " If the girls had pets, they had to look after them. If they were going to have rabbits, the gardener's boy wasn't going to look after them – they were going to look after them," recounts Sara Delamont.

Chapter Ten: Success in the Mille Miglia

trousers," remembered Jim Simpson[3]. "Everyone told me what a terror Kimber was. I'd not been there very long and I was coming into the factory with a wall on one side and a fence on the other and coming towards me was Kimber. I was terrified. I literally shook. I'd done nothing wrong as far as I knew, but that was the effect he had. I thought that with a bit of luck he wouldn't notice me. Just as I got to him he stopped and called me. He looked at me – he did glare at people, with a bit of a baleful look – and then he suddenly smiled and said 'Hello laddie. How are you getting on now? Alright are you? Good – keep it up!'. I walked on, feeling ten foot tall. He could be a bit of a tartar but he was basically a nice man."

A NEW MAGNA AND A LEGENDARY RACING MODEL

M.G. entered 1933 with a four-car range: the J-type Midget, the F-type Magna, the K-type Magnette and the 18/80 MkII. Admittedly the continued listing of the MkII was merely a question of disposing of stock, the last chassis number having been issued in October 1932; all the same this was an ambitious programme

---

[3] Interview recorded by David Burgess-Wise. The same story is told in *The Other Tack* and in Simpson's 1997 interview for the *Triple-M Yearbook*.

ABOVE: *An advertisement for the L-type Magna Continental Coupé. The catalogue referred to 'pleasing and dainty lines' but the buying public were not convinced and the sanction of 100 cars proved hard to shift. (Author's collection)*

LEFT: *The 'fiacre' or horse-cab styling of the Continental Coupé caused one wag at the 1933 MGCC Motor Show dinner to come up with this cleverly doctored photo, as* The Autocar *reported. (Author's collection)*

Chapter Ten: Success in the Mille Miglia

THE L-TYPE MAGNA

The L-type Magna that replaced the F-type in March 1933 used a detuned 41bhp twin-carb ('KC') version of the more robust 1086cc engine of the Magnette, in a largely unchanged chassis. The four-speed manual gearbox, mated to a twin-plate dry clutch, continued to be sourced from Wolseley. There were now flowing front and rear wings with integral running boards, and the body of the tourer was completely redesigned. The coupé, meanwhile, switched body manufacturer to Abbey Coachworks, and gained rear side windows. In September 1933 the Continental Coupé with its controversial French-style coachwork became available.

The L-type never received the 1271cc power unit and lasted barely 18 months before the N-type Magnette replaced both it and the K-type, production stopping in January 1934. Abingdon assembled 576 L-types, with the most popular body style, by a considerable margin, being the L1 open four-seat tourer, with a recorded 258 made. In contrast, 90 of the L2 sports two-seater were built. Of the closed cars, 97 Salonette two-door saloons were made and 96 Continental Coupés; examples of the latter were still being sold as late as 1936, some two years after they had been manufactured. In addition 35 chassis went to outside coachbuilders.

Although not envisaged as a competition car, a trio of tuned L2 two-seaters took part in the Light Car Club Relay Race at Brooklands in July 1933, carrying off the team award. It was these same cars that subsequently participated in the Alpine Trial.

The Magna tourer in L1 form now had a dual-cowl scuttle, more deeply cut-away rear-hinged doors and a different rear treatment with a bolster tank and a more inclined spare wheel. (Magna Press Library)

for a small company. With the Magnette entering production at the beginning of the year, it might have been expected that the Magna would quietly fade away, leaving Abingdon with one four-cylinder model and one six-cylinder model.

Instead, March 1933 saw the F-type being replaced with a revised model using a slightly de-tuned version of the 1086cc Magnette engine. The three principal body styles for the new L-type Magna were as before, but with subtly revised lines. There were now elegantly sweeping full wings and the L1 tourer had a dual-cowl scuttle, while the Salonette was a new design built by outside supplier Abbey Coachworks and featured more saloon-like glazed rear quarters.

A newcomer was the Continental Coupé, a close-coupled two-door model that picked up on styling themes seen in France and Italy. Finished in bright colours and with flamboyant Art Deco interior detailing, the model was certainly striking. It proved too daring for conservative British tastes, however, and sales dragged out over several years until Kimber's over-optimistic 100-car body order had been exhausted.

If the Continental Coupé was aimed at the carriage-trade sector of the market, and intended to attract the gentleman or lady about town, the K3 Magnette introduced in March 1933 was in contrast an off-the-peg racer designed uncompromisingly for the competition successes it would soon achieve. Even before the car was unveiled, plans were afoot for its racing debut in the Mille Miglia road-race. Indeed, George Eyston suggests in *Flat Out* that the K3 was conceived specifically with participation in the arduous Italian event in mind.

Chapter Ten: Success in the Mille Miglia

THIS PAGE: *The first K3s had a slab-tank body very similar to that of the J4 Midget. This is the second prototype, as used on the Mille Miglia recce, and has a sloping radiator not found on any other K3.*

OPPOSITE: *The L-type moved the game on from the original F-type Magna; just 90 of the L2 two-seater were made. (Magna Press)*

Chapter Ten: Success in the Mille Miglia

GLORY IN ITALY

In 1932 a supercharged Montlhéry Midget had been entered in the Mille Miglia by Lord Edward de Clifford and T.G.V. Selby. It had retired with a sheared camshaft drive but had been lying second in class, and this suggested that M.G. might be in with a chance for a class win with the more potent six-cylinder K3. Well-known racing driver Earl Howe put to Kimber and Sir William Morris the idea of an M.G. team for the 1933 event. Quite possibly to his surprise, he received the full backing of Morris, who was known for his scepticism about the value of motor racing[4]; that Howe agreed to bankroll the exercise doubtless sealed the deal.

Howe's first move was to put together a crack team of drivers: George Eyston with Johnny Lurani, 'Bentley Boys' Sir Henry Birkin and Bernard Rubin sharing a car, and Howe himself, paired with Hugh Hamilton. Kimber was concerned about taking a new and untried model, but Howe set up a 3,000-mile development-testing practice run to Italy in January with the second K3 prototype[5]. The weather during the exercise was appalling, but helped highlight areas where the design needed to be improved. Back in Abingdon sundry modifications were incorporated in the three team cars that were built up – an exhausting race-against-the-clock that had Hubert Charles (and he was not alone) at one stage working for 72 hours without a break.

This careful preparation – and good organisation when in Italy –

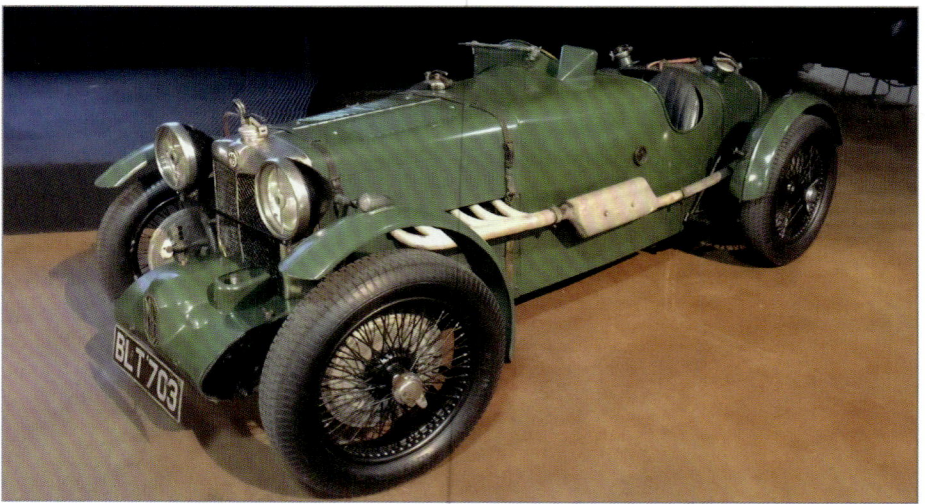

ABOVE: *Hugh McConnell, the manager for the 1933 Mille Miglia team (left) with Sir Henry Birkin (in overalls) and co-driver Bernard Rubin. Birkin's task was to act as the 'hare' and push rival cars so hard that they broke. (M.G. Car Club)*

TOP: *The K3 in its later pointed-tail form, this revised body being fitted from the 20th car onwards. 'The extremely successful K3 cost £795 and was worth every penny,' observed John Bolster in 1981. This particular example is the car that came home fourth in the 1934 Le Mans 24-hour race. (John Nikas)*

---

[4] The specialist press wrote what it suited them to say. When they wanted to talk up Morris's support for a venture, he was portrayed as having an interest in motor sport. When there wasn't this context, they suggested – more accurately – that he was anything but an enthusiast. 'It has been said, quite incorrectly, that Sir William is against motor racing,' wrote Tommy Wisdom in a January 1933 issue of *Sporting Life*. 'He is not…He is very much in favour of motor racing when it is done properly'. In contrast *The Motor* wrote in its 25 December 1940 issue 'Here was a man who was completely convinced that racing as such was without real value to the British motor industry and to British prestige, and despite every argument, he stuck to his guns.'

[5] The first prototype, meanwhile, achieved fastest time and a class record on the Mont des Mules hillclimb part of the 1933 Monte Carlo Rally.

From left to right in this photo can be seen Eyston, Hamilton, Howe, Birkin, Kimber and Rubin inspecting one of the K3s being prepared for the 1933 Mille Miglia. Kimber was to claim that the only deviation from the standard specification was a counter-balanced crankshaft. (M.G. Car Club)

Chapter Ten: Success in the Mille Miglia

Earl Howe and Hugh Hamilton receiving their time at an official checkpoint. The duo came in second in the up-to-1100cc class, behind Eyston's car. (M.G. Car Club)

paid off when the race took place in April: Eyston came home first in the up-to-1100cc class, with Howe close behind in second place, against strong competition from what *The Motor* described as 'two hot-stuff Maseratis'. The Birkin/Rubin car had been forced to retire with valve trouble, but as no complete teams had finished the event, M.G. claimed the team prize, plus a gold medal for the fastest time in class for the leg to Florence and a silver cup for the first foreign car home.

'That British small cars, properly prepared and organised, could beat the best Continentals of like size was proved conclusively,' wrote *Motor Sport* when it looked back on the event ten years later. 'When it is remembered, too, that this was the first racing appearance of the supercharged K3 M.G. Magnette, one's admiration knows no bounds. Lord Howe, by his inspiration in picking on the M.G. Car Company Ltd to produce him a team of cars, by his willingness to meet the not inconsiderable expenses involved, and his splendid powers of organisation, enabled British prestige to be indisputably upheld in the world's most exacting road-race.'

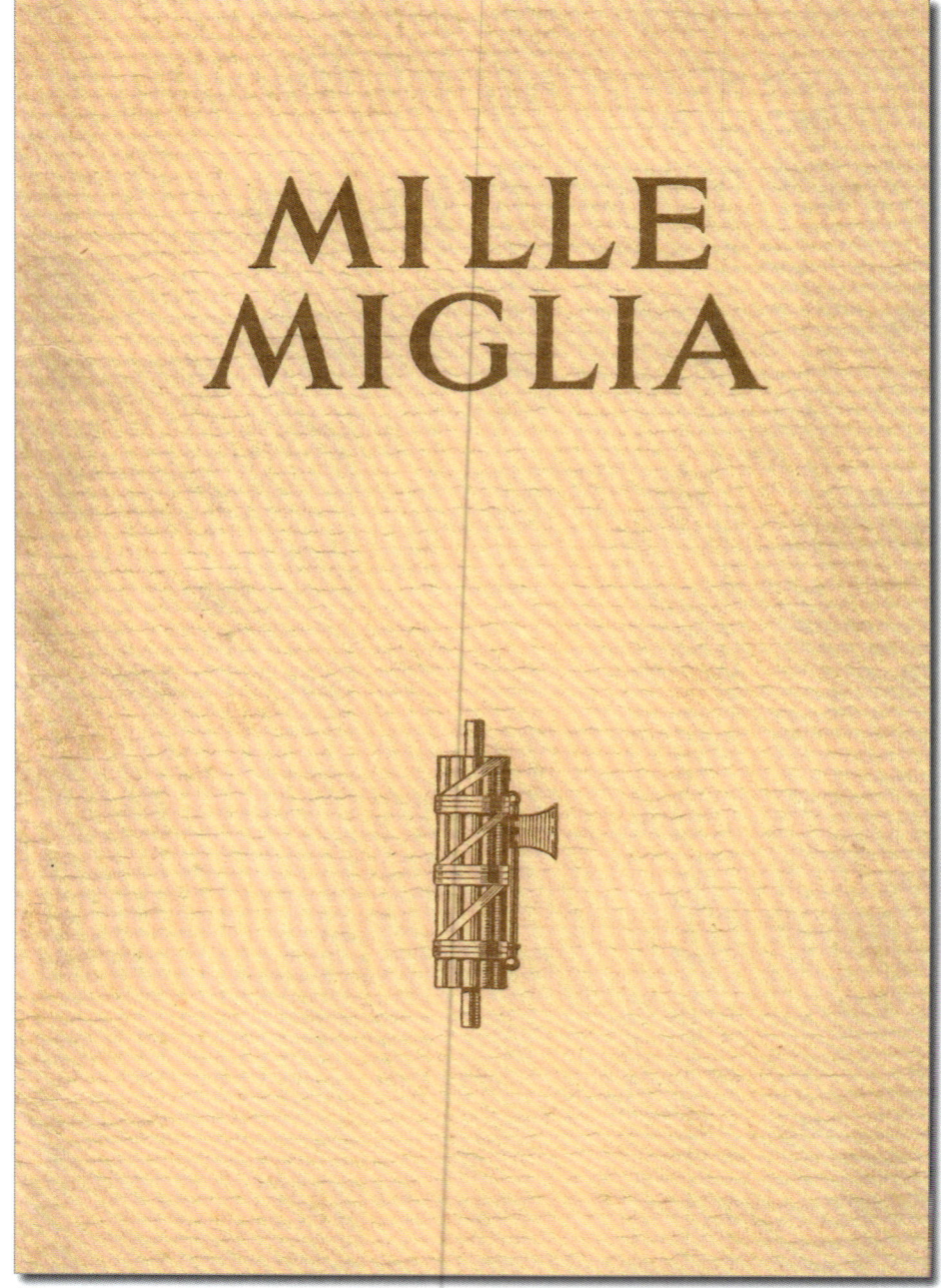

The M.G. publication celebrating the Mille Miglia achievements was adorned with the fasces, emblem of Italian ruler Mussolini's Fascist state – and, until 1935 – of Sir Oswald Mosley's British Union of Fascists. William Morris, who had briefly given financial support to Mosley's preceding New Party, would presumably not have found this objectionable.

The Mille Miglia team photo. Left to right on the back row are Bernard Rubin, Clifton Penn-Hughes, who drove Howe's Mercedes SSK in the race as a tender car to the K3s, George Eyston, and Hugh McConnell, the Italian-speaking chief scrutineer at Brooklands who looked after organisation; on the front row are 'Hammy' Hamilton, Earl Howe, Cecil Kimber, and Sir Henry Birkin. Missing is Johnny Lurani, as the aristocratic Giovanni Lurani Cernuschi, Count of Calvenzano, preferred to be known.

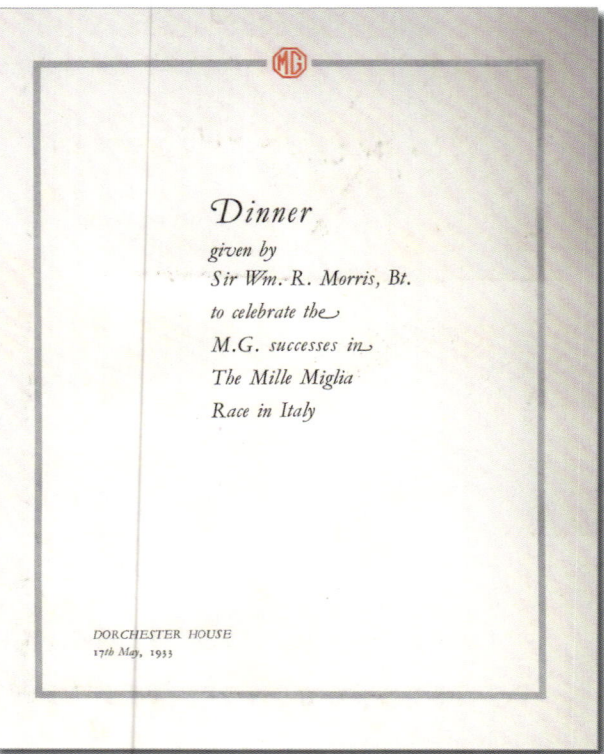

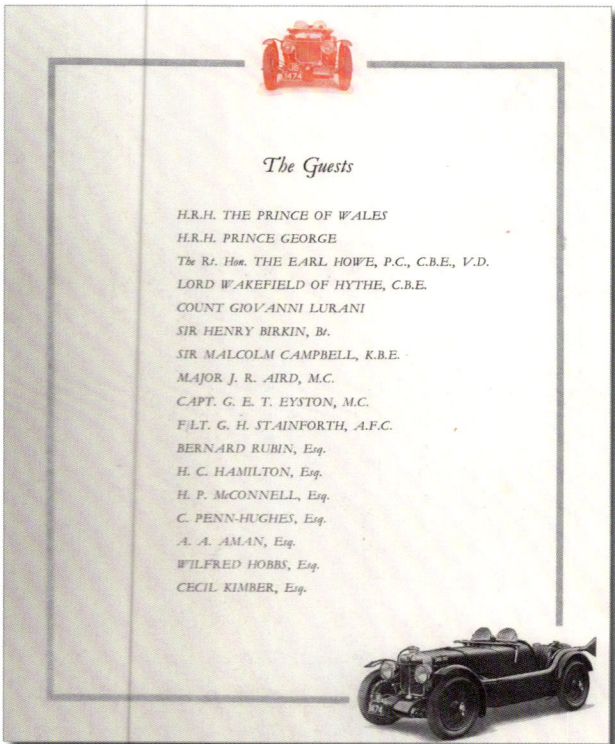

Chapter Ten: Success in the Mille Miglia

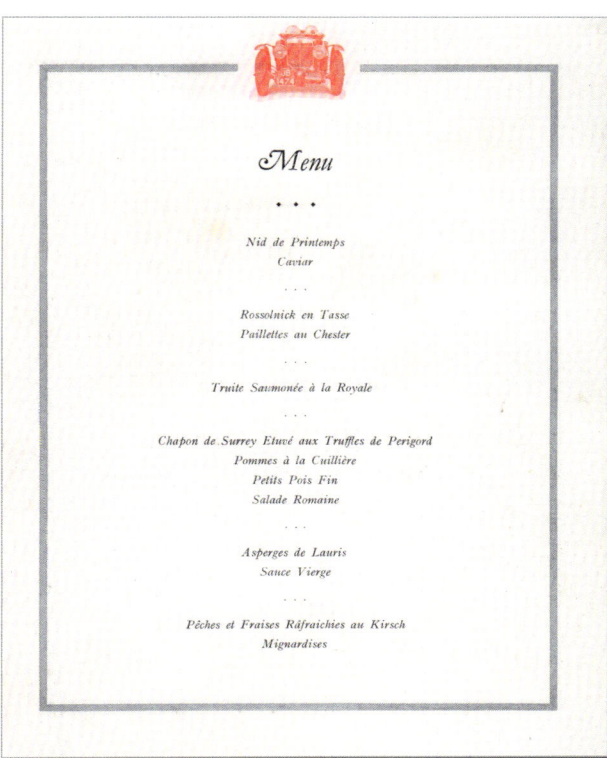

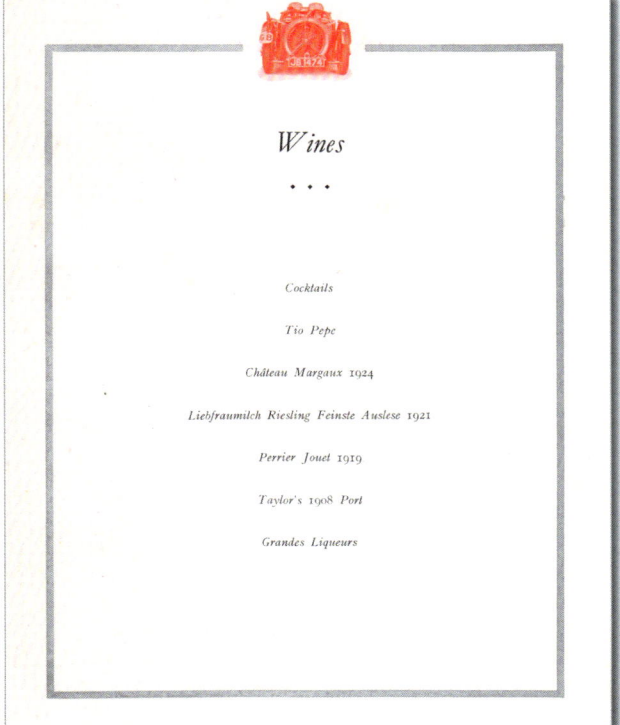

THESE TWO PAGES: *Sir William Morris threw a celebratory dinner at the Dorchester, attended by the Prince of Wales (the future Duke of Windsor) and his younger brother Prince George, a royal with an even more turbulent private life, including a relationship with notorious socialite drug-addict Kiki Preston – 'the girl with the silver syringe'.*

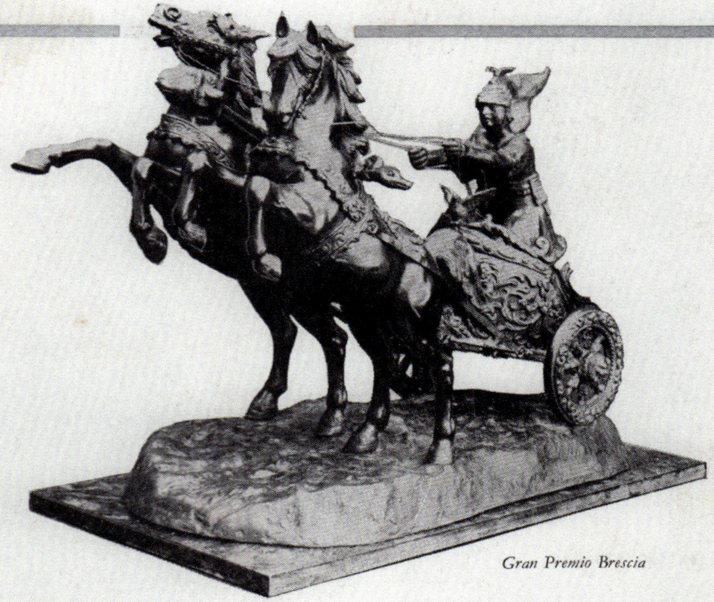

ABOVE & RIGHT: *House monthly* The M.G. Magazine *was launched in 1933, with an editorial from Cecil Kimber and featuring a scene from the Mille Miglia on its inaugural cover; renamed* The Sports Car *in April 1935, publication lasted until the outbreak of war.*

ABOVE: *After the 1933 International Trophy Race, M.G. had a good set of results to advertise. (Author's collection)*

Kimber at the 1933 Brooklands JCC International Trophy Race with second-placed Eddie Hall and the K3 of Elsie Wisdom, who finished third; the only woman driver entered, Wisdom was 'steadiness personified' according to the report in The Autocar.

NUVOLARI CHOOSES AN M.G.

Further adding to Abingdon's laurels in 1933 was a headline victory in that year's Tourist Trophy. Having been impressed by the M.G. performance on the Mille Miglia, which he had won in his Alfa Romeo, Italian ace Tazio Nuvolari mentioned to Earl Howe that he would welcome the chance to drive a K3 in the TT. Sir William Morris reputedly dug into his personal pocket to pay a fee to Nuvolari, and he would be present in Ulster for the race, for which he put up a £1,000 cash prize[6]. One of the Mille Miglia cars was prepared, and although he had never raced a British car, or used a pre-selector gearbox, Nuvolari drove a masterly race enlivened by a duel with Hamilton's J4 Midget, which came home second. Cecil Kimber was at the track with his camera, and recorded the Italian's triumphant taking of the chequered flag – followed, in fourth place, by Eddie Hall in his K3.

The Mille Miglia and the TT were merely the pinnacles in a year where M.G. cars were omnipresent on the track at home and abroad, securing victories, high placings and class wins in everything from the Brooklands International Trophy race (second and third places going to K3s) to the Grosse Bergpreis von Deutschland hillclimb (class win and third-fastest time for Hamilton's J4), not to forget a class win and sixth overall for a C-type at Le Mans. Even the L-type got in on the act, with a trio of works entries – this despite normal Abingdon policy – collecting Glacier Cups and the Team Award in July's Alpine Trial. Keeping this essentially touring model in the competition limelight, Kimber in addition had the PR savvy to lend ten Magnas for a race at Brooklands between 'veteran' pre-WWI racing drivers.

---

[6] 'The prize is offered by Sir William with the object of encouraging private owners of cars to compete in races; he is, however, opposed to manufacturers building cars with racing as the main objective,' cautiously explained M.G. in-house publication *The M.G. Magazine* in its first issue of May 1933.

THESE TWO PAGES: *Kimber took this photo of Hamilton in his J4 Midget (car 19) and Nuvolari in his K3, during the dramatic 1933 Ulster TT, also capturing Nuvolari as he took the chequered flag.*

In his Epilogue to Barré Lyndon's 1933 book *Combat* – to be followed in 1934 by *Circuit Dust*, devoted to the 1933 season – Earl Howe was generous in his praise for Kimber's achievements as they stood at that particular moment.

'Motor racing in England has passed through difficult times, although, happily, interest seems to be greater than ever before and I think that, in a large measure, the revival is due to the fact that Cecil Kimber provided amateur drivers with cars they could race and maintain. Invariably amateurs are men eager to carry on the traditions of those who drove in the dangerous dawn of the sport, and the friendly assistance which Cecil Kimber has always tried to give them is in keeping with that chivalry which makes motor racing such a fine thing. Right from the beginning, he followed an ideal, and I think that he has done much – more, perhaps, than many of us appreciate – for those who like fast driving and fast cars.'

ABOVE: *A photo dedicated to Cecil Kimber by Nuvolari. 'I liked Nuvolari, he was sweet. He was terribly jolly and played with us children in the garden,' recounted Betty to Wilson McComb.*

TOP RIGHT: *Nuvolari (left) and his M.G. mechanic Alec Hounslow celebrate the Italian's victory; Hounslow has his arm around colleague Reg 'Jacko' Jackson. (Author's collection)*

OPPOSITE TOP: *Kimber's Corsica-bodied K-type. Under the heading 'Mr Cecil Kimber's Ideal Car' the May 1934 issue of The M.G. Magazine described it as follows: 'A standard M.G. Magnette touring chassis fitted with a supercharger and a special all-weather body. It has a maximum speed of 94mph and yet is perfectly normal to drive in traffic without any trace of oiling-up troubles, usually associated with a "blown" engine.'*

OPPOSITE BOTTOM: *The Corsica wasn't totally civilised, suffering not least from engine fumes in the cockpit. John Thornley apparently said to a subsequent owner that it was essentially a racing car with touring bodywork. Vic Derrington, the well-known purveyor of tuning accessories, who owned the M.G. just before the war, nonetheless had fond memories of the machine. "It was literally a perfectly made car in every way, and had an exceedingly good performance," he recalled.*

Chapter Ten: Success in the Mille Miglia

ABOVE: *The dispatch bay with a Continental Coupé to the fore, doubtless waiting in vain for a purchaser. 'When we visited the factory, I am sorry to say that my sister and I were often very naughty, and stole illicit rides on the goods trolleys, running them down the ramps from floor to floor. It was spotlessly clean with a quiet hum of activity,' writes Jean. (Mike Allison)*

OPPOSITE: *An L-type chassis having its brakes set up on the rolling road at the end of the production line. (Mike Allison)*

TOP (BOTH) & ABOVE: *Boundary House and a view of Jean in the sitting room. The car is not the K-type Magnette tourer shown in the previous chapter.*

RIGHT: *Kimber's 'Change of Address' card after the move to Boundary House demonstrates his eye for design and graphics.*

ABOVE LEFT: *Jean with horses in the field behind Boundary House.*

ABOVE RIGHT: *Kimber relaxing at Boundary House. 'Cecil Kimber was very much one of the famous then, in the mid-thirties. One remembers him as a small man, usually smoking a pipe, dressed in tweedy clothes and wearing a somewhat battered trilby hat. Also he was often seen in that long-forgotten fashion, plus-fours,' writes John Dugdale.*

LEFT: *Goldie Gardner visiting Boundary House in his Alfa Romeo 8C-2300; he had two of these cars.*

Chapter Ten: Success in the Mille Miglia

11

COWLEY TAKES CHARGE

As 1933 turned into 1934, Cecil Kimber could feel proud of M.G. and its position in the motoring world. In just ten years he had established the marque as Britain's major producer of sports cars and as the country's leading flag-waver in international competition. The cars were now distinctively M.G. rather than Morrises in a party frock, and had achieved an aesthetic rightness that would never be bettered among traditional open-wheeled sports cars. The pace of development had been rapid, with a cascade of different models introduced in the 1931 to 1933 period; now it was time for things to settle down a little.

TIDYING UP THE MODEL RANGE

In January the L-type Magna was discontinued, although the Continental Coupé continued to be offered, to enable stocks to be run down. In February a P-type Midget replaced the J-type, bringing with it a more robust three-main-bearing crankshaft[1]. A month later the K1 and K2 Magnettes were replaced by an improved Magnette, the N-type; the K3 remained available, but the last chassis would be laid down in August. There were thus in essence just two models: the P-type and the N-type.

---

[1] A crankshaft needs to be rigid, and to be rigidly mounted in the engine block. A two-main-bearing crank in a four-cylinder engine will lack sufficient support and thus be prone to 'whip' – especially at high revs. The unwanted movement will put the big-end journals out of alignment with the bearings, causing bearing wear and stressing the crankshaft to the point where it could well break. This proved to be a problem with the J-type Midget.

OPPOSITE: *Lord Nuffield and Leonard Lord. 'On a personal level Kimber and Lord managed to remain quite friendly, but they both knew who was boss,' writes Wilson McComb. "Remember, Kim – the higher you are, the nearer you are to your hat," Lord reportedly observed to Kimber. Just a year later and it was Lord who was reaching for his headwear.*

ABOVE: *George Eyston continued to wave the flag for M.G. with his 'Magic Midget' record-breaker; for this November 1933 sortie to Montlhéry the driving was entrusted to former racing motorcyclist Bert Denly, Eyston's chief mechanic and co-driver.*

Chapter Eleven: Cowley takes Charge

It was a tidier and more financially sensible line-up, although the price lists were all the same filled out with leftovers such as those hard-to-shift Continental Coupés and the KN pillarless

ABOVE: *Kimber photographed near Northcourt Farm, Abingdon, with Rinty, the family's wire-haired terrier.*

RIGHT: *This cartoon, in the style of renowned caricaturist Ralph Sallon, appeared in* The Morris Owner *at the start of the 1934 racing season. It pokes fun at the differing physiques of Cecil Kimber and John Cobb.*

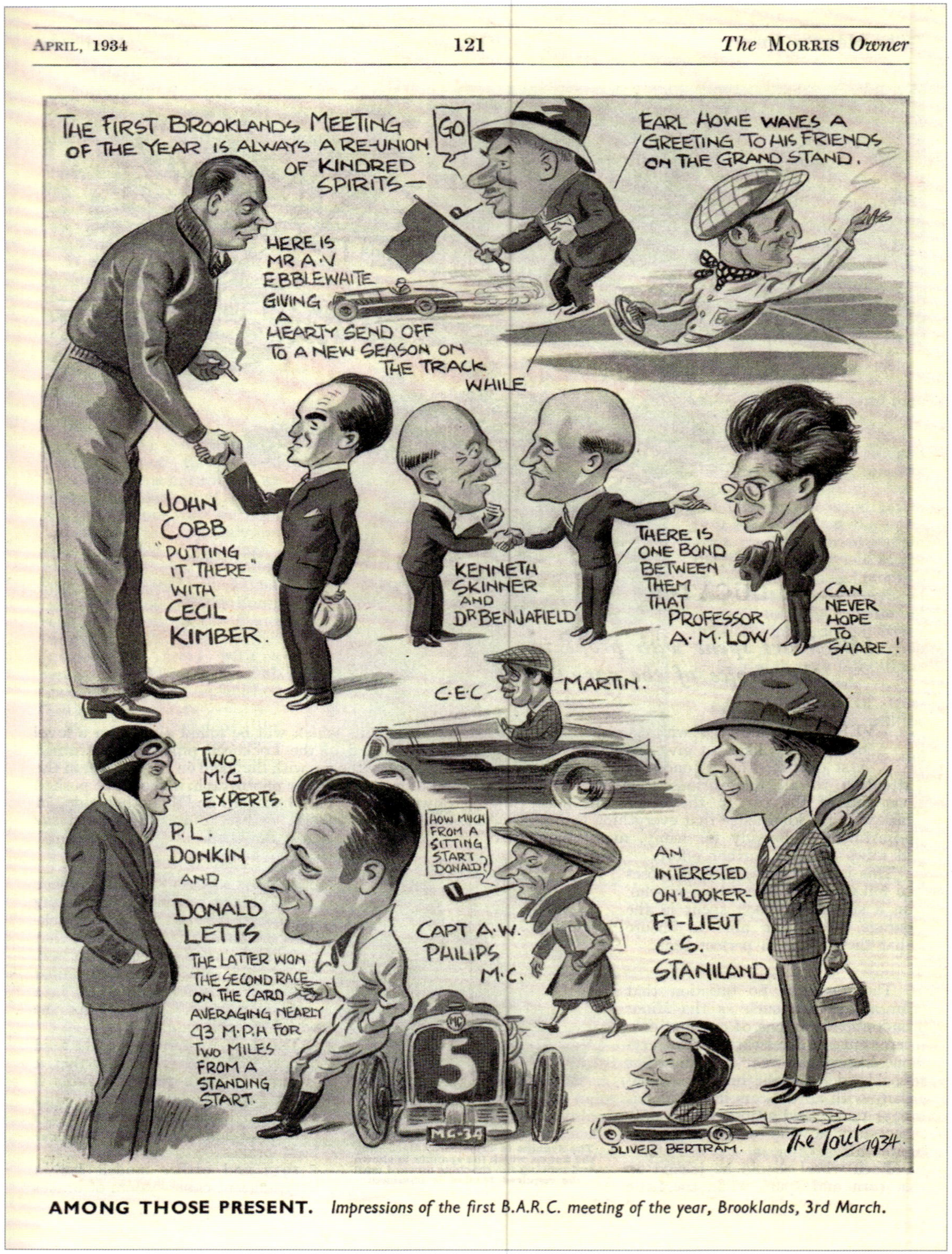

Chapter Eleven: Cowley takes Charge

THE P-TYPE MIDGET

Introduced in February 1934, the P-type addressed the problems of the J-type – and moved the game on in other areas. The key change was to go over to a crankshaft with three main bearings. This was accompanied by an increase in brake diameter from 8in to 12in and by an uprated gearbox and back axle, the whole housed in a strengthened longer-wheelbase chassis. The Midget now had road manners that were largely irreproachable and reserves of reliability. The revised engine, wrote *The Autocar* in its road test, offered 'an enormous gain in smoothness' and the M.G. was judged 'a most desirable little sports car'.

With the resultant increase in weight the power output of 35bhp was on the low side, however, and for the 1936 model year the engine was up-gunned to 939cc – giving an output of 43.3bhp. With a weight of 15.6cwt, this was sufficient to give the new PB, announced in August 1935, a top speed of roughly 75mph and measurably improved acceleration. Other changes were a closer-ratio gearbox (still unsynchronised), Bishop cam-and-peg steering, and a slatted grille. With its crisp engine, responsive steering and nicely easy gearchange, the PB was a thoroughly pleasing small sports car. It was replaced in June 1936 by the T-type Midget – a very different machine.

Both the PA and PB were offered in three catalogued styles: an open two-seater, a four-seat tourer, and a new Airline coupé. Designed by Henry Allingham and built by Carbodies, this was a striking two-seat fastback. Introduced at the 1934 Motor Show, only 42 were made, 28 as a PA and 14 as a PB: the extra weight of the body inevitably blunted performance, especially in the case of the 847cc PA, and the price, £290 at launch, against £222 for an open two-seater, also counted against it. In comparison, 1,396 PAs and 408 PBs were made as two-seaters, and 498 PAs and 99 PBs as tourers; 57 chassis went to outside coachbuilders.

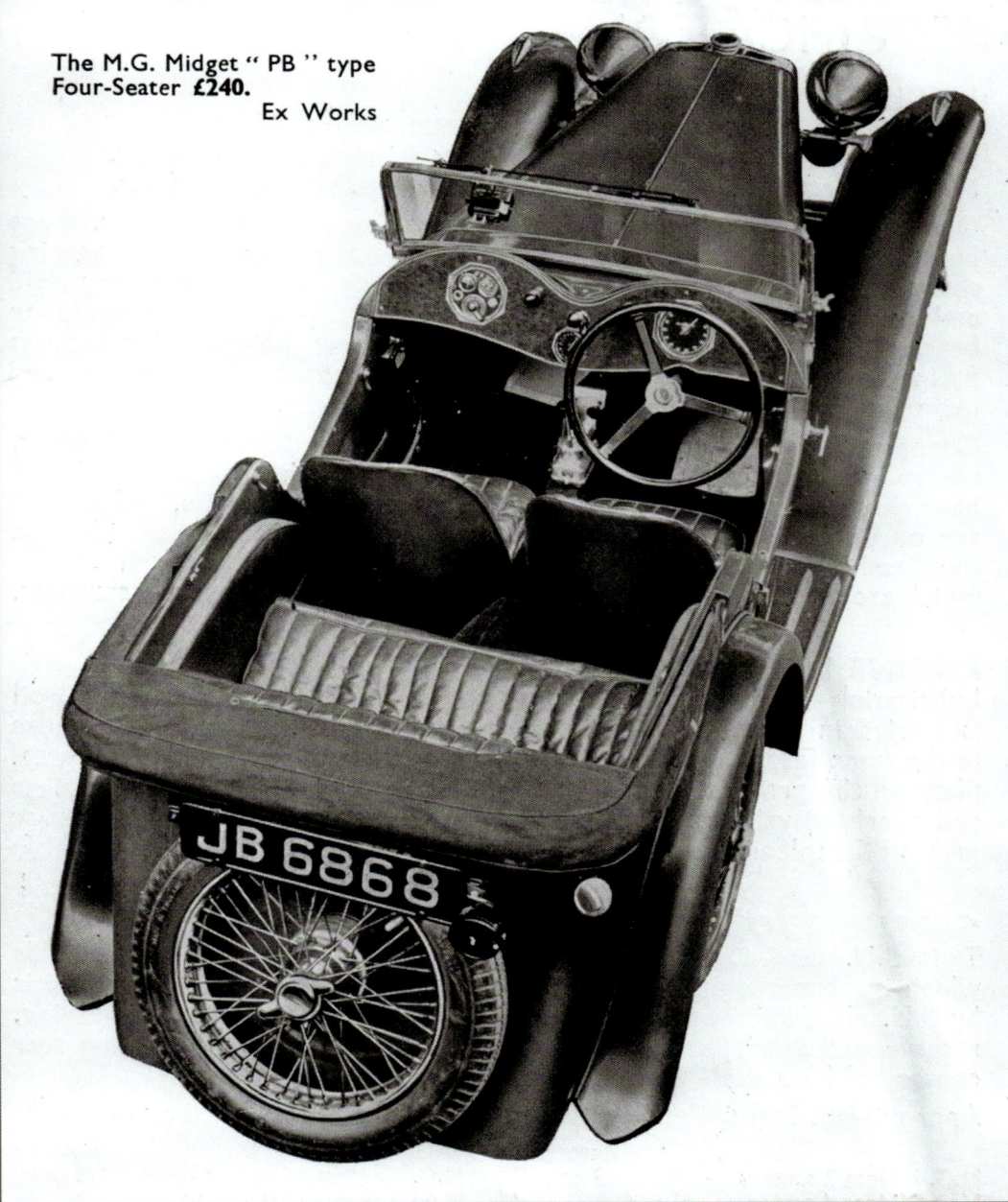

The PB in four-seater tourer form. The Midgets continued to be the bedrock of M.G. sales: 4,962 of the J-type and P-type were built (excluding J3s and J4s), against a little over 3,000 of the smaller six-cylinder road cars.

Chapter Eleven: Cowley takes Charge

saloon. Plugging away with these two models was doubtless laudable, but the other side of the coin was that every additional car leaving the factory was welcome, as sales in 1933 had started to fall from their previous peak in 1932.

A final detail was that for the 1934 season the construction of M.G. bodies moved from Carbodies to Morris Bodies Branch, industrially an eminently logical change. The only exceptions – as far as the catalogued models were concerned – were two limited-production models: the contract for the P-type and N-type Airline coupés went to Carbodies while the N-type Allingham 2/3-seater, a dickey-seat open car, was built by Whittingham & Mitchel.

A NEW RACER – AND MORE COMPETITION LAURELS

As for the competition models, there was a new racing '750' for 1934, the Q-type unveiled during May. The J4 had proved to have too much power for its chassis so the supercharged engine, now with three main bearings and mated to a pre-selector gearbox, was decanted to a new frame with a longer wheelbase, to which wider axles and N-type brakes and steering were fitted.

Despite this, the Q-type remained something of a beast: Reg Jackson remarked to Mike Allison that it was "almost undriveable – all that power and no roadholding worth the name." Respected tuner Robin Jackson (no relation to his namesake) improved

The P-type was the ultimate evolution of the overhead-cam Midget series. Ernest Appleby of The Autocar *in his guise as 'The Scribe' wrote in glowing terms of the P-type owned by 'Junior' – presumably his son Barry. 'What a pleasant little car it is; with it, it is so easy to maintain a high average without any suggestion of speeding or fancy work. It takes bends like a monoposto Alfa, and, in my hands, keeps up a steady fifty which feels like thirty in most other cars.' (LAT Images)*

Cecil Kimber participating in one of the mid-1930s 'old crock' stunts at Brooklands. The M-type Midget looks somewhat battle-worn.

matters by moving the engine and gearbox back in the chassis, and also devised a bronze-alloy head to cure problems with the cast-iron head cracking, but the 'Q' was not one of Abingdon's more glorious moments; just eight would be built.

The first major competition fixture of 1934 was April's Mille Miglia. After the previous year's success, Kimber had persuaded William Morris to support a second foray into Italy. Given Morris's ambivalence – at best – concerning the value of racing, this was quite an achievement. Perhaps this accounts for the way the venture was described in the press, the team being presented as financed by Morris and run by Earl Howe, with little or no mention of M.G. or of Kimber: a massaging of the Morris ego seemed more

Sir W. Morris To Run Racing Team

WOMAN DRIVER IN HARDEST EVENT

By THOMAS H. WISDOM

MOTOR-RACING is booming, and Britain's chance of success next year in the international speed arena is better than ever.

Many British motor-racing syndicates have been formed, for in 1934 victory on road and track promises to pay handsome dividends.

As a sporting gesture, and for the sake of this country's prestige abroad, Sir William Morris is financing a team which is to compete, under the leadership of Lord Howe, one of our best-known racing motorists, and president of the British Racing Drivers' Club, in the famous Mille Miglia, the Italian 1,000-mile race, which takes place in April.

This year Earl Howe's team scored a great success by winning its class in this most strenuous of all motor races. Next year the same cars will compete.

DANGEROUS ROUTE

The team is to consist of Mr. E R Hall, winner of the 500 miles race, and his wife, Earl Howe, Count Lurani, the Italian driver who was in this year's team, and Mr. C. Penn Hughes.

Mrs. Hall, who has always acted as her husband's team manager, will be the first woman to drive in the Mille Miglia, which is regarded as one of the most dangerous races.

Other important motor-racing news is that Mr. John Cobb, our foremost track driver and owner of the Napier-Railton, the 180 m.p.h. car that is too fast for Brooklands, is to return to road-racing next year.

He is to drive the Monza-type Alfa-Romeo driven by the Hon. Brian Lewis this year.

Mr. Lewis, most successful British driver in 1933, has obtained the 3-litre Maserati raced by the late Sir Henry Birkin at the beginning of the year. This was the car in which Sir Henry received the injury which resulted in his death.

HELP FOR MOTOR RACING.

SIR WILLIAM MORRIS TO FINANCE A TEAM.

Sir William Morris has decided to finance a team, under the leadership of Earl Howe, president of the British Racing Drivers' Club to compete in the Mille Miglia, the Italian 1,000 miles race which takes place in April.

The team is to consist of E. R. Hall, winner of the 500 miles race, and his wife, Earl Howe, Count Lurani, the Italian driver, and C. Penn Hughes.

Mrs. Hall, who has always acted as her husband's team manager in his races, will be the first woman to drive in the Mille Miglia, which is regarded as one of the most dangerous races since it takes place over open roads not closed to ordinary traffic.

OPPOSITE TOP LEFT: *The Airline was styled by independent designer Henry Allingham. In P-type guise, as here, it cost £290 when a two-seater cost £222 and the four-seater £240. The body had a surprisingly complex wooden structure with square-tube steel windscreen pillars. (RM Sotheby's)*

OPPOSITE RIGHT: *Two stories from the press about Abingdon's return to the Mille Miglia for 1934 both manage to avoid any mention of M.G. or of Cecil Kimber. The PR spin centred on generating publicity around the participation of Joan Hall as co-driver to husband Eddie Hall. 'Woman Driver Faces Mountain Thrills' ran the suitably catchy headline in the* Sunday Express. *(National Motor Museum)*

OPPOSITE BOTTOM LEFT: *The Q-type used a Zoller supercharger, as opposed to the Roots type on the K3; this was developed by Laurence Pomeroy and Michael McEvoy, two of Kimber's circle, in conjunction with Hubert Charles. The result was a 750cc power unit that developed 'about 111bhp' according to* The Autocar. *The body was a simple lightweight aluminium affair. (Magna Press Library)*

TOP: *The rule established by Kimber was that all M.G. racing cars had to be to customer order. If a car was loaned, it was usually a development vehicle. An exception was the batch of six unsupercharged NEs fielded in the 1934 TT: three were financed by George Eyston and three by Kaye Don. (Magna Press Library)*

MIDDLE: *Cecil Kimber and George Eyston inspect Eyston's K3-based offset-driveline EX135 single-seater. It was given two interchangeable bodies, one for racing and one for record-breaking. The chassis was later used for Goldie Gardner's streamliner. (Magna Press Library)*

RIGHT: *The car with its body for track racing and record-breaking. The nickname 'Flying Humbug' came naturally to the wags at the factory. (Magna Press Library)*

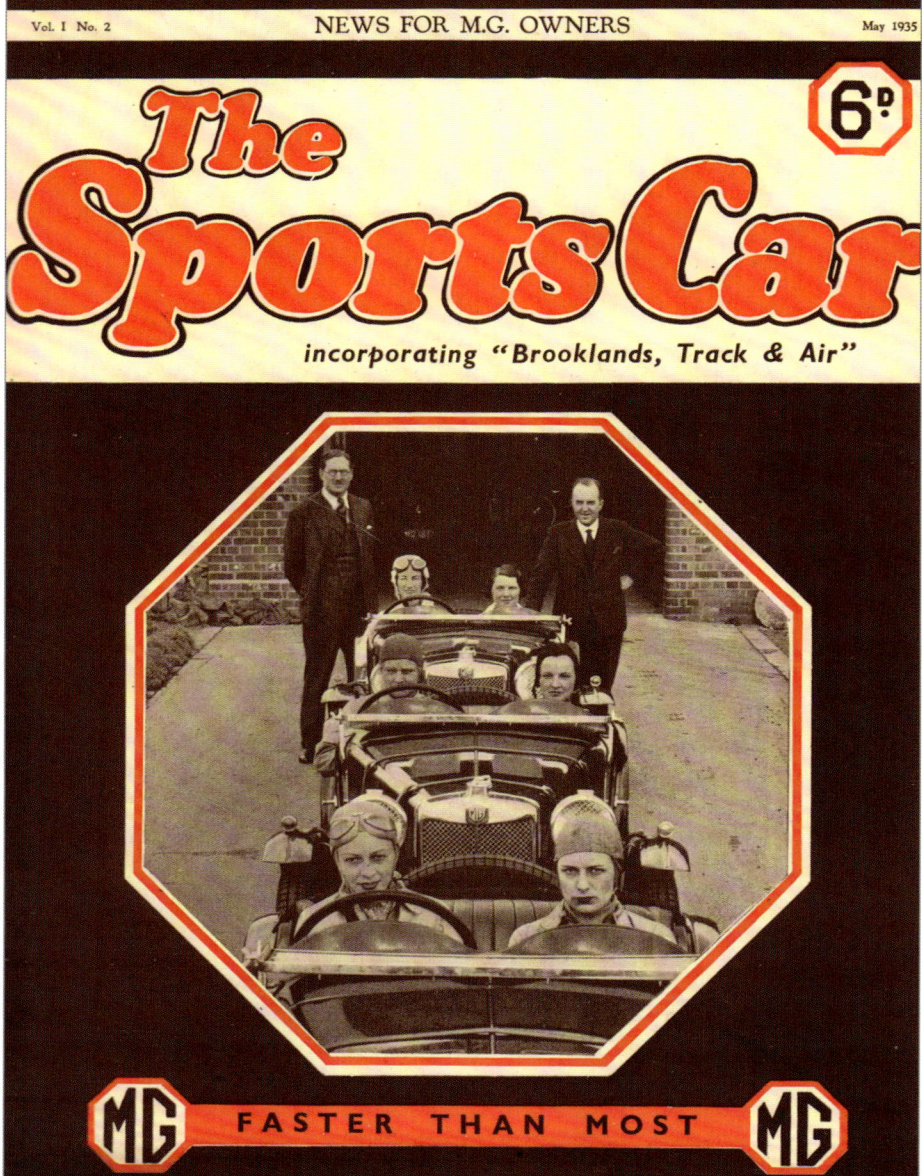

For 1935's Le Mans George Eyston sponsored an all-ladies team of P-types – jokingly referred to as 'Eyston's Dancing Daughters'. In the front car are Doreen Evans (at the wheel) and Barbara Skinner (of the Skinner family behind the SU carburettor business). All three cars finished, but the best M.G. result was a class win for ninth-placed Frenchmen Philippe Maillard-Brune and Charles Druck in their K3.

Amongst his business interests George Eyston was a director of Morris and M.G. agents Jarvis of Wimbledon. This was the result of his friendship with fellow director Jimmy Palmes, with whom he had rowed in the Trinity College first 'eight' while at Cambridge studying engineering. The financial support Eyston brought to M.G. racing and record-breaking was considerable. He was also behind the creation of the Powerplus supercharger.

On a visit to Boundary House, Goldie Gardner and lady friend pose with Jean, Betty and Rene Kimber, in front of Gardner's Mercedes – which he was later to wreck when he turned it over in an unfortunate accident.

important, and was doubtless a price worth paying. The result was a second place in class (and 11th overall) for the K3 of Johnny Lurani and Clifton Penn-Hughes.

The Mannin Beg race on the Isle of Man saw M.G. filling the top five places, George Eyston took his offset-drivetrain K3 special to victory in the British Empire Trophy, with K3s in five of the first ten places, and Charlie Dodson won the Tourist Trophy in a non-supercharged NE-type Magnette[2]. Throw in a 1-2-3 in the Coppa Acerbo, a win in the French GP, a fourth place at Le Mans and a batch of international Class G one-hour records in a Magnette, and one can say that in the course of the 1934 racing season M.G. had acquitted itself more than honourably.

---

[2] The regulations for the TT had changed, and supercharging was now banned. Kimber, as a champion of small-capacity cars that were reliant on superchargers to boost their power, had opposed the new rules, but ended up building a small batch of unblown N-type racers.

LEFT: *Forward-hinged doors with plated hinges identify this N-type as an NB – along with the slatted grille and a slightly lower scuttle.*

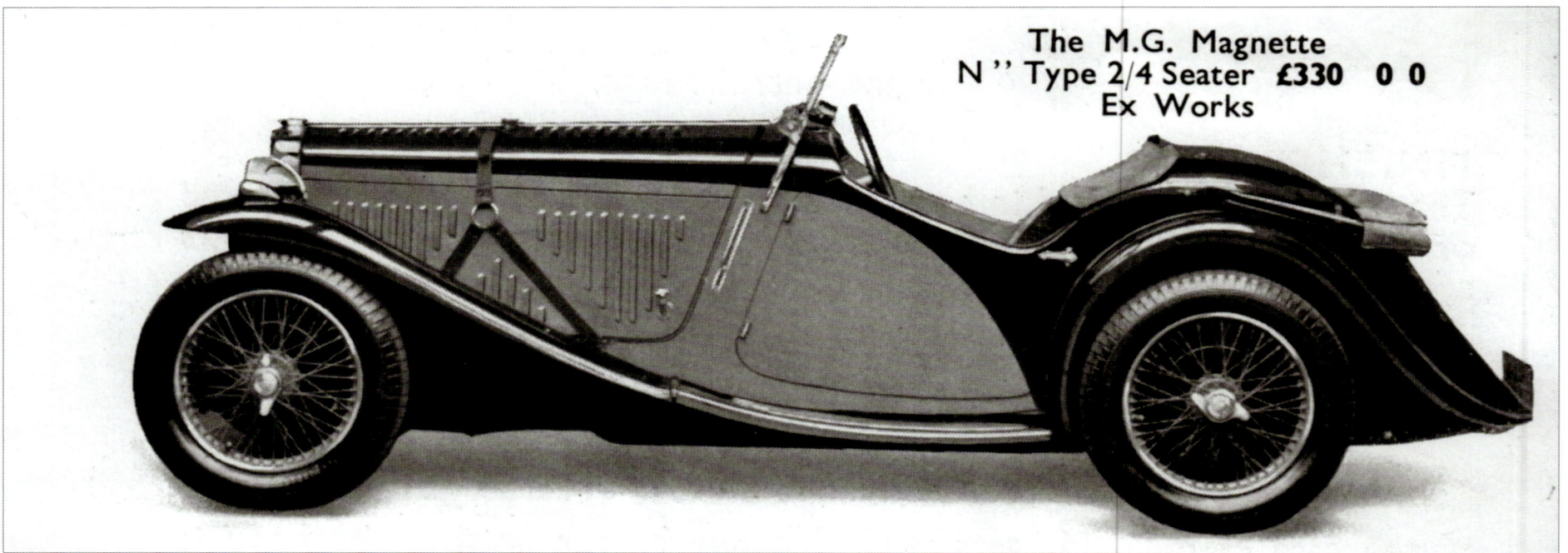

ABOVE & OPPOSITE BOTTOM: *Designed by Henry Allingham, the N-type 2/4-seater was built by London-based Whittingham & Mitchel, who also bodied Hornet Specials for Wolseley dealer Eustace Watkins. (Author's collection and RM Sotheby's)*

THE N-TYPE MAGNETTE

Announced in March 1934 as a replacement for both the K-type Magnette and L-type Magna, the N-type represented a welcome rationalisation of the M.G. range. The cars featured an improved and lighter chassis, Bishop cam-and-peg steering in place of the Marles-Weller type, and a 56.6bhp version of the 1271cc KD engine with a revised block, more efficient cylinder head and better cooling; the gearbox was a conventional unsynchronised four-speed type. The NA gave way to the NB in August 1935, front-hinged doors, a lower scuttle and a slatted grille being the principal innovations.

The two mainstream N-type bodies were made by Morris Bodies Branch, and the two-seater now featured a concealed fuel tank. A clever detail was the mounting of the bodies using Silentbloc rubber bushing, to help insulate the body from direct road shocks. Two further catalogued models had bodies designed by Henry Allingham: a version of the Airline coupé built by Carbodies and announced at the 1934 Motor Show, and an open 2/4-seater, with a folding rear seat, built by Whittingham & Mitchel. Finally, another stock-clearing exercise saw the last 21 slab-tank K2 two-seater bodies being mounted on N-type chassis and sold as the ND – sometimes referred to at the factory as the NK.

Over and above these regular N-type models there were the NEs, specialist racers built for the non-supercharged formula adopted for the 1934 Tourist Trophy. The high-compression engine had a sharper camshaft and triple valve springs, amongst other modifications, and delivered a healthy 74bhp running on petrol. Just seven NEs were built.

The final N-type was delivered in February 1937, bringing to an end the line of 'cammy' MGs. Total production had been 745 cars, with the open four-seater being the more popular of the two principal styles: 232 NAs and 135 NBs were open tourers, against 174 NAs and 98 NBs with two-seater coachwork. This very much suggests that M.G. enthusiasts wanting a two-seat sports car were tending to go for a Midget, whereas those looking for more of a family touring car were more inclined to opt for a six-cylinder model. Of the more specialist bodies, seven in all were Airline coupés and 11 were Allingham 2/4-seaters (NA and NB combined, in both instances); further to this, 48 chassis went to outside coachbuilders.

The N-type was also available as a four-seat tourer. Heavier than the earlier ohc six-cylinder cars, the NA and NB were nevertheless well-regarded, and considered by many as the best of the breed.

LOOKING TO THE FUTURE

Abingdon's model range was the most coherent it had ever been, and the cars technically at their peak; for 1934 the company would even post a respectable net profit, despite a further fall in sales. Cecil Kimber was pushing forward with an advanced new racing single-seater designed by Hubert Charles – a car whose engineering was every bit as up-to-date as anything being conceived in Germany, France or Italy. The design was intended to be adopted for a new series of M.G. models, starting with a big saloon known by the EX150 internal code. There was every prospect that M.G. would join the technological avant-garde, whether on the road or on the track. Such, at any rate, is how an optimistic evaluation of the company's future direction would have looked by mid 1935.

Given the backdrop of conservatism permeating the British motor industry, it is worth pointing out that Kimber, although no engineer himself, was very much aware of the direction in which car design was moving. In a 1932 article in *The Autocar* he was already envisaging that in a not-too-distant future cars would have all-enveloping streamlined bodies, engines (possibly V8 or V12) mounted at the rear, perhaps transversely, and a hydraulic automatic transmission. German and Czechoslovakian designs of the later 1930s proved he had his finger on the pulse, although the rear-engined configuration would prove a technical dead-end. In fairness, Kimber was aware of the dangers of concentrating too much weight at the rear, and seems to have been thinking of something closer to a mid-engined layout.

Interestingly, a few years later, in the course of discussing an Institution of Automobile Engineers paper, Kimber would reject the front-wheel-drive approach exemplified by the Traction Avant Citroën. He was not alone: in 1933 Sir William Morris spent £10,000 of his own money to buy the British patent rights to the German-made front-wheel-drive Adler, only to do precisely nothing with a concept that – as with the Citroën – genuinely did represent the future of automotive design. By the end of the 1930s the British motor industry would be turning out the most technically backward vehicles of any major European car-producing nation. The evidence suggests that Kimber would have wished things otherwise.

Whilst his new projects were bubbling away at Abingdon, Cecil Kimber took a break at the end of May for what was evidently a slightly harum-scarum boys holiday on the water, crewing on a friend's converted Falmouth quay punt with the cheery Bill Gibbs as third member of the team. Based at Bradwell-on-Sea in Essex, the trio spent Whitsun cruising around the East Coast, punctuated by running aground, wrapping the painter of the auxiliary dinghy around the boat's propeller shaft, nearly colliding with a large yacht, and – much to Kimber's pleasure – enjoying hearty fry-up breakfasts.

EARTHQUAKE: THE 1935 RESTRUCTURING

Kimber wasn't long home from his holiday when his professional life came tumbling down. On 1 July 1935 M.G. and Wolseley ceased to be the personal property of William Morris, their ownership being transferred to Morris Motors Ltd. Naturally enough, this also meant that direct control passed to Cowley, ending the way the two businesses acted as quasi-independent fiefdoms within the group. 'The activities of the Wolseley and M.G. concerns will remain unchanged, but in future will be carried on under the direct control of Morris Motors, although all will derive the advantage of centralized research and development facilities,' reported *The Motor* in its 25 June 1935 issue.

As a consequence Cecil Kimber was no longer Managing Director of M.G. but returned to his previous title of General Manager. Leonard Lord, Managing Director of Morris Motors at Cowley, added to his responsibilities that of Managing Director of the Abingdon factory. Lest this be thought a slap in the face for Kimber, it should be pointed out that at the same time he was elevated to the board of Morris Motors, along with former Morris Sales Director Miles Thomas, who in 1934 had been promoted to General Manager of Morris Commercial Cars.

There was no pretending, all the same, that this was just a largely meaningless game of musical chairs: the changes fundamentally altered how M.G. was run, and downgraded Kimber's role in steering the business. Henceforth he would have to play the game by a different set of rules, a less than congenial prospect for such an individualistic manager. 'Kimber's personality flourished only when he had freedom of action, when he was in a position to make quick decisions,' writes Wilson McComb. 'He was anything but a committee man; still less a company man. M.G. owed their success to his personal control and direction, under which the Abingdon factory had become a close-knit unit owing loyalty to him, the personification of M.G.'

The reorganisation was more than a piece of financial and administrative realignment, as it brought with it the transfer to Cowley of the design of future Wolseley and M.G. models. Hubert Charles, Jack Daniels and George Cooper in the Abingdon drawing office were accordingly moved straightaway to Morris Motors. "We had absolutely no notice of this, no warning. It all happened over a weekend," Daniels told author Graham Robson. For M.G. the upheaval additionally signalled an end to Abingdon's racing programme, which it was felt had contributed to the uneven state of the company's finances; this will be discussed further in the next chapter.

The process would be completed in October 1936 by Morris Commercial Cars, the SU Carburettor Company and Morris Industries Exports all being transferred from Morris's personal proprietorship to ownership by Morris Motors. This meant that only The Morris Garages and Wolseley Aero Engines Ltd were left as private businesses within the Morris empire[3].

---

[3] Regarding the garage business, it was apparently felt that it was undesirable for Morris Motors to own a distribution company in competition with private distributors – although such an arrangement was hardly unusual. Sentiment may also have played a part, as The Morris Garages was Lord Nuffield's original business. As for Wolseley Aero Engines, this was a new concern, only established in 1935, and was yet to find its feet. In common with other such investments, Morris seemed to be following a policy of supporting the enterprise personally until it had been built up into a viable entity.

IT'S ALL IN THE FIGURES...

Were the changes to the status of M.G. some form of punishment for profit-denting profligacy on the part of an irresponsible Kimber who was spending too much of William Morris's money on over-specialised M.G. models and expensive racing cars? This is often said, but if such accusations have a grain of truth, they are in no way anything like the whole story. Former M.G. boss John Thornley – an accountant by training – confirmed to the author that accusations of poor profitability were broadly fair. "Every other year Kim went cap in hand to Morris for a bag of gold to bail him out, but the intermediate years showed a profit," Thornley said in a 1989 interview. "Even so, the Old Man got tired of this, and so that's why he sold us to Morris Motors in 1935."

This touches on one inescapable truth: M.G. had survived essentially as a result of William Morris's personal largesse. His account books show regular loans to the M.G. Car Company, including two loans totalling £40,000 in 1933. The company's annual accounts, meanwhile, bear out Thornley's analysis. The net profit figures – in other words the profit (or loss) after all expenses have been deducted but before tax – show a clear pattern of profits every other year, culminating in a loss of £28,156 (first eight months only) for 1935, against a profit of £14,122 for the previous year.

A key element in these statistics is what is termed 'Satisfaction of Customers' – in other words warranty and out-of-warranty 'goodwill' costs. They make sobering reading. These figures represent more than six times the cost of record-breaking and competition activity in 1930, dip a little in 1931, and then start to run away, only being brought under control in 1935. The more than doubling of 'Satisfaction of Customers' costs for 1933 comfortably exceeds the net losses posted that year. The truth is that 1932 and 1933 were sticky years for M.G., when it came to keeping customers happy.

The new six-cylinder overhead-cam cars were bound to have added substantially to warranty costs in their first full year, as there were plenty of teething difficulties. Not least, the pre-selector gearbox in the K-type gave trouble, while the pillarless Magnette saloon was less than rigid and was prey to dreadful body problems as well as many quality niggles – a great many having to have major body repairs or rectifications early in their life. Then there were all those disgruntled J2 owners who had to be placated after their car couldn't achieve the 80mph managed by the souped-up press car lent to *The Autocar* magazine, or who had contrived to break the two-bearing crankshaft that was the Achilles heel of the engine. Even without this, setting up an overhead-cam M.G. so that it gave of its best was not a job for the amateur, and there were many owners who were disappointed by the performance of their car.

Given the high labour costs of some of the rectification work[4], and that in some instances complete replacement engines and gearboxes were fitted to K-type Magnettes, the sums involved were not insubstantial. In retrospect the K-type was an exercise of dubious commercial value, and a costly one in financial terms. That 'Satisfaction of Customers' costs nearly halved in 1934 reflects that the N-type Magnette and the P-type Midget were manifestly better cars than the models they replaced; having a simplified range after the complications of earlier years can only

---
[4] Sam Bennett recalled having to re-shim the bevel gears for the drive to the engine's overhead camshaft, which was quite a job, and similarly re-shimming rear axles. He also had to rectify noisy oil pumps by relieving the backplate with a file.

With its 'clap-hand' doors open, the pillarless construction of the Magnette saloon allowed easy access; the penalty was poor rigidity, exacerbated by the firm suspension and flexible chassis. Warranty claims were a continuing headache.

ABOVE: *As this 1935 advertisement demonstrates, an important leg of M.G. marketing was the marque's success in competition. With racing activities axed, the new challenge was to keep alive the connection between M.G. and motor sport.*

FAR LEFT: *Jean at Eastleach, where Kimber used to go fly-fishing; the photo dates from the 1933-35 period.*

LEFT: *Betty and the family spaniel, Nipper, at Keble Bridge, Eastleach, at the same time.*

BELOW: *Rene and Jean at Bridge Farm Cottage, home of the Monk family with whom the Kimbers were friendly.*

have helped, too, when it came to the Abingdon factory producing trouble-free vehicles[5].

But it had been a roller-coaster ride to reach this point, something that would not have escaped the attention of the Morris accountants and senior management in Cowley. A look at trends in M.G. gross profit for 1935 – in other words profit by sales – would without doubt have further sharpened their perception that M.G. needed bringing under closer financial control: the figure was on course to fall from £452,448 in 1934 to £175,571 in the first eight months of 1935.

M.G. now had some serious rivals in the marketplace – which wasn't really the case beforehand. Triumph had its sassy-looking Gloria Southern Cross newly on sale – and it was good. Singer was riding a wave, with its Nine Le Mans nicely established after a

---

[5] At least M.G. was on the ball when it came to tackling customer problems. "I had a daily meeting with H. N. Charles, when I'd been through the incoming correspondence, and I took in the complaints which had come in – that was immediate instant feedback to design, something which was lost down the line so much in later years," John Thornley told the author.

German M.G. agent and racer Bobby Kohlrausch presented this photo album to Cecil Kimber after a successful season campaigning a J4 and a K3. Kohlrausch went on to purchase Eyston's Magic Midget, had it rebuilt with a new aluminium body with full undertray, and broke several speed records in the car. "The preparations were made much easier by the kindness of Mr Cecil Kimber," he said.

In the Gabelbach hillclimb Kohlrausch took first place and set new class records in both the J4 (shown) and the K3.

strong performance at the 1934 Le Mans 24-hour race. In-house, Wolseley's Hornet Special had been available since April 1932 and had been significantly improved for the 1934 season. Finally, since 1934 there was the chirpy Austin Seven Nippy for those wanting a bargain-basement small sports car.

At a time when the British new-car market was performing more strongly each year – and would have its best year yet in 1935 – M.G. sales were in the process of dropping off a precipice, quite possibly in part as a result of this increased competition. After a fall of 8.1 per cent in 1933 and 6 per cent in 1934, sales dropped by a huge 40 per cent in 1935, to 1,231 units.

Kimber himself put the blame on the introduction of a 30mph speed limit in built-up areas in March 1935, and on increased insurance costs. At a Scottish Motor Show function, reported on in the 26 November 1935 issue of *The Motor*, he is quoted as saying that the introduction of the 30mph limit had caused the sales of

M.G. cars to drop by 50 per cent. Then there was the insurance question. 'Insurance premiums for sports cars have been increased to an alarming extent so that a sports car fitted with an ordinary saloon body is subject to ordinary rates, but if fitted with a sports tourer body there is a 50 per cent increase in the premium. The trouble is that insurance companies differentiate between cars instead of between drivers,' he told his audience.

Whatever the reasons for the fall in M.G. sales, the company's disappointing results were sufficient justification for Morris management to act tough with Abingdon. Dial in a substantial increase in expenditure on motor sport and a huge leap in new model development costs – seemingly linked in large part to the R-type, the new racing model which will be discussed in the next chapter – and one imagines you could almost have heard Leonard Lord sharpening his axe[6].

---

[6] As mentioned earlier, it seems that relations between Lord and Kimber were cordial, and family recollections corroborate this. 'I can remember the advent of Leonard Lord as the new overall boss. We had to go to tea with his children, and they came riding at our friendly local riding school in Marcham Road. Leonard Lord had a ride with us one day dressed in his business suit, perhaps out of bravado,' recounts Jean.

A QUESTION OF CORPORATE HOUSEWORK

Ultimately, however, the failings of M.G. – real or apparent – were incidental to the restructuring of 1935; after all, a loss of a little over £28,000 was a drop in the ocean for a Morris organisation that would record a pre-tax profit of £1.4m in 1935 and of almost £2.2m in 1936. The consequences for Cecil Kimber and the business he had created would not be anodyne, and would set the company on a very different path, one that would not be welcomed by many parties and least of all by Kimber himself[7]. But the reorganisation was at its base something that had to happen, for very straightforward administrative and financial reasons.

Now that William Morris was increasingly delegating day-to-day management, it was clearly desirable to unify control of all his businesses. But the changes were implemented for more than

---

[7] Wilson McComb, seemingly picking up on a remark made to him by Hubert Charles, writes that at this juncture Kimber had the opportunity to leave the Morris organisation and set up on his own. 'Shortly after the change in M.G. management he had been approached by a group of London financiers to form the C. K. Car Company, in which he would again enjoy control of design and marketing. He decided not to pursue the idea,' says McComb.

At the Kesselberg hillclimb Kohlrausch again won the first-place prize and set a class record with the J4 and in the K3 (shown) was the fastest up-to-1100cc car.

Chapter Eleven: Cowley takes Charge

mere reasons of administrative tidiness. During the 1920s Morris had triumphed in two legal cases where he had been pursued for payment of a so-called 'Super Tax', his successful defence being that extensive funds were needed for the survival and future development of the company. But he was worried that he might in the future be judged liable for this tax, thereby threatening the well-being of the firm. He therefore began to think of a flotation – which would also have the advantage of freeing money for personal benefactions. But the timing, after winning the second 'Super Tax' case in 1929, was not propitious, with the onset of the slump, so he had decided to delay action until the economy had demonstrably recovered.

So it was that the structural reforms to his business in 1935 and 1936 were accompanied by the issuing of Ordinary shares in the company. These were 'placed' – at a cost of some criticism in City quarters[8]. Only a quarter of the company's Ordinary stock was offered, Morris retaining the rest himself, whether personally or through charitable trusts. The shares all sold at a strong premium, reflecting Morris's wisdom in riding out the recession before offering the shares in a more buoyant Stock Market.

Miles Thomas provided Andrews and Brunner with another reason for the restructuring and its linked share issue. "What bothered the legal and financial pundits was that violent exception might be taken by shareholders to Sir William, as chairman of a public company, buying a considerable value of components from companies of which he was the private owner." Arguments such as this were kept from the public. "We saw they were not forcibly fed with facts," commented Thomas.

Equally, the public was not appraised in detail of another key explanation for the share issue: that it freed up large sums of money for Morris to spend on his multitudinous charitable activities, putting as much as perhaps £20m at his disposal. The

---
[8] 'Placing' is the practice of selling shares to a particular institution (in this case a 'jobber' rather than, for example, a merchant bank), for selling to the public.

Kohlrausch used an Opel Blitz lorry to transport his two cars, which were painted in white, the official German racing colour.

part-flotation represented, said Thomas, a 'nodal date' in Morris's personal fortune. Doubtless aware of the potential for adverse publicity relating to his multi-millionaire status, Morris would redirect some of his gains back to his personnel: in early 1937 he set up a special trust with one million Ordinary shares, dividends from these going to his hourly-paid employees as a bonus on top of their wages.

Riding on the back of all this would come a new range of Cowley-originated M.G. models and a new approach to participation in motor sport. If Kimber had lost in freedom of action, he would prove that he was by no means down and out. Indeed, he displayed a canny mix of imagination and pragmatism that – even through gritted teeth – would take Abingdon to new heights.

12

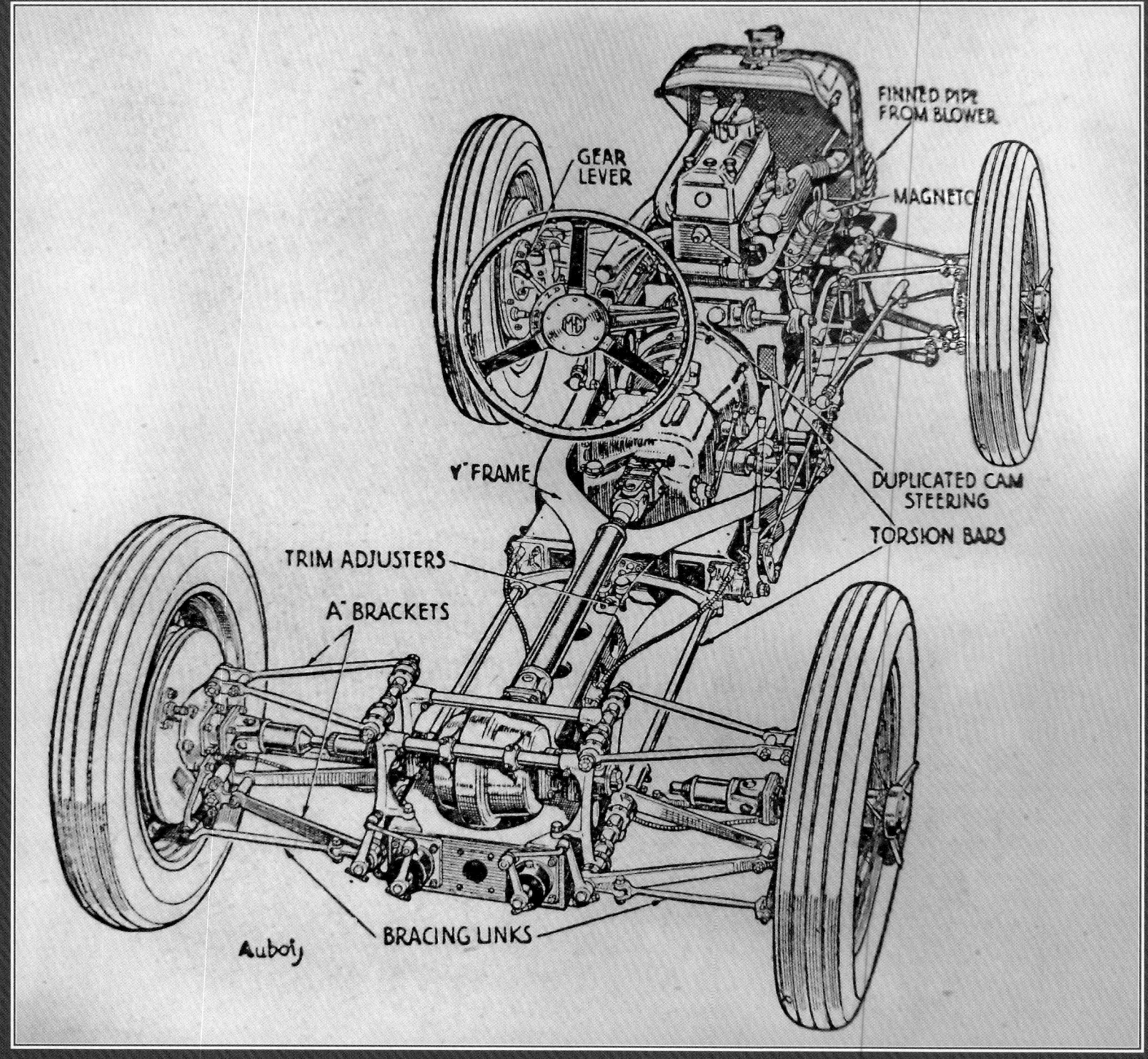

GOODBYE TO MOTOR RACING

Motor sport was an important part of the M.G. identity by 1935, and had done much to give Cecil Kimber an elevated status in the closed little world of the British motoring. 'In 1933 when I first came to *The Autocar*, Kimber was already a very big presence in the industry,' writes John Dugdale. 'By 1934 he had put Britain completely back into the forefront of international motor racing, winning the team prize in the Mille Miglia beating Italy's own Maseratis; winning Britain's premier race the Tourist Trophy; also the Isle of Man races; the 500 Miles Race at Brooklands at 105mph, faster than that year's Indianapolis.' Despite this, and with the benefit of only a very limited measure of hindsight, it is possible to see that the end of manufacture of racing cars by M.G. was inevitable.

At the end of 1934 Abingdon's approach to racing was outlined in the 25 December 'On Road and Track' column of *The Motor* in the course of a review of the season[1]. 'The whole point about M.G. racing cars is that they are built and sold in the same way that Ettore Bugatti made his racing cars for years. That is to say, you pay your money and take delivery of a complete racing car.

'Cecil Kimber is proud of the fact that he does not run works teams. All his successes are won by outside drivers. His job is to build and prepare the car, and he leaves the driving to those with no factory connection. With the exception of the ERA, the M.G. is the only racing car you can buy in this country straight out of the catalogue, either the 750cc Q-type Midget, which produces as many bhp per litre per thousand as is reckoned possible, or the 1100cc Magnette.'

---

[1] The author 'Grande Vitesse' was Rodney Walkerley, the Sports Editor, who was one of Kimber's longstanding press friends.

OPPOSITE: *The R-type with its 'tuning-fork' chassis was conceptually brilliant. The frame was electrically welded, internally braced, and liberally sprinkled with lightening holes. Control arms helped locate the twin-wishbone rear and the steering used twin drop arms and long drag links, thereby eliminating the track rod.*

RIGHT: *The 1934 M.G. pamphlet* Supremacy *obligingly featured Lord Nuffield – and misspellings of Donington and Montlhéry; a few months later it was all over for Abingdon's competition programme.*

Chapter Twelve: Goodbye to Motor Racing

THE DANGERS OF THINKING ALOUD

Kimber's policy[2] was followed against a background of a constantly evolving technology – in other words, M.G. was involved in a continuing race for better performance. 'The speeds of which these cars are capable would have been considered impossible even a couple of years ago, and yet they go up and up almost monthly,' concluded the magazine.

Where this might lead Abingdon was hinted at when in the 12 February 1935 edition of the same column there was a story headlined 'Mr Kimber pleads for 1½-litre GP Formula' in which Kimber gave his views on the then-current discussions on a new formula for Grand Prix racing for the three years commencing 1937.

---

[2] See Appendix 4 for Kimber's exposition on this subject in his 1934 IAE paper *Making Modest Production Pay in Motor-Car Manufacture*.

'The present regulations have produced a car which is too fast for reasonable safety in road races, and few drivers are capable of piloting them,' he said, going on to propose a 1500cc maximum engine capacity and a minimum weight of 600kg without fuel. This would result in easier verification and fewer disputes and in safer cars, capable of being handled by a greater number of drivers. It would also make racing more affordable, so more firms across Continent would end up participating, and would thus lead to the end of racing's domination by five firms, most of which, he pointed out, were heavily government-subsidised.

Personalities as prominent as Nuvolari supported similar ideas, but nothing came of them. Was Kimber saying that if a 1½-litre formula were accepted, Abingdon would seek to enter the Grand Prix arena? 'He was speaking publicly about the Grand Prix and one could anticipate his ambitions,' John Dugdale would later write. Such a venture would put M.G. up against the expense-no-object Nazi-sponsored Mercedes and Auto Union teams and would be hugely costly in terms of technical development. It is hard to believe that Kimber's proposals did not ring alarm bells in Cowley.

REVOLUTION – THE R-TYPE SINGLE-SEATER

Whatever was or was not coursing through the consciousness of Lord Nuffield and Cowley's senior management, April 1935 saw Kimber seriously ratchet up M.G.'s game, with the announcement of his advanced new racing model. Priced at £750, the R-type was a radical response to the shortcomings of the Q-type, which above all suffered from having unyielding suspension in a rudimentary and flexible traditional chassis. Independent front suspension was becoming commonplace on the Continent, and some manufacturers were even essaying independent rear suspension. But in order for these installations to give of their best they needed to be mounted in a rigid structure; for a racing car, such a structure also needed to be light.

OPPOSITE: *Kimber was a keen observer of the German scene, and had a particular interest in the Auto Union racers designed by Ferdinand Porsche. (Goldie Gardner courtesy Mike Jones)*

RIGHT: *The bare bones of the R-type: with its body it had a dry weight of just 11cwt, or 13cwt in long-distance form. Output of the Zoller-supercharged engine was given as 108bhp at launch, a figure later to rise to 113bhp; the twin-cam adaptation was good for 160bhp.*

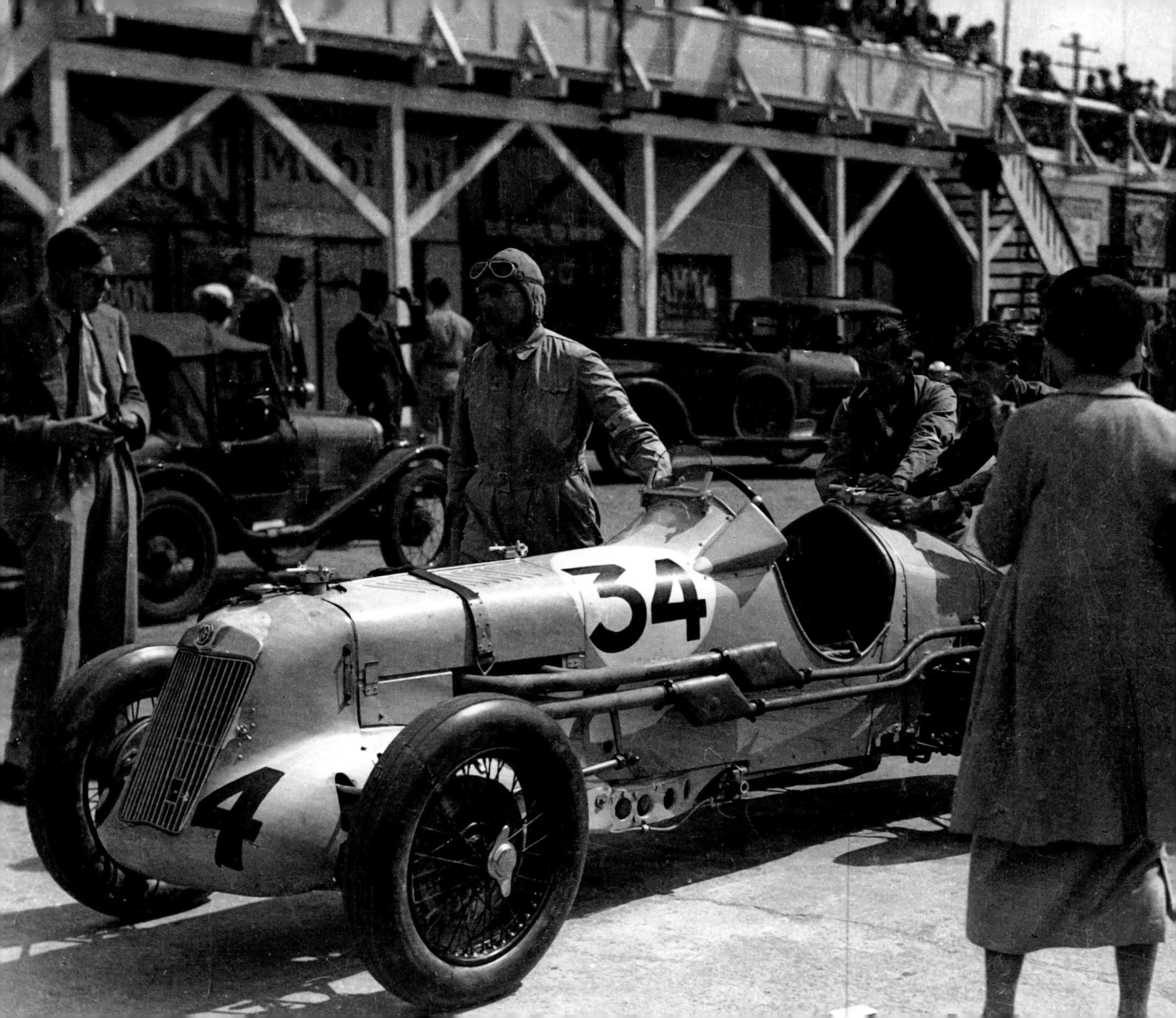

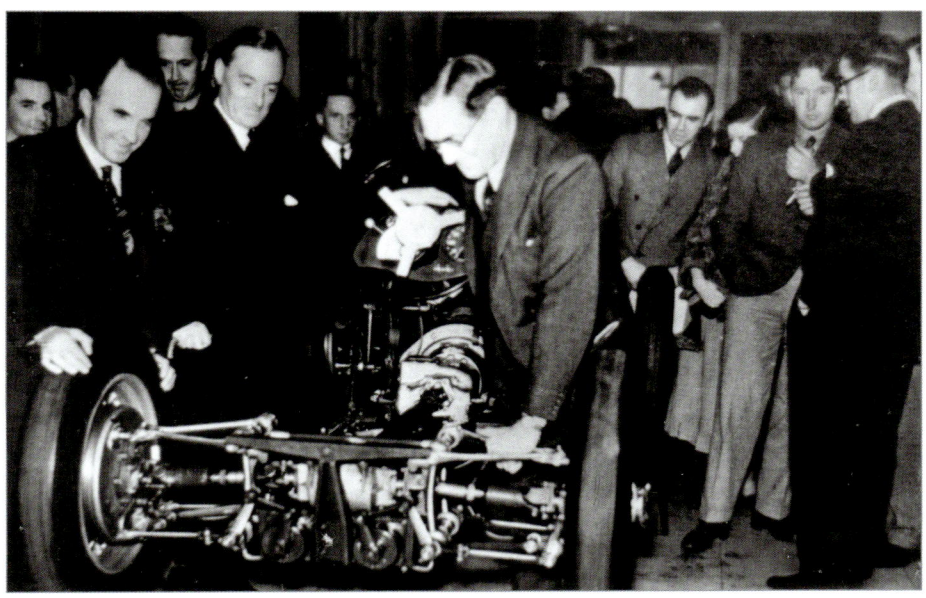

ABOVE: *Kimber and George Eyston studying an R-type chassis. All but one of the ten R-types made were sold to privateers, with Eyston – a long-time backer of the racing department – buying three cars. (Abingdon County Hall Museum)*

OPPOSITE: *Eyston and one of his R-types at the start of the British Empire Trophy race at Brooklands, on 6 July 1935 – the last occasion in which the cars were entered under his name. (National Motor Museum)*

Hubert Charles had devised four-wheel independent suspension using equal-length wishbones and longitudinal torsion bars, and for this to work effectively he came up with a welded-steel backbone chassis that drew in particular on German and Czechoslovakian practice. Stiff in torsion, it was said to be more than 50lb lighter than the Q-type's frame. Into this state-of-the-art chassis was slotted the Q-type's supercharged 746cc engine and pre-selector gearbox. It was, in the view of John Dugdale, 'the sort of specification which we journalists were pressing the conservative British makers to adopt'.

The press was indeed breathlessly excited. 'April 25th, 1935, may well rank as a milestone in British automobile history. On that day a little gathering of racing personalities assembled at a Piccadilly showroom, where Mr Cecil Kimber had invited them to inspect the latest product of the M.G. Car Company,' wrote *Motor Sport* in its May 1935 issue. 'And what a magnificent engineering achievement this new car is! The Monoposto M.G. Midget Racing Model (Type R) stood in the centre of the large room, almost submerged by the peering heads of the guests, while those who had already examined the remarkable features stood around and unburdened their enthusiasm on their equally enthusiastic listeners.'

In its conclusion the magazine also put its finger on the R-type's significance to the future evolution of M.G. road cars. 'No description of this outstanding racing car would be complete without a tribute to Mr Cecil Kimber for his courage in breaking away from orthodox design. The result is a car which will be the admiration of the rest of the world,' it wrote. 'Is it too much to hope that, following the tradition of the M.G. Company of incorporating in their production cars features tested in racing, that we shall see independent springing on M.G. sports cars?'

That this was not a wild thought was confirmed by Abingdon's house magazine, who discreetly trailed the company's coat. 'As the last word in small racing cars from Britain's most eminent sports car factory, it has quite rightly startled the motoring world,' commented the editorial in the June 1935 issue of *The Sports Car*. 'Does its design foreshadow the sports car of the future?'

A QUESTION OF MONEY

Unsurprisingly, the R-type wasn't successful 'straight out of the box'. In particular the suspension needed further development time – and thus money – as the equal-length wishbones had been found to promote excessive roll. Equally, the bold single-seater was another salvo in the Austin-versus-M.G. battle, and this inevitably costly duel showed no sign of abating. It was a friendly rivalry, but one in which M.G. was not above goading its Longbridge opposition to match Abingdon's technology, something likely to

lead to an equally inevitable upward spiral of spending, as each party sought to best the other.

Illustrating this is a comment in the July 1935 issue of the M.G. in-house magazine. The performance of L. P. Driscoll in beating the two quickest Abingdon cars up Shelsley Walsh in his blown Austin Seven was duly hailed. 'Every M.G. and Austin enthusiast has rejoiced for years in the keen competition between the two marques. This brilliant show of Driscoll's has put us all on our toes,' commented *The Sports Car* – and then went on to take a dig at the Austin's old-fashioned engine: 'Maybe he was fired with some of the enthusiasm which accounts for Bobby Kohlrausch's amazing Midget records. A bit over 130mph with 750cc will take some beating with a side-valve engine.'

The following year Austin would abandon its side-valve power unit in favour of an advanced twin-cam engine in a brand-new racer designed by the talented Murray Jamieson. With this in prospect, all the indications were that competition on the track between Longbridge and Abingdon would soon move up a gear, with the racing budgets for both companies rising to match. That three of the R-types were later given a twin-cam head designed by Laurence Pomeroy and Michael McEvoy indicates how these friendly hostilities might have evolved.

An examination of the M.G. accounts suggests that Morris management was right to be concerned about the cost of M.G. involvement in racing, as a proportion of its overall turnover. From the figures that can be found in Appendix 1, immediately apparent is a nearly five-fold rise in 1931, the £3,891 jump accounting for nearly 30 per cent of that year's losses. An informed

The R-type of D.L. Briault holding off Eddie Hall's K3 in the 1935 British Empire Trophy race at Brooklands. The angle of lean of the R-type's wheels is very noticeable: the envisaged remedies were dampers better able to cope with the suspension travel, uprated torsion bars, and an adjustment of front-to-rear spring rates. (National Motor Museum)

Hubert Charles (left, nearest camera) and team running an R-type up on the rolling road – a noisy process. A six-cylinder derivative was planned but the closure of the racing shop put paid to the idea. (M.G. Car Club)

Chapter Twelve: Goodbye to Motor Racing

ABOVE: *Murray Jamieson's twin-cam Austin Seven racer was Longbridge's intended rival to the R-type: it was a little lighter, marginally more powerful...and had works support. (BMIHT)*

OPPOSITE: *A portrait of Sir Malcolm Campbell in the works development R-type in which he finished sixth in the 1935 International Trophy race. The car is in Campbell's habitual pale blue, but this may be artistic licence, as there are stories that the car was in fact painted cream. Back at the end of the 1920s Campbell had run a 14/40 M.G. – a fact the company proudly advertised at the time.*

guess is that the introduction and successful campaigning of the C-type had something to do with this. After slipping back in 1932, competition spending then rose to £5,863 in 1933. As this was the year of the K3's introduction, and was a notably active and successful year for M.G. in motor sport, maybe again this is no great surprise. It should also be pointed out that when Wolseley – an admittedly shoddily-run company – indulged in a short-lived racing programme in the 1921-23 period the total bill was in the region of £13,000.

All the same, the fact that after this the M.G. spend on competitions and record-breaking didn't fall back to anything like the 1932 level, and then rose sharply in 1935, suggests that things were indeed getting a little out of hand. Corroborating this is the massive leap in expenditure on 'Development of Models'. It is reasonable to assume that the lion's share of this sum was accounted for by

Miles Thomas was, it seems, instrumental in closing down the racing operation. That said, attempts to portray him as a pantomime villain, engaged on a long campaign to destroy Cecil Kimber and all his works, are frankly nonsensical.

the R-type, given the somewhat embryonic state of the EX150 saloon – which all the same must have contributed something to the red ink. Whatever the potential long-term benefits of this investment, both for M.G. racing and road cars, it can only have occasioned an intake of breath at Cowley, especially as both Leonard Lord and Miles Thomas[3] were known to be sceptical about the benefits of racing.

THE KAYE DON AFFAIR: A NASTY TASTE IN THE MOUTH

The abandonment of overt factory support for racing and the closure of the racing shop may well have been in part a question of saving money and of avoiding an escalating and costly technological joust with Austin. The reasoning advanced by Kimber in his announcement of the cessation of racing (pages 269-270) may equally have been factors, despite their air of reluctant special pleading. But there is also one further motivation for the decision, one that has generally been accepted over the years. This is Kaye Don's accident on the Isle of Man in May 1934, one that cost the life of long-serving M.G. mechanic Frankie Tayler and saw Don convicted of manslaughter due to 'culpably negligent driving'.

Dublin-born Don, a well-known racer with many Brooklands records to his credit, was to drive a K3 in the Mannin Beg race on the Isle of Man. He was relatively new to M.G. cars and according to Reg Jackson kept complaining about the car's behaviour. "Frankie had a really good look at Don's car, and even got me to test it with him, and we agreed it was fine," Jackson told Mike Allison many years later. Tayler reported back to Kaye Don late in the evening before the race, when Don had just finished dinner and was about to start a game of bridge.

At 10 o'clock at night, in failing light, Don took the

Dublin-born Kaye Don – real name Kaye Ernest Donsky – was famed for his exploits at Brooklands. He also held the World Speed Record on water and attempted the Land Speed Record in the Sunbeam 'Silver Bullet'. (Wikipedia)

---

[3] Thomas certainly had form. When he was editing *The Morris Owner* he wrote several pieces hammering the notion of motor sport as having any value. Examples are 'That Demon Speed – Its Fascination and Futility' (December 1925), 'The Lure of that place called Brooklands' subtitled 'A Vivid Pen Picture of Track Racing – Its Futilities and Absurdities' (May 1926), and an editorial headed 'The Madness of Motor Racing' and subtitled 'Too Many Deaths – No Useful Results' (November 1926). Such polemics made sense, admittedly, when Morris was offering no products that had competition potential.

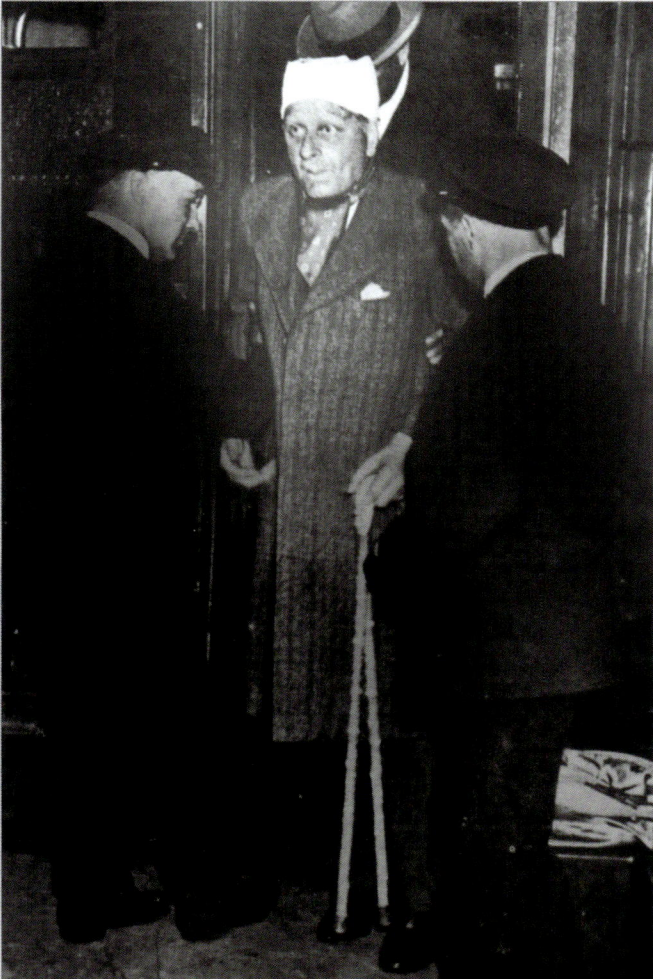

ABOVE: *Kaye Don theatrically wrapped in bandages during his trial for manslaughter. (Author's collection)*

RIGHT: *The obituary in* The M.G. Magazine *for Frankie Tayler. The death of the M.G. mechanic was one of the factors behind the further cooling of Sir William Morris's generally lukewarm enthusiasm for motor racing.*

JULY 1934

FRANK TAYLER—

An appreciation of the late Frank Tayler, the best of friends and the finest of sportsmen.

WHEN you lose the companionship of one with whom you have worked side by side for a number of years, it is very difficult indeed to become reconciled to the gap so created; the more so after a little while, when the first shock of the loss has passed and the actual manner of its happening is put into the background to some degree, and the absence of a departed friend who can never be replaced becomes really felt to the fullest extent.

Those of us whose good fortune it was to associate with Frank know that he prepared the racing cars under his care with no thought other than that they should go out to win, completely ignoring time and forgoing all pleasures in the enthusiasm of motor racing, and who stepped into the background at the moment of victory, proud, above all, that the car had responded to his labours. We were apt, perhaps, to treat his work too much as a matter of course, overlooking the dangers he gladly faced, and the great share of victory, if victory it was, which really was his to claim.

Frank was one of the six mechanics with the M.G. concern right from the very start in 1923, he was also with the *équippé* when the Midget won the Junior Car Club's Double Twelve Hours' Race; again at the Phœnix Park Race the same year, and in many events too numerous to deal with here. Probably his greatest race was at Ulster in 1931, when he rode to victory in the Tourist Trophy Race, with Norman Black, in the Midget he had fostered. We know too, above all, how dearly he loved to handle a really fast racing car, and this makes the manner of his departing still the more poignant.

Life to Frank had been good of late, and solace must seem remote to the one who made it so, but if there be any small measure of consolation in these few words, penned in the fullness of sincerity with the heartfelt sympathy of a friend, then they are not in vain.

426

M.G. out with Tayler for a test run, with the apparent intention of testing the steering under braking, an aspect of the car about which he had been concerned. The car was without any lights, and was on roads that were open to the public – unlike during official practice during the day, when they had been closed to other traffic. Rounding a blind corner at speed, Don collided with a taxi coming the other way. The Magnette mounted the grass verge, crashed into a hedge and overturned, pinning Don and Tayler underneath, *The Oxford Times* reported. Don was said to have just suffered facial abrasions, but Tayler was more seriously injured and died in hospital the next day.

Kaye Don's trial in July, which received relatively extensive publicity, was a messy affair. The prosecution made much of the fact that the M.G. had no lights or horn, and that Don was not insured for practicing on the road outside official practice hours[4]. He was, said the Attorney-General, 'utterly indifferent to anything else on the highroad'.

Kaye Don – dramatically swathed in bandages and reported by *The Times* as 'still suffering from the effects of injuries he received in the accident' – tried to back-track on his statement that he was doing 60mph at the time of the impact, whilst maintaining this was a perfectly safe speed and that he had the car 'under perfect control' whilst attempting a braking test as he approached the bend.

Notwithstanding this, he said the M.G. had heavy steering and a tendency to wander – thereby raising discussion about whether the car had been in some way defective, with this contributing to the accident; as part of the cross-examination, H. N. Charles was called as a witness, so there was a very direct M.G. involvement in the trial. Following the conviction, an appeal was heard in September, but was not successful, and Don was sentenced to four months imprisonment. He was released a month early, on medical advice.

But this is only part of the story. In October 1934, after the failure of Don's appeal and whilst he was still in gaol, jobbing writer James Wentworth Day, already the author of a sycophantic biography of Sir Malcolm Campbell, published his book *Kaye Don – The Man*. In an introduction, Campbell speaks of 'the latest misfortune to have overtaken my old friend and gallant competitor' and goes

Frankie Tayler's grave in St Sepulchre's Cemetery, in the Jericho quarter of Oxford. Married just ten months before his death, he had promised his wife that he would give up racing after the Isle of Man event. (Andrew Whitehead)

---

[4] There was no suggestion that Don had been drinking. 'It is a case where you have not disturbed your senses with drink or anything of that sort,' observed the presiding judge. It is legitimate to question whether this was really the case: Don did after all take the car out after a dinner in which alcohol would most likely have been consumed. In this connection the view of Tayler's great-nephew Mark Hotson merits recording. "It is etched into family history – with absolutely no doubt at all – that Don had been drinking," Hotson told the author.

on to write 'We all of us take risks, we all of us face death, we all of us face disfigurement, broken limbs and shattered lives in this peculiar game of motor racing which is our chosen business or hobby…Kaye Don is weathering a gale of misfortune which might very well have struck any other racing motorist in the full flower of his career.' No mention is made of Frankie Tayler, who had been overtaken by a somewhat greater misfortune than that to have befallen the gallant Mr Don.

Then, in the chapter devoted to the accident, Wentworth Day launches into an intemperate diatribe against the Isle of Man – 'that insignificant little piece of goat-infested hill set in the Irish Sea' – and its supposedly inbred population, cynically enjoying 'the money-drawing capacities of a butcher's holiday' by promoting road-racing in which 'our best and finest motor drivers can legally kill themselves to the plaudits of the tourist crowd beneath the benignant eye of the Manx law.'

In any case, he wrote, Tayler was taking a reasonable professional risk. Wentworth Day had himself passengered Don in numerous practices and races. 'Each time I took the risk of being killed, as hundreds of others have done before me. It was a sporting and a reasonable risk…Kaye Don is not unique in that a man died because he took the ordinary risks of everyday motor racing. Yet the Manx authorities saw fit to prosecute.'

This argument was also articulated in an article in *The Autocar* by well-known racing driver and journalist S. C. H. Davis, who was closely associated with M.G., designing the badges and overalls worn by its racing mechanics and helping with M.G. entries at Le Mans. As with Wentworth Day, there was no expression of sympathy for the dead Tayler: risking one's life was part of the racing mechanic's job, and for Sammy Davis the notion of a driver being charged with manslaughter in the event of death 'caused by any error of judgement of the driver at any time' was in his eyes ridiculous. No consideration was given to the criminal negligence of which Don was convicted, having driven a car at high speed at night on a public road, without lights.

The article resulted in a flurry of hostile letters to the magazine, the publication of a riposte by an Isle of Man resident, and a statement by Don on his release disassociating himself from the attacks made on the Isle in the press and in his biography. But the damage had been done. For many people the racing fraternity must have appeared as privileged playboys with a disdain for the lives of the lower orders who served them as mechanics.

Perhaps it was just as well that the general public was not aware that Don – as *The Autocar* admitted – had a reputation for treating his mechanics 'a little autocratically' and that amongst the racing fraternity he was not, the magazine said, the most popular of drivers. The main thing, though, was that the whole episode evidently stuck in the craw of William Morris. 'From then on, Billy Morris didn't want to be connected with racing,' Hubert Charles observed to Wilson McComb[5].

Whilst the Don affair was rumbling on, Hugh 'Hammy' Hamilton, a regular competitor in M.G. cars, died at the Swiss Grand Prix in August 1934, his Maserati going head-on into a tree after a tyre burst at speed. Hamilton had suffered severe internal injuries the previous year in an accident in his M.G. at an event in Czechoslovakia; now he was dead, and Abingdon had another racing fatality to mourn, something that would not have been lost on William Morris.

---

[5] The fact that Cecil Kimber (as reported in *The Autocar* for 22 January 1932) had proposed the races in the Isle of Man, ahead of the first events in 1933, might possibly have been a further influence on Sir William Morris.

The deaths of Hugh Hamilton and Frankie Tayler were a double blow to Abingdon, and were sure to have distressed William Morris; here Hamilton (behind the wheel) is seen at the 1933 TT, with his mother and Goldie Gardner. (M.G. Car Club)

THE EXECUTION CONSUMMATED

So it was that whilst work was underway on sorting the R-type, the axe fell. "We had a car dismantled...There were bits and pieces everywhere. Then word came from 'HN' that Kimber was coming round the factory with Len Lord and Miles Thomas. We all knew that Thomas was a nasty piece of work, and had heard that Lord was a tricky one to deal with," Reg Jackson related to Mike Allison. "The party arrived, and as Lord walked through the door he said to Thomas 'This bloody lot can go for a start!' Then he walked out, just like that. 'HN' told me afterwards that he and 'CK' had tried to talk to him sensibly about independent suspension but Lord said he didn't want any of this suspension nonsense on any of his cars... Thomas came back to us, and I was told by him to return all privately-owned stuff to their owners, and anything that hadn't been sold could go for scrap."

In the opinion of John Thornley, the cessation of work on the R-type put a stop to a line of development that could have redefined the M.G. design ethos. "The R-type would probably have seen the birth of a new breed of vehicle. It could have led automotive engineering for the nation – it was way ahead of its time. Through the medium of the R-type we were on the way to the Porsche style of vehicle. With the 1935 takeover we thus took quite a step back, development-wise. But we became much more financially viable...I don't think anybody ever realised the extent to which we were running into expense, as the models never ran for long enough."

Kimber sought to make the best of the situation

Kimber's statement on racing in The Sports Car *carried with it an element of special pleading, but he had to make the best of an awkward situation.*

in an 'official statement' published in *The Sports Car* magazine. Claiming that 'racing for the purpose of development has...served its useful purpose,' he went on to say that the handicapping system operated to the detriment of M.G. in British racing and that as a result the company intended to rest on its laurels and 'let the production type catch up with the extremely advanced ideas incorporated in the present racing car'.

Kimber made sure that his friends in the motoring press were suitably briefed, so that a positive spin could be put on the situation. So it was that, for example, *The Motor* for 9 July 1935 ran an item under the heading 'M.G. Cars May Race Again' in its 'You'll be Interested to Know' column. 'Some people are attributing the announcement that the M.G. Co has dropped making racing cars to the absorption of this business by Morris Motors Ltd. Mr Cecil Kimber assured me last week that this is not correct,' wrote the anonymous journalist. 'Long before the merger he had come to the conclusion that, for the time being, there were no records which they did not already hold that they could go for, nor races in which any useful purpose would be served by competing, and so he decided upon recommending a policy of concentrating upon production of cars that ordinary users can buy.'

The magazine was clearly sceptical of this reasoning. 'Nevertheless, if you produce real sports cars you must be continually putting up performances that maintain their prestige,' it concluded. Readers were clearly being made aware that Kimber's remarks were to be taken with a pinch of salt, and that – wishful thinking, no doubt – the door remained open for a return to making racing cars.

Meanwhile there were enough M.G. cars being campaigned for it to seem to the untrained eye that nothing much had changed: for the remainder of the 1935 season and throughout 1936 the marque would continue to be a significant presence at Brooklands and elsewhere, and development of the R-type would carry on in private hands, notably with the twin-cam head mentioned above. In January 1937 *The Sports Car* would write that in 1936 privately-owned M.G. cars had won 24 events around the world, including, with a total of 11 victories, a quarter of all Brooklands races.

PERSPECTIVE: WHEN 'TOMMY' WROTE TO LEN

There is an interesting postscript. In the Thomas papers preserved at the British Motor Museum can be found a friendly correspondence between Len Lord, then heading Austin[6], and Miles Thomas, by this stage his counterpart at Cowley. In a letter to Thomas of 22 December 1943, Lord broaches the question of motor-racing after the war: 'I had just been reading the report in *The Autocar* of the luncheon of the Sports Car Enthusiasts, and it prompted me to ask you what were your ideas regarding post-war racing. As you know, I have never been very keen on it, and as far as the Austin Motor Company is concerned I would like to give it a rest for a year or two after the war. Obviously I may find difficulty in doing this if you intend to race from Riley or M.G., so I thought I would risk asking you a direct question,' he writes.

In a letter of 3 January 1944, Thomas confirms that M.G. and Riley had no wish to participate in immediate post-war racing events. 'I, personally, will always strongly set my face against racing programmes – an opinion that is fortified since I have had the opportunity of looking at some of the M.G. accounts dealing with various Continental exploits and special car sales transactions with the experts involved,' he goes on to say.

'I know exactly what you mean when you say you had a bit of a shock when you saw the M.G. accounts,' says Lord in his reply of 5 January 1944. 'I myself of course had seen them previously, and well remember what they looked like. I have since had the opportunity of seeing the cost of racing to the Austin Company, and if they were laid side by side I doubt which would win.

'To my mind the whole thing is crazy. One has only to go to Brooklands and see the crowd of hangers-on that we are supporting by racing to realise what fools we have been in the

---

[6] See Chapter 14.

past; in fact I think it would pay us to buy some horses and support a few gentlemanly bookmakers, as I believe they are a preferable type!'

TAKING BREATH, BOUNCING BACK

That Cecil Kimber was knocked back by the withdrawal of M.G. from active participation in racing is not in doubt. He was able to regain equilibrium with one last family holiday in Instow, surrounded by friends and with the relaxation of more sailing. "The sea is a clean enemy," he is said to have remarked.

For the children, the holidays in North Devon were as fun as ever. '[He] took us for picnics in the lovely local fishing boats…We knew all the fishermen, and rowed pram dinghies which belonged to the delightful family hotel where we stayed for seven years running. I now realise that my father was recreating the happiness of Runswick Bay for himself as well as for us,' recounts Jean.

By the time of the annual Motor Show dinner and dance Kimber was even able to joke about things, saying in his speech that he hoped that a day would come when Lord Nuffield would offer him £100,000 to produce a racing car to beat the world – "but he is just as likely to give me the sack instead." As he would demonstrate, there were other ways to keep the M.G. name prominent in motor sport, at rather less risk to his position.

In a friendly 'Dear Tommy… Dear Len' exchange of letters in 1943-44, Leonard Lord and Miles Thomas (here with wife Hylda) agreed that motor racing was a financial drain and something best not to be countenanced after the war. By this time Thomas was Sir Miles, having been knighted at the beginning of 1943. (Ken Martin collection)

LEFT (BOTH): *Bill Gibbs continued to join the Kimbers for their holidays in North Devon. In the lower image he is believed to be with a young lady known as Alsace Lorraine, remembered by Jean as 'a girl from Harpenden Co-Ed School – very advanced'.*

BELOW: *Rene in a hired lugsail boat, with Betty gathering up the sail, probably during the 1935 summer holidays at Instow: it is difficult to date exactly these various photos in an album from the 1933-35 period. The notion that Rene did not gain pleasure from the sailing that was one of her husband's passions does not stand up to scrutiny.*

TOP LEFT: *Rene and Jean, relaxing in the garden of the Marine Hotel.*

ABOVE: *A radiant Betty in the dunes, most probably at Braunton.*

LEFT: *The summer of 1935 would see Rene's last family holiday in Instow. Despite a failing marriage and looming health problems, she gave the appearance of enjoying herself. Whether, in contrast, she appreciated to the same degree attending the M.G. Car Club's end-of-year 'Downstage Dinner' with its loud brass band and fireworks is another matter.*

13

RECONSTRUCTION AND DISINTEGRATION

The direction in which M.G. road cars would evolve, after the P-type and the N-type, was a perplexing question. Kimber must have known how expensive the overhead-cam engines were, given that they were special adaptations, made in penny-packet numbers, of an engine family that was already a low-volume product. He had been fortunate indeed to have access to personalised power units for an output of barely 2,000 cars a year, but such good fortune could not last for ever.

The four-cylinder M.G. unit had already lost its principal mass-production sister in 1932 when the Morris Minor had ceased using the ohc engine. Kimber would have known – or at least suspected – that Leonard Lord was planning to abandon both the four-cylinder and six-cylinder overhead-cam Wolseley engines when his commonised ranges of Morrises and Wolseleys were ready for launch, beginning for Wolseley at the 1935 Motor Show.

This was a matter of undebatable industrial logic. There was no point in making small quantities of a costly overhead-cam design, primarily for Wolseley, when the average Wolseley owner probably wouldn't have cared where his car's camshaft was situated. Equally, there was no point in having Wolseley making its own distinctive design of engine when production of closely related engines for Morris, Wolseley and M.G. could be more efficiently achieved at one location, the Morris Engines Branch factory in Coventry. Making specialised engines at Wolseley's Ward End works was a nonsense, and one that was inevitably going to be eliminated as Leonard Lord dragged Morris back to manufacturing coherence and financial profitability.

OPPOSITE: *A drawn-looking Rene caught unawares by the camera at the 1936 MGCC Abingdon Trial. The car on which Kimber is leaning is a Singer, a great many of the Coventry marque being fielded at these trials.*

RIGHT: *These renderings were prepared by Mulliners of Birmingham (not to be confused with H.J. Mulliner), for EX150, Kimber's stillborn independently-sprung saloon.*

'QUEEN MARY' AND OTHER STORIES

Quite how M.G. would have replaced the Midget and Magnette remains a mystery. Perhaps Kimber hoped to hang on for another year – as did in fact happen – and find a suitable solution in the Morris-Wolseley parts bin. Even the press was scratching its head. 'Rumour has been rife concerning the future of the popular M.G. models. It has even been suggested that in future the M.G. range would be but special bodies on existing Morris chassis,' wrote *The Autocar*, before continuing almost with a sigh of relief to describe the improved P-type and N-type models that would continue for the 1936 season.

Chapter Thirteen: Reconstruction and Disintegration

What is not a mystery, but a certified fact, is that Kimber was planning to move substantially upmarket with EX150, which was seen as having a 3½-litre engine. The car would have been a sort of 'Poor Man's Bentley' and it was not a coincidence that Kimber borrowed a 3½-litre Bentley for a few weeks. There was talk of sourcing an engine from an outside supplier, and even of a V8 devised from putting together two P-type blocks. Such discussion can only have been theoretical to the point of fantasy: it is certain, as far as the author is concerned, that neither option would ever have been permitted by Lord Nuffield. All the indications, indeed, are that the car was intended to have a tuned version of the physically massive 3485cc pushrod engine of the new Wolseley Twenty-Five[1].

A key part of the specification was all-independent torsion-bar suspension based on that of the R-type. A prototype irreverently nicknamed 'Queen Mary' was built, possibly with a backbone design of chassis, and temporarily fitted with – so it is said – a regular Morris or Wolseley body[2]; meanwhile Mulliners of Birmingham was commissioned to come up with a range of definitive body styles.

There was a logic to developing a higher-cost and one assumes higher-profit range-topper: after all, this was the direction in which William Lyons at SS was moving. It would also have been following in the wheeltracks of Triumph, who had already made a decisive move up the price range with their Gloria series; additionally Riley, another rival, would introduce a V8 model for 1936. All the same, this was an ambitious programme for Kimber to undertake – over-ambitious, almost certainly.

It was surely a disappointment when the project was cancelled, in the wake of the closure of the racing department and the abandonment of the R-type. But it cannot have been wholly unexpected. In its best year of 1932 M.G. had made roughly 2,400 cars; this dropped to approximately 2,100 in 1934 and to a slender 1,250 or so in 1935. At those volumes, maximum parts-sharing with mass-production Morrises and Wolseleys, conventionally engineered though they were, was the only financially viable way forward. Cancelling EX150 wasn't the act of a crew of uncultured barbarians from Cowley determined to smash plucky little M.G. to smithereens.

COWLEY'S FIRST M.G. – THE TWO-LITRE

In place of EX150 the M.G. Two-Litre was announced at the 1935 Motor Show. This was a resolutely conventional design, with rigid axles front and rear, and used the running gear – engine, gearbox, back axle – of the new Super Six Wolseleys. "Four of us were sent over to Cowley to 'design' the Two-Litre saloon. What happened was that we were told to make an M.G. out of the 18/80 Wolseley," remembered former Abingdon draughtsman Stewart Daniels[3].

At least the newcomer looked the part, with an elegant body that was a direct development of one of the Mulliners coachwork proposals for EX150. That this is manifestly the case – early advertisements even seem to crib the original Mulliners artwork – is a reasonable indication that the story of Kimber being responsible for the car's styling is wide of the mark.

Quite how this notion gained currency is difficult to say, as nowhere in print does Kimber claim such paternity. Daughter Jean may well have prompted the idea. 'He was responsible for the beautiful lines of these cars – Winifred, now our housekeeper since my mother was in a nursing home, remembers him bringing

---

[1] Former M.G. draughtsman Stewart Daniels recalled in an interview (M.G. Car Club SVW Register newsletter, 1994) that this was the engine proposed. As for its heft, Anders Clausager in *MG Saloon Cars* gives a weight of 780lb for the overhead-valve Wolseley version, with its clutch and gearbox – almost 155lb more than the weight of the assembly used for the Two-Litre that would take EX150's place.

[2] The specification of the lashed-up prototype is seemingly confirmed in a review of experimental and one-off M.G. models in an article 'Cars that never were' published in *The Motor* for 27 February 1963. Author D. B. Tubbs writes of EX150 being 'a very large motor car with Morris 25 engine and body but a central box frame with footwells and independent suspension with equal-length wishbones all round.'

[3] SVW Register interview cited above.

The initial artwork for what became the M.G. Two-Litre or SA was clearly derived from one of the proposals from Mulliners.

the designs home to work on until he was satisfied,' she writes, for instance, in *The MG Log*.

In reality, what the family housekeeper may have briefly observed while going about her business, and then recounted some good few years later, can hardly be regarded as conclusive evidence. Kimber had an artistic sensibility, could sketch and draw, and certainly had an eye for a line. That doesn't make him a car stylist. What does seem to be the case is that he had ideas, communicated them, and helped shape the form of the cars for which he was responsible – notably through working with his friend the commercial artist Harold Connolly.

Abingdon PR man George Tuck explained to Norman Ewing how the process worked. "Kim kept this drawing block in his office at a big table near his desk; he was always drawing bold lines, and when Harold Connolly came down to the works they sat down at this block and played around with ideas. Kim would give a

THE M.G. TWO-LITRE OR SA

The tourer (discontinued in April 1939) would receive a further-modified body in time for the 1937 show, gaining cutaway front doors and a swept tail, the spare wheel migrating to the left-hand front wing. Another late 1937 change to the SA was the substitution of louvres for the line of bonnet flaps, in a bid to cut down on the bugbear of excessive engine heat penetrating the cockpit.

The Two-Litre or SA was for many years looked down upon as not being a true M.G. – whatever that might mean. The truth is that it was a perfectly honourable rival to the SS Jaguars and big Triumphs of the time. Nobody criticised William Lyons for using a converted Standard engine in his cars, so taking pop-shots at the M.G. for having a Wolseley engine seems misplaced.

The Two-Litre was announced in October 1935 with the same 2062cc pushrod engine as used in the new 16hp Wolseley Super Six, but before production began the capacity for the M.G. (but not the Wolseley) was increased to 2288cc; in this form, with two SU carburettors unusually laid horizontal, output was 75.3bhp. A further capacity change, to 2322cc, took place in February 1937, so that it shared its engine with that of the Wolseley 18/80. The gearbox was initially described as having synchromesh on third and top but when the M.G. went on sale it had lost its synchromesh – only to have it restored in August 1936. The chassis, unique to the SA, was not underslung at the rear and was of semi-cruciform construction, and had a substantial 10ft 3in wheelbase; brakes were hydraulic.

During 1936 both a Tickford-built drophead and a four-door open tourer by Charlesworth became available, with both models having their tail lightly restyled by the time of that year's Motor Show.

The constant modifications to the SA's specification – and there was a further round of minor changes for 1939 – cannot have helped production. As will be discussed, this was substantially bettered by that of the 2½-litre SS Jaguar, which was not a perceptibly superior car and which was not the bargain-priced proposition it was made out to be, when a more stylishly turned-out 2322cc SA cost just £4 more.

According to the SVW Register of the M.G. Car Club a total of 2,745 examples of the SA were made, the last in September 1939. This output was split between 1,945 saloons, 696 dropheads, 90 tourers, and 14 chassis. Most of the chassis – ten, it seems – went to J. H. Keller in Switzerland, who had them bodied as dropheads or open tourers by Reinbolt & Christé; two of the remainder are known to have gone to Australia, one being bodied as a saloon and the other as a fixed-head coupé. Output of the SA more than halved between 1938 and 1939, from a peak of 1,045 units to just 447 in the latter year, but add the WA to the tally and for a nine-month year the 1939 figures look pretty stable, suggesting that buyers made a switch to the bigger-engined car.

Chapter Thirteen: Reconstruction and Disintegration

rough outline of what he was after, and Harold would then make a proper three-dimensional drawing of the thing and add people and so on…I wouldn't say that's how all our bodies were designed, but the general character and outline of the thing was basically Kimber, and the development by Harold. That's how a lot of the flowing lines and general appearance came about…It was Kimber who put the feel into M.G., although Harold had a lot of influence on the body styling…"

Putting the Two-Litre into production took time: hardly surprisingly, given that it was an all-new design. The very fact that a car was ready to be displayed at Olympia in October 1935, not even four months after Cowley assuming responsibility for M.G. design, was already an impressive achievement, even if it leaves one with the suspicion that work was already underway before July, with or without Kimber's knowledge.

Before sales could begin, a factory re-fit was required, at the substantial cost of £20,000. There were now four assembly lines instead of two, and a new paint shop, but the consequence was that quick-on-its-feet SS had its Jaguars rolling off the lines well before year-end, but Abingdon only stumbled into production with the SA in spring 1936, by which time there was a 500-person waiting list. When they were able to sample the Two-Litre, the press were predictably generous. 'Typically M.G. as regards roadworthiness' was the verdict of *The Autocar*. 'The car as a whole gives a strong impression of the fact that M.G. racing experience has been drawn upon most successfully as regards roadability, and also that a degree of refinement has been added that will render these cars very attractive indeed.'

As a relaxed touring saloon the new M.G. did indeed have much to commend it. Cecil Kimber was no doubt able to confirm this for himself when in March 1936 he used a pre-production example for a trip to Germany and Switzerland to visit M.G. agents. As usual, he took plenty of photographs, including some of quirky old vehicles he encountered along the way, conserving the images in an album devoted to the trip. Accompanied by Managing

The same image as that on page 277 was used in launch-time publicity. Talking up the competition heritage of the new model was somewhat brazen – but the press fell for it.

Editor of *The Autocar* Ernest Appleby[4] and his old friend Russel Chiesman, Kimber was taking a break from an increasingly tense domestic situation: his marriage to Rene was now on the rocks.

---

[4] Not to be confused with his son, cartoonist Barry Appleby, best known as creator of the *Daily Express* cartoon strip 'The Gambols' and a longtime contributor to *The Autocar* magazine.

ABOVE: *The final style, created by Cowley's design department, was tautly drawn and suitably sporting. (Author's collection)*

LEFT: *The SA engine was initially based on that of the 2062cc 16hp Wolseley Super Six but ended up being of 2322cc, as in the Wolseley 18/80. (Author's collection)*

RIGHT: *Kimber doing the smiling PR routine with the new Two-Litre, at the time of its 1935 Motor Show launch. In attendance are Lord Nuffield and M.G. racing driver Doreen Evans.*

OVERLEAF: *The drophead version of the SA had a body by Tickford. Kimber was not happy with the initial styling, which included a higher windscreen and a different tail treatment. These were swiftly changed. Additionally, the line of the rear wing was made more harmonious, as Kimber recounts in his IAE paper on design; see Appendix 2.*

ABOVE: *The SA Charlesworth tourer in its original form had flat-topped doors. (Magna Press Library)*

LEFT: *An M.G. publicity image showing an SA on test at Brooklands.*

OPPOSITE: *Later tourers were given cutaway front doors and a swept tail. (Magna Press)*

OPPOSITE TOP LEFT: *A pause on the Geneva trip in the pre-production SA. The M.G. was reported as cruising happily at an indicated 70-75mph and giving 'an impression of quality and power found only in a few cars in the 3-litre class'.*

OPPOSITE TOP RIGHT: *By Lake Geneva. Kimber's third companion on the trip was the manager of Morris operations in Belgium, a Mr Gouvy.*

OPPOSITE BOTTOM: *At the Franco-Swiss border – note the delightful and typically French Art Deco lettering on the front of the Customs building.*

RIGHT: *The split rear window was a design fad of the time, and was also found on Triumph saloons.*

BELOW: *Ever one with an eye for an interesting curiosity, Kimber snapped this rear-engined buggy with its all-independent wishbone suspension.*

BOTTOM RIGHT: *This smiling duo with what looks like an adaptation of a veteran vehicle of some sort also caught his attention.*

A WORM ENTERS THE APPLE

It is difficult to be sure when Kimber and Muriel Dewar began their relationship: perhaps as early as 1933[5]. Certainly by 1935 it had become a serious affair, but conducted with sufficient discretion for the inevitable tensions between their parents only rarely to surface in front of the children. 'I only witnessed one major confrontation between my parents and that was when my mother, who had begun to have suspicions that there was "somebody else" taxed my father with his "unkindness" and I burst into tears saying he was "horrible". He remained very quiet and contained, however, and refrained from getting angry because he realised that I ought not to have been there,' writes Jean.

'I sometimes wonder what real feelings might have been ventilated if my parents had had the benefit of modern family therapy. It might have relieved their burdens, but I suspect it would not have healed the breach; it was too wide, and my father had started to look for comfort in another direction. He apparently asked my stepmother in the initial stages of their relationship "Will you be my friend?" – which points to the sad reality that my parents were not friends. My stepmother also told me that my father had felt my mother's almost obsessive interest in M.G.s to be "not interest, but a whip to drive him". It seems likely that she continued to make suggestions which, helpful as they may have been in the early days, he now felt were criticism and resented.'

A different side of the same coin was that a demoralised Rene Kimber, now suffering from ill health, was in addition less inclined to share her husband's enthusiasm for his principal means of relaxation outside work. A spot of sailing at Instow was one thing, but his love of fishing was another. This Jean observed when he was proposing to buy his own stretch of trout-fishing water at Pangbourne.

'He had taken my mother, my sister and me to see The Retreat way back in 1936 when it was still just a bus. He tried to explain what he wanted to do, but my mother angrily rejected the idea; she was quite unable to see the potential. It was pouring with rain, which didn't help. She, of course, far preferred to continue going to Eastleach where she could call on the friends she had made locally, and talk to Mrs Monk about gardening while my father fished... She could not feel enthusiastic, already feeling tired and ill, and my father, of course, not realising the reasons, again felt that his wife would not enter with enthusiasm into any of his dreams.'

By 1936 Kimber was playing a more active role in the life of Gillie's daughter Bobbie, paying all expenses in connection with her education, clothing and travelling, including the costs of sending her to study in Heidelberg – and on her return from Germany he would pay her £2.10.0 weekly while she was working in London.

It was against this backdrop that in June 1936 the second Cowley-originated M.G. model was announced. The T-type Midget, retrospectively named the TA, followed the chassis and body design of the preceding P-type, but was slightly larger and was powered by a slower-turning 1292cc pushrod engine taken from the Wolseley Ten, in conjunction with a cork-in-oil clutch; there were also hydraulic brakes, for the first time on an M.G. sports car. 'The sports die-hards were aghast,' writes

Bobbie Dewar in 1936: Kimber was now a more constant presence in her life.

---

[5] In support of this date, in *The MG Log* Jean writes of 'the gentle, witty, wholly supportive divorcee, Muriel Dewar, nicknamed Gillie, whom he had loved since 1933.' Quite how she is able to give a precise date is not known.

THE T-TYPE M.G. MIDGET

Introduced in June 1936, the TA Midget was a bigger car than the PB it replaced. 'On the road the "feel" of the car has undergone a change; the new Midget is softer, quieter, and more flexible at low speeds,' commented The Autocar *in its road test.*

The 1936 remodelling of the Midget, the most consistently successful M.G. model in the 1928-35 period, was an exercise in pragmatism – or plain old-fashioned prudence. The aesthetics were barely changed, and the same went for the chassis. The wheelbase was longer by a little over 6in and the track (the same front and rear, as before) was increased by 3in, but the same basic underslung ladder-frame design was used.

The engine, gearbox and back axle were regular Morris/Wolseley units, the 1292cc long-stroke 'four' borrowed from the Series II Wolseley Ten being a pushrod version of the side-valve Morris Ten unit. The gearbox was initially unsynchronised but was soon given a synchronised third/fourth, and was combined with a cork-in-oil clutch. Power was up from the PB's 43.3bhp to an unstressed 52.4bhp, but had to cope with a kerb weight that had jumped from 13.5cwt to 17.3cwt.

Initially just an open two-seater was offered, but in August 1938 a drophead coupé was announced, with a body built by Tickford. Additionally Park Ward made a single drophead and Carbodies are understood to have given two TAs an Airline coupé body; the days of bespoke coachwork were drawing to a close.

After 2,741 two-seaters TAs and 260 dropheads had been assembled, in May 1939 the TB arrived. This was physically identical to the TA it replaced but had an over-bored 1250cc version of the new 1140cc short-stroke 10hp engine introduced for 1939 in the integral-construction Series M Morris Ten. Also found in the unrelated Wolseley Ten announced in early 1939, it would go on to power the TC, TD and TF Midgets of post-war years. The new engine, developing 54.4bhp, was mated to a conventional dry clutch and the gearbox now had a synchronised second gear. Just 319 two-seaters and 60 Tickford dropheads would be made before war stopped production. The TB would be revived after the war as the TC, with a slightly wider body tub, and would be made until 1949.

John Dugdale. Sales proved to be roughly the equal of the P-type, however, at approximately 1,000 cars a year, and descendants of the TA would be made until 1955. "It must have been right," John Thornley commented to the author.

FUN IN FALMOUTH

The summer holidays of 1936 were spent in Falmouth – but without Rene, who at the last minute, on medical advice, and possibly in order to follow a controlled diet, went into a nursing home in Oxford for treatment of the colitis from which she was suffering[6]. She may have already developed the cancer that would soon prove fatal, although this may not have been officially diagnosed. In Rene's absence, accompanying Kimber and his daughters were his brother Vernon and his wife, his brother-in-law Billy Sutton, and long-time friend Bill Gibbs and his new wife Nan. He was also joined at one stage by veteran sailor and Morris colleague Hans Lanstad.

In later life Jean pondered why Kimber did not cancel the holiday. She assumed that he was too heavily committed with deposit-paid bookings, but also that he did not want to forego the adventure of a fortnight on the first boat of his own, freshly acquired a short time before. The craft was a 27ft scaled-down Bristol Channel pilot cutter, registered as the *F.L.B.* – which Kimber changed to *Falcon*, reportedly after Rene suggested the initials stood for 'Family Left Behind' – and some of the holiday was spent with everyone mucking-in for a 'scrubbing party'.

Staying in a modest hotel owned by North Country friends, it was clearly a jovial holiday, judging by Jean's recollections. 'I was by now such a self-reliant tomboy in boats, that I spent most of my time on the water, but I remember Uncle Vern playing the piano as if music was his very soul, and then making us laugh until we

A photo by Cecil Kimber of the river at Eastleach, where he had rented some trout-fishing rights.

---

[6] This inflammatory bowel disease, which can affect the whole colon, may flare up when the person is under stress, which can influence how the immune system operates. It is not unreasonable to consider Rene Kimber's disintegrating marriage as a factor in the breakdown of her health.

Kimber's first boat, Falcon, *was a Bristol Channel pilot cutter.*

TOP: *Scrubbing party at Greeb Cove in Cornwall, for Kimber's new boat* Falcon: *Bernard and Nellie, owners of the hotel where the family were staying, are on the left, with Nan and Bill Gibbs and Betty; atop the boat is Jean.*

ABOVE: *Off to St Mawes, Kimber and a happy boatload: Jean is far left, Betty second right, with Nan Gibbs waving.*

ABOVE: *At the age of 17, Betty was developing into a self-assured young adult – which would lead to tensions with her father.*

RIGHT (BOTH): *Betty and Jean below decks on* Falcon.

Chapter Thirteen: Reconstruction and Disintegration

ached as he imitated the immortal Stanley Holloway's classic Lancashire monologues about Albert and the lion.'

Further enlivening the summer was the presence of a certain 'Captain Cowper' who on occasion joined the Kimbers on the beach, with the hotel owner, but turned out to be a confidence trickster and ended up leaving the hotel without paying his bill. Kimber, meanwhile, took pleasure in teaching Jean and Betty the rudiments of how to sail a cruising yacht, as they explored St Mawes and up the River Fal.

'The last of the clipper ships, the *Cutty Sark*, now a museum, was in those days moored off her former captain's house, opposite Falmouth, and I shall never forget rowing my father across to visit her. It was entirely typical of him to let me row, not to be impatient with me, and to show his delight in every detail of that wonderful morning,' recalls Jean in *The Other Tack*.

'The next day we sailed out of the harbour, across Falmouth Bay to Helford River, and I slept aboard a boat for the first time. The moon shone on the calm water and the wash of passing boats lapped gently against the pitch pine planking. *Falcon* might [have been] old and slow, but she taught us a lot.

'We fished for mackerel; on a windless day we rowed ashore and explored mysterious sea caves, and at the end of the holiday we voyaged from Falmouth to Plymouth. In spite of motoring all the way in a flat calm, nothing will ever eradicate my memory of the Yealm when we followed the leading marks up that incomparable Devon river. When my husband and I called there on our own boat in 1981, my father's photographs were not really out of date, though there are more houses, and hundreds, not dozens, of boats. The magic is still unmistakable, and what my father gave me on that holiday has lasted a lifetime.'

TOP: *Faithful Morris hand Hans Lanstad, who had drawn up the very first Morris car, was a visitor during the Falmouth holiday. The Norwegian-born Lanstad was an experienced sailor.*

LEFT: *Bill and Nan Gibbs in typical good spirits.*

SLIPPING AWAY: DIFFICULT TIMES FOR RENE

Hardly surprisingly, given the unpleasant side effects of colitis, the summer of 1936 was less happy for Rene Kimber, whom Jean described as being hysterical and difficult. 'My mother was the life and soul of a party, but in private, if things weren't going her way, she was capable of emotional blackmail...Eileen Kingerlee confirmed these feelings and also shared them. Although Eileen was a lifelong friend of my parents, she was appalled to find herself invited to tea, and then turned on and falsely accused by my mother of "helping my husband to deceive me."

'I don't think my father realised that her illness was taking a more serious turn. If her doctor knew, of course, he would not have said anything, but I think now that my mother had begun to suspect that not only was her marriage collapsing, but her health too, which closed her escape route into another relationship. Though she was supposed to live on a bland diet, she would suddenly feel better, go out to a dinner party and eat something forbidden, such as crystallised ginger, and of course have a relapse. I realise now that she was fighting back in the only way she knew, but at the time it was very frightening.'

This wasn't all, according to the memories of both Jean and those handed down by older sister Betty. Their father was a non-practicing Quaker and their mother, who came from a High Anglican background, had been similarly non-observing. But now Rene sought spiritual support. 'We also had to endure her desperate attempts to find solace in religion,' writes Jean. 'There were experiments with Roman Catholicism and Christian Science, which banished the kindly vicar of St Helen's at Abingdon who taught us all games of patience.'

OPPOSITE TOP: *The fishermen's wharf at Falmouth.*

OPPOSITE BOTTOM: *Jean and friends – including Carl Kingerlee's daughter Felice – pose with Cecil Kimber's SA saloon on the quay at West Looe.*

RIGHT: *During the 1936 Falmouth break Kimber turned to his old love, and on August Bank Holiday attended a motorcycle race around Pendennis Head, where he took a series of photographs.*

14

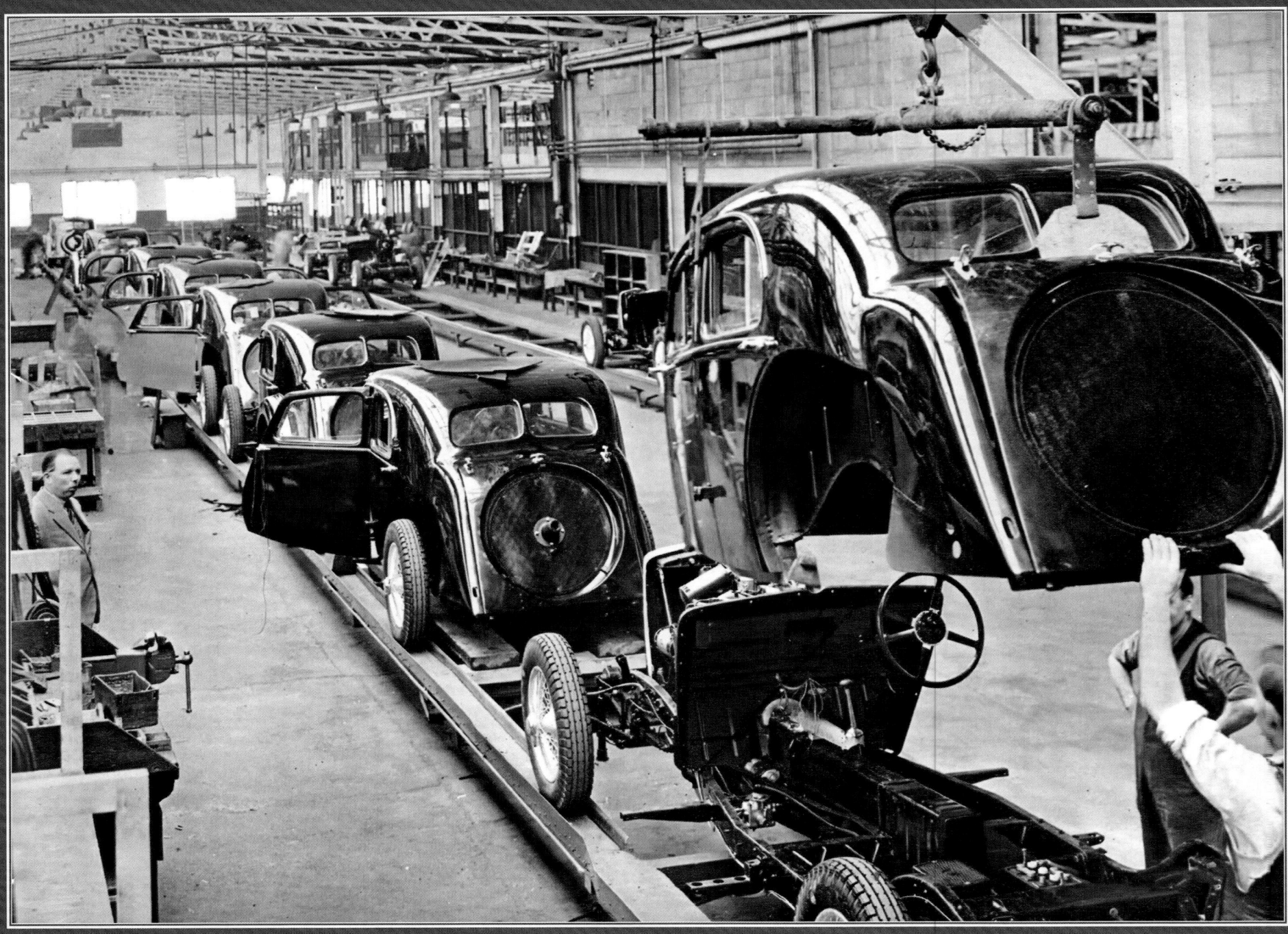

A MARRIAGE ENDS, A NEW CAR ARRIVES

Turbulence wasn't in this period restricted to Kimber's personal life. During that same summer of 1936 the Morris empire was rocked by what *The Motor* described as 'quite the biggest sensation in the motor industry for some years' when on 24 August Leonard Lord resigned from Morris Motors. It has always been understood that Lord's departure was because he had requested a share of the profits that were being generated largely as a result of his own endeavours, and was not prepared to accept Nuffield's refusal to entertain this. "I make the money. He just sits there and does nothing," Lord was reported as observing. According to Miles Thomas, writing in *Out on a Wing*, Lord requested a salary 'which was quite surprisingly high' and a percentage of all profits over and above a figure that at the time was not being realised but which had been achieved in previous years.

But it wasn't just a question of money. Nuffield had seen how Lord had been making decisions off his own bat, effectively running the business when Nuffield felt that this was his job. According to Thomas, he felt he was losing control of the company he had created. Worse, there was a fierce difference of opinion over Morris participation in the government scheme for the motor industry to build aircraft engines in secondary or 'shadow' factories paid for by the state. Lord Nuffield wanted the government instead to buy his Wolseley aero-engines. He returned in spring 1936 from one of his overseas trips, forced Lord to pull Wolseley out of the shadow-factory scheme in the early summer, and ultimately, in a fit of petulance, closed Wolseley Aero Engines Ltd. It is impossible to believe that the tensions between the two men during this affair cannot have contributed to the final rupture.

OPPOSITE: *Production of the Two-litre took time to begin. In May 1936* The Autocar *reported that cars were coming off the line 'at the rate of about one an hour' and that this rate would be increased. 'Although some 500 orders are still outstanding, it is hoped that the delivery situation will be considerably relieved during the next few weeks,' wrote the magazine.*

There was a further element to Lord's resignation, which will be discussed in a future chapter; suffice it to say that such high-level disputes were often due to a combination of genuine and contrived grievances, brewed up in the cauldron of Cowley's internal politics. What is undoubtedly the case is that letting Lord go was a dreadful misjudgement on the part of Lord Nuffield. For Kimpton Smallbone, the Morris Motors company secretary, the departure of Lord constituted the biggest loss the firm had ever suffered. In his opinion, Lord "had saved the business" – an analysis with which it is difficult to disagree. Charles Nichols of instrument supplier Smiths would later say that it had broken his heart when Lord had left Cowley. For Cecil Kimber the verdict was more positive: the exit of Lord redressed his position within the organisation, as in the resultant reshuffle he was re-appointed Managing Director of the M.G. Car Company on 30 November 1936, answerable to new group Vice-Chairman Oliver Boden, the former MD of Wolseley.

A SMALLER SISTER FOR THE TWO-LITRE

In time for the 1936 Motor Show, the next car in the series of Cowley-designed M.G. models arrived: the 1½-Litre or VA. There was graceful saloon, open four-seater or Tickford drophead coachwork, but underneath was a 1548cc pushrod engine derived from that of the Morris Twelve and Wolseley 12/48, mated to a Morris/Wolseley part-synchromesh gearbox via – until 1938 – a Morris cork-in-oil clutch of the type first seen in the Bullnose. With other key components such as the hydraulic-braked front and rear axles also derived from those found on the 12hp Morrises and Wolseleys, it all seemed a long way from the delicate overhead-cam Magnettes with their crash gearboxes, cable brakes and lightweight if fragile construction: the rolling chassis alone weighed as much as an entire four-seater N-type Magnette.

Offering a belated riposte to the 1½-litre version of the SS Jaguar, the mid-sized M.G. was most probably designed with Cecil Kimber exerting a measurable influence. In his Institution of Automobile Engineers paper *The Trend of Aesthetic Design in*

ABOVE: *SA chassis on test on the factory cinder track, in an image from M.G. brochure* Safety Fast in the Making. *Each car also received a road test.*

RIGHT: *Test reporting, in another photo from the same publication. The brochure stresses the 'individual assembly' of the cars. 'Every M.G. is hand-built, there is no conveyor to give a rigid time limit to each of the several hundred operations. The personal element enters into the building of an M.G. car more than ever at this stage and every man in the M.G. factory is a skilled craftsman,' runs the text.*

OPPOSITE: *A line-up of SAs, in an image from* Safety Fast in the Making. *The year 1937 would see record M.G. profits.* "When Kimber got a few octagons on the pushrod cars he really quite liked them – and then, of course, we got some money in the bank. I don't think we'd ever have done it under his control," *Reg Jackson observed to Wilson McComb.*

Chapter Fourteen: A Marriage Ends, a New Car Arrives

Motor Cars he concludes with a lengthy description of how the lines of the VA saloon were evolved, and says that four sample bodies were produced before the design was finalised. He also takes pains to highlight the car's most distinctive and perhaps most aesthetically debatable feature, the plain doors denuded of any moulding. All this suggests that on this particular M.G. his role was more hands-on and closer to that of William Lyons when overseeing the shaping of his SS and Jaguar bodies.

The VA, production of which began in February 1937, was talked up by the press as being a different type of M.G. in character. 'The new M.G. is designed for those who require economical high performance combined with silence and refinement,' observed *The Motor*. It developed this theme in its road-test of a tourer: dubbing the M.G. 'a car of infinite charm', it went on to comment that 'if one wanted to term it a sports model, then it would have to be classed with the new régime of silent sports motoring which is becoming so popular.'

M.G. in-house magazine *The Sports Car* went further, pronouncing the VA 'a sports car of modest dimensions and ladylike mien...a car which a wife or girl friend could be allowed to handle without grievous noises coming from the gearbox'. Such comments must have had the purists weeping into their scotch-and-sodas, because the truth wrapped up in these circumlocutions was that with a power output of 54bhp and a weight in saloon form of roughly 25cwt the new mid-sized M.G. was hardly in danger of stripping the rubber from its smart Rudge-Whitworth wire wheels.

The VA or 1½-litre had unusual plain doors without any mouldings or pressed ridges; the chassis, semi-cruciform and no longer underslung, was not shared with any other car from the Morris group.

THE M.G. 1½-LITRE OR VA

The VA evolved only in detail during its life of a something under four years. The gearbox, initially with synchromesh only on third and top, soon gained a synchronised second gear; the 'wet' clutch was replaced by a dry-plate unit in early 1938; a fully counterbalanced crankshaft was fitted from later in 1938, followed towards the end of production by a move to shell bearings. Additionally the drophead was given a revised and wider body ahead of the 1939 model year. Manufacture ended soon after the outbreak of war, probably by October 1939.

Although latter-day enthusiasts were for a long time as snooty as the 1930s marque purists about the VA, the buying public were less picky: first-year sales of 913 cars, increasing to 1,045 in 1938, compare more than favourably with the 945 N-type and KN Magnettes made between early 1934 and late 1936.

As for the tepid performance, Abingdon's little-publicised response was to fit a bored-out 14hp engine of 1708cc capacity. Achieved by using pistons common to the later six-cylinder 2.6-litre WA, and complemented by a high-lift camshaft, this resulted in a 63bhp power output. These engines were used in the works-supported 'Cream Crackers' trials TAs but also in some of the 1½-litres used by the police. One of Kimber's personal VAs had the 14hp unit, and it seems the odd private customer also profited from this never-advertised option.

In common with its bigger sisters, special bodies were, with the odd exception, no longer fitted to the VA chassis. A single car was given drophead coachwork by Reinbolt & Christé of Switzerland, and at least two 'woody' shooting-brakes are known – one being used by M.G. record-breaker Goldie Gardner.

With 2,407 VAs made, against 2,738 of the six-cylinder SA and 3,003 of the TA, the Abingdon mid-ranger amply justified its place in the range – even if pre-war sales of 7,285 SS Jaguar 1½-litres show who was really making the running in this class. Had production begun sooner, perhaps that gap would have been closed at least a little.

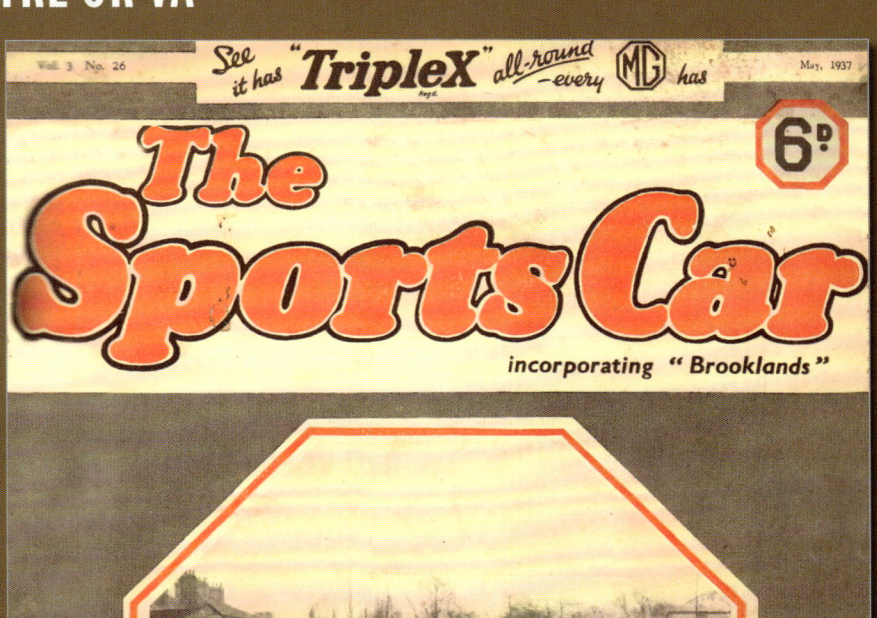

Duo-tone paint finishes were available on the VA saloon and drophead, and many saloons were painted in duo-tone green. Cars in metallic grey had wings in a non-metallic finish, to aid subsequent touching-in.

CREAM CRACKERS AND MUSKETEERS

At the same time as the nature of M.G. cars was being redefined, the company's approach to competition was also taking a new direction. Trialling was still a popular form of motor sport, and one that received good coverage in the motoring press. Kimber had of course been a keen practitioner himself, and was well aware of the potential publicity dividends – not least as M.G. cars were a dominant presence on any British trial one might care to name. But as individual privateers the various M.G. drivers had less media impact than they might have had if competing under a single banner.

Espousing this logic, in 1934 three enthusiasts, Maurice Toulmin, Jack Bastock and 'Mac' MacDermid, put together a team of J2s. By the end of the year, the trio having moved on to PAs, the cars were painted in the same cream with brown wings as George Eyston's racers and became known as the 'Cream Crackers'. Although the drivers owned the cars, the venture was supported financially by the factory and the 'Cream Crackers' were regarded as an official M.G. team. In a similar process a team of three ex-TT Magnette NEs were campaigned as the 'Three Musketeers'.

More than twice as many VA saloons as tourers would be built – 1,238 against 591; a drophead (564 made) would later join the range. The tourer body was sourced from Morris Bodies Branch.

Captained by an Abingdon garage-owner, all the drivers were M.G. employees and the factory again supported the team.

In 1936 the two teams dominated British trials, the 'Cream Crackers' in supercharged PBs and the 'Three Musketeers' in supercharged 1408cc cars based on the L-type Magna chassis. In both cases the factory built the cars, and in addition the works extended support to regional M.G. Car Club trials teams. For 1937 both teams would use unblown TAs while for 1938 the 'Cream Crackers' would run TAs fitted with a VA engine (subsequently bored out to 1708cc) and the 'Three Musketeers' supercharged TAs with a Laystall crankshaft. All this was achieved at minimal cost to Abingdon, something that doubtless won the approval of Lord Nuffield. As the M.G. presence on British and Continental race tracks quietly tapered downwards, Kimber was masterfully succeeding in keeping the marque visible in motor sport.

TOP: *One of the 1936 'Cream Crackers' team in action; although not an official works venture, the cars were supported by the factory.*

RIGHT: *Archie Langley with Aramis, one of the cars forming the 'Three Musketeers' trials team, with cups garnered by the summer of 1936, when this photo was taken. (National Motor Museum)*

SEPARATION FOR RENE – AND A NEW LIFE IN BOURNEMOUTH

Rene had recovered sufficiently by the end of 1936 for Kimber to organise a family Christmas at the Palace Court Hotel in Bournemouth. During the holiday Kimber took his daughters skating, where they met John Walkinton, who became a close family friend and would marry Gillie's daughter Bobbie. She later recalled how Kimber and Walkinton took to each other at once, after Kimber gave the young Walkinton a cigarette which exploded in the middle, one of his favourite jokes[1]. At the Christmas Eve dance, meanwhile, Betty met her eventual husband Dean Delamont, at that time a reporter on the local newspaper.

Six years older than Betty, Delamont, the future head of the RAC Motor Sport Division, had left school at 14 to join *The Bournemouth Daily Echo* and not long after his 17th birthday he had become

---

[1] "He was childish, in a lot of ways. Simple things amused him. I'd never seen him laugh so much as when he went to see *Charlie's Aunt* – he was roaring with laughter," Vernon Kimber told Wilson McComb.

the paper's motoring correspondent, apparently because he was the only reporter with a driving licence. "Dean's mother was very severe Plymouth Brethren – only cold food on Sunday, and no reading, no nothing. His father, who wasn't Plymouth Brethren, although he went along with it, was accounts clerk at the paper," relates Sara Delamont. "Bournemouth was very fashionable but a bit raffish. People with a lot of glamour and money would come down for the weekend to the Royal Bath Hotel. Maybe Dean was going to the hotel and finding out who was staying that weekend and writing snappy paragraphs about glamorous people. I really don't know. Jean remembered Dean with enormous affection – he treated her as if she were a grown-up person, listening to her carefully and making sure they did things she enjoyed. She used to say that when she went down to the flat Dean was always lovely to her."

Given the strains of his personal life, Kimber was doubtless relieved to take a break abroad in March 1937 and depart for the Geneva Motor Show with a prototype VA, in the company of old friends Russel Chiesman and managing editor of *The Autocar* Ernest Appleby. Bobbie was staying with a family in Heidelberg, so he paid her a visit and also took her to meet racing driver Bobby Kohlrausch and his wife. Kimber took the same VA to Scotland for a fishing trip and on a holiday in Devon with Gillie and Gladys, and he clearly had an affection for the mid-sized saloon, running examples as his personal car right up to his death, rather than a more flashy model.

ABOVE: *John Walkinton was briefly Betty's boyfriend but would end up marrying Bobbie Dewar; this image dates from 1937.*

LEFT: *Ernest Appleby, who accompanied Kimber on the VA trip and on that in the WA the preceding year. 'Our Managing Editor E.J. Appleby was…a professional journalist probably trained on newspapers. He wrote a weekly column under the pseudonym The Scribe… Appleby was a big fan of Kimber, saw him often, drove his cars, and if you researched those columns now you would learn much of Kim's doings,' writes former* The Autocar *journalist John Dugdale.*

OPPOSITE: *George Propert's daughter poses with an M.G. VA drophead; the body was again by Tickford.*

A VA tourer photographed by Kimber in Derbyshire, during a rally organised by the North-Western Centre of the M.G. Car Club.

In the spring of 1937 Cecil and Rene Kimber separated. Quite possibly this was not a legal separation, but it was most definitely a geographical one. Kimber moved to the Crown and Thistle hotel in Abingdon, while Rene and Jean and Betty settled into a flat in Lilliput, just outside the Bournemouth suburb of Parkstone.

'My sister, now 17½, no doubt feeling it was better to face facts, told me long afterwards that she thought she was doing the best thing in persuading my mother to accept the situation,' writes Jean. '[She] swept my mother off to a sunny flat overlooking Poole Harbour, and enrolled herself at Poole Art School. This step freed my father from the burden of my mother's care, and, incidentally, ensured a great deal of freedom for my sister.

'I only learned about all this in detail when my sister, now a qualified driver, came to fetch me for the Spring half-term to take me down to the new flat where she had already installed my mother. My sister had organised my transfer to the boarding house at Oxford High School, where I had been a day girl for two terms in the autumn of 1936; she bought all my required clothes without telling me what they were for. My father informed me I was to be a boarder on the afternoon of the day I was due at the boarding house with my trunk.

'Curiously, I did not consciously resent this decision at the time, though I was very unhappy at first[2]. I accepted that my father thought it would be best. He was quite Victorian in his discipline, and I had a healthy respect for the spanking I would get if

---

[2] Rather a different perspective on Kimber's approach to Jean's education is provided by her son Peter. 'He sent my mother to boarding school where she was bullied and unhappy, and then he did nothing to ensure that she went to university, which she should have done,' he says.

Russel Chiesman and the prototype VA in Rouen, during the March 1937 trip to Germany and Switzerland; as a German-speaker, Chiesman was a handy companion on these jaunts.

ABOVE: *The duo-tone green VA beside the Basilique de Vézelay in France's Yonne département.*

TOP RIGHT: *Kimber inspects the autobahn near Darmstadt: the VA was reported as maintaining an average of nearly 70mph when the group sampled a section of the new German motorway system that Hitler was rapidly constructing.*

RIGHT: *Outside the Heidelberg house of a Dr Horsch, with whom Bobbie may have been staying. The VA combined, said Ernest Appleby, 'the attributes of both sports car and touring car'.*

TOP LEFT: *The VA on France's Col de Faucille, in the Jura mountains. After 1723 miles of very mixed driving the overall fuel consumption of the M.G. worked out at 23mpg.*

ABOVE: *Another sight on the seven-country trip: one of the castles on the River Neckar.*

RIGHT: *Michelstadt, a town in the Odenwald between Darmstadt and Heidelberg.*

I rebelled[3]. He no longer spanked me at 12 years old, but his word was still law, which meant it was to be obeyed without question.'

Jean had fond memories of this time. 'The new flat was marvellous: very light with sunshine flooding in all day and a stunning view of one of the most beautiful harbours in England. At first, my mother seemed to take on a new lease on life. She had ARX 710, one of the new 1½-litres[4]…She enjoyed exploring the Dorset coast and reading guide books about its history. My future brother-in-law, Dean Delamont, was extremely good to her and she blossomed in his cheerful company. She was also stimulated by Betty's friends from art school.'

BETTY KIMBER AND THE CHALLENGES OF PARENTHOOD

The memories of this period passed down by Betty to her daughter Sara Delamont are less idyllic than those of her sister. "What made her really angry about her childhood was that she hadn't been allowed to go to Oxford. She'd been sent down to Bournemouth to look after her mother. The way she told it, Kimber packed Rene off so he could live with Gillie, whom he was flaunting, with her sister, all over Oxford. He had sent my mother to Oxford High School for Girls – a very intellectual, hothouse sort of school, so she must have been clever. She won a scholarship to St Anne's College, to read English, and he wouldn't let her go, because he didn't believe in educated women.

"She told me that when I was 16 or 17. Not being allowed to take up that Oxford scholarship was for her a burning, blinding injustice. She felt that she had not been properly educated, that if she's been to university she'd have been a better person. She felt a real resentment, as she had passionately wanted to go to Oxford – although I can imagine that she would have been a very rebellious undergraduate. I was brought up with a narrative that my great-grandfather had stopped my grandmother from going to university and then my grandfather had forbidden my mother from going to university. From when I was in nappies the abiding message I had was that nothing would stop me going to university."

It wasn't just her father with whom Betty was in conflict when in Parkstone, says Delamont: in addition Rene had social aspirations for her elder daughter that were never going to be welcomed. "They had a big difference in opinion because Rene wanted my mother to be a deb and be presented at court, and she thought the idea dreadful. Rene was apparently very cross with her about that. She had wanted her to be a deb and have her marry well – and my mother had no time for that[5]."

In all this there is an element of that perpetual trap for parents: not adapting to an offspring's fragile transition from childhood to being a young adult. Jean picked up on this when she came across an entry in her father's sailing diary for 7 August 1937. 'Rene insisting on them returning for her birthday which was a flop. Kids very disappointed,' writes Kimber. 'The word "kid" applied to a daughter of nearly 18, who was not only attending art school full-time, making all her own clothes, and all the soft furnishings

Betty in a portrait from March 1937.

---

[3] According to daughter Sara Delamont, neither of the girls was spared the odd spanking when they were young. "He certainly spanked my mother – pulled her pants down and spanked her with a hairbrush. I think he thought of her like a boy."

[4] This is almost certainly incorrect, as ARX 710 was only registered on 7 January 1938. If Rene did use the car, it would only have been for a very brief period; the photos in this chapter suggest in fact that the VA she drove when living at Parkstone was DEL 303 – this being a Bournemouth registration.

[5] Cecil Kimber also had hopes for his elder daughter's future, says Sara Delamont. "What my mother always said – the story I always remember from my earliest childhood – is that Lord Nuffield and Kim thought it would be lovely if she married the young man who was Nuffield's favourite nephew. Kim thought it would be wonderful if they were to fall in love. But they had no interest in each other. Nuffield set the nephew up in a travel-agency business – I don't think he was interested in cars at all."

Betty on a horse in 1937, at the Abingdon Riding School; as a teenager she was a keen rider.

Kimber with Jean (and black cat), in 1937 at Bucklers Hard, where his new boat was kept.

ABOVE: *A joyful Betty in 1937; the notion she had a grim time looking after her ailing mother needs to be nuanced.*

TOP LEFT: *A spot of make-up going on, on a Dorset beach: at nearly 18 years old, Betty was now a young lady, something her father seemingly found difficult to assimilate. Kimber agreed to Betty enrolling as an architecture student at an art school in Bournemouth.*

LEFT: *With the author's apologies if he has misidentified the subject of this photo, this is believed to be Sybil Leek, who became a friend to Betty when she was living in the Parkstone flat.*

Dean Delamont (left) brought laughter to life in Parkstone, as this happy image shows. It is surely one of the last photographs taken of Rene Kimber.

Chapter Fourteen: A Marriage Ends, a New Car Arrives

TOP: *Rene by the VA saloon she used when in Bournemouth; she was no longer the 1920s flapper with the cloche hat.*

ABOVE: *This photograph is the only one that has surfaced that shows Rene Kimber wearing spectacles.*

RIGHT: *Betty (at the wheel) and Rene in the VA; the car's sliding roof was part of a VA saloon's standard equipment.*

Chapter Fourteen: A Marriage Ends, a New Car Arrives

for her bedroom, but also caring for a dying woman and a child of 12, is very revealing. In this piece of self-deception lay the seeds of future conflict,' Jean comments.

Kimber was also in all likelihood unaware of some of the burdens he had indirectly placed on Betty's shoulders. One wonders, too, what he would have thought had he known that his daughter was consorting with white witch Sybil Leek, who in her later life was to become High Priestess of the Horsa Coven in the New Forest and a media celebrity known for walking through the Hampshire village of Burley in a black cape, with her raven 'Mr Hotfoot Jackson' perched on her head.

"As her unwilling carer and companion, my mother was dragged around a succession of gloomy churches to indulge Rene's religious mania, something she hated and resented very much," says son Jonathan. "My mother was already some sort of pioneering neo-pagan in her own heart and soul, and used to bus off from Poole to Burley whenever she could to hang out with witchy Sybil Leek, who must have been about 20 or 21 at the time. She found much respite in Sybil's company, but stopped short of actually joining the Horsa Coven, though Sybil apparently encouraged her to do so."

WIND IN THE SAILS: A NEW BOAT ARRIVES

In April 1937 Kimber bought a new boat, *Fairwind*. 'My father had obviously been doing some homework during the winter. He had discovered that a pilot cutter was designed to keep the sea in all weathers, hove-to on station, so that the pilots could wait for their ships in comparative comfort. This type of boat did not make a good cruising yacht, however, as she needed a gale to move her,' writes Jean. His new boat, she recounts, was a rather more dynamic affair, designed by Dr Harrison Butler, a famous eye specialist, 'who drew the lines of handy little yachts that really sailed and yet took care of their crews in bad weather'.

Constructed of copper-fastened pitch pine on oak, *Fairwind* had been built just a year or two before at Barton-on-Humber. 'My father and my stepmother were sitting on Cracknore Hard, just outside Southampton, at 11am when they saw in *Yachting World* that she was for sale, so they drove up to Hull, catching the last ferry across the Humber at 7pm, and phoned the owner from a hotel. Another buyer was expected the next morning, so they gulped down their dinner and dashed round to see the owner and his family,' recounts Jean.

It was too dark to see the boat that night, but Kimber and Gillie retired for the night with plans and drawings. The next day Kimber paid £350 for *Fairwind* and had her brought down by rail to Southampton. 'He and my stepmother were so excited that they climbed aboard when she was still on the railway truck in the siding and had a picnic in the cockpit.[6]'

Both daughters were to have their own boats down at Parkstone, as Jean recalls. 'Betty had her 12ft Lymington scow transferred from Abingdon to Parkstone Sailing Club, and took me out in it… Later, my father gave me the pram dinghy from his new boat… and I used to fish with a handline out in deep water. Typical of those days, nobody worried about me. Life jackets were unknown for yachtsmen, let alone for children; it was accepted that I knew what I was doing in boats.'

By this stage Kimber's daughters had been introduced to *Fairwind*, aboard which they spent a week, including sailing to Cowes. 'His Sailing Diary details every day of that not very adventurous week, judged by the standard of most cruising people nowadays, but to me it was all wonderful. My stepsister agrees that he had a gift for making simple things magical. We became very fond of Mr Downer, the Harbour Master, and his wife and daughter, from whom we collected our milk and letters, and also of Frank Hendy, the shipwright,' writes Jean.

'My father still had much to learn, but he had very little time off from work to learn it. He was not, perhaps, the most competent

---

[6] Jean is reprising here the story told by her father in *The Patient's Condition Remains Unchanged*, a short article written in 1944 or thereabouts for *Yachting World* magazine.

yachtsman, but he coped with all the engine breakdowns with great patience...From his diary, he seemed to go aground a great deal, but then he was not armed with an echo sounder, a modern diesel engine, and up-to-date charts and pilot books compiled specially for the small-boat sailor. There were no Yachtmaster courses, or navigation classes in Further Education Colleges all over England, which have helped us so much. What he did have was a real love of boats and the sea, which he transmitted to me. I can never sufficiently thank him for this. Typically, he had the patience to teach himself to splice a rope, and then to teach me.'

The Abingdon Sailing Club and its scows. Kimber had been a founder member of Abingdon Sailing Club in 1936, and his dinghy had originally been kept there after his daughters had gone to live in Parkstone.

THESE TWO PAGES & FOLLOWING: *It is difficult to be certain of the date of this sequence of photos depicting a trip to Dartmoor in a VA by Kimber, accompanied by Gillie and Gladys: Jean attributes it to 1938 but the author inclines more to 1937. Certainly the car, here outside The Drewe Arms in Drewsteignton, is the prototype used for the March 1937 trip to Germany and Switzerland.*

Chapter Fourteen: A Marriage Ends, a New Car Arrives

Chapter Fourteen: A Marriage Ends, a New Car Arrives

Chapter Fourteen: A Marriage Ends, a New Car Arrives

LEFT: Fairwind, *Kimber's second boat, which he purchased in April 1937 for £350: as he had bought* Falcon *for £195 and sold her for £295, he only had another £60 to find.*

TOP LEFT: *Kimber engrossed in writing perhaps the ship's log for* Fairwind. *He was gradually advancing in his skill as a yachtsman.*

ABOVE (BOTH): *Betty and Jean on* Fairwind – *it was known as a 'Bogle' and was rigged as a Bermudian cutter, with a tall triangular mainsail that was only just becoming widely accepted, and two foresails.*

THE FIGURES START TO ADD UP

The 1937 Motor Show brought no changes of import for M.G., which now had three complementary models in production. The real news of the autumn was Goldie Gardner coming within a whisker of achieving 150mph during a session of record-breaking in Germany, on the Frankfurt autobahn. Gardner had been racing M.G.s since 1931 and in 1934 had bought the single-seater K3 successfully campaigned by Ronnie Horton, another M.G. stalwart. After capturing two up-to-1100cc records in June, on the same stretch of autobahn, and a further four later that month at Montlhéry, Gardner now raised four of these Class G records even higher. This achievement would be the catalyst for one of Abingdon's most famous projects.

By the end of 1937 two and a half years had passed since M.G. had been brought under the wing of Cowley. The results were now evident. "We became much more financially viable," John Thornley told the author. "I don't think anybody ever realised the extent to which we were running into expense, as the models never ran for long enough." The figures bear this out. For the year ending 31 August 1936 net profit was £16,033, the best since 1932. The following year (this time up to the end of December 1937), net profit rose to a record £25,436, helped by both the SA and VA being in full production alongside the TA Midget.

But there is a twist to this. The accounts for 1937 record that 'The directors recommend that a dividend of £25,000 free of Income

Tax be declared, leaving a balance of £7,758.2s.9d to be carried forward to next year.' In other words, instead of ploughing the additional profit back into the company, most of it went into the shareholders' pockets. That's business, one might say. All the same, it is worth recording that in 1932 all profit after tax – amounting to £23,900 – had been carried forward. Maybe, though, Lord Nuffield and his fellow shareholders felt they should get some return on their investment. Nuffield's personal holdings company Morris Industries Ltd had after all basically kept M.G. going in the 1930 to 1935 period, with a continual infusion of loans. This would persist, with Abingdon owing a cumulative total of £81,000 by October 1938.

ABOVE: *Goldie Gardner's ex-Horton single-seater on the Frankfurt autobahn. In 1936 he had already lapped Brooklands at 124.4mph in the car, taking the up-to-1100cc lap record. (Goldie Gardner courtesy Mike Jones)*

OPPOSITE: *On this first visit to Germany, Gardner took the up-to-1100cc class records for the flying kilometre and flying mile, the latter at 148.5mph. (Goldie Gardner courtesy Mike Jones)*

RECORD-BREAKING IN GERMANY – AND A LIFE RENEWED

The year 1938 would prove a momentous one both for Cecil Kimber and for the M.G. company. In the case of the car company, it saw what has to be regarded as one of the biggest publicity coups achieved by Kimber: the creation of a streamlined record-breaker for Goldie Gardner, who then went on to secure a number of speed records in Germany up until the outbreak of war. On a personal level, meanwhile, the genesis of the Gardner streamliner would coincide with the final chapter in Kimber's marriage to Rene.

RENE'S DEATH, AND RE-MARRIAGE FOR CECIL KIMBER

Over the last months of 1937, the health of Kimber's estranged wife further deteriorated. In the spring of 1938 Rene was persuaded, against explicit advice from her Oxford doctor, to go into Poole General Hospital for a bypass operation of the colon. At the time this was an innovative procedure, so the doctor's caution is understandable; there were not, as there are today, drug treatments for the problem.

After coming through the operation quite well, Rene had an unexpected relapse and died on 21 April; her death certificate gives the cause as ulcerous colitis[1]. 'My father came to fetch us, and left me at the Crown and Thistle while he and Betty attended the funeral,' writes Jean. 'It was thought, quite wrongly, that children should be shielded from grief and death. I have always been sorry that I was not allowed to go and say goodbye properly.'

---

[1] Today more commonly known as ulcerative colitis.

TOP: *Kimber with Bobbie at the Pangbourne fishing hut The Retreat, in 1938 or possibly earlier.*

RIGHT: *Bobbie, Gillie and Gladys, seen at the same time.*

OPPOSITE: *The Gardner streamliner on the autobahn, streaking by the Zeppelin shed. (Goldie Gardner courtesy Mike Jones)*

Gladys (left) and Gillie; the lady behind Gillie is believed to be her mother.

The crisis in Czechoslovakia that would ultimately lead to the Munich agreement was now brewing. Convinced, according to Jean, that war with Germany was coming, Kimber abandoned his plan to wait until his daughters were older before he married Gillie. Now his idea was for a swift and essentially secret marriage. He planned to go to Lee-on-Solent, near Portsmouth, with Gillie and her mother, and live there for the statutory period necessary to gain residential qualifications, so that they could be married in Fareham. They would then honeymoon on the new boat. Things did not go quite as had been intended.

One day, on the road between Southampton and Fareham, Kimber lost control of the M.G. Two-Litre he was driving, described by Jean as 'an experimental model with riveted, not welded front suspension'. At 70mph, she writes, 'the steering literally came apart and the car veered off the road and hit a bank.' Kimber

The SA saloon in which Kimber had an accident just before his marriage to Gillie. It seems the car was fitted with experimental independent front suspension.

Tommy Wisdom and wife Elsie entered the 1937 Mille Miglia in this M.G. SA, which is believed to be the car in which Kimber had his pre-wedding accident.

broke his nose, Gillie had minor cuts and bruises, but her mother was quite seriously injured, breaking several ribs and cutting her head open. It was a traumatic moment, not just on account of the injuries all three incurred but because Gillie was terrified, according to Jean, that news of the proposed marriage would leak out. In the end it remained a secret, and when Kimber's future mother-in-law was out of danger, the marriage duly went ahead on 25 June, witnessed by Bobbie and Gladys; only a few trusted friends such as Goldie Gardner were in the know.

The boat, being worked on at a yard on Hayling Island, was not ready in time, so the honeymoon was spent on land, after which the couple returned to the Crown and Thistle in Abingdon. Betty remained at the Parkstone flat for a while, but by the autumn she was a full-time student at the London School of Interior Decoration in St Johns Wood and living, it appears, in London.

Returning to Kimber's accident, the rather vague reference to 'riveted, not welded front suspension' on the car is most intriguing. It is quite feasible that this may have been some form of independent suspension. For M.G. this would have been a logical step forward, as its cars at the time all retained an old-fashioned beam front axle on semi-elliptic leaf springs.

In possible corroboration is a 1940 column 'For M.G. Owners' in *The Motor* that takes a look at potential post-war developments for the marque. 'Much research work has also been done in springing. It need no longer be kept secret that several experimental cars were built with independent front-wheel suspension,' writes the magazine. 'Some of them had torsion-rod layouts on the general lines of the R-type Midget. Others had more conventional systems.'

In the case of the Kimber car, the mention of riveted suspension

Bobbie, photographed on Hayling Island in 1938, most likely at the time of the marriage.

may well be a reference to the long control arms of a Girling-type independent front end. An arrangement of which Kimber particularly approved (see page 466), its installation in an SA features in an entry under the number EX158 in the Abingdon experimental drawing register, making the use of such a suspension in the Kimber car a very strong possibility.

ADVERTISING WITH THE PERSONAL TOUCH – AND A NEW BIG M.G.

There was now a new advertising campaign for M.G. cars, devised by Crawfords, who were responsible for the advertising for up-market clothing firms such as Simpsons and Daks. Each advertisement took the form of a signed message from Cecil Kimber, an astute way of putting a human face to the cars and hinting at the clubby intimacy that Kimber sought to foster with M.G. customers. Within the Morris organisation the advertisements were however regarded in some quarters with a different eye, being seen as an exercise in self-promotion. As will be discussed in a future chapter, the campaign would turn around and bite Kimber.

August 1938 saw Cecil Kimber's last sailing holiday with both his daughters, the trio spending a fortnight on *Fairwind* – including an unofficial race against its designer, Dr Harrison Butler, in his latest boat *Vindilis*, Kimber being delighted to meet the designer he so much admired. Gillie, meanwhile, spent much of the time in lodgings on dry land, so she could visit her mother, who was still in hospital after the pre-wedding accident.

The same month saw the announcement of a new M.G. model. Since the entry into production of the Two-Litre, principal rival SS had moved on. For the 1937 season its Jaguars had received countless improvements, and then for 1938 had changed over to a slightly bigger all-steel body on a new and stiffer chassis. Making things worse for the competition, a potent new 3½-litre model had joined the range, the 1½-litre had gained a 1776cc overhead-valve engine, and a drophead body had been introduced. The new

THE M.G. 2.6-LITRE OR WA

The WA was a mildly revised SA, nothing more; at one stage there had been thought of moving to the Wolseley 25hp engine to offer a more direct rival to the 3½-litre SS Jaguar, but perhaps thankfully this idea was rapidly nipped in the bud. Instead the new M.G. used an overbored 2561cc version of the 18hp SA straight-six, developing 95.5bhp; now with a counterbalanced shell-bearing crankshaft and an oil cooler, the engine was mated to a conventional dry clutch.

The body was essentially the same as that of the SA, albeit now equipped with a secondary bulkhead in steel-faced plywood in response to the SA's unfortunate habit of excessive engine heat frying its occupants' feet. The rear – sitting on a wider and more robust axle – was however pulled out at the bottom by 2in each side, and the base of the scuttle moved outwards by a little less.

The bonnet was also extended, purely in the interests of looking more impressive, and this brought with it a taller and more vee'd radiator shell. Doubtless for similar reasons the spare wheel migrated from a vertical position exposed on the tail to a new emplacement on the nearside wing – with the option of a second side-mount if you wanted to be really flash. A final detail was a 'dress guard' attached to the rear doors and overlapping the rear wing; this was intended to avoid passengers' clothes being dirtied when entering or exiting the car via the narrow-at-the-bottom rear doors.

With around 3cwt of extra weight, the WA wasn't much faster than the SA, but it was a better car.

Series production began in November/December 1938 and just 369 were made before the onset of war stopped manufacture. The tally was 265 as saloons, 86 as dropheads, and nine as tourers (with all but one of these going to the Glasgow police); additionally Swiss importer J. H. Keller had Reinbolt & Christé body one WA as a drophead and another as a four-door open tourer. One further car was supplied in chassis form, but further details are not known.

The dashboard of the WA marked a return to octagon-mania. The exuberantly stylish interior also featured octagon-embellished door furniture and (on the saloon) an octagon-inscribed roof lamp. In its bespoke hand-built feel the big M.G. genuinely did have the aura of a cut-price Alvis or Bentley. (Author's collection)

M.G. 2.6-Litre or WA was Abingdon's response to the 3½-litre SS Jaguar. An extrapolation of the Two-Litre, it was available as a saloon, a drophead or – briefly, as only nine or so were made – as a Charlesworth four-door tourer. If, however, you couldn't reach to the £450 that was asked for a WA saloon, the SA remained available in all three body styles, and gained many of the WA's detail enhancements.

FAMILY LIFE RE-FOUND

By autumn the secrecy surrounding Kimber's wedding had been cast aside – and Jean had accepted Gillie's new role. 'I too fell under her spell and I remained under it until her death in 1980. My stepmother was described by her third husband, Eric Graham, as the kindest and most generous woman he had ever met. She was a true mother to me, not hesitating to be strict when it was necessary, but usually managing with humour to point out that there were better ways to do things! She talked to me as if I were grown up, and let me work through all my feelings about the tragedy of my own mother's early death.'

The change in her father was amazing, Jean writes. 'I could not believe all the laughter, the teasing and fun that went on constantly, which was perfectly normal for Bobbie. She had never known anything else.' This was something his younger daughter had also described to Wilson McComb. "He used to be so grim, so stern. I can remember him sitting there for ages, not saying a word," she recalled. "He changed so much after he married my stepmother, I sometimes felt I couldn't recognize the same man. She was very good for him. Liberated him. He was more relaxed, happier. I loved Gillie on sight – she had that sort of charm and spirit.'

All this was taking part against the backdrop of the Czechoslovakian crisis, which would reach a climax at the end of September with the Munich agreement that forced the Czechs to accept the German annexation of key parts of the country. Having been whisked out of Germany, according to her daughter Easter, lest she got caught up in the Hitler Youth movement, Bobbie was working in London for the Midland Bank. As she recalls in her memoir, Kimber seemed to panic.

'Kim gave strict orders to myself and anyone else in the family working in London that if war started and things were difficult we must start walking for home and he would find us on the way. It didn't quite happen that way for me, but more dramatically. I was working in a bank in the City of London, and I suddenly received a telephone call: "This is University Motors here. Mr Cecil Kimber says you are to resign from your job, pack your belongings and be ready to leave London at 6.45pm, when Mr Dean Delamont[2] will pick you up and drive you home." All other bank employees were making plans to stick to their posts, come what might, but I knew Kim was not a man to be defied, and I was out of the place in ten minutes. My chauffeur frightened the life out of me all the way to Oxford...'

When the threat of an imminent war receded[3], Bobbie secured a job working for the organisers of the London Motor Show, in its second year at the new venue of Earl's Court. 'I went with Kim to my one and only M.G. Motor Show dinner-and-dance, and what a thrill it was for me. There were some very well-known names in the party of about 40 who had a traditional breakfast with Kim in his hotel at 5.00am, including a rather shy 18-year-old who partnered my stepsister...and whose name was Donald Campbell[4].[...]

'We went to a vaudeville show at one of the big London theatres that week too; Kim knew one of the comedians and went backstage

---

[2] By this stage Kimber had apparently taken on Delamont as a press officer or similar.

[3] As will be discussed, Kimber's attitude fluctuated as to whether or not there would be a war. But he did want to make sure that M.G. was suitably prepared for the eventuality. Accordingly, Reg Jackson was dispatched to the Gloster aeroplane factory to familiarise himself with the government inspection standards that might need to be applied to work on ministry contracts secured by Abingdon.

[4] Betty's dancing partner Donald Campbell was the son of Sir Malcolm Campbell, and would follow in his father's footsteps as a record-breaker.

to see him. During one of the comedy sketches the hero exhorted the audience "How shall I save my darling from the clutches of this villain?" Kim's friend shouted from sidestage "Buy an M.G. Midget!" and our delight was complete. At that time, it seemed fame indeed.'

PUBLICITY COUP: RECORD-BREAKING WITH GOLDIE GARDNER

Not long after the Motor Show junketings came the media blizzard occasioned by Goldie Gardner's record-breaking in Germany. Gardner had no qualms about using Nazi Germany as the location for his record-breaking, and in his book *Magic MPH* he takes pains to stress how helpful and hospitable were the Germans during his visits to the country. His attitude was at odds with that of George Eyston, whose relationship with Kimber had cooled because of just this issue, according to John Dugdale.

'What had happened was that he had got the Magic Midget up to these remarkable speeds, when Kimber went and sold the car to the German driver Bobby Kohlrausch, who was also an M.G. distributor in Germany. George felt offended because of his very close personal association with this car; also he had a strong – shall we say British – feeling about dictatorships. When in Italy for the 1933 Mille Miglia he had pointedly not met Mussolini with the rest of the team. His experience as a young man in the terrible trench warfare of the Western Front in World War I never left him…He could not take this Kohlrausch incident and he never drove for Kimber again. Looking back there is some justification for his feelings. Kohlrausch took George's record away, at 140mph, and the Magic Midget finished up in Mercedes-Benz's racing department for examination[5].'

---

[5] This is also said by Kimber, in his article *The Future of Motor Racing* in *The Autocar* of 21 January 1944. 'From reliable information I was able to obtain, there is no doubt the new 1500cc Mercedes Grand Prix racer was, in effect, two banks of the 750cc M.G. engine in the form of a vee-eight. It's nice to know that we can teach Germany something about racing engines,' he writes.

The Gardner project had commenced in the New Year, following an exchange of letters in December 1937 between Gardner and Lord Nuffield. This had resulted in Kimber being authorised to construct an aerodynamically-advanced new car for Gardner. The basis for the car was EX135, George Eyston's former K3-based racer. This was given a lightweight all-enveloping aluminium body drawn up by Reid Railton, who had latterly been responsible

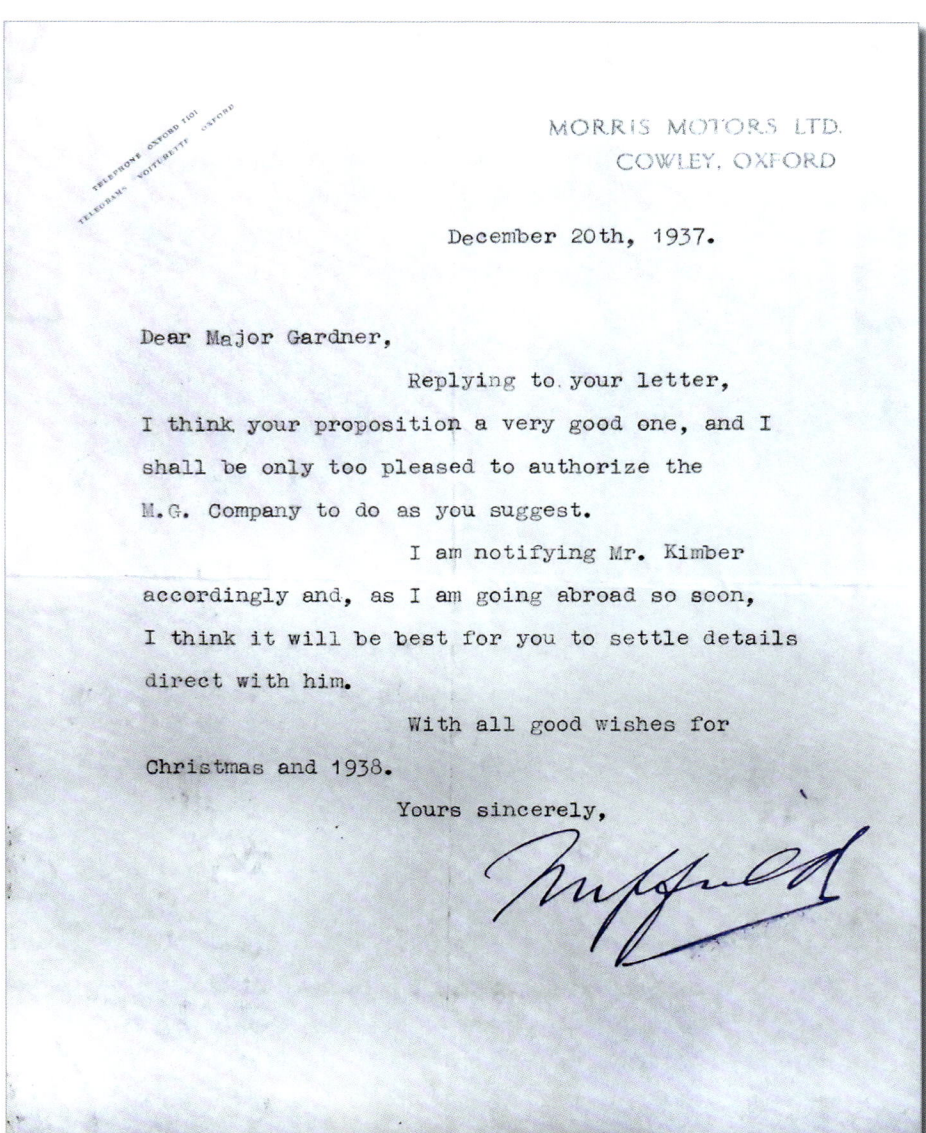

The letter from Lord Nuffield that kicked off the construction of the Gardner streamliner. (National Motor Museum)

Initial artwork by Harold Connolly shows how Reid Railton envisaged the body of the Gardner streamliner. (Goldie Gardner courtesy Mike Jones)

The chassis of EX135 was that of George Eyston's offset-driveline K3 special, but the engine, mated to an ENV pre-selector gearbox, came from Gardner's ex-Horton single-seater; it ended up developing 193.5bhp from just 1086cc. (Goldie Gardner courtesy Mike Jones)

ABOVE: The Duralumin body frame weighed just 52lb – and the completed alloy-skinned body only 228lb. *(Goldie Gardner, courtesy Mike Jones)*

TOP LEFT: At Frankfurt, Syd Enever behind the car with Reid Railton (in sunglasses). The body design was produced under patents registered to Hungarian aerodynamicist Paul Jaray. *(Goldie Gardner courtesy Mike Jones)*

LEFT: Kimber looks on as Lord Nuffield tries EX135 for size. The venture was seen, John Dugdale later wrote, as demonstrating 'Lord Nuffield's ready enthusiasm for the sport' and that he was 'thoroughly keen that Britain should be adequately represented' – but not in Grand Prix racing against the Germans. *(Goldie Gardner courtesy Mike Jones)*

for the design of Sir Malcolm Campbell's Bluebird record-breakers and that of John Cobb. Meanwhile the engine to be used, the supercharged 1086cc six-cylinder unit of Gardner's ex-Horton K3, was carefully honed to develop just shy of 200bhp – an extraordinary output for such a small-capacity engine.

Built to the accompaniment of breathless press coverage and regular name-checking of Lord Nuffield as the project's backer, the car was completed in June 1938 and demonstrated at Brooklands in August. During an autumn trip to Berlin, Kimber arranged with the German authorities for use of the same stretch of Frankfurt autobahn as had been made available to Gardner the year before. The declared target was 170mph, and on 4 November Gardner achieved an average of 186.6mph over the flying kilometre and 186.5mph over the flying mile. This beat his previous year's figures by 38mph, and proved the value of the new streamlined coachwork. Next up, said Gardner at the celebratory lunch in London, would be a bid to crack 200mph – another sure publicity coup in the making.

Remaining in Germany for the record bid, Kimber took many photos on his Leica – not least of a streamlined Mercedes-Benz that was clearly of some interest – and in the course of his stay visited the Auto Union factory. This helped inform his thoughts when

Sailing was predictably one of the themes in the series of signed advertisements Kimber initiated in 1938.

THESE TWO PAGES: *A series of images from the 1938 Kimber summer holiday, shot mainly by Betty, who had developed a keen interest in photography. 'The weather was generally much more blustery than the previous year, and* Fairwind *having been lightened and re-rigged, we had some good sailing, culminating in a memorable run back in a Force 6/7 from Yarmouth,' writes Jean. 'We had developed into quite a competent crew...'*

Chapter Fifteen: Record-breaking in Germany – and a Life Renewed

he contributed to a debate in *The Motor*, following an article in a November issue entitled 'Building British Racing Cars to Beat the World'. Kimber highlighted the value of aerodynamics and signalled the Mercedes-Benz switch from a rear swing-axle to a more secure-handling de Dion suspension for its racing cars – proof that he was attentive to engineering advances on the Continent that seemed to pass by most engineers in the rather more staid British motor industry.

ABOVE: *At a glance there was little to distinguish the WA from the small-engined SA. In fact the body was slightly wider, the bonnet longer, and the radiator slightly vee'd. Details included an M.G. octagon cover for the starting-handle hole, a chrome mount for the spare wheel, octagonal sidelamps and octagon-embossed door handles, and be-trumpeted 'Mellotone' horns.*

OPPOSITE TOP: *Kimber and Laurence Pomeroy of The Motor, somewhere in Germany. Technical journalist 'Pom' was a friend, and always wrote favourably of M.G. products; he was partially responsible for the design of the twin-cam head for the R-type.*

OPPOSITE BOTTOM: *The WA from the rear, with the dress guard on the rear door just visible. The big Cowley-designed M.G. models gave nothing away in style to the competitor cars from Riley, SS and Triumph. (Author's collection)*

Chapter Fifteen: Record-breaking in Germany – and a Life Renewed

TOP (BOTH): *Gardner sets out on a warming-up run; in the white overalls is Syd Enever.*

ABOVE LEFT: *A tense Gardner in the car. Note the rectangular wheel, and how it has been removed for access to the cockpit. (Goldie Gardner courtesy Mike Jones)*

ABOVE RIGHT: *Coming in after a run. By 1937 Hitler had built 800 miles of autobahn, a figure equalled only in 1971 by Britain.*

MAIN: *Gardner and some of the team, with his personal WA. To his left are Reg Jackson (not to be confused with Robin Jackson, also present), Les Kesterton of SU Carburettors, and Syd Enever.* **INSET:** *Gardner's team mingling with some gentlemen of the press.*

Chapter Fifteen: Record-breaking in Germany – and a Life Renewed

TOP: *Pomeroy looks skywards whilst a group of curious German soldiers inspect the innards of the Gardner M.G. streamliner.*

LEFT: *All smiles from the Nazi officials who helped facilitate the record-breaking venture. (Goldie Gardner courtesy Mike Jones)*

ABOVE (BOTH): *Kimber's interest was evidently piqued by this 5½-litre supercharged Mercedes-Benz, on test ahead of the Berlin-to-Rome race.*

LEFT: *A cigarette break for Goldie Gardner and Auto Union chief engineer Robert Eberan von Eberhorst. George Eyston described Gardner as 'an extremely reserved and calm individual' and said that one journalist once observed "the only thing about Goldie that remains unbroken is his silence".*

ABOVE: *Away from the modernity of Germany's new autobahn network Kimber photographed a rather less gleaming scene at Freudenstadt in Baden-Württemberg.*

OPPOSITE LEFT: *Former Brownshirt Adolf Hühnlein, head of the Nazi motor-sports organisation, and Prince Richard of Hesse. The German civil and military authorities gave the Gardner team every possible assistance. (Goldie Gardner courtesy Mike Jones)*

OPPOSITE TOP RIGHT: *Gardner ponders the Segrave Trophy, awarded for what Pomeroy termed 'the finest technical achievement ever put up in the history of record-breaking.' (Goldie Gardner courtesy Mike Jones)*

OPPOSITE BOTTOM RIGHT: *Gardner received this album from Prince Richard of Hesse. (Goldie Gardner courtesy Mike Jones)*

PERMISSION FOR RENEWED RECORD-ATTEMPTS WAS READILY GRANTED BY THE GERMAN MOTORSPORTS-LEADER

KORPSFÜHRER A. HÜHNLEIN.

THE «ONS» (SUPREME NATIONAL OFFICE FOR THE GERMAN MOTORSPORTS) ORDERED THE NSKK-MOTOR-GROUP HESSE UNDER THE COMMAND OF

TO TAKE CHARGE OF THE ENTIRE ORGANISATION FOR THE RECORD-ATTEMPTS OF MAJOR GARDNER ON THE RECORD-SECTION OF THE REICHSAUTOBAHN NEAR FRANKFURT ON MAIN.

GROUP-LEADER **RICHARD PRINZ OF HESSE**

RACING: THE DEBATE CONTINUES

All this was part of an enduring discussion in the British press about the direction of Grand Prix racing, and what hope there might be of British participation; inevitably the main block was that the exercise looked largely futile so long as the Nazi government in Germany was prepared to invest whatever it took to achieve supremacy.

In an October 1937 issue of *The Motor* in which Kimber and Sunbeam engineer Georges Roesch discussed the new GP formula, Kimber had said that no British concern could justify the expense – and if the government put a quarter of a million pounds into a project, what benefit would the producer of the cars derive from the exercise?

In February 1939 an editorial in M.G. house magazine *The Sports Car* said that a national GP racing team would bring in prestige, but that it would take three years before there were a reliable, full-developed contender – by which time the foreign teams would have moved the game on. Where, too, would Britain get the drivers? Not only that, but publicity gained on the Continent would be of little value, and the British press probably wouldn't give the home-grown cars decent coverage – a perpetual and puzzling Cecil Kimber complaint – while a lack of success would make a British team a laughing stock.

All this was clearly echoing Kimber's speech at the January 1939 celebratory lunch for Gardner. 'On the subject of Grand Prix racing, Mr Kimber said it had become too costly for individual firms to embark on it and justify the cost to its shareholders,' the magazine related. 'It was a matter for national rather than individual expenditure. He thought we would do better to concentrate on the air, water and land speed records and that a co-operative motor trade scheme to run a team of GP cars would be foredoomed to failure. The manufacturers' subscriptions would not be repaid by extra export business.'

Intriguingly, Lord Nuffield, admittedly never shy of demanding

Gardner's congratulatory letter received from Lord Nuffield. (National Motor Museum)

state intervention to support his business interests, chimed in to suggest that maybe the time was ripe for a national team. 'Lord Nuffield was on top of his form and said he could see no reason why our Government should not subsidise racing cars in the same manner as do the governments of certain continental countries. The expense of Grand Prix racing was so tremendous that no normal concern could stand it,' he was reported as saying.

This position neatly encapsulates the ambivalence – and the pragmatism – of Nuffield's approach to M.G. and racing: if the company were not risking its money and the chances of success were reasonable, then he would support a venture. Otherwise, leave it to those with deeper pockets. Cecil Kimber had played a shrewd game, even if the withdrawal of M.G. from racing had hurt. He had known when to draw his horns in, whilst still keeping the debate alive, and instead had persuaded Nuffield to back Goldie Gardner's record-breaking, which brought in equal amounts of publicity with rather less expenditure or financial risk.

Kimber's menu from the celebratory lunch at the Trocadero Restaurant in London's Theatreland. Signatories include Oliver Lucas, John Cobb, Sir Malcolm Campbell and George Eyston.

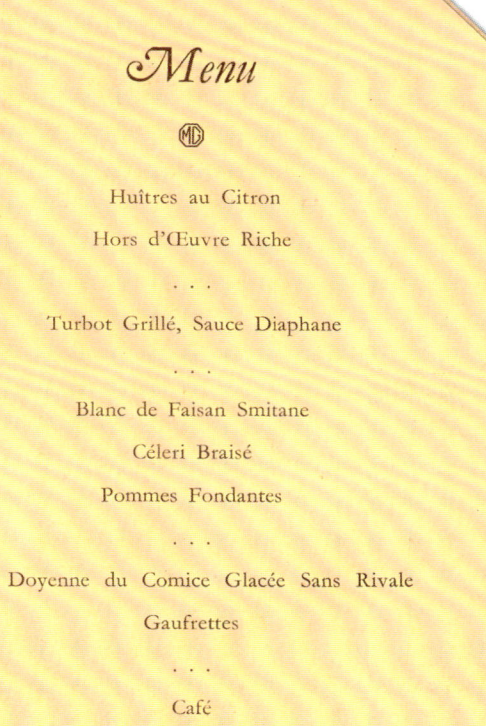

Left to right: Gardner, Nuffield, Cobb, Campbell and Kimber, celebrating Gardner's achievement. (National Motor Museum)

Chapter Fifteen: Record-breaking in Germany – and a Life Renewed

THIS PAGE: *A pamphlet was published by M.G. to celebrate the Gardner records, and there was the expected magazine advertising to capitalise on the achievement, including an advertisement with a signed message from Kimber.*

Chapter Fifteen: Record-breaking in Germany – and a Life Renewed

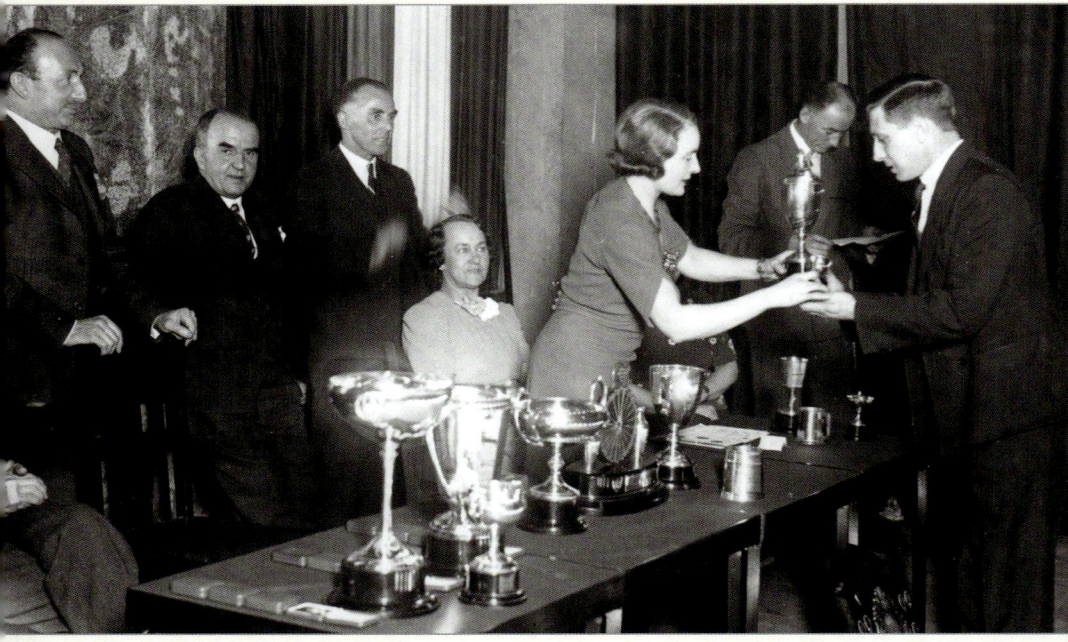

TOP: *Gillie presenting prizes at a 1938 M.G. social club function. To Kimber's right is George Propert and to his left Edward Tobin, General Manager of The Morris Garages.*

ABOVE: *Betty accompanied her father to the MGCC South-West Centre dinner-dance at the Spa Hotel, Bath. Goldie Gardner is third from the left in the front row.*

ABOVE: *Shillingford Bridge, Christmas 1938: 'We all spent Christmas at a hotel, where in typical style Kim smuggled in a canary for my mother and two white mice for Jean, all concealed by the staff until Christmas morning,' writes Bobbie, who it is believed took this photo of Kimber with Gillie and Gladys.*

OPPOSITE: *Kimber's Christmas card for 1938 featured the Gardner streamliner in embossed aluminium.*

16

SUNSHINE BEFORE THE STORM

In the spring of 1939, Cecil and Gillie Kimber moved into Kimber's first home of his own; until then, Kimber had always lived in rented accommodation. The Miller's House was in the Berkshire village of Pangbourne, where, as Jean recalls, Kimber had his stretch of fishing water. 'The Miller's House stood on an island in the River Pang, a tributary of the Thames, in the middle of Pangbourne village where I could fish for coarse fish from the garden. By walking half a mile up river through the grounds of the pumping station, which supplied Reading with water from an artesian well, we came to the stretch of the Pang that my father had owned for some time; it still had its delightful "Retreat" made out of a London bus with a thatched roof added, and was set in a large field which he had landscaped with trees. This is where he fly-fished for trout,' she writes in *The Other Tack*.

OPPOSITE: *'Kim was very colourful, his leisure clothes way ahead of his time – he favoured short-sleeved shirts in rust, apple green or deep shades of blue, which was most unusual at that time for a man: no wonder his cars were colourful too,' writes Bobbie in her memoir* Remembering Kim.

ABOVE: *The Miller's House in the village of Pangbourne, six miles west of Reading, with Gillie at the door. "It was obvious that Gillie and Kim loved being there – that was their retreat," says Bobbie's daughter Easter Kirkland.*

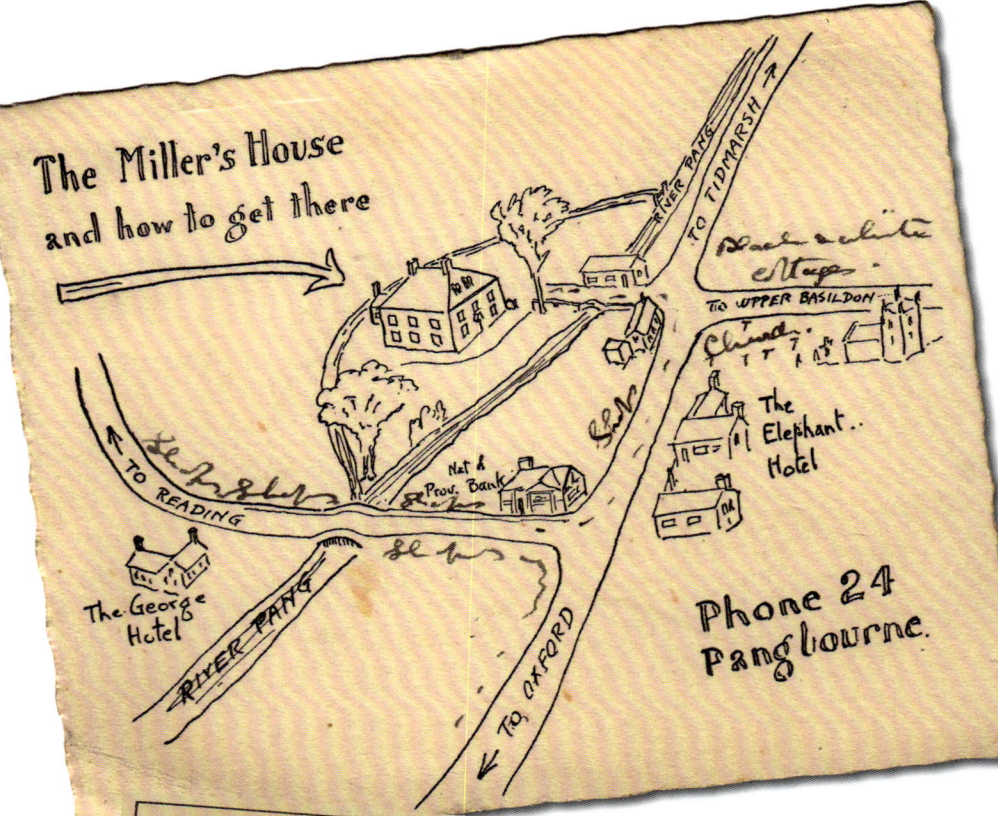

LEFT (BOTH): *Two of Kimber's pieces of artwork following the move to Pangbourne.*

TOP: *The 'Long Room' created from the old kitchen and wash-house. The fireplace is modern, having been designed by Betty, but the beams are authentic. The Welsh oak carver on the left is still in the family.*

ABOVE: *Gillie in the dining-room end of the 'Long Room'.*

Daddy has I expect written about this. I hope this sketch of what he wants is satisfactory. I think it ought to look very good in the room.

Yours sincerly

Betty Kimber

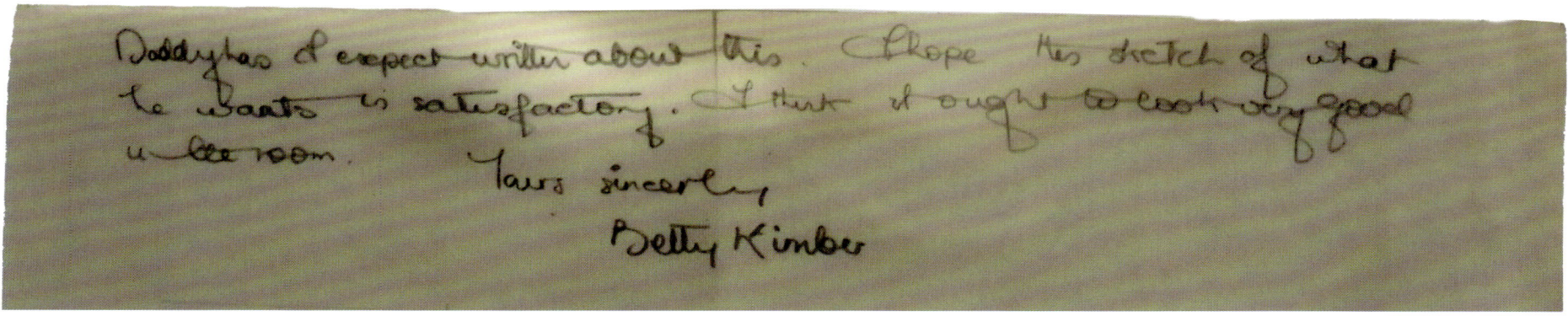

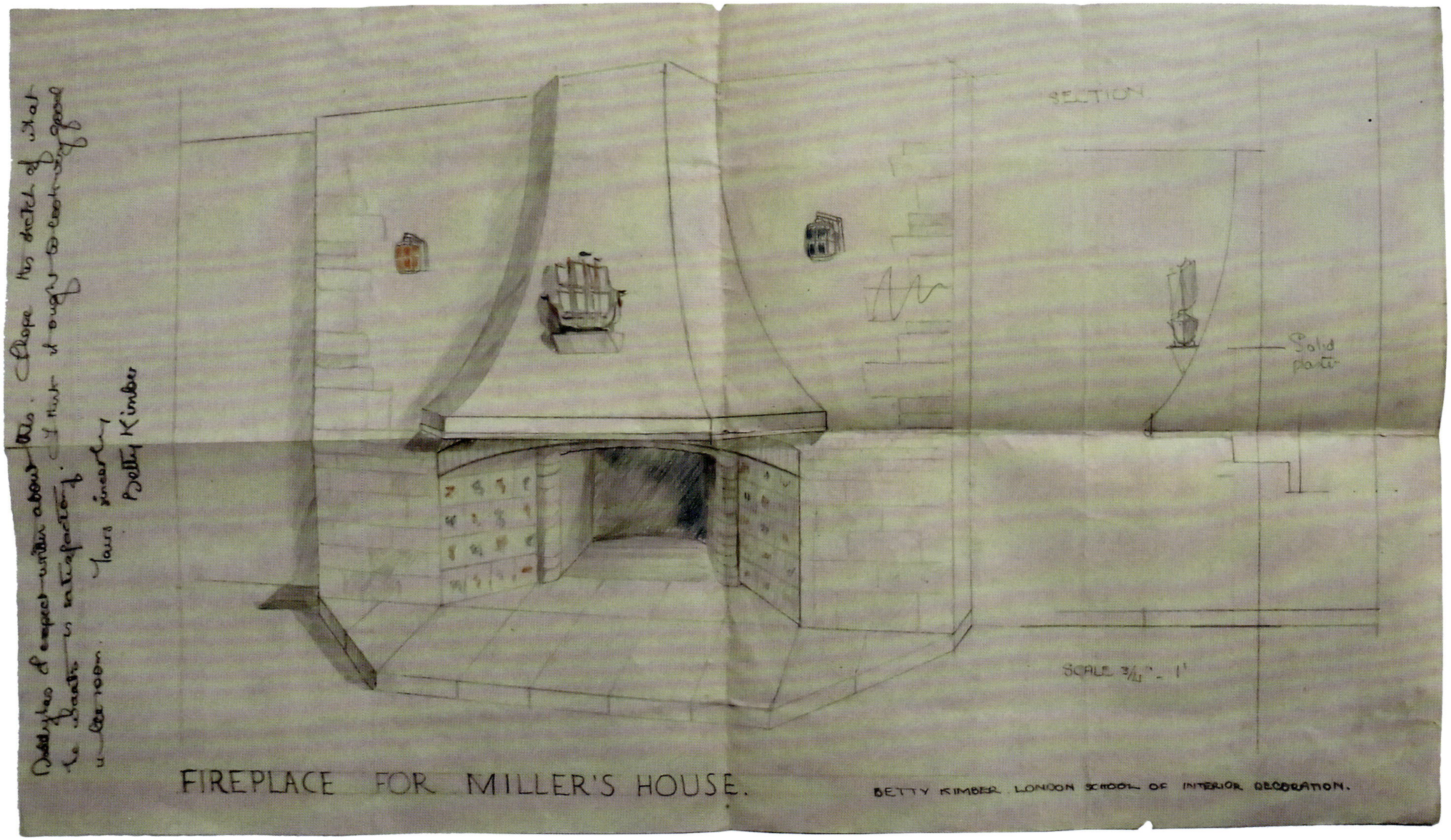

The design by Betty for the fireplace at The Miller's House.

Kimber must have had his eye for a while on the 18th century house with its four bedrooms and two reception rooms, as in his surviving papers is a survey dated July 1937 for Mill House, Pangbourne, as it was described by the surveyor. The property, which was conveniently situated for both Abingdon and Oxford, was clearly in need of some attention, and Kimber put some effort into improving the modestly-sized but comfortable house, not least creating a pleasant living room out of the old kitchen and the washhouse.

'The genuine beams went quite well with my father's Welsh oak furniture and Indian carpets, but my sister, Betty, who had designed the hooded fireplace, criticised the inevitable Tudor motifs plastered into the walls and the reproduction refectory table. She was attending a school of interior design in London and was totally committed to rules: it must be all antique, or all modern furniture in bent plywood and chromium, but not reproduction. She could not see that the mixture actually worked very well,' writes Jean.

TOP: *"Gillie was lovely to look at – she was no statue, but she always looked neat and tidy," son-in-law John Walkinton observed to the author.*

LEFT: *Kimber looking nautical, in a yachting cap, with Gillie and Bobbie. Gillie dressed in a slightly less classical style than Rene.*

Chapter Sixteen: Sunshine Before the Storm

TOP LEFT: *Gillie and Bobbie by the pond – built by Kimber.*

ABOVE: *Jean and family dog Roger by the mill leat. "My mother told me that the dog was so well trained that it would sit by the fishing basket and wait for his master. One day Kimber forgot about the dog and when he went back the next morning the dog was still there by the basket," recounts Sara Delamont.*

LEFT: *The Retreat was a converted London bus, complete with a thatched roof. Jean has written of how Gillie thought it wonderful, whereas Rene couldn't see the attraction.*

WHEN JAZZ MET GILBERT AND SULLIVAN

Relations between Kimber and his elder daughter continued to be tense, as Jean could observe. 'Betty had been completely in charge at the flat at Parkstone. Now she was a daughter again, and expected to conform to my father's very Victorian ideas about how young ladies should behave. Her views, particularly about the traditional relationships, culled from wide reading and mixing with free-thinking art students, were bound to horrify him... My sister felt that he of all people had least right to tell her how to live her life. My stepmother, trying hard to keep the peace, was rather relieved when eventually there was a total breach.'

The same picture was handed down by Betty to her daughter. "She talked about what really angered her was his old-fashioned double-standards. He had entirely different ideas about what was appropriate for men and women. That really annoyed her. Her whole socio-political stance was very oppositional to him," Sara Delamont told the author. "She had turned into someone who listened to jazz and read books he didn't think suitable. She wanted a life he was frightened by and didn't think suitable. The way she told it, the sort of adult she wanted to be was absolutely not what he wanted and that became a problem. I think he was very jumpy about what she was turning into, as an adult."

It wasn't just a question of an inter-generational conflict of values: equally important was the fact that Kimber was no high-brow and had unimaginative and not particularly cultured tastes. This may well have been one element in the unravelling of his marriage to Rene – and a key element in the success of his relationship with the cheery and unintellectual Gillie. "He quite enjoyed a sort of beer-drinking jolly party, like those M.G. Car Club affairs when we once had a band of buskers in from the street," Betty told Wilson McComb. "They once pushed a grand piano down seven flights of stairs, and he related this as quite OK. When they all got going on a jolly party like that – a bachelor party, not a mixed one – anything went."

His literary preferences were home-spun, confirmed Betty to McComb. "He loved that Owen Wister[1] book, *The Long Rifle*. Oh, and Adrian Bell's farming one, *Corduroy*. Yes, he loved that, and *Owd Bob*, the sheepdog thing. I had a volume of Rupert Brooke's poems...so I showed him the poem about the trout – 'In a cool curving world he lies/And ripples with dark ecstasies'. He read those two lines and said 'Rubbish!' and threw it in the fire; he advised me to read Izaak Walton instead. He had a habit of throwing books of mine in the fire if he didn't like them. Another he chucked in the fire was a biography of Bix Beiderbecke, the jazz trumpeter – he hated anything to do with jazz. That was a library book, too, and I had to pay for the damned thing; I was most annoyed."

Sara Delamont has a different version of this incident. "Kimber had very narrow middle-brow unimaginative tastes. The only music he liked was Gilbert and Sullivan[2]. My mother was a great jazz enthusiast. She was playing a jazz record and he snatched it off the record-player and smashed it on the floor, because it was black man's music and he didn't want her listening to that. Similarly, she was reading a library book and he took one look and threw it on the fire." Perhaps both a book on jazz and a jazz record were victims of Kimber's ire, but this does illustrate the danger of taking handed-down stories as gospel, when they seem sometimes to change in the telling.

Jean, who would celebrate her 14th birthday in May 1939, had more positive memories of the Pangbourne house, coloured by the joie de vivre imparted to the home by Gillie. 'She transformed my father's life, which now became full of jokes, teasing and hilarious parties which blossomed out of solemn business dinners. To

---

[1] In fact by Stewart Edward White.

[2] Whilst this might be an exaggeration, a collection of a dozen of his personal records that survives in the hands of the M.G. Car Club suggests that Kimber's tastes were certainly conventional: the records include light classical music (Verdi, Bach, Greig, Mendelssohn, Schubert), a recording by Harry Lauder, two 78s of Wurlitzer organ music, and one of the well-known WWI song 'Roses of Picardy'.

By 1939 over 50 constabularies had M.G. cars on their fleet. The Lancashire police took a batch of 120 cars – TAs and VA and SA tourers, while the eight WA tourers ordered by Glasgow accounted for all but one of the total production of this style. Kimber was known to flag down M.G. police cars and ask the officers if they were satisfied with their car.

this day, I treasure the memory of a rather pompous guest who ended the evening crawling under the table, almost weeping with laughter, to find the cherries he had dropped. Gillie had taught us all to "bob", i.e. to nibble up from the end of the stalk and try and hook the fruit into our mouth,' she writes in *The MG Log*. A further attraction for Jean was the presence of a sailing dinghy – 'another Lymington scow, this one salvaged from the bottom of Sowley Pond near Beaulieu, and bought for 30 shillings'. A new mast and sail cost £5 and the handmade wooden boat was scraped and painted, and christened 'Gladys'.

GERMANY CALLING: MORE RECORD-BREAKING WITH GARDNER

In February 1939 Cecil Kimber was in Germany for the Berlin Motor Show. He does not seem to have taken photographs at the show, but amongst his surviving photos are some images of Volkswagen Beetles, taken when the international press were given the chance to drive a dozen examples of the KdF-wagen – as it was now called – on the autobahn from Berlin to Dessau. Kimber, having predicted that streamlined styling and a rear-mounted engine would be the most likely future direction for car design to take, clearly had an interest in the Beetle. Following his trip to Berlin, a two-page feature on the show and the VW featured in the April 1939 issue of M.G. house magazine *The Sports Car*, accompanied by an editorial on the Beetle.

The article's writer, Michael McEvoy, had tested the car. 'If some readers are surprised that I devote most of this article to KdF matters, let me say that this remarkable little vehicle is a remarkable car in the fullest sense of the word,' he comments[3]. It is interesting to speculate on the reason for this coverage of the Volkswagen in the magazine, other than as a demonstration of an openness of mind. Was Kimber perhaps sending out a coded message to Cowley that the design of its cars could be more adventurous?

After the Czechoslovakian crisis of the previous year, the attitude towards Germany emanating from Abingdon was one of optimism. In the company's *Sales Letter* for March 1939 Sales Manager Bill Slingsley, writing of the Berlin Motor Show, said that 'the general atmosphere and buying confidence dispelled any feeling one might have expected to exist as a result of the International situation of the last six months.' M.G. was on a roll, said Slingsley. 'It is strange that as people are looking towards Germany as the cause of trade depression and general unrest, they are, at all events as far as M.G. is concerned, the best European buyers at the present time...Our old friend Jack Woodhouse, the Distributor over there, is doubtless responsible to a very large degree, plus the good impression Major Gardner left behind after his wonderful

---

[3] Given the snootiness with which the Beetle was regarded by the British motor industry after the Second World War, it behoves one to record that back in 1939 other commentators were equally impressed by the Volkswagen. "The car wasn't at all a crude job. It was a pretty well-developed machine by the time they displayed it to the press. It was quite an achievement for the time. But people in England weren't convinced by the concept of a rear-engined air-cooled car, while psychologically it had a hard time in England in 1939 because the clouds of war were gathering and the attitude to German ideas and products was not universally cordial," journalist Gordon Wilkins, one of those present at the 1939 event, told the author in a 2002 interview.

Chapter Sixteen: Sunshine Before the Storm

LATER RECORD-BREAKING WITH EX135

Buoyed by the success of the Dessau runs, Gardner and Kimber decided to attack the records for the up-to-750cc class. For this a new cylinder block was cast, and by August 1939 the engine was ready for assembly, ahead of a planned return to Dessau in October.

The war intervened, but in 1946 Gardner picked up where he had left off. The streamliner was rebuilt with the 750cc 'six' and on a section of an uncompleted motorway near Jabbeke in Belgium he claimed the records for cars of up to this capacity, with a best average speed of 159.2mph. In doing so, Gardner delivered on the last M.G. project of the Cecil Kimber era.

Re-engined with a six-cylinder 1100cc unit reduced to three-cylinder 500cc format, the Gardner-M.G. went on to take records in this class in 1947 and 1949, achieving 154.8mph as a best average speed. In 1950 the engine, running as a twin-cylinder of 332cc capacity, managed a best of 121.048mph and claimed the up-to-350cc records for the flying-start mile, kilometre and 5km distances. One last class remained untackled, and in 1948 Gardner pocketed the 2-litre records. With the car equipped with one of the stillborn four-cylinder Jaguar XK engines, a best of 176.76mph was achieved, this over the flying-start 1km distance.

Gardner returned to M.G. power in 1951 for an attempt at the international and North American Class F (up to 1500cc) records. Intended to help promote M.G. TD sales in the United States, the runs took place at the Bonneville Salt Flats in Utah. Two supercharged versions of the TD's 1250cc XPAG engine were prepared, one only mildly modified and one to a higher stage of tune. With the less powerful engine over 139mph was achieved, and 16 class records broken, but problems with the timing gear put paid to attempts on the high-speed records with the more potent engine.

The car returned to Bonneville in 1952 and took a batch of 2000cc records with a supercharged and much-modified version of the overhead-cam six-cylinder engine found in the Wolseley 6/80 and Morris Six. It was then fitted with the lower-powered of the two 1951 XPAG units, picking up a further set of records. Attempts to add to the score with the higher-output XPAG resulted in failure, however, when a piston collapsed.

Retired after the 1952 Salt Flats sessions, EX135 had under its belt the records in every class from 350cc to 2000cc, an extraordinary achievement for a car that had started out in 1934 as a K3 Magnette. Ultimately purchased by the British Motor Corporation, Abingdon's overlords after the 1952 merger of the Austin and Nuffield companies, the car survives in the British Motor Museum at Gaydon, a testament not only to Goldie Gardner's record-breaking abilities but also to the vision and enthusiasm of Cecil Kimber that made these ventures possible.

OPPOSITE: *Gardner with the EX135 streamliner, post-war; holding the steering wheel is famous M.G. figure and future Chief Engineer Syd Enever. (Goldie Gardner courtesy Mike Jones)*

record run. The product is no less admired due we are told to its ability to stand up to high speed on the *autobahnen*. News of this sort goes to strengthen one's belief that the present "uncertainty" is much more newspaper sensation than actual fact.'

This state of mind presumably informed the decision by Cecil Kimber and Goldie Gardner to return to Germany for a further bout of record-breaking on Hitler's autobahns – this time with a target of breaking 200mph. Not only that, but it was decided to attempt the short-distance records in the 1100cc to 1500cc class by the simple – in theory rather than practice – expedient of over-boring the 1086cc Magnette engine to take it to a whisker over 1100cc in capacity. This was to be done on site, using an electrically-powered boring machine.

This time a stretch of the motorway near Dessau was chosen – a section that according to Gardner had been prepared for an intended attack on the World Land Speed record by Mercedes-Benz. The M.G. party arrived in Germany at the end of May, on this occasion without Kimber. With no drama, Gardner on

Kimber photographed these Volkswagens during the 1939 Berlin Show: for him they showed the future of car design.

had received a severe compound fracture in his accident at the 1932 Ulster TT, and he had narrowly avoided having to have it amputated, after it had turned septic. But for all his life he was equipped with the normal complement of legs.

Thanks to Gardner's endeavours, Cecil Kimber's last summer before the war thus began on a high note. The subsequent holidays were split between Pangbourne and a final bout of sailing. John Walkinton, who had been working in London in the wholesale fruit-and-vegetable business, had departed to Palestine to become involved with orange-growing, putting on pause an affair with Betty Kimber. During the summer he spent some time at Pangbourne and the seeds of a romance with Bobbie were sown; the two would marry in 1945. With Betty pursuing her own interests in London, and Bobbie working in a bank, it was just Jean who accompanied Kimber and Gillie to Bucklers Hard for some sailing on *Fairwind*. In fact, says Jean, her father spent more time relaxing and entertaining friends than actually sailing *Fairwind* – leaving her to enjoy herself sailing the Kimber dinghy, or, more excitingly, a 15ft Seagull belonging to the son of another sailing family.

By now Gillie had been initiated into the social side of M.G. life as the wife of the Managing Director. Having been kitted out in fancy dress for the M.G. Car Club's Tramps Party earlier in the year, in May she was in Scotland to present the prizes at the Scottish M.G. Car Club rally at Taymouth Castle.

Kimber sailing the scow he had rescued and renovated.

MISSION ACCOMPLISHED?

If Cecil Kimber took time during these holidays to reflect on the four short years that had elapsed since the reorganisation of 1935, he would have had reason to feel modestly cheered. The blow of M.G. being brought under the direct control of Cowley and of car design being moved to the mother factory had not been anything like mortal. Kimber was surely disappointed to have lost some freedom of action, and to have been obliged to step back from motor racing. The chance for M.G. to be in the technological avant-garde had also been strewn to the winds. But there is no reason to believe that Kimber – or many other people, for that matter – held the new M.G. products as in any way unsatisfactory, whatever their sharing of parts and engineering with more prosaic Morris and Wolseley models.

Leaving aside the fact that the change in the status of M.G. had been eminently reasonable in management terms, the results spoke for themselves. The company had made a thoroughly honourable showing in the later pre-war years, with the T-type Midget and the larger VA, SA and WA models. Sales had jumped from 1,250 units in 1935 to 2,845 in 1937, falling back a little to 2,497 in 1938. In the same period, exports had risen from 9 per cent of output to 15 per cent, dropping to 10 per cent in 1938.

For some perspective, however, it behoves one to look at the performance of SS Cars during the same period. Getting its all-steel bodies into production nearly bankrupted SS – there were disasters with the component panels simply not fitting together – but in the end the company pulled through, and pre-war production of both wood-framed and steel SS Jaguars amounted to 14,079 units. Post-war another 12,042 would be sold.

In contrast, pre-war output of VA, SA and WA models came to only 5,514 cars. The real success for SS was the 1½-litre, which sold 7,368 units pre-war, against 2,407 of the M.G. VA. The 3½-litre, at 1,306 units, was a relative minority interest. As for the 2½-litre, its overall sales of 5,300 – plus 105 SSI-derived tourers – compare

Chapter Sixteen: Sunshine Before the Storm

with a total of 3,107 SAs and WAs sold by Abingdon, putting the Coventry concern ahead of its M.G. rival by a considerable margin.

Without the hesitant entry into production of the Cowley-designed bigger models, allowing M.G. to be beaten to the punch in the marketplace by the new SS Jaguars, the scenario would surely have been rosier. At least, though, M.G. had fared well in comparison with its in-house sister marque: Wolseley had a good 1936, but by 1938 its sales had slipped back almost to their 1935 level. As car manufacture ceased in autumn 1939, with the advent of war, both Cecil Kimber and Lord Nuffield had every reason to feel content with the performance of the modestly-sized Berkshire factory.

Tickford drophead bodywork for the TA was announced in August 1938 and the style carried through to the TB when this was announced in May 1939. Author Anders Clausager estimates production to have been 260 as a TA and 60 as a TB.

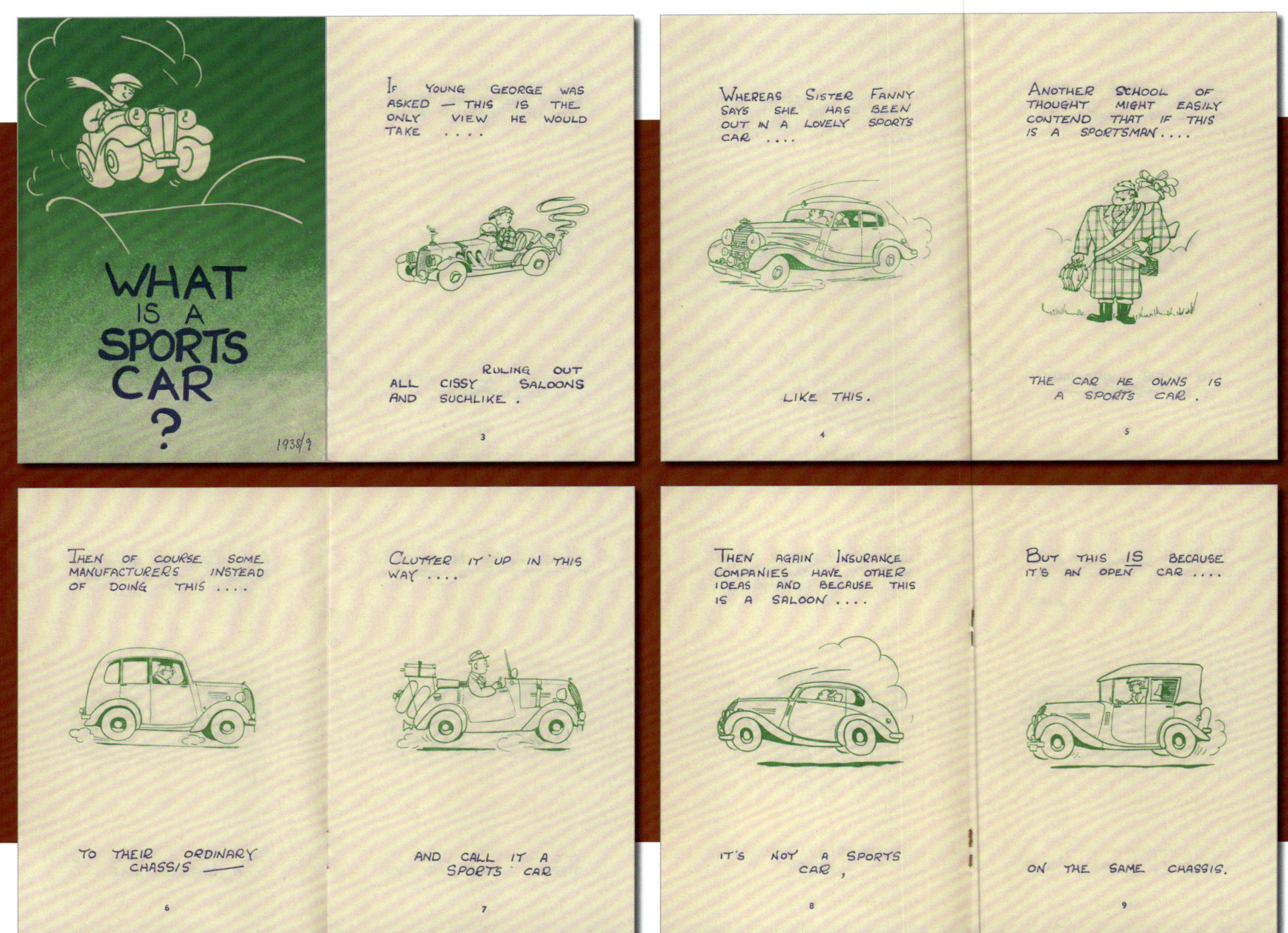

Then again some companies contend that this is a sports car too....

Even though it is a saloon.

10

Just because the makers used to win lots of races with cars like this....

And therefore know how to make fast and safe cars.

11

Our outlook on the other hand is pretty clear and we contend a sports car is simply one which is faster, safer, more comfortable, corners and road holds better, and is in fact superior in lots of ways to an ordinary car.

12

This for instance is one but we don't say so....

Because the term is so misunderstood, and

13

Because M.G.s are fast cars with a high performance, many people have been misled on the question of Insurance. They thought that the Midget Coupé 1½, 2 and 2·6 Litre models would be rated as purely sports cars — with consequently higher premiums. This is not so. The emphasis on the famous M.G. slogan is as much on the word 'safety' as on the word 'fast.' Many of the leading Insurance Companies will accept M.G. Cars at standard rates. This is, of course, subject to the usual provisos concerning the age, status and accident record of the individual proposer, and in some cases certain open body styles. If you have any difficulty, write direct to the M.G. Car Company Limited of Abingdon-on-Thames, Berkshire.

14

Drawings by "App"

Produced by the Publicity Dept.
THE MG CAR
Company Limited
ABINGDON-ON-THAMES
BERKSHIRE

Printed in England by Wood, Rozelaar & Wilkes Ltd., London, N.W.10.

THESE TWO PAGES: *Barry Appleby, son of Kimber's old friend the journalist Ernest Appleby, was commissioned to illustrate this tongue-in-cheek* What is a Sports Car? *pamphlet.*

Chapter Sixteen: Sunshine Before the Storm

LEFT: *Kimber and Lord Nuffield inspect a VA chassis. In 1938, around when this photo was taken, Kimber was on a salary of £2,750 a year, which by the standards of the time was a respectable sum; today it would be equivalent to over £236,000, so he was not being underpaid by Nuffield. (Author's collection)*

ABOVE: *Kimber and Gillie at Pangbourne in 1939. "A lot of this is guesswork and hunches, from things my mother said, but when Gillie turned up I think it was like the lights going on. She loved sailing, and went sailing with him, and she would go fishing with him. I think Kimber for the first time in his life found a companion who shared his interests, would muck around in boats, fall in the river with him, and so on," observes Jean's son Kim McGavin. "Kimber had a wonderful sense of fun – which Gillie had in spades."*

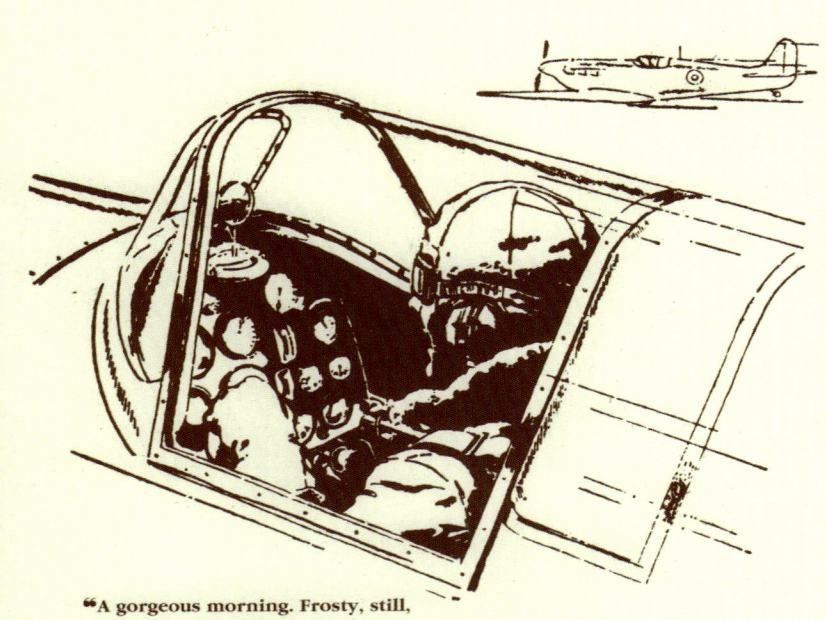

WAR ON TWO FRONTS

ABOVE: *What is thought to be Kimber's second VA; uniquely for the model, it has rear-hinged rear doors, and there is a wind-deflector on the driver's door.*

OPPOSITE: *Two advertisements from a series instituted in 1940: establishing a link between fighter aircraft and M.G. cars was an astute move, with so many RAF pilots having an affection for Abingdon's products.*

The declaration of war on 3 December 1939 perforce had an impact both on Kimber's personal life and on the functioning of the M.G. business – although in the case of the latter it came too late to prevent the announcement in the motoring press of Abingdon's 1940 models.

As the reported minor changes had virtually without exception been implemented some time previously and the only genuine novelty, the TB Midget, had been formally launched in May 1939, there was in reality little that was newsworthy. In any case, car production was run down immediately and to all intents and purposes had ceased by October – with some vehicles still being registered in 1940.

In the case of the his life outside work, Kimber was forced to abandon a 'boys-only' sailing trip with Carl Kingerlee. The idea had been to take *Fairwind* to the Scilly Isles, winds permitting. If faced with westerly winds, on the other hand, the duo would take advantage of these to spend a fortnight visiting such Devon and Cornwall sailing ports as Brixham, Dartmouth, Salcombe, Fowey and Falmouth. Sunday 3 September was finally fixed for the departure, but events dictated otherwise, the Admiralty clamping down immediately on all maritime movement.

Kimber and Kingerlee instead spent the first few days of their planned holiday putting *Fairwind* into a mud berth at her Bucklers Hard home and stripping her of all equipment, down to her engine. 'At last everything was done, and stretching a tarpaulin over her we bade a sad farewell to our little ship. It felt like a funeral,' Kimber later wrote.

In those early months of the 'Phoney War' life continued almost as normal at The Miller's House. Jean went back to school in Oxford. Betty, it seems, initially continued her architectural studies in London. Bobbie almost immediately joined the Women's Auxiliary Air Force, where she was soon able to profit from the pull the M.G. name had amongst the Air Force community, something of which she had already become aware.

'At the beginning of the war I went to a dance at an RAF station with Kim and my mother, where we were guests of the Commanding Officer. A very young officer was told to look after me, and during the course of the evening I told him who Kim was as he seemed very keen on cars. When he saw us off, he shook Kim's hand and said, "Goodbye, King of Cars!" I've never forgotten that, because after all it's what we all thought at the time,' she writes in *Remembering Kim*.

'A few months later I was in the women's branch of the RAF myself. Wherever I was stationed Kim always knew someone nearby who was happy to entertain me for his sake, often because they owned or had an M.G. and taken it to the works to talk to Kim about it, as everyone was welcome to do and frequently did. They all thought the world of Kim – my mother said he had no acquaintances, for everyone who met him was his friend.

'I was working on radar, which was very secret for the whole of the war – Kim would have been so interested in it, and I always regretted I was never able to tell him about it. I met one very clever young technical officer during the war from time to time, who had an M.G. he was allowed to use as he travelled between the various radar stations, so of course I was always glad to see him, and introduced him to Kim as soon as I could. He became a great friend of the family, and when Kim died my mother gave Clive the gold cuff-links which Kim wore so often, presented in 1925 for qualifying in the London-Land's End trial[1].'

During 1940 Betty moved out of the Pangbourne house, marking a further deterioration in her relationship with her father. After her affair with John Walkinton and – according to Kim McGavin – 'a fairly major flirtation' with Jean's future husband Eric McGavin, Kimber's elder daughter, to celebrate her 21st birthday in October, had embarked on a serious liaison with Dean Delamont.

This provoked Kimber's ire, to the point – it is said – that he forthwith sacked Delamont. Given that his job at Abingdon was apparently to look after press cars and relations with the press, it is equally possible that Delamont's position was quite simply redundant in a time of war; he went on to work for the Inspectorate of Fighting Vehicles under Stanley Barnes, the former manager of the Singer racing team who had briefly competed in M.G. Midgets. Whatever the truth, by later that year Betty was living in Hamble, just outside Southampton; whether this was with Delamont is not known. In November she narrowly escaped with her life. She had started attending life-drawing classes at the Southampton Civic Centre, but on 6 November she missed her class because she was fire-watching. That day a direct hit by a German bomb destroyed the Centre, killing 35 people.

---

[1] This has been frequently said, even by Kimber himself, but is not correct. He accepted the cuff-links in lieu of a gold medal in 1923 not 1925; see Chapter 4.

FIGHTING FOR ABINGDON

Whilst all this was going on, Cecil Kimber's main task in his professional life was to keep the M.G. factory turning and the maximum number of its employees in work. Some inevitably lost their job – and if a man were called up for military service then the Morris organisation's policy was that there was no severance pay. John Thornley tells a tale[2] that reflects upon Kimber's generosity of spirit. He had been told by Kimber that he was to stay, but then the following morning he received his Emergency Reserve call-up papers. 'I took them in to show Kim. Somewhat abruptly he sent me out of his office, saying he couldn't see me just then and I was to come back next morning. He fired me that afternoon. So I left M.G. with my severance pay and left the town of Abingdon without a blemish on my financial escutcheon.'

With car production halted, the premises were cleared of all their plant, including the paint shop so expensively installed at the time of the introduction of the Two-Litre. Storing all this, and a large quantity of car parts including several hundred chassis frames, was solved by acquiring a dilapidated former factory a mile and a half from the works. This was restored to a usable state

---
[2] 'Forever Abingdon' in *Motor*, 13 December 1969.

Kimber's message to M.G. Car Club members in the last issue of The Sports Car *magazine.*

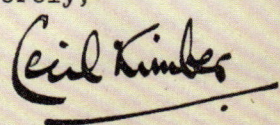

ABOVE: *Making hay in June 1940 at The Retreat.*

OPPOSITE TOP: *Kimber, third from left, with the Upper Thames Patrol, in the summer of 1940.*

OPPOSITE BOTTOM LEFT & MIDDLE: *Kimber and Gillie at Pangbourne, and both espousing the nautical look. Kimber's cap carries the Royal London Yacht Club badge.*

OPPOSITE BOTTOM RIGHT: *Bobbie in her WAAF uniform: she worked in radar, about which she had to keep a discreet silence.*

Gladys, Jean and a friend, during a 1940 half-term.

Chapter Seventeen: War on Two Fronts

Bobbie with 'ARX 710'. As well as wartime headlamp masks, it has white-painted bumpers to give it some visibility during blackouts.

Goldie Gardner remained a good friend. Here he is with his second wife Una, whom he married in 1940, and his WA drophead. Suffering a cerebral haemorrhage in 1952, Gardner would die in 1958 at the age of 68.

and by early 1940 the M.G. works was empty. Meanwhile the press shop, which had previously been a minimally-equipped operation making small runs of components or one-off fabrications, was re-fitted for more serious presswork.

The challenge was to secure government contracts in the chaotic early days of the war. Businesses were desperate to find work but government departments were overwhelmed and unused to functioning with the reactivity to which industry large and small was accustomed. Whilst Whitehall fumbled, a premium was put on the resourcefulness of company Managing Directors obliged to knock on door after door of the Civil Service until they were granted a manufacturing agreement.

Kimber and his team began by obtaining orders for small quantities of shell racks, bins and other similar items, in runs of 50 to 100 pieces, low-scale operations suited to the M.G. press shop; soon the department was running at full capacity. According to Wilson McComb 'the most menial tasks were gladly accepted, such as making fish-frying pans for a local military depot'.

To occupy the main factory, once it had been emptied, a contract was obtained from the Ministry of Supply for the overhaul of the Vickers-Armstrong MkV and MkVI Light Tank. This commission was apparently obtained via John Howlett, the founder and managing director of Wellworthy, a leading manufacturer of piston rings, who had become friendly with Kimber through a shared passion for fishing. Howlett had been appointed a regional chairman of the Emergency Services Organisation in 1940, under Lord Beaverbrook, Churchill's hard-nosed Minister of Aircraft Production, and thus had some influence in the higher echelons of government.

TOP: *A Vickers Light Tank of the type that was reconditioned by Abingdon. (Alamy)*

LEFT: *During 1941 M.G. took on assembly of the Matilda tank, as notably used in the earlier Western Desert battles. (Alamy)*

Initially the Ministry insisted on the needless dismantling of the tanks almost to the last nut and bolt, but after much discussion it was finally accepted that most of the time all they required, in the words of one official, was 'a hair cut and shave'. The overhaul of bigger Matilda tanks followed, along with the assembly of several consignments of trucks shipped from the United States.

There was also a brief period in 1940 when a large quantity of Browning machine-guns were passed to M.G. for reconditioning. Typical of the orders and counter-orders flying about at the time, no sooner had Abingdon got into the swing of this contract then it was transferred to another enterprise. Meanwhile the press shop was bursting at the seams, primarily with the manufacture of small pressings for the aircraft industry. As a result the Maintenance Department doubled the shop's surface by building an extension using timber from the crates in which the US trucks had arrived, topping this with a roof made of tarred felt laid over chicken-wire.

It was during 1940 that Kimber obtained for M.G. its most important wartime contract, in terms of physical size and technical complexity. This was to build the G1 nose unit of the Albemarle medium bomber. A whole range of processes had to be learnt, tools and fittings had to be constructed, and the complicated electric and hydraulic systems mastered. M.G. was one of four firms undertaking the same job, and it was the first to enter production, a major achievement. The Abingdon factory would manufacture 653 Albemarle nose units and carry out conversion work on a further 285, all this constituting a major contribution to the war effort. Kimber had been brave to hold his hand up for such a contract, but he would pay the price for this buccaneering audacity.

THE MOVE TO FYFIELD

During 1941 the Albemarle contract gradually fell into place and M.G. also took on the assembly of the Crusader tank. Meanwhile petrol rationing made it unrealistic to continue living 20 miles from the factory, so in the course of the year Kimber let The Miller's House, and he and Gillie become tenants of John Howlett at Fyfield Manor, about five miles out of Abingdon on the Faringdon road.

The bonds between the two men had strengthened when Howlett had set out in 1940 to find additional factory premises to boost his production of rings and pistons for – above all – the aircraft industry. Kimber put him onto M.G. neighbour the Pavlova Leather Company and Wellworthy ended up taking over its tanning shop. The factory proved a great success. 'One reason why things went well was because a Mrs Hamilton, Cecil Kimber's sister-in-law, took a job with us as a sort of personal assistant, with an office in with the Pavlova people,' says Howlett in *The Guv'nor*, his autobiography.

Howlett did not own Fyfield, but had leased it from St John's College as a convenient stop-over for Wellworthy people visiting his Abingdon works and as a centre for informal business conferences, entrusting its running to Gillie's sister Gladys alongside her duties at the Pavlova works. 'We had regular technical meetings there with, for instance, the Rolls-Royce men about the development of pistons and rings for Merlin and Griffon engines. They would often stay the night and fit in a call in London before going back to Derby, and they appreciated the chance of a good night's rest since accommodation in the area was very scarce,' he writes in *The Guv'nor*.

The Kimbers had a top-floor flat, shared with Gladys. The atmosphere seems to have been relaxed, with for the first time no children intruding into daily life. "At Fyfield, Kim would be at one end of the table and Gillie at the other, and she'd up sticks and put arms around him and give him a kiss," John Walkinton recalled. "He must have wondered what had happened to him. She was a real breath of fresh air."

Jean had reached the age of 16 and had left Oxford High School for Girls with her School Certificate, following which Gillie had

Fyfield Manor, leased from St John's College by John Howlett, was briefly home for Kimber and Gillie. Restored in 1868, the property retains some elements of the original house, which dates from the 14th century.

ABOVE: *Gillie at Fyfield Manor. With Pangbourne over 20 miles from Abingdon, and petrol being rationed, Kimber decided to rent out The Miller's House and move closer to the M.G. factory.*

LEFT (BOTH): *The couple had a top-floor flat; they shared this with Gillie's sister Gladys, who ran the house for Howlett, whom she would marry after the death in 1950 of his first wife.*

persuaded Kimber to send her to Châtelard, a Swiss finishing school that had been evacuated to Wales. There she would learn secretarial skills and study English and History, before going on to a college in Crewkerne, Somerset, to hone her abilities as a secretary.

She had fond memories of the manor, which was evidently a charming place. 'Fyfield was a beautiful medieval manor, originally a small religious house, and then it gradually evolved through the centuries into the kind of place England does best, with gracious lawns, a mulberry tree, and a clipped yew hedge with an archway through to the church where both Bobbie and I were later married,' she writes in *The Other Tack*.

BETTY GETS MARRIED

Betty, meanwhile, had continued to plough her own furrow, and this led to a definitive rupture with her father. The cause was straightforward: in March 1941 she married Dean Delamont. It is not clear whether Delamont had sought Kimber's approval. His grandson, also called Dean, thinks this likely. "Dean was a gentleman – the sort of person who would have gone to Cecil Kimber to ask for his daughter's hand," he told the author. "I don't think he would have done anything that would have gone against the etiquette of the time."

Whether or not this was the case, Kimber did not give his accord. "He may have thought Betty was much too young to get married. She must have been hell on wheels for someone of his generation. I imagine she had turned into precisely what he didn't want," says Sara Delamont. "When she said she wanted to marry Dean, I assume he realised they were sexually active. I don't know. She never said that explicitly. For her it was a case of old-fashioned sexual double-standards. I remember her saying they had a blazing row and she accused him of being a hypocrite. She said he had been living with Gillie when they weren't husband and wife, and everybody knew."

Delamont was desperate to be married, says his daughter. "I think

Betty in a glamorous studio portrait. "Apparently she did a great deal to wind her father up, whereas my mother was more mousey and played the game," says Kim McGavin.

people did things in the war that otherwise they wouldn't have done. As for my mother, she always said she married Dean as much as anything because she didn't think it was her father's business, or anyone else's. All her aunts assumed she was pregnant, but she wasn't. She did it primarily because Kim forbade it.

"It was a terrible mistake. Dean was not intellectual. He wasn't interested in serious theatre, or serious films. His idea of theatre was 'Salad Days'. It wasn't 'Hedder Gabler' or whatever. He was tone deaf and had no interest at all in classical music. My mother invested in a good radio. It was tuned to the Third Programme, and we listened to a lot of classical music. Dean wouldn't have known where to find the Third Programme on the radio dial. She had an interest in drama and was active in the Unity Theatre[3]. She subscribed to Penguin 'New Writing' – she had a complete set. I don't think they had a single thing in common, ever."

Naturally enough, Kimber was profoundly upset by the breach, which he recounted to his uncle Sydney in a letter of September 1941. 'I too am disappointed about Betty. She was such a nice kiddy and showed promise,' wrote Sydney Kimber in reply, mentioning that he had had similar concerns about his daughter Ruth. 'There is nothing one can do about such things. Frequently they turn out all right and let us hope it will be so in Betty's case, so don't cut all bonds. You know that we had a hectic time over Ruth's marriage but it has turned out quite all right and Win is now doing better than I could have imagined. So cheer up. I am so glad you are so happily married – that takes the sting out of the other affair.'

It does not appear that Sydney Kimber's advice bore fruit: all contacts seemed to break down between Kimber and his elder daughter. Lisa, as Betty now preferred to call herself, spent the war working on the camouflaging of important buildings, disguising factories and the like so that they avoided getting bombed. Displaying a radical and feminist streak to her character that she would always retain, she fought what her daughter terms 'gender-related battles' over the unequal allowances given to men and women. At some stage in the war she found herself living at Chislehurst in Kent, and it was here that John Ramsbottom, a famous expert, taught her about edible fungi. "We would go and pick things in the woods when we were kids," remembers Sara Delamont. "People thought she would poison us. But she knew all about edible fungi because John Ramsbottom had taught her about them."

Betty's marriage to Dean Delamont led to a complete rupture with her father.

---

[3] Born out of 1930s agitprop street theatre in London's East End, the Unity Theatre became a leading outlet for left-wing drama in the post-war years, with associate branches around the country.

Chapter Seventeen: War on Two Fronts

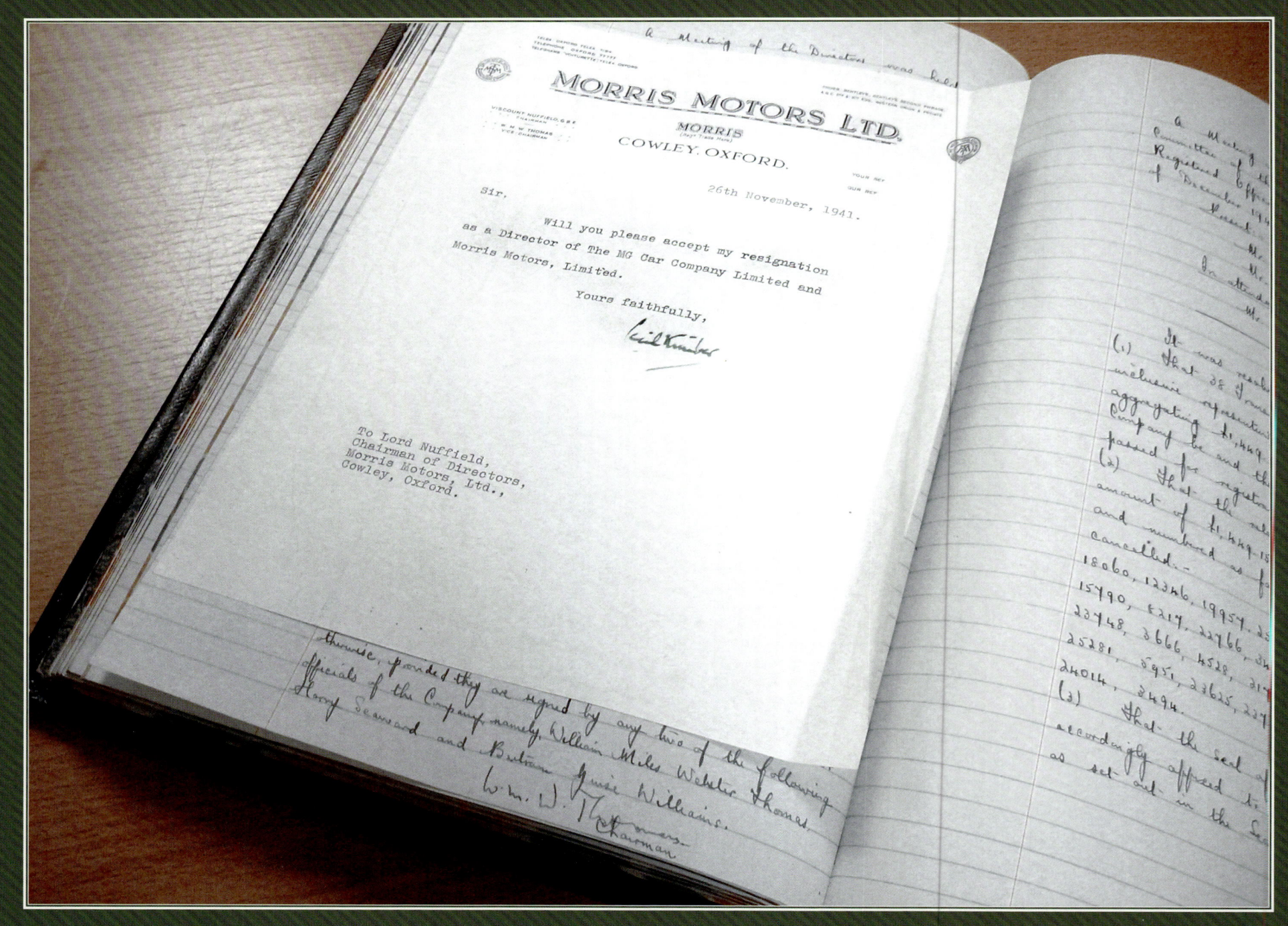

18

VICTIM OF THE SNAKEPIT

Slipped into a volume of Morris boardroom minutes is a single sheet of paper that it is hard not to find extraordinarily poignant. It is the resignation letter of Cecil Kimber. Dated 26 November 1941, it is on Morris Motors Ltd notepaper, rather than on M.G.-headed paper – suggesting that it was dictated and signed immediately after Kimber's final meeting with Lord Nuffield, in which he tried to discuss his intended dismissal.

It opens with a coldly impersonal 'Sir' rather than a more personal 'Dear Lord Nuffield'. The letter simply reads 'Will you please accept my resignation as a Director of the M.G. Car Company Limited and Morris Motors Limited.' It is then signed 'Yours faithfully', with Kimber's characteristically neat signature in his trademark green ink. There is no reference to happy days creating and building up the M.G. marque, to shared memories of those pioneer times, immortalised by so many photos of the two men together, smiling for the camera. Kimber had been sacked, and he wasn't disposed, it is evident, to waste his time on niceties.

Building the Albemarle nose section was a fearsomely complex operation. M.G. workers were justifiably proud of mastering this challenging contract. (Author's collection)

ABOVE: *The Armstrong Whitworth AW41 Albemarle was designed as a medium bomber but was soon used instead for transporting paratroopers, towing gliders, and other general duties. (Wikipedia)*

OPPOSITE: *Kimber's resignation letter to Lord Nuffield: less is more. (Author)*

So how did this sad state of affairs come to pass? It is generally accepted that it was largely because Kimber secured on his own initiative that government contract for M.G. to build the front section of the Albemarle bomber – although John Howlett, writing in *The Guv'nor*, makes no mention of this, and attributes the sacking to the obtaining of the earlier contract to repair tanks. Perhaps Kimber had exceeded his authority in these two matters. But it seems that there were personal factors at play. The Albemarle affair surely entered into things, but it was probably merely the final – or maybe the penultimate – straw.

For some time Kimber had been seen as exalting his own personality, and forgetting that within the Morris group there was only one hero to be worshipped – and that was Lord Nuffield. In particular, Kimber had run that series of very personal M.G. advertisements before the war, each one signed with his name. "He put all the directors at Cowley against the M.G. because of that," family friend Carl Kingerlee told Andrews and Brunner.

"Kimber...was tactless, and got so that he rather forgot that if it had not been for Nuffield he would not have been able to do it... It was Kimber says this and Kimber says that, and he was advertising himself."

This is one way of looking at things. But Kimber had built up M.G. on the basis of personal attention to his customers, whether getting to know them himself or simply taking a generous attitude to their wishes when they brought their car to the Abingdon service department[1]. With M.G. design having become the responsibility of Cowley, and the perception that the cars were now of less individual character, it was sensible marketing practice to try to convince the enthusiast M.G. customer base that in fact nothing had changed and that Cecil Kimber was still a listening hands-on presence one could look upon almost as a friend. Such notions didn't wash, however, when it came to fragile egos in the Morris organisation at large.

PINK-EYED RATS: INSIDE THE COURT OF KING WILLIAM

Here a bit of context is required. By the 1930s the Morris business had grown to a size where former garage-owner Nuffield could no longer control it. He resented this reality, and one of the ways he tried to reinforce his authority was by dismissing key members of management on often spurious grounds. Making matters worse, he had become a semi-absentee boss, away for long periods on sea cruises. When he was away, there was a power vacuum. This led not only to management having to second-guess his likely intentions, but to an atmosphere of intrigue at Cowley that made the court of the Borgias look like a Sunday School.

Jostling for the favours of Lord Nuffield involved vicious power-plays, and the circulation of injurious gossip until it reached the ear of Nuffield or his wife; perceived failings in one's private life were a particularly lucrative currency with Lillian Morris, a shrewish prude who would gladly retail to her husband the

Unsparingly described by senior Morris manager George Dono as "a woman with a small village mind who had never grown up," Lillian Morris, Lady Nuffield, was a conduit for Cowley gossip. The private life of Cecil Kimber would not have met with her approval. (Author's collection)

---

[1] "Anyone who buys an M.G. buys a brick out of the wall," Kimber is said to have remarked.

Chapter Eighteen: Victim of the Snakepit

personal peccadillos of a manager whose card his rivals had marked. Those who paid the price were without exception men of talent whom Nuffield had recruited in his early days, when amongst his qualities he had a fine eye for spotting such people. Cecil Kimber perfectly fitted this profile.

"It was very difficult to sort out those people who were using you and those who were not," observed Frank Woollard to Andrews and Brunner[2]. "[Morris] was a strong man, but he was the centre of warring factions." Everyone fought their own corner, jockeying for position. Lady Nuffield and her brother, Bill Anstey, who ran the transport department, were an acknowledged conduit for damaging talk to reach Morris. "She had her spies all over the place," said Kimpton Smallbone, the one-time company secretary who latterly headed the Export division. "The atmosphere at Cowley was lousy. Everybody was cutting each other's throats."

"Tale-bearing and tittle-tattle in this company [were] dreadful and [did] irreparable harm," concurred George Dono, post-war head of the Nuffield pressings business, blaming Smallbone himself for much of the ill-feeling that prevailed. He was, said Dono, "a snake in the grass" and "fair game for any trouble". Meanwhile, Harry Seaward, MD of Morris Bodies Branch, was in his opinion "a somewhat embittered man" and "violently antagonistic" to colleague and future Vice-Chairman Reginald Hanks. Carl Kingerlee had no time for either man. As far as he was concerned, Seaward and Smallbone were "pink-eyed rats".

---

[2] The subsequent quotations are also taken from the Andrews and Brunner transcripts.

Frank Woollard with his special-bodied Morris Six. The portly engineer liked a snooze after lunch – which helped seal his fate. (LAT Images)

Although this is rarely acknowledged, holding the ring in this arena of squabbling Midlands manhood was another wily political operator whose hands were less than clean: Miles Thomas, the journalist who had joined Morris in 1924 and would rise without interruption to the highest ranks of the company. Thomas was not just a dynamic manager who seemed to get things done. He was also a proficient courtier, anticipating and accommodating Lord Nuffield's wishes and if necessary carrying out the sackings that his master demanded but himself lacked the courage to implement.

It was a difficult line to walk, but all the same Thomas's apparent involvement in cabals with the likes of Seaward and Smallbone leaves a nasty taste in the mouth. "He was able and ambitious and not very scrupulous and went out of his way to ingratiate himself with Morris," former Cowley production director Arthur Rowse told Andrews and Brunner.

That William Morris latterly developed dictatorial tendencies and ended up preferring yes-men around him seems to have been acknowledged as part of the problem[3]. When this fused with conspiratorial hissing from the Cowley snakepit, the venomous cocktail resulted in the departure of men that Morris could ill afford to lose.

THE PERILS OF AN AFTERNOON SIESTA... AND OTHER STORIES

The first high-up manager of undoubted ability to bite the dust for dubious reasons was Kimber's old friend and colleague Frank Woollard. Influential in applying flow production principles across the entire company, Woollard's role in the development of the Morris business should not be under-estimated. Yet Morris sacked him. The supposed reasons were design failings in the Oxford Six engine and not pulling his weight as a senior manager, but the real gripe with Woollard was that he ate copiously at lunchtime, and so was not in a fit state for afternoon board meetings. Possibly exacerbated by his suffering from diabetes, he needed a post-prandial nap, and as a result preferred to retire to a small room where he had a couch. He locked the door, set his alarm clock, and had a two-hour snooze, it was said. "That was not good enough," snorted Nuffield to Andrews and Brunner.

The next to fall on his sword was Arthur Rowse, the director in charge of production, who was forced to resign in 1933. As superintending engineer for the Ministry of Munitions, Rowse had set up the lines at Cowley for the efficient manufacture of mine sinkers during the First World War. Joining the Morris company after the Armistice, he got the factory re-equipped and ready to make motor cars again. He went on to become the prime mover behind the dramatic price-slashing of 1921 that saved the company – which in a long-perpetuated self-serving myth was presented as a stroke of inspired genius on the part of William Morris himself.

The supposed cause for the demise of Rowse was a minor teething problem on the Morris Ten, to become a highly successful model that would restore Cowley's fortunes after a rocky few years. Seaward and Smallbone used their influence to convince Morris that there was nothing right with the Ten. The ground was fertile, because Morris, with his habitual insecurity, felt that Rowse was guilty of being condescending towards him.

There were other trivial matters. Rowse fitted his office with carpet and a posh fire grate; he spent the firm's money on an elaborate 'progress board'. But above all – and this was the ultimate reason for his downfall – he had supposedly undeclared interests in a business that supplied Morris Motors. The charge was manifestly trumped-up, but constant whispering in Morris's ear about Rowse's alleged financial impropriety had its effect. "I seem to be very unpopular. I had better put my hat and coat on and go," he is reported as having said. He was phlegmatic about

---

[3] 'Some of those to whom he delegated authority may not have been brilliant or even conscientious: but then, it is not every first-rate businessman who would choose to work for a querulous and unpredictable despot,' industrial commentator Graham Turner would write in *The Leyland Papers*.

his departure, saying that he owed his life to Lord Nuffield – because had he stayed at Morris he would surely have died on the job. "Life at Cowley would drive you to the grave," he commented.

Finally there was Leonard Lord. Here again, as discussed earlier, there was a mixture of explanations for his departure. But there was also the usual political intriguing at Cowley, doubtless fuelled by the fact that Lord's brusque manner did not always make him friends: Oliver Boden, the Wolseley works manager who would rise to become Morris Vice-Chairman before dying in his boots in 1940, and William Cannell, in charge at Morris Commercial Cars, both apparently loathed him.

There was additionally the small matter of the married Lord allegedly showing an improper interest in a young lady in the drawing office. Having surprised the two in Lord's office, Smallbone made allusion to this over lunch. As Smallbone's wife had already started to spread tittle-tattle about Lord's friendship with the lady in question, there is every possibility that word reached Nuffield, doubtless via Lady Nuffield, who would have been sure to have talked up the affair to Lord's detriment.

EGOS AND JEALOUSY – A FATAL COMBINATION

This background is important, because the dismissal of Cecil Kimber has clear parallels with those just discussed. Kimber was merely one of a chain of gifted managers that Lord Nuffield decided to sack, and his dismissal fits with distressing neatness into a pattern of ill-considered behaviour that disfigured the management landscape at one of the country's leading industrial concerns.

A key motor behind Kimber's departure was Thomas, who in 1940 had been elevated to Vice-Chairman of what would soon be known as the Nuffield Organization, and who was thus the de facto head of the entire Morris business. Nuffield was by this time taking more of a back seat in the running of the enterprise, not always attending board meetings and broadly leaving essential decisions to Thomas. He would still intervene, but increasingly in a negative way more likely to impede the smooth functioning of decision-making rather than to lead from the front; this would become particularly apparent after the war.

Thomas would inevitably have picked up on Lord Nuffield's feelings, and the disgruntlement of other high-ups in the Cowley vipers nest. It is also pretty clear that Thomas did not warm to

Relations between Kimber and Thomas are difficult to fathom; what is not in doubt is that Thomas was a wily political operator. "One person John Thornley didn't like was Miles Thomas," says Mike Allison. "He thought he was a bastard of the first order. Thomas would follow Morris around on factory visits saying 'Yes, Sir William...No Sir William,' someone once told me."

Kimber, although they were outwardly friendly according to Jean, who remembered going to tea with the Thomas children. According to former M.G. chief John Thornley, one of the things that irked Thomas was the very fact that Nuffield and Kimber got on so well together.

"Kimber went on the basis of petty jealousy. I don't think there's any doubt about that," Thornley told the author. "Thomas was green-eyed about the extent to which Kim had the Old Man's ear…Getting the aircraft contract gave Miles Thomas the excuse to fire him – or gave him the story to tell the Old Man to get him fired. All the war contracts were supposed to go through a central office in the organisation, and there was 'That Man Kimber' going off on his own again…"

Injured egos may well have been a part of this. In 1938 Lord Nuffield had swung an extraordinary deal with the government to build a factory at Castle Bromwich for the manufacture of the Supermarine Spitfire fighter. The project turned into a nightmare, with clear evidence of massive incompetence on the part of the Nuffield managers. In May 1940, at a stage when shockingly not a single Spitfire had been built, the aggressive and abrasive Lord Beaverbrook, newly appointed as Minister of Aircraft Production, had taken the running of the factory away from Nuffield.

Alongside this unfolding drama Nuffield had been asked to take control of all repair work for the RAF, and had been appointed Director-General of Maintenance at the Air Ministry. What was called the Civilian Repair Organisation was then set up as a new unit of the RAF, under the civilian control of Morris Motors.

Miles Thomas with William Morris. In 1947 it would be Thomas's turn to be sacked, when he was deemed to have become too big for his boots in taking on a government job alongside his vice-chairmanship of the Nuffield Organization. Appointed chairman of BOAC in 1949, multi-tasking networker Thomas, never a shrinking violet, was known as 'The Aplombable Showman' by colleagues at the state airline. (Author's collection)

Chapter Eighteen: Victim of the Snakepit

The CRO was to become a huge enterprise of crucial importance to the war effort, but once more the perception in government was that Nuffield was out of his depth trying to run it. The result was the same: in 1940 Beaverbrook transferred responsibility away from Morris Motors and Nuffield ceased to be Director-General of Maintenance.

Always touchy about being condescended to by what he thought were upper-class nabobs in the government and the civil service, Nuffield rightly or wrongly emerged thoroughly bruised from the Spitfire and CRO affairs. From that stage on, writes Miles Thomas in *Out on a Wing*, his chief 'had begun to sulk in his tent'. He can only have felt more grouchy watching Cecil Kimber make a success of the Albemarle contract – no doubt seen as having been secured via Beaverbrook, the man who legendarily had snatched away from him the Castle Bromwich factory after a brusque exchange on the telephone.

According to Jean, there was also a dispute about a minor administrative reorganisation, and this gave Thomas the pretext to act. 'Because of the connection with Lord Beaverbrook and John Howlett, Thomas could not quite use…the complicated building of the noses of Albemarle bombers as an excuse for getting rid of a thorn in his flesh, so he bided his time,' she writes in *The MG Log*. 'According to my father's story, a directive came from Morris…to centralise the issuing of unemployment and insurance stamps, which would mean sacking a faithful M.G. employee, a single woman who supported a widowed mother. My father refused. Next day, Miles Thomas arrived to demand his resignation.'

THE PRICE OF 'ACUTE INDIVIDUALISM'

In a letter to Lancashire garage owner and M.G. specialist Edward Lund, dated 2 January 1942, Kimber recounts what happened. 'It has been a terrible wrench for me as you can imagine but, right out of a blue sky, the Vice-Chairman of the Group deliberately created a false situation that left me with no option but to resign. I feel very bitter about it because of the gross injustice especially after over twenty years' service.'

In *Out on a Wing* Thomas describes the sacking as 'the first of several unpleasant executive duties I had to perform'. Talking of the M.G. founder as an incorrigible individualist, he goes on to say that 'when Kimber wanted to maintain his acute individualism after the war had broken out and adopt a policy of nonconformity when he was supposed to be working to Ministry specifications it was clear that there must be change.' Thomas knew what the consequences should be: 'I therefore went to see him at Abingdon in November 1941, and told him that he had better look for another outlet for his energies because he did not fit into the war-time pattern of the Nuffield Organization.'

According to Thomas, Kimber was 'thunderstruck…but accepted the situation with brave grace'. He goes on to say that he felt sorry for Kimber. 'He was completely unorthodox, even in his domestic life, which did not endear him to Lord Nuffield or, in particular, to Lady Nuffield.'

Thomas was alluding to what almost certainly was another element to the dismissal: his affair with Gillie, the separation from Rene when she was seriously ill, and then his second marriage – to someone understood to be a divorcee, to boot – a mere two months after Rene's death in April 1938. This would have been pretty racy by the standards of the time – and not least for Lady Nuffield. Thomas might well have felt a certain distaste, too, as apparently his wife had been friendly with Rene Kimber.

John Howlett had seen how Nuffield operated. 'It made me angry the way Nuffield used up people,' he writes in *The Guv'nor*. 'Poor

little Cecil Kimber was just one of the great majority who seemed to give their very souls into his keeping, and Nuffield, for all his great public benefactions, was a rather awkward sort of god in private.'

Howlett saw Kimber when he returned to Fyfield Manor after Thomas's visit. 'He was white-faced and stunned – he just couldn't understand why he had deserved the sack.' Encouraged by Howlett, Kimber went to see Nuffield, and came back, according to Howlett, 'more bewildered than ever'. Lord Nuffield had been evasive when he had received Kimber at Cowley.

"He had me in his office for an hour...but he wouldn't let me get anywhere near the issue I'd come to talk to him about. He talked generalities for an hour," Kimber told Howlett. "He just kept me talking about things he wasn't interested in to stop me from saying what I'd come to say. And then he indicated it was time for me to go. He evaded me. He tiptoed all around me. He didn't give me a chance."

This comes across as a boss trying not to get dragged into taking to pieces a decision made by one of his senior managers, whom he does not wish to undermine. Admittedly Lord Nuffield wasn't averse to asserting his authority, but given his increasing distance from decision-making, it seems wholly probable that even in this rather special instance he wasn't prepared to get involved.

A hard-nosed but fundamentally decent person, but also acknowledged as someone with little grace or finesse, if this were indeed the case, then Nuffield must have felt desperately awkward – hence his round-the-houses conversation with Kimber. It was presumably on closing the door after this fruitless interview that Cecil Kimber dictated that terse letter, heavy with unspoken words.

John Howlett and Gladys Hamilton, after their marriage.

Howlett said that he ought to sue for unfair dismissal, but Kimber told him he was not prepared to do this. "I don't feel I could do a thing like that to him, not to Morris, not after all this time. Nearly twenty years, and me a director for six of them. You see, John, he gave me the chance to be someone in the motor trade; none of us would have been up to much without him. And if he thinks it right to put me back on the market now, well I must admit he puts me back with better prospects than I had when he took up with me. I ought to be able to find a job easily enough, it's just the way he's treated me, the way he's gone about doing this to me, that's what's so difficult to take."

FAREWELL TO ABINGDON

Returning to the M.G. factory, Cecil Kimber called his staff together and with quiet dignity told them he was leaving. 'There were no explanations, no recriminations,' writes Wilson McComb. 'One member of the staff, Reg Jackson, was out on a service job, so a message was left asking him to call at the Kimber home that evening. On that occasion Kimber revealed something of what had occurred, but Jackson always respected his chief's confidence. Not until more than twenty years later, when *Out on a Wing* was published, was the story made public.'

The workforce paid a touching farewell to Kimber, relates Jean in *The Other Tack*: '[A] deputation from the works came to present my father with a pair of silver candelabra, and a tobacco cabinet made by the jig and toolmakers, which I am sure meant most to him. It was quite terrible to see such a respected and honourable man with tears in his eyes, plainly bewildered by what had happened.'

Also bewildered were Kimber's friends in the motoring press. 'It will be hard, indeed, to think of M.G.s without Cecil Kimber,' wrote *The Motor* in its 10 December 1941 issue. 'The M.G. car has kept a distinct and traditional character of its own, and this character has been almost entirely a reflection of CK's ideas of what a car should be like. That large numbers of others agree with him is quite evident from the fact that there must be more M.G. cars on the road than any other British sports car – probably more than any other sports car in the world…

'[He] can look back with pride and pleasure on the record of his cars up to the outbreak of war. Not only have they given pleasure to their owners but the marque has always been remarkably successful in upholding British prestige abroad. It was interesting to note when travelling on the Continent that M.G. was a household name in estaminet and lokale, whereas many other British cars of far larger output were completely unknown.'

Tractor supremo Harry Ferguson wrote to Kimber from the United States with his views on Lord Nuffield. 'I am not surprised at anything he would do. It appears to me you got shameful treatment, but I should put the blame on Nuffield rather than upon Thomas, who may only have been the tool,' he says in a letter of 3 September 1942[4]. 'Over in this country that kind of man is described as a man without background. Under the circumstances, I think you are well clear of him but unquestionably you have been very, very badly treated indeed, as far as I can see.'

In his reply, Kimber tells Ferguson that when he left the Morris group he received an offer of financial backing and enquired about taking over the M.G. business[5] – 'but Nuffield would not consider it'. Ferguson's rejoinder is sour: 'It was just like this man to refuse to sell you the M.G. Company. I do not suppose he wants it particularly, but he has a very mean streak, of which I have had sad experience,' he writes.

---

[4] This view accords with that of Kimpton Smallbone. "Nuffield never had the pluck to get rid of a man on his own, but always someone else did it for him," Smallbone observed to Andrews and Brunner.

[5] One wonders whether the story retailed by Hubert Charles to Wilson McComb about Cecil Kimber having backing to set up on his own in 1935 (see Chapter 11) in fact relates to what happened after Kimber's sacking – this being unambiguously documented in correspondence in the author's hands.

19

STARTING OUT AGAIN

THE M.G. TWO-LITRE TOURER
Four seater open model by Charlesworth
£385 *(ex works)*

ABOVE: *Charlesworth provided tourer coachwork for the M.G. Two-litre (or SA); this is the earlier type with flat-topped doors.*

OPPOSITE: *Bobbie, Jean and Gillie, at Elstree, January 1943, Bobbie adjusting Kimber's tie for the camera.*

After a pause of four months, Kimber had recovered sufficiently from the shock of his dismissal to take up a new job. This was with Coventry-based coachbuilder Charlesworth. Established in 1907, the company, which had been restructured in 1931 after a period in receivership, had latterly been bodying mainly Alvis cars, these representing something in the order of

80 per cent of 1937-38 output. Charlesworth had also bodied a hundred or so of the M.G. SA and WA as open tourers, and plant manager and chief designer John Cannell was a former Abingdon engineer. Kimber thus had connections with the business, and was friendly with Managing Director John Reynolds.

The company had been manufacturing aircraft components at its Much Park Street premises in Coventry, but in November 1940 the factory was destroyed in the blitz. Its wartime activities were thereafter centred on a 50,000 sq ft facility in Newent, Gloucestershire, established in 1939 by Hawker Siddeley subsidiary Gloster Aircraft. The works were managed by Charlesworth, and specialised in sheet-metal work.

FROM CHARLESWORTH TO SPECIALLOID

Kimber joined Charlesworth on 1 April 1942, taking a substantial drop in salary, to £900 per annum; tasked to reorganise the factory for more efficient production, he moved with Gillie into accommodation at a local hotel. 'My stepmother was very good at making the best of whatever befell her and had soon subjugated the entire staff of the Bell Hotel at Tewkesbury, where my parents lived for six months, with her charm and humour,' recounts Jean.

'By the time I arrived to spend my summer holidays, the Irish waiter was dashing up to our table announcing "Four gooseberry fools and I'm one of them!" We went on the river, and I paddled my father in a Canadian-style canoe, or we all paddled a punt, so water again was helping him regain his balance.'

Despite such diversions, this was not a happy period for Kimber, who was brought low by health problems. During the summer he went into hospital for a hernia operation and also had the little finger of his right hand amputated, as it had curled up. 'This hurt him almost more as a "phantom finger" than it had before,' writes Jean. He then went down with tonsillitis. Finally, whilst under the pressure of tackling the backlog of work that had accumulated in his absence, he suffered an ulcer on one eye which, he reported in October, prevented reading or writing for some weeks.

Kimber's time at Charlesworth, interrupted as it was by ill health, was of short duration, as in autumn 1942 he was offered the position of Works Director at piston manufacturer Specialloid, with a starting date of 1 December and the brief to run the main factory in Finchley, North London, and subsidiary facilities in Boreham Wood. At a salary of £1,500 per annum, plus a quarterly bonus that would put annual earnings up to around £5,000, the package was a generous one in comparison to the £2,750 salary he had latterly enjoyed whilst in the employ of Morris.

The new job seemed to get off to a good start when Kimber and Specialloid director Eric Graham had lunch at the RAC Club to finalise the appointment, and the two men ended up talking mostly about boats. There was a steering problem on Graham's vessel, and the next day he received a drawing from Kimber that apparently led to the problem being resolved.

As a new home, a large five-bedroom furnished house at 6 Barham Avenue in Elstree was rented, and Kimber threw himself into his new job – although not, it would appear, with any great enthusiasm. 'As far as I can see now, my future will be wrapped up with this concern, which is a highly progressive and prosperous firm and one of the largest piston manufacturers in the country,' he wrote somewhat flatly to Harry Ferguson in April 1943.

JEAN FINDS HER FEET

Both Bobbie and Jean were now away from home, Bobbie in the WRAF and Jean completing her year at St James's Secretarial College in Crewkerne. Equipped with a full Secretarial Diploma, Jean had a brief interim job during 1943 as assistant secretary to Geoffrey Smith, a managing editor at magazine publishers Iliffe. Smith was a friend of Kimber's, and was happy to give his daughter a job. During this period Jean briefly lived at the Elstree house, before entering the Women's Royal Naval Service in September 1943 to train as a signaller. 'We soon knew all the neighbours, and in spite of food shortages and bombing, I can remember some happy times there when I finished at secretarial college, and was travelling up to London every day,' she writes.

ABOVE: *Jean in 1942, in which year she celebrated her 17th birthday.*

LEFT: *A letter to Cecil Kimber from the Specialloid company secretary; on the letterhead Kimber's position as Works Director is given as well as his membership of the Institution of Automobile Engineers.*

ON AIR MINISTRY WAR OFFICE AND ADMIRALTY LISTS

  Specialloid
LIMITED

DIRECTORS:
H.N. BATES, M.I.MECH.E., CHAIRMAN AND MANAGING DIRECTOR
C.F. RUSSELL, GENERAL MANAGER & DIRECTOR
E.B. GRAHAM, TECHNICAL DIRECTOR
C. KIMBER, M.I.A.E., WORKS DIRECTOR
I.C. FLOWER, DIRECTOR

NORTH FINCHLEY
LONDON N·12

SOLE MANUFACTURERS OF
SPECIALLOID
PISTONS

TELEPHONES:
HILLSIDE 2233 7 LINES

TELEGRAMS:
SPECIALOID·LONDON

OUR REF.   YOUR REF.   DATE

LHM/IP   4th October 1943.

C. Kimber Esq.,
6, Barham Avenue,
Elstree,
HERTS.

Dear Mr. Kimber,

    A cheque has today been forwarded to your Bank value £69. 3. 9. made up as follows:-

September Salary	£125. 0. 0.
Car Allowance	29. 3. 4.
	154. 3. 4.
Less Income Tax	84.19. 7.
	£ 69. 3. 9.

    We enclose herewith cheque value £62.10. 0. being in respect of Expenses for the Quarter to 30th September.

    We are,

        Yours faithfully,

FOR AND ON BEHALF OF
SPECIALLOID LIMITED

SECRETARY
(L.H. Maidman)

THIS PAGE: *Bobbie, Jean and Gillie, in some further shots taken at Elstree in January 1943; the gentleman in uniform is Clive Lacey, an RAF officer who had become a family friend, as related on page 374.*

Chapter Nineteen: Starting Out Again

LEFT (BOTH): *Jean and Bobbie at the piano, on the same day.*

ABOVE: *A sober-looking Kimber at home in Elstree; gentlemen in those days did not consider wearing a suit in the house to be over-dressing.*

By this stage Jean had a serious boyfriend, Eric McGavin, a First Officer and Conductor of Music on the training ship *Mercury* near Southampton. She had met McGavin though Betty, which risked causing a problem. 'I had some difficulty over introducing Eric to my father and stepmother as we had met when I had gone to spend a weekend with my sister, whom I was expressly forbidden to see,' she relates in *The Other Tack*.

'Oh dear. I do wish there wasn't all this wretched business of Bett's being a bad influence on me,' she says in a letter to McGavin in March 1943. 'I don't blame her for her way of life, but it does make things just a bit difficult for me to cope with. I suppose all parents are as particular as Mummy and Daddy but sometimes I have a sneaking desire just to dope them one day, so that I can do things without having to say where I'm going and whom with!'

Thankfully for Jean, other aspects of her private life remained a secret between the two sisters – and a source of amusement to Jean. In a pause in her relationship with McGavin, who was ten years older than her, she took up with someone closer to her age who was a professed adherent of what was then called 'free love'. Betty, 'who had indulged herself, was the one to save me,' writes Jean in an unpublished memoir of her wartime years. 'We went to stay for a weekend, and she was horrified and warned me to be wary and not let myself get caught. It is interesting that my sister, so advanced in her own ideas of female sexual emancipation, could not handle her anxiety about my sexual freedom!'

SAILING CLOSE TO THE ROCKS

At around this juncture Kimber and Gillie decided to find a cottage somewhere on the coast where they could spend the winter – and at the same time to purchase a bigger boat on which they could live during the summer. In June 1943 a suitable boat was found in Scotland; a 17-ton ketch that measured 39.2ft on the waterline and 46ft overall, it was given the name *Sea Witch*. During this period Kimber was also continuing to follow what was going on in the sailing world, and in the correspondence columns of *Yachting World* he contributed to a debate about luffing rules – the conventions regarding steering a boat towards the wind when racing.

Meanwhile, overwork and a psychologically unrewarding job had taken their toll on Kimber. '[In] August I crocked up and the Doctor ordered me a month's rest as he said I was heading for a nervous breakdown,' he wrote to Ferguson in January 1944. 'This lengthened into two and then they discovered a streptococci [sic] in my tonsils which were traced to my back teeth. This had been poisoning my system, added to which a lack of vitamins in the food these days prevented my resisting them as I might otherwise have done. Anyway, my back teeth had to come out and this has been a long and painful process as each extraction flooded me with poison and made me thoroughly ill. I had the last three out at the beginning of the year so now I hope to go from strength to strength. So all this time, since August, I've been on sick leave.'

What Kimber did not reveal to Ferguson was how unhappy he had become in his job at Specialloid, something he made clear in a letter around the same time to his uncle Sydney. 'I have an aching jaw and feel very low…[Although] I am still on the Board and am on the friendliest terms, I do not expect to go back,' he writes. 'My job as Works Director did not work out as expected as the Managing Director just could not bring himself to delegate any authority and interfered with petty matters which was alright when the firm was a small one with only about a hundred employees, but he couldn't get used to the idea that different methods are necessary with 1,400 men and six factories…[The] frustration I suffered…the worry and strain…were not worth the handsome remuneration…and I think it was this, more than anything, that brought me to the edge of a nervous breakdown.'

Jean recalled how low was her father's morale at this time. 'I remember him playing patience for hours, always a sign that he was battling against depression,' she writes in *The Other Tack*. To Wilson McComb she said that she thought he was 'brokenhearted' and that playing patience was something he had a habit of doing 'when he wanted to think.'

Artist Harold Connolly picked up on Kimber's state of mind when the two re-established contact at around this time: it seemed he was still brooding over his dismissal by Lord Nuffield. 'He said, "Look, I'm with Specialloid Pistons now, would you like to do some drawings for me?" So I picked up with him again,' Connolly related to McComb. 'He hadn't changed a bit – still just as nice. Kind, thoughtful, and never, never went up-stage. But he was very unhappy. He wouldn't discuss it with me, I'll say that for him – he was loyal enough. But I knew they had hurt him badly. After all, he did found the firm, he'd put it where it was, and they could afford to put up with his peccadilloes.'

In despair, but also with the hope of better times ahead, Kimber had in fact handed in his resignation from his post at Specialloid. Some light did however penetrate this gloom, as in the second half of 1943 at least two future career paths appeared to be opening up. Meanwhile, despite his differences with the company, Specialloid did not want to lose Kimber and refused to accept his resignation. 'I told you about having resigned from Specialloids. However, this shattered them so much that they first asked me to remain on the Board, and now they want me back on full time and at the same handsome salary to look after Sales Promotion,' he says in a February 1944 letter to Sydney Kimber. 'As I know, literally, everyone in the Motor Industry, they know how valuable I can be to them. I haven't decided yet as I can't altogether ignore over 5,000 dollars a year, but the allure of making cars again is very strong.'

All this was equally outlined in Kimber's January 1944 letter to Harry Ferguson. 'During this period I have had several approaches made to me not unconnected with the making of fast motor cars after the war which induced me to tell Specialloids that I did not think I would come back to them. The thought of making nothing but pistons for the rest of my life, in spite of it being well paid, was too grim a prospect to contemplate with something so much more exciting in view. However, they asked me to remain on the Board and providing this does not interfere with my future activities, it suits me alright,' he writes.

'It is too early to tell you anything about it, even if I could, but I have several possibilities in mind, and have not decided in which direction to go. Meanwhile I am a free lance and if there are any commissions you would like me to execute for you, just let me know…

'There is a possibility that I may be invited to join one of the biggest independent engine manufacturers in the Country, which, if I do, might be interesting from your point of view.

'Anyway, I am not going to be in any hurry as, if it had not been for the present high scale of taxation, I might have been tempted to retire though I think I am still too active seriously to consider this.'

JOINING FORCES WITH HEALEY?

The references to returning to 'the making of fast motor cars' is intriguing. Although confirmation has not proved possible, it seems likely that Kimber was in conversations with Donald Healey about the possible revival of the Triumph marque. The two men had known each other for many years, dating back to the time when Healey was a keen trials driver and was running a garage in Cornwall. Healey had gone on to become Technical Director at Triumph, and under his supervision the company had briefly blossomed before falling into receivership in 1939 and being acquired by Sheffield steel company Thomas Ward.

What Ward's intentions were for its new acquisition was never clear. The bigger of the Triumph factories was soon compulsorily purchased by the government and used for the manufacture of Claudel-Hobson aircraft carburettors and the smaller Stoke facility, which turned to sub-contract work for Armstrong Whitworth, was badly damaged in the November 1940 bombing of Coventry. The remaining spare parts for Triumph cars were bulldozed into the ground or sold for scrap and the marque's future looked uncertain.

In 1941 Healey had moved to the Rootes Group, and in his spare time was scheming a car of his own. His hope was that the

Triumph name could be revived, and that he would be able to use it for his vehicle. Talks began with Thomas Ward, being most likely underway by the end of 1943 or very early in 1944. It seems that at this stage Kimber and Healey may have started talking about a possible collaboration.

But then Healey's plans fell apart. 'Donald and I began to feel that our little team was really getting somewhere and we now felt that we very nearly had a good enough design to think about production and that the time had come for us to try and sell our ideas to Triumph's,' wrote former Triumph sales director James Watt, then working on the Healey project and also serving with Donald Healey in the RAF Volunteer Reserve[1].

'I had already made two fairly successful approaches to Triumph's and in February 1944 the opportunity arose for another meeting. Very conveniently my Commanding Officer had a new aeroplane to collect at Doncaster that week so I reckoned that this would be a handy way to get to Sheffield. So I flew up to the all-important meeting.

'At first things seemed most encouraging and they genuinely thought that our scheme and ideas had merit. However, Triumph's had had a board meeting recently and I was tremendously downcast to learn that they had decided not to back Healey, mainly for the very simple reason that we were not motor-car manufacturers…And so we had to put aside all thoughts of building our car at Triumph's…'

---

[1] Watt's oft-quoted memories were put down on paper for author and former BMC Competitions Manager Peter Browning and first given exposure in his 1970 book *Healeys and Austin-Healeys*.

OPPOSITE: *Donald Healey, here with the Healey Westland in which he finished ninth in the 1948 Mille Miglia; it seems possible that the former Technical Director of Triumph, in the process of creating what would become the Riley-engined Healey, was talking to Kimber about the two joining forces.*

Possibly prompted by the Healey project, if he was indeed involved with it, May 1944 saw Cecil Kimber authoring two articles in *The Autocar* that explored his thoughts on the future design of sports cars. In an October 1944 talk delivered to the Institution of Automobile Engineers he further developed his ideas, which demonstrate a wide-ranging and forward-looking mind but at the same time a sensible pragmatism.

Retaining a separate chassis, to allow for differing bodies, Kimber's proposed post-war sports car was seen as having an optionally-supercharged alloy-block four-cylinder in-line engine with bevel-driven overhead camshaft, mated to a gearbox with either overdrive or a fifth gear. Independent front suspension of the André-Girling type would have torsion-bar springing, there would be a de Dion back axle, and the chassis would have welded sheet steel elements, including a bulkhead as part of the structure.

By the time of the October talk Kimber had inclined to using leaf springs with the de Dion rear, and was advocating the adoption of disc brakes, having picked up on their use on US aircraft. These two features would only appear on mainstream cars in the 1950s (disc brakes, on the 1955 Citroën DS) and the 1960s (de Dion rear axle, on the 1963 Rover 2000), so he deserves credit for proposing engineering details that were advanced for the day.

Kimber, who in 1944 also had an article published by *The Autocar* outlining his vision of post-war motor racing, was evidently proud of these magazine articles. 'I'm glad you liked my article in *The Autocar* but the second instalment is more interesting and I hope you have been able to get hold of a copy. It has been very well received and created a lot of favourable comment in the trade,' he commented in a September 1944 letter to Harry Ferguson. Despite this, he told Ferguson that he felt that nothing would emerge from his propositions for a well-engineered sports car for the connoisseur. 'I doubt if anybody is going to be interested in making this in the immediate post-war years as all the manufacturers will be so occupied in trying to supply a car-hungry nation who will be prepared to buy anything as long as it has four wheels and an engine.'

THE TEMPTATION OF TRIUMPH: TALKS WITH SIR JOHN BLACK

The future of Triumph was ultimately resolved when in November 1944 the Standard Motor Company purchased the remains of the business for £75,000. The bombed Stoke factory was supposedly 'not worth a farthing', but the Standard boss could see the value of the Triumph name. According to a press release, 'the experience and technique gained in the production of aircraft' would be used for 'the production of Triumph cars of character and distinction.' Soon – perhaps even before the agreement had been formalised – Black was commissioning sketches of a new open Triumph, which he wanted to be an amalgam of pre-war SS at the front and dickey-seat Dolomite roadster at the rear; the result would be the blowsy Triumph 1800 Roadster announced in March 1946.

Whether Kimber and Healey were still talking about joining forces – if indeed they had ever started – is not known. What does seem to be the case is that Black was keen to have Kimber on board for his proposed revival of Triumph, if Harold Connolly's recollections, recorded by Wilson McComb, are any guide.

'[Kimber] told me…he'd love to be back doing cars again. I know he was longing to get out of the piston business. "Y'see," he said, "there's nothing to it, you just make a piston and there it is, it's either a good one or a bad one."

'He was going to take me up to see Black for the weekend, to talk about cars and shapes and designs. I felt Black thought Kimber would make a lovely head for Triumph, with the reputation he had…in spite of the bloody awful thing he was trying to sell, with its coal-scuttle mudguards; it was a dreadful-looking crate. And that's what Kimber said to me. He said, "You come up with me, we'll talk to Black, we'll get some shape into that Triumph"…'

Kimber did indeed pay Sir John Black a visit, and he was not reassured by the plans for his newly-acquired prestige marque, as he lamented to journalist Harold Hastings in a letter of 30 January 1945. 'I feel somewhat pessimistic about the future of the real enthusiast's car. Sunbeam-Talbot, Riley and now M.G. have been or will be wrecked by the soul-deadening hand of the big business interests, and recently I have been staying with John Black who has just bought Triumph's, and what he proposes to do with that old name makes me want to weep. Lea-Francis appear to be the only concern left to cater for the real enthusiast…Singer's may come into the picture, but I think this is doubtful.'

MORALE RE-FOUND – AND A NEW LIFE PLANNED

In fact Kimber seems to have been oscillating between enthusiasm for a return to motor-manufacturing and a decision to seek at least semi-retirement. Possibly pushing him in the latter direction was his purchase of that seaside cottage that he and Gillie had promised themselves. Early in 1944 they had found just what they were looking for in Itchenor – 'built around 1600-something, old oak beams and old Sussex brick' – but the owner hadn't wanted sell. 'We haven't recovered from the disappointment yet,' he wrote in February to his uncle Sydney.

By August of that year he was able to tell Sydney that he had found a suitable substitute, still in Itchenor. 'We've got our little cottage at Itchenor. Not the one I told you about in my last letter but a much nicer one and, all being well, in three or four years' time we hope to retire to it though we intend to live on our boat during the summer. Itchenor is a lovely unspoilt village beloved by yachtsmen and situated on Chichester Harbour, and yet only two hours from town which will enable me to keep on with a part-time job if I feel like it. However when I get busy in my workshop and doing jobs on the boat, I shan't feel like doing much work. I want to take up painting again. I did a bit whilst I had a week's holiday which I spent with another fellow in this caravan but situated by the side of my little Cotswold trout stream at Eastleach…

'I'm back again with Specialloids in full harness and have put aside any thoughts of getting back into the motor car game again. If I did I should never be able to retire when I want to as I should get involved and be an old man before I knew where I was.'

Kimber says pretty much the same thing to Harold Hastings in his January 1945 letter. 'I don't think you will find me making cars again as I want to retire, or semi-retire, in a very few years, and if I once got caught up in the whirl, heaven knows when I should be free again,' he wrote. 'Instead we have bought a cottage at Itchenor, that delightful little yachting centre on Chichester harbour, and we are looking forward to getting down there after the war – and we can get the present tenants out! – and, until I can give up working altogether, having a small flat in town. I'm determined to retire whilst I am still young enough to enjoy going off sailing or fishing when I feel inclined.'

Back at work at Specialloid, Kimber needed, at least in the short term, to retain a principal home close to the company's factories. With Jean and Bobbie on war service, the rented Elstree house was proving needlessly large and, with no maid to help, Gillie was finding running it a chore. This was all the more so when hordes of youngsters descended on the house for jolly weekends; there was also a billeted airman to be looked after. So it was that in June 1944 the couple moved to Rose Cottage in Barnet Lane in Totteridge, a semi-rural suburb in the borough of Barnet.

'It's rather a nice little place with a delightful garden full of fruit trees and bushes – rather too much work for me – and not so large as the house at Elstree which was far too much for my wife to look after in these maidless days and far too great a temptation to the girls to bring home masses of friends at the weekends. They, of course, didn't appreciate the amount of work that eight or nine

Kimber had talks with Sir John Black, whose proposals for what became the Triumph Roadster horrified him. (BMIHT)

people in the house meant for one pair of hands, not to mention the strain on rations,' Kimber told Hastings.

He was now in a better frame of mind, he confirmed. 'Having had most of my teeth out, I'm glad to say that I was quite fit again by last April and am once more back in harness. The firm are making use of the many friends I have in the industry and in consequence I get about a lot and thoroughly enjoy my lot.'

Home on leave in October 1944, Jean could see a transformation in her father. 'I can still see him meeting friends at the RAC, full of energy and enthusiasm. He limped across to speak to a rather tall man, and as he looked up at his friend, I suddenly thought he was like a small terrier at a rabbit hole, full of expectant bounce. In that moment, I realized I had grown up, and that I understood and loved my father whatever his faults, or whatever differences we might have in the future,' she writes in *The Other Tack*.

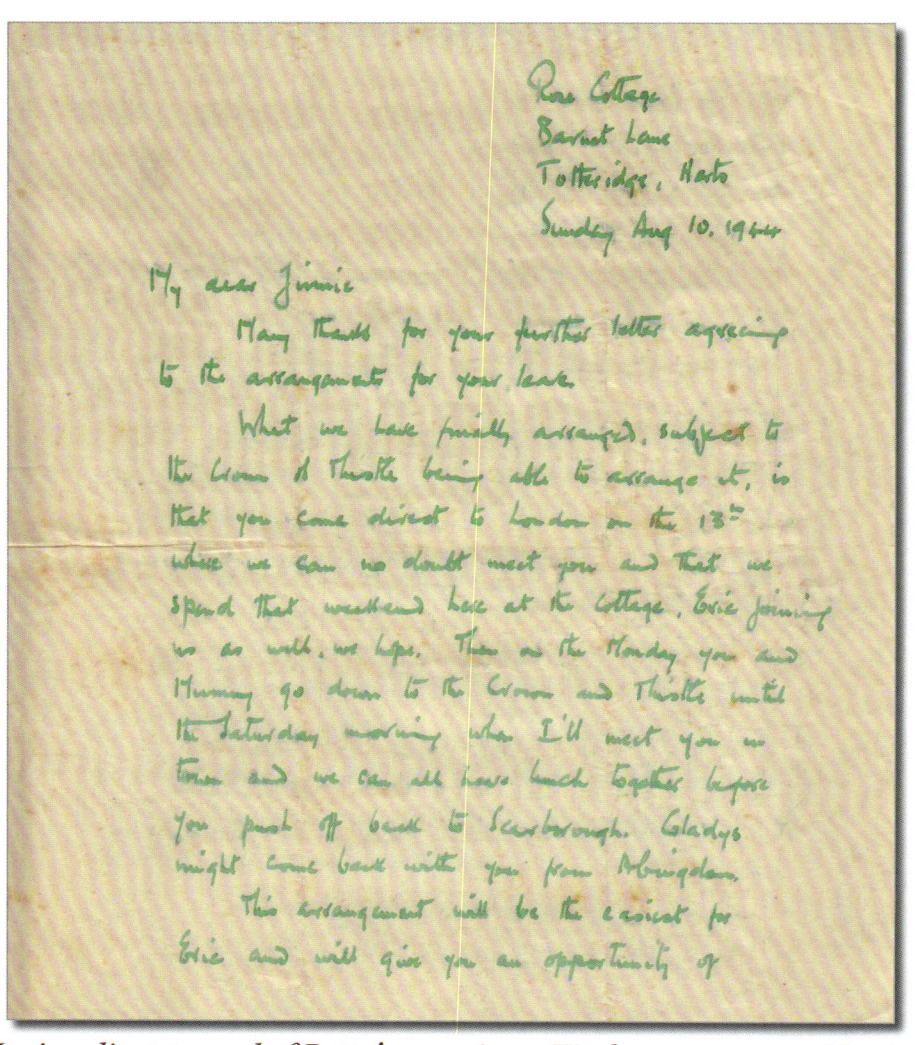
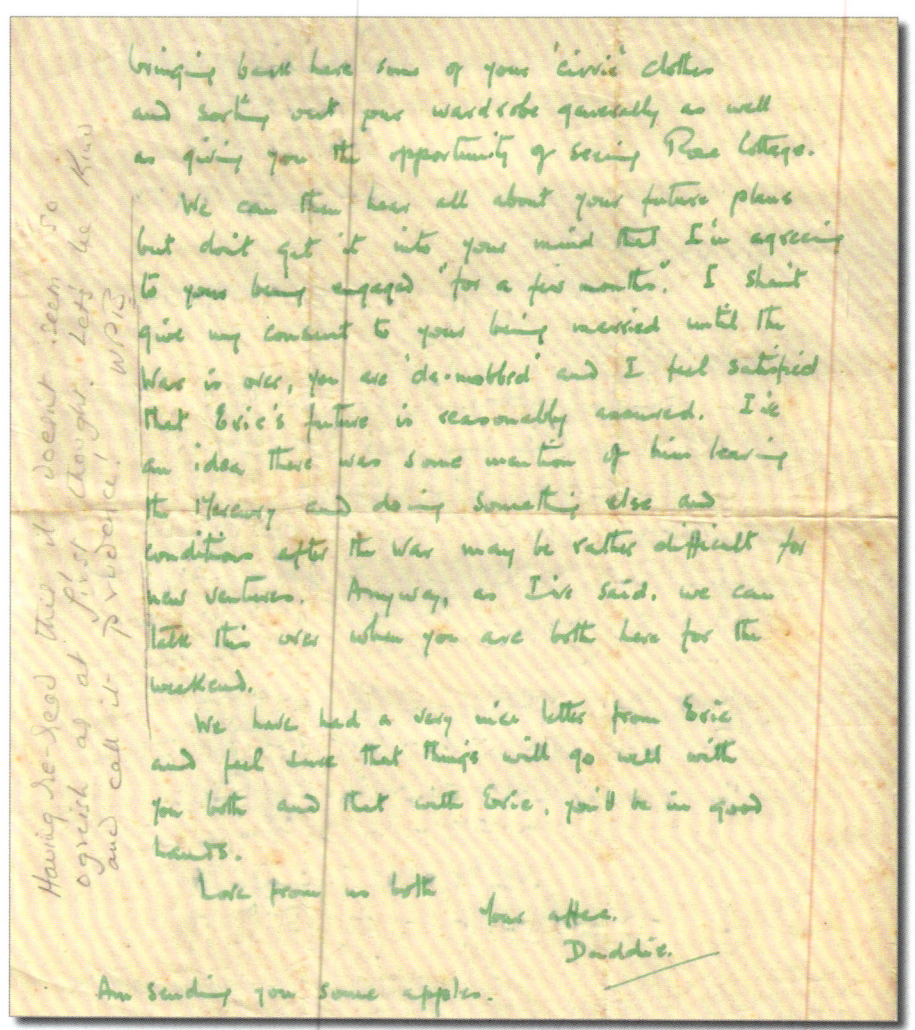

Having disapproved of Betty's marriage, Kimber now seemed hesitant about giving his accord to that of Jean. 'I shan't give my consent to your being married until the war is over, you are de-mobbed and I feel satisfied that Eric's future is reasonably assured,' he wrote to Jean in August 1944. He ends the letter, however, on a positive note, saying that he and Gillie thought that with Eric McGavin she would be in good hands. McGavin, a musician, was ten years older than Kimber's younger daughter.

Harold Hastings of The Motor *(far right) had a correspondence with Kimber in 1944/45. On the left in this photo can be seen Abingdon MD John Thornley and journalist and racing driver Tommy Wisdom (with glass); looking straight at the camera is BMC Technical Director Alec Issigonis. (Suzanne Hankey)*

Life wasn't without stresses, however. Soon after the move to Totteridge, Germany started to attack Britain with its V1 flying bombs – the infamous 'Doodlebugs'. The nervous strain these provoked brought on attack of sciatica in Gillie. Rather than carry on sleeping in the cottage cellar, Kimber and Gillie repaired to the George Hotel in Silsoe, described by Kimber as a 'delightful little village about halfway between Luton and Bedford'. This was only a temporary arrangement, recounts Jean. 'My father, resourceful as always, remembered the caravan he had been keeping at Eastleach for brief war-time holiday breaks. First, he moved it to a field north of Hertford. This proved to be still within the danger zone, so he prudently retired to an apple orchard at Tring, on the edge of the Chilterns, 34 miles north-west of London, where he and Gillie could at least sleep at night.'

CONVERSATIONS WITH THE TRACTOR KING

It was during 1942 that Cecil Kimber and tractor engineer Harry Ferguson began a correspondence that would stretch until late 1944. The two had known each other for many years. Ulsterman Ferguson had run a garage in Belfast before developing first a plough for use with Fordson tractors and then his own tractor and matching hydraulically-actuated implements. He had also been an enthusiastic racing motorist, and had been a major force in establishing the Ulster TT races.

When Ferguson started to devote all his efforts to perfecting his tractor system, his brother Victor took over the Harry Ferguson Ltd garage business, at the time an Austin distributor, before setting up on his own as Belfast-based Victor Ltd at the beginning of the 1930s. Victor Ferguson took on the main M.G. agency in Northern Ireland, and had close relations with Kimber. An active member of the Ulster Automobile Club, he competed in the 1931 Craigantlet hillclimb in a C-type thought to be works demonstrator and press car, and his workshops were used by M.G. during the TTs; in particular Nuvolari's K3 and Hamilton's J4 were prepared there for the 1933 event.

As well as there being this Ulster connection, Kimber had intervened on Harry Ferguson's behalf when the latter was demonstrating his coupling system to various parties at the beginning of the 1930s. The Norfolk estate of Sir Henry Birkin, with whom Ferguson had become friendly as a result of the TT, and who was of course well-known to Kimber, was used for tests and demonstrations. Further to this, the Prince of Wales and the Duke of Kent were shown the system at demonstrations held at a farm near Ascot racecourse. Kimber had previously arranged a meeting between Ferguson and Sir William Morris, as he then was, and Morris had sent a representative to the Ascot event. Subsequently he had offered to collaborate in developing the tractor and implements. An agreement was drafted but then Morris pulled out, something that had continued to rankle with Harry Ferguson.

RIGHT: *Ferguson was a talented engineer but his nervous energy, leech-like persistence and incurable perfectionism made him an impossible business partner. (Alamy)*

OPPOSITE: *Harry Ferguson with his arm around Sir John Black, at the wheel of a Ferguson tractor of the sort manufactured by Standard. The paths of both men crossed that of Cecil Kimber during the war years. (BMIHT)*

In the end, the first Ferguson tractors had been produced by David Brown in Huddersfield, starting in 1936. Their failure to sell led to a break with David Brown, who ended manufacture in 1939. By this stage Ferguson had entered into a gentleman's agreement with Henry Ford whereby the tractor would be made in the United States by Ford.

There was the prospect of manufacture also being undertaken by Ford of Britain at its Dagenham factory, but in the end Ford of Britain's General Manager Patrick Hennessey stuck to making the Fordson tractor for the duration of the war, bolstered by a deal with the British government. The failure to come to an agreement with Dagenham ultimately led Ferguson into an alliance with Standard's Sir John Black.

Meeting of minds: Henry Ford (left) and Harry Ferguson both had something of the messiah in their make-up. Ferguson's mission to mechanise agriculture immediately struck a chord with Ford, who agreed on a handshake to seal the deal to make the Ferguson tractor. (Author's collection)

PROPOSITIONS FOR A 'PEOPLE'S CAR'

Ferguson's animosity towards Lord Nuffield is evident in the first letter in the surviving correspondence, one dated 3 September 1942. 'I do not know whether you know it, but Nuffield treated me disgracefully. He promised the Prince of Wales – as he then was – and a few others and me that he would do certain things with regard to the development of a tractor for our System. I had a few doubts about him and I got him to confirm his promises so that there could be no possible doubt about what he had agreed to do. He put us to a lot of expense, delay, and trouble, and then without the slightest excuse brazenly broke his promise to us and refused to see me or discuss the situation,' relates Ferguson.

Having vented his spleen with regard to Nuffield, he moves on, in his somewhat awkward English, to the main purpose of his letter: would Kimber like to collaborate with him on the design and manufacture of a 'people's car' to be sold alongside his tractors?

'All this new Tractor and System of ours has been developed on a close study of automobile racing and now I want to talk to you about developing a real automobile to be developed on the marvellous foundation we are laying through agriculture,' he writes.

'If people are going to be very poor when the war ends the automobile business will not be worth much. The agricultural machinery will be the real thing, and on that business can be founded cars and trucks which will meet the Reconstruction Period.

'We shall want a small four- or five-seater car for the home and export trade of outstanding performance, light, powerful, durable, and which will operate with an economy that has not yet been approached.

'I cannot see how such a car could be developed other than by experience of racing, and if you and I can get together with this we may find a real joy and success in future years. Think it over and write me your views. [...]

Kimber was not convinced by Harry Ferguson's desire to make a people's car. He felt that Ford had a perfectly serviceable low-priced vehicle in its Anglia and Prefect models. This is a post-war Anglia, a stripped-out version of which became Britain's cheapest car when introduced as the Popular in 1953. (Author's collection)

'If you are thinking of a real utility automobile designed primarily for farmer's use, then I think you have something there but I doubt if there would be sufficient volume in this Country to get down to an attractive figure. Perhaps you are thinking in terms of a European market?

'The other day I spent some time examining one of the American Army's "Jeeps" and the thought came to me then what an ideal farmer's car it would make fitted with a smaller and more economical engine. With its four-wheel drive a farmer could literally go anywhere on his land with it, it could haul heavy loads to market and for the poorer type of farmer and small-holder who could not afford a conventional saloon, the "Jeep" would at least provide utility transportation for him and his family.'

Here Kimber is well ahead of the curve, anticipating by at least three years the thoughts of Rover's Wilks brothers, which were to lead to the creation of the Land Rover. Ferguson didn't buy into the idea. 'This subject is too big to be discussed by letter, but my general plan is already for a real volume car to be founded on agriculture. The car that would suit the farmer's needs would be

'There is an easy market in the British Isles for about one million tractors and about ten million implements, and there is something like 115 million farms in the whole of the world so you will realize the magnitude of the opportunity we have. What a foundation on which to build a car and truck business!'

ANTICIPATING THE LAND ROVER

In his reply of 12 October 1942, Kimber pours cold water on the idea. 'Your remarks about this want a little understanding as with the Ford Company at Dagenham turning out such an excellent car for the Masses and at prices that defy serious competition, it is difficult to imagine what you have in mind,' he writes. At the same time, though, he presciently puts his finger on a possible alternative more closely aligned with the needs of the farming community, an adaptation of the Jeep:

There was more mileage, Kimber felt, in creating a farmer's car derived from the Jeep – exactly as Rover would do with its Land-Rover, of which this is a Series I example. (Author's collection)

Chapter Twenty: Conversations with the Tractor King

also the car which would sell in the greatest volume throughout the country and there will be no trouble on this account,' he replies in a 22 October letter in which his thoughts can only be described as woolly. 'Surely with a big project like ours all ready to go when the war is over we should be able to get a factory and machinery on unheard-of good terms because of the great good we could do for the Country,' he continues.

What Ferguson envisaged, it appears, was something that could be a genuine popular motor car and at the same time suitable transport for the farmer. It is difficult to grasp exactly what he had in mind, and how he would reconcile two contrasting types of buyer. A drop-tailgate open tourer, sparsely trimmed, of the sort the French abandoned in the 1930s, would have hardly met the bill. A remodelled Jeep wouldn't be suitable: 'Your suggestion is quite intriguing and worthy of more thought, but I fear it would not work out unless a complete new model were made up and this would be costly because it would not sell, except for farmer's use. You see the farmers must have plenty of room in their cars. The car I have in mind is the thing for him and he will be able to buy it easily because of the greater profits he can make with low production costs made possible by our new System.'

Ferguson didn't let up, and tried to bring Ford of Britain into the equation. He talked to Dagenham boss Rowland Smith about the car project, and brought up Kimber's name – 'I also told him that you were a man whom I thought should be linked up with us in the future' – before setting up a lunch meeting in early 1943 between the two men. Kimber remained unconvinced by the proposed venture.

'Frankly, I would hesitate, if I were in your position, very strongly before I attempted to get into such a highly competitive field and I really do not think there is room for another quantity car manufacturer in this country. Personally, I cannot see why you should not link up the production of a new car with your already established Tractor,' he writes on 8 April 1943, concluding 'I do hope that you will hesitate a long time before you even consider making a motor car.'

DENIS KENDALL ENTERS THE PICTURE

Come 1944 and Kimber was still trying to discourage Ferguson. 'With regard to your idea of coming over here and producing a car for the masses, the more I think of this, the more I think it a terrific gamble,' he writes on 21 January. 'You've got to remember that there are already some big car producers whose works and facilities have been greatly increased under War production and, in addition to this, there is the huge aircraft industry who will be looking around for some outlet for their big resources and some of them are bound to think of making motor cars. Then there is a go-ahead fellow over here – something like your ship-building Kaiser[1], only smaller – who has announced his intention of making a People's Car after the War. No, unless you go in for the specialty market, as I intend to do, I don't think you have a dog's chance of surviving against the established interests and others.'

The 'go-ahead fellow' was Denis Kendall, a flamboyant self-publicising industrialist and would-be politician who was at the time very much in the public eye. The Halifax-born son of a Quaker mill-owner, in 1921 Kendall had jumped ship in the United States while serving in the Royal Fleet Auxiliary and after a number of odd jobs had ended up a few years later with automotive-pressings specialist Budd. Having liaised with Citroën on its use of Budd-patent all-steel bodies, in the 1933 to 1935 period he worked at the French company's Quai de Javel factory supervising the entry into production of the famous Traction Avant Citroën. It is said that by 1935 he was in England working for Pressed Steel, in which Budd was until 1936 a partner[2]. By 1938 Kendall was running a

---

[1] Henry Kaiser was a major US public-works contractor with many large-scale projects to his name. In the war he diversified into ship-building with the mass-production of the 'Liberty Ships' and started a project to create a low-cost motor car. Ultimately he established the Kaiser-Frazer car-manufacturing business.

[2] It is difficult to separate fact from self-serving fantasy in the story of Kendall; whether he actually worked directly for Citroën, for example, is not clear, let alone whether, as has been stated, he was a close personal friend of André Citroën. Many of the same tales are repeatedly retold, and for the Kendall car all too many writers take on trust the misleading account in Jean-Albert Grégoire's notoriously inaccurate *50 ans d'automobile*.

Denis Kendall MP in the first version of his Kendall; it had a rear-mounted radial engine and was supposed to sell at £100. Kendall also came up with a small three-wheel tractor. (Karl Ludvigsen)

newly-established British offshoot of Hispano-Suiza, set up in Grantham, Lincolnshire, to make the company's 20mm canon fitted to aircraft such as the Hurricane and Spitfire.

During the war the business expanded, Kendall became MP for Grantham in 1942, as an Independent, and in November 1944 the motoring weeklies carried details of the £100 popular car he had announced he was to produce after the war. In summer 1945 a gimcrack device powered by a rear-mounted three-cylinder air-cooled radial engine was shown to the press. It was delusional stuff. After a second prototype had been built, Kendall turned to another self-promoting figure best held at a safe distance, and agreed to manufacture under licence Jean-Albert Grégoire's alloy-hulled Aluminium-Français Grégoire[3]. Kendall's supposed

backers evaporated, nothing came of the AFG-based Kendall, and after losing his parliamentary seat in 1950 Kendall decamped to the United States, where he made lightweight diesel engines and electronic devices to help alleviate arthritis.

There is no reason to believe that Kimber felt any warmth towards the braggardly Kendall, whom he does not seem to have known personally. Nor is it credible, either, that the ascetic Ulster messiah would have been able to establish any meaningful rapport with such a bombastic showman. But for Kimber the introduction of Kendall's name into these discussions allowed him to fend off Ferguson's advances, whilst at the same time appearing to offer constructive advice. Ferguson took the bait. Perhaps working with Kimber should be something to consider a bit further down the line, he pondered.

'I just cannot say whether you could help by joining us now. We want a very brilliant business man, manufacturer, salesman

After it became apparent that his rear-engined car was a no-hoper, Kendall proposed to put into production Jean-Albert Grégoire's little twin-cylinder front-wheel-drive car, with its cast-aluminium hull. (Marc-Antoine Colin)

---

[3] Hawked around the French motor industry, the ingenious AFG was never a realistic proposition for series production. In the end it served as the basis for the design of the Dyna-Panhard, but only after its salient technical feature, the cast-aluminium hull, had been rejected as impractical by Panhard's engineers. Henry Kaiser was one of those to have a brief involvement with Grégoire; nothing tangible resulted from their discussions.

and organizer to take charge of our Eastern Hemisphere developments, provided we can straighten out our difficulties. I am sure you would not take this job because I do not think it would suit you, but you might help us to find someone and I am willing to talk to you about any job in the company,' writes Ferguson in a letter of 23 February 1944.

'Who is this "Kaiser man" to whom you refer? Might he not be the man for us? This is the greatest opportunity in the world. Feel free to have a talk with him, provided you have confidence in him.

'There is just nothing that I can offer you that would definitely get us working together at this time, so, Kim, if any promising offer comes your way in the work you like, do not miss it. You may get into something such as the engine company where we could still work together, or perhaps in a car company where I could be interested.'

Ferguson was still bubbling with enthusiasm for his car project. 'All the difficulties you mention only create the opportunity. All are child's play compared with what we had to face in the tractor industry...

'If I could talk to you about a car, I could quickly show you what a marvellous opportunity we have by doing things differently from the way others do them...

'What an opportunity your "Kaiser man" would have if he combines honesty and sincerity with brilliant ability.'

Ferguson even talks – music to Kimber's ears? – of a participation in motor racing: 'If all goes as we hope, we are going to encourage racing in a highly practical form. Indeed, in every country where we are having success, we should like to subscribe to racing to help build up international teams for a Grand Prix.'

After a further letter in which Ferguson evokes involving the Duke of Richmond in his projects, Kimber responds in May 1944 to the appeal for more information on his hitherto un-named industrialist. 'You asked who is this Kaiser man to whom I made reference in my previous letter. He is a man named Kendall who is a very go-ahead type,' he writes. 'He started business in Grantham making machine guns, had a row with the Ministries on price and production and won; put up as a member of Parliament and got in and now I hear he has been promised some very considerable financial backing with which he intends to break into the Morris, Austin, Standard, Ford and Vauxhall market and I think we shall hear more of him.'

DISENTANGLEMENT FROM 'THE GREATER PLAN'

Kimber by this stage can be presumed to have had his mind on other things, following his return to full-time work at Specialloid and his continuing hunt for a seaside cottage. 'I am afraid I can help you but very little in the big plan that you have ahead of you,' he writes on 8 May 1944. Ferguson was not deterred. Indeed, Kimber's articles in *The Autocar* prompted thoughts of an even-deeper collaboration.

'You have incorporated many of my own ideas, and there is not a doubt in my mind that you and I could work together on what I call the "Greater Plan". I could not begin to tell you in writing all the details of what is in my mind. If I do not go home before long, I may give you a cordial invitation to come out here at my expense and talk over this "Greater Plan" with me...I can see all that is in your mind about cars, and if this were coupled with what is in my mind, we would indeed have something of immense National value,' Ferguson writes on 26 June 1944.

'It would be a great pity if you got linked up with a poor crowd for the development of your ideas. Next time you want to start something where your good work will not be lost to you.

'If Kendall continues to be promising, why not keep in contact with him, and we may all work something out together of very great value. I would say that your ideas about a sports car should unquestionably be linked with a volume-producing concern which could handle this and carry your ideas out to the fullest.'

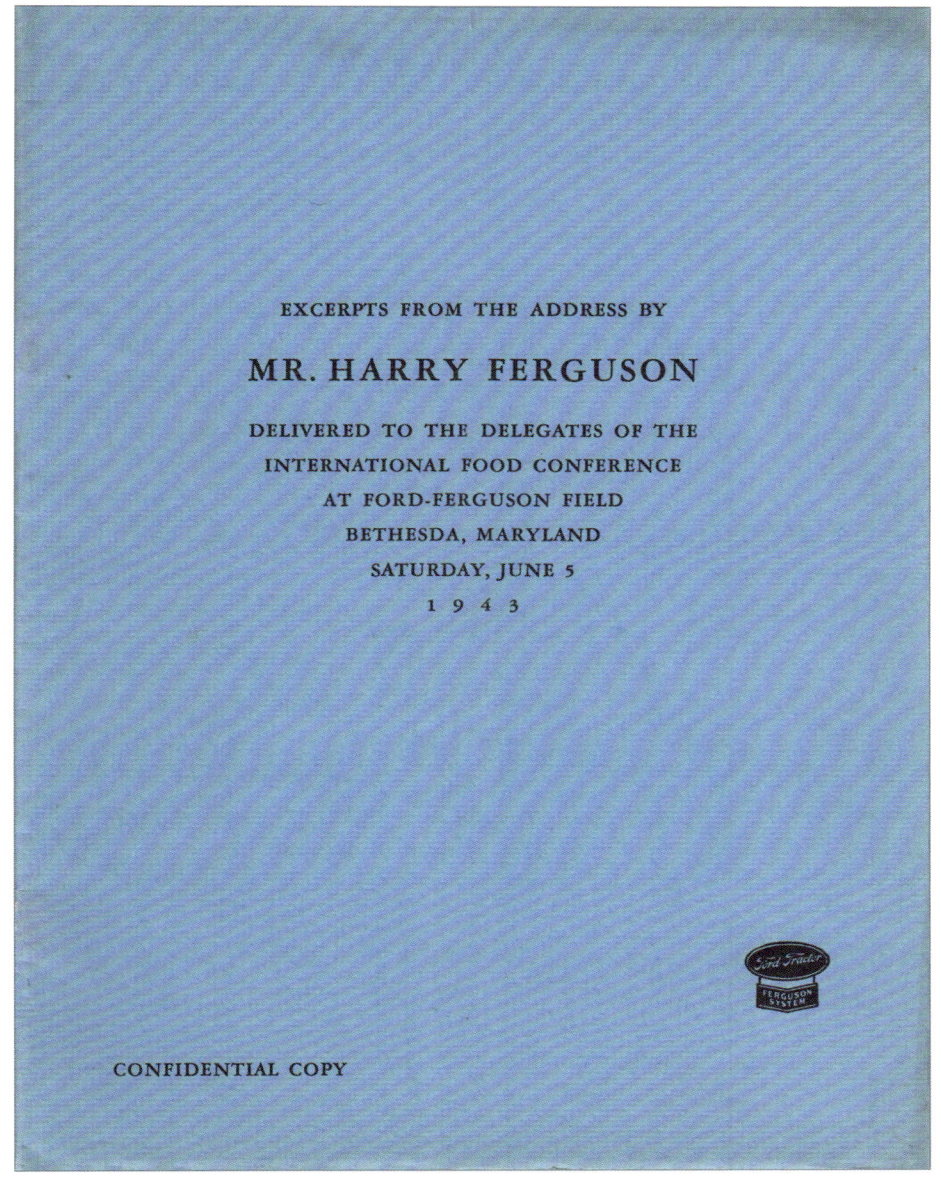

As well as bombarding Kimber with long letters, Ferguson sent him copies of his address to the International Food Conference, in which he outlined how his 'Plan' – and his tractor – would end world poverty.

Perhaps the Duke of Richmond could be involved. 'I am delighted you think so highly of Freddie Richmond. He is fairly well informed of my plans, and do try and see him and have a private talk with him,' he enjoins Kimber. 'I feel sure Freddie would be just as keenly interested in your plans for a car as I am, and let me assure you again if my plans were added to yours, it would make something of immense value.

'If you and Freddie agree about it, why not have a talk with Kendall, and put your ideas before him? You are free to show him just what you wish.'

In this effervescent but seemingly interminable letter, in which Ferguson would appear to have a rather tenuous grip on reality, he then moves on to talk of his plans to make a 'big tractor for the world' in Britain. 'If Kendall would seem to be a likely source, then here is the greatest opportunity that will ever come his way. On the foundation that the tractor will lay for us in all the Eastern Hemisphere, we can build a car business and a truck business that will eclipse anything that has ever been done,' he bubbles. 'We do not need to worry in the least about getting into big production after the war on a car. We can take our time about that and build on the sure foundation of a good product first and rapidly develop volume as we are justified.'

Kimber did his best to help Ferguson, who by this stage had broken with Ford in both Britain and the US and was searching for new partners. '[The] fact that my job with Specialloids keeps me pretty busy makes it hardly possible to do much in cultivating and contacting a man like Kendall, particularly as I have no official standing as far as the Ford-Ferguson tractor is concerned,' he explains in a letter of 3 September 1944 in which he also says that he has not been able to get in touch with Richmond.

But he had tried a further avenue. 'When I got your letter telling me of your break with Dagenham, I did drop a line to my friend Len Lord of Austin's in case they had any thoughts of doing something after the War in their big aircraft shadow factories. This was, of course, in confidence but he wrote and said they had decided to confine themselves to cars only and produce in their original works.' Meanwhile, he writes, what about approaching Kendall for the car?

The last letter from this correspondence – enclosing two copies of an address on agriculture that Ferguson had given in Washington – dates from 19 September 1944. 'I think it would be best if we would leave our common ideas until we have the joy of meeting again,' writes Ferguson. 'Do have a talk with Freddie Richmond when you meet him. If we don't do anything else together, then we surely can help to get the ground sport of motor racing going again, and that would be all to the good.'

Ferguson says that he was still keen for contact to be made with Denis Kendall, but otherwise this is a low-key letter, suggesting that he had rather given up hope of recruiting Kimber to either tractor-manufacturing in Britain or to his frankly pie-in-the-sky automotive project. It is hard not to imagine Cecil Kimber heaving a sigh of relief.

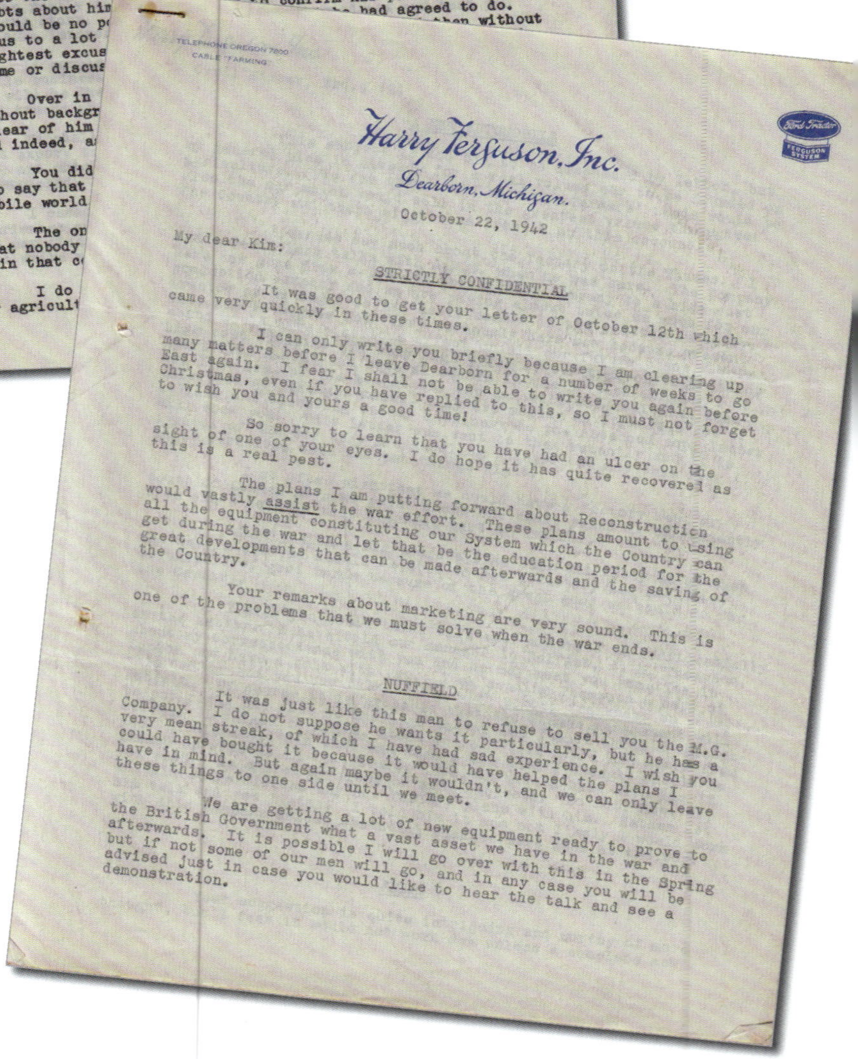

Ultimately, Harry Ferguson Research was created, and came up with this four-wheel-drive saloon, the Ferguson R4. It was a long way from Ferguson's notion of a car for the farmer. (Vauxford)

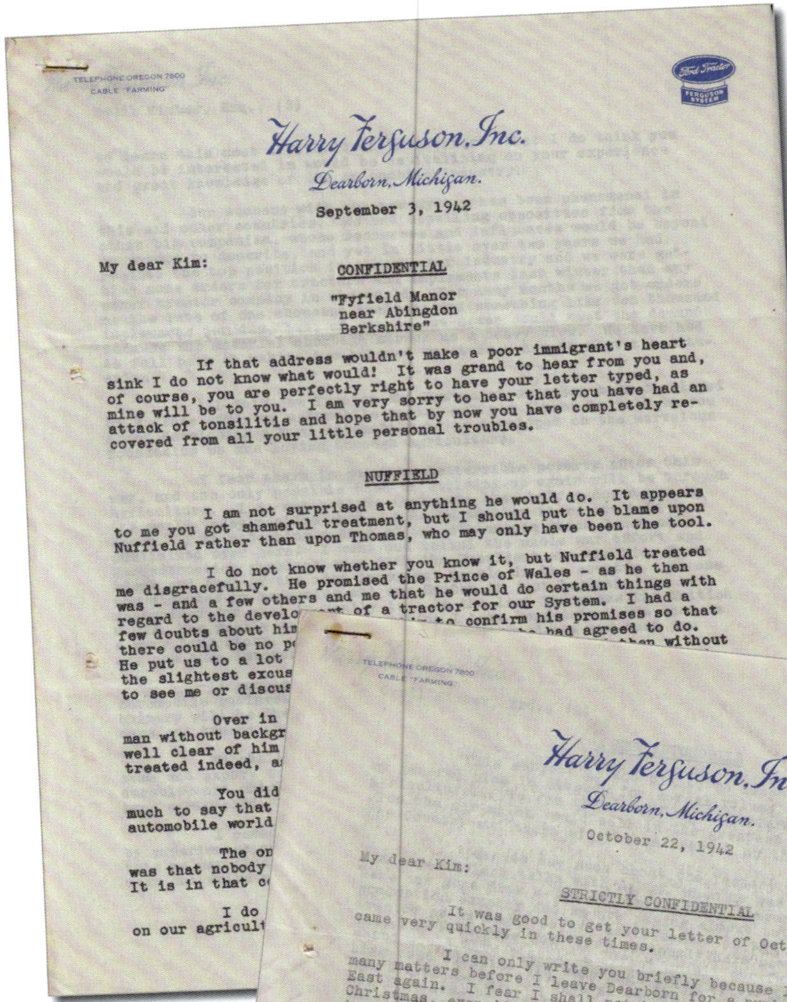

Chapter Twenty: Conversations with the Tractor King

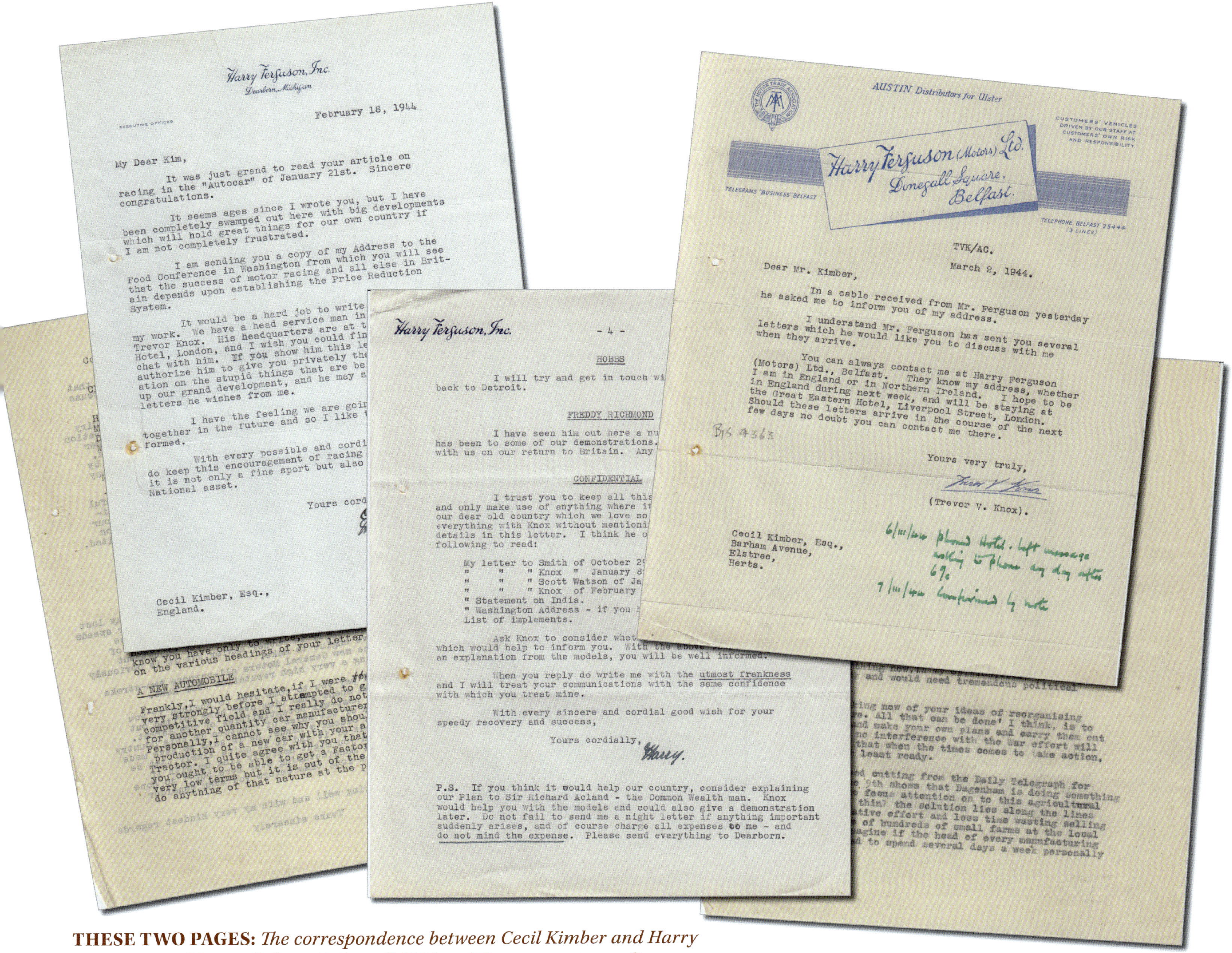

THESE TWO PAGES: *The correspondence between Cecil Kimber and Harry Ferguson would stretch from 1942 until 1944 – with no concrete result.*

21

THE DEATH OF CECIL KIMBER

As 1944 turned into 1945, life for Cecil Kimber must have taken on a new shine. The war was some way from being over, but the threat from V1 flying bombs had receded after the Allies had neutralised the last launch site in October. Kimber and his wife had an agreeable rented home in Totteridge and a seaside cottage in Sussex. Jean and Bobbie were shortly to be married, to men of whom Cecil Kimber approved. There was the prospect of taking up sailing again, and maybe spending summers at sea. Meanwhile Kimber was amusing himself writing whimsical short articles for *Yachting World* magazine.

Despite his well-received contributions to *The Autocar* there was no longer a gnawing desire on Cecil Kimber's part to get back into the motor industry: Sir John Black seemed to have taken the wind out of those particular sails. Retirement beckoned – or at least nothing more onerous than a part-time job. Meanwhile, he was back in good health and earning a substantial salary in a post which he had come to regard with slightly more equanimity.

LAST JOURNEY – BY TRAIN

Whatever his general state of mind, it is easy to imagine that Kimber might have been disappointed not to have the petrol to take his M.G. VA when he needed to visit engine specialist Perkins in Peterborough, on Specialloid business. Instead, on the evening of Sunday 4 February 1945 he boarded a First Class compartment in the rearmost coach of the 6.00pm London-to-Leeds express.

RIGHT: *Kimber and Gillie in the snow; the date is uncertain, but certainly during the 1942-44 period.*

OPPOSITE: *An A4 Pacific locomotive of the type pulling the fatal train, which had to pass through three tunnels on an uphill gradient. Wheelspin was common, and trains were often helped by a second engine. The rails, which wore heavily on this section, had just been replaced; the first train through had slipped to a standstill in the tunnels, but four others managed without trouble. (Science Museum)*

Hauled by a streamlined A4 locomotive, the train steamed out of a rainy Kings Cross five minutes late. The track, newly-laid, was wet. As it entered the second of the three uphill 'Gas Works' tunnels the train stopped and began to slip backwards, without either the driver or the guard realising. "We were just picking up speed when suddenly the train seemed to begin to slip. It jerked forward and then went backwards at speed," passenger John Moore, a US Army sergeant, told the *Daily Express*.

The points having been re-set, there was now a risk of collision with the express for Aberdeen, waiting at its platform. To avoid this, a signalman hastily threw the points. The Ministry of War Transport report relates what happened next. Unfortunately the signalman was just too late, and the points moved between the bogies of the rearmost coach, with the result that it was derailed and fell on its side against a steel stanchion of the main signal

Kimber's last Christmas card, from his final London-area address, in Totteridge. (Early M.G. Society)

bridge, which cut into the roof and demolished one of the two First Class compartments.

'Soldiers, airmen and railway workers used hatchets to break open the overturned coach and rescue passengers,' recounted *The Daily Telegraph*. It was recorded that 25 passengers escaped with nothing more than shock and light injuries. Two, however, remained trapped in the wreckage, and flame-cutters were used to free them. It was too late: both were dead. One was Cecil Kirk of Blackpool, described as manager of the St Andrew's Steam Fishing Company of Hull and a director of the Boston Deep Sea Fishing Company, Fleetwood. The other was Cecil Kimber.

'At that moment, I lost a very great friend, whom it would be impossible to replace. A brilliant and kindly enthusiast, who had done so much to prove that a British car would hold its own against the products of any other country in the world,' Goldie Gardner would later write.

The obituary in *The Autocar* surely spoke for many in the motor business. 'Although Cecil Kimber resigned from the managing directorship of the M.G. Co in 1941, and since December 1942 had been works director of Specialloid's, the piston and components specialists, it is impossible in the minds of those who had known him, as I had, since the late twenties, to dissociate the man and the car. His career with the M.G. was in the nature of a motor industry dream come true,' wrote editor H. S. Linfield. 'Regarding the man himself, he made many friends, and kept them, and I am glad to have been counted among them. Only last week I was in touch with him, and his death came as a profound shock, removing as it did a personality that was always essentially friendly and helpful – in short, human. In his new post, too, he had endeared himself to those with whom he was associated.'

ABOVE LEFT: *How* The Manchester Guardian *reported the train accident; only the* Evening Standard *picked up on Kimber's death, headlining its story 'M.G. Car Designer Killed In Crash'. (British Library)*

ABOVE MIDDLE: *With the war still in full swing,* The Daily Telegraph *gave minimal coverage to the accident. (British Library)*

ABOVE RIGHT & FAR RIGHT: *This was the report in* The Times, *which ran this unfortunate advertisement from four railway companies in the same issue. (British Library)*

This generous tribute contrasts with the mealy-mouthed 86-word news item that appeared in the Nuffield Organization's house magazine. 'We deeply regret to announce the death, in his fifty-eighth year, of Mr Cecil Kimber, who was killed in a railway accident outside King's Cross Station on 4th February. In 1929 he became Managing Director of the M.G. Car Co. Ltd., Abingdon, and it was through his energy and initiative that the Company scored its many brilliant successes in racing and record breaking. It seems a tragic twist of fate that such a keen exponent of racing as "Kim" should be killed in a railway accident,' wrote *The Morris Owner and Nuffield Mail*, as *The Morris Owner* had become.

Had Kimber had sufficient petrol coupons, he could have journeyed to Peterborough in his final VA, seen here with Jean outside the Eastleach home of Bill and Ethel Monk, in the early days of the war. The same car, probably by then fitted with a 1.7-litre 14hp engine, features in the 8 November 1940 issue of The Autocar. *It is also mentioned in the 21 August 1940 issue of* The Motor – *described as having 'sundry improvements to suit a hypercritical owner' and as being 'an uncommonly nice car'.*

LEGAL WRANGLES: THE AFTERMATH OF KIMBER'S DEATH

Following Kimber's death, damages were sought from the railway company, the London & North Eastern Railway, who had admitted 'substantive liability'. Negotiations would carry on until November. Surviving papers not only chart the process but in addition throw a certain light on family affairs; it goes without saying that there was a degree of special pleading, as the Kimber lawyers sought the most advantageous settlement.

A copy, dating from 1952, of Cecil Kimber's death certificate, giving the cause of death as 'compression injury of chest'.

The exchanges in essence related to Kimber's likely future earnings and to the status of Jean and Bobbie. The estranged Betty was omitted from discussions from the start, as being in no way dependent on her father, and no monies were sought for her.

Jean, executor L. F. Herbert informed Counsel on 19 March 1945, was 19, unmarried, and in one of the services, 'and it is apprehended that, but for the incidence of the war, she would have been wholly dependent on her father'. As it was, she had been receiving from him a weekly allowance of ten shillings. This summary glossed over the fact that Jean was engaged, and was due to marry within a matter of weeks.

Described as 'Pauline Dewar, now 25 years old', Bobbie was portrayed as in a similar situation: 'once again, but for the incidence of the war, this child would have been wholly dependent on Mr Kimber, since her mother was without personal means. As it is, Pauline holds a commission on [sic] the WAAF, and all she received from Mr Kimber was 10 shillings a week pocket money.' That Bobbie's marriage to John Walkinton was also imminent was again not mentioned.

Turning to Cecil Kimber, his average annual salary including bonuses was given as £5,210.14s.3d, plus a car allowance and expenses. 'At the time of his death Mr Kimber was in the best of health, and instructing solicitors apprehend that he had a working life of many years before him. He enjoyed consistently good health,' said Herbert, not totally accurately, and he went on to estimate Kimber's estate at 'about £15,000 to £20,000' – a sum he characterised as 'fairly substantial' and which in 2023 money would be equivalent to approximately £800,000 to £1.1m. Assets included £7,405.18s.4d in stocks and shares, The Miller's House, Puck's Cottage, the yacht *Sea Witch*, a '12hp M.G. motor car' and – surprisingly – a Triumph motorcycle. This is the only indication that Kimber may have continued to have been at least an occasional motorcyclist.

In a letter of 14 August 1945 to the LNER's Chief Legal Advisor, Herbert expanded on this information and announced the marriages of Bobbie and Jean. Eric McGavin, whom Jean had married in April, was described as a music master on board the training ship *Mercury*, earning some £300 a year. 'It is unlikely

CECIL KIMBER
Killed in Railway Crash

WITH deep regret we have to record the death of Cecil Kimber, who was killed in a railway accident on Sunday, February 4; he was 60 years of age. Although he spent the last two years of his life as a director of Specialloid, Ltd., he will always be remembered for his long association with Lord Nuffield, and in particular with the birth and success of the M.G., which took its name from the Morris Garage that Cecil Kimber managed in the early days. "Kim," as he was known to a very wide circle of acquaintances, was a keen sportsman: more than that, he was a Good Companion. We tender our sincere sympathies to his widow and daughters.

Cecil Kimber.

72

Mr. Cecil Kimber

WE deeply regret to announce the death, in his fifty-eighth year, of Mr. Cecil Kimber, who was killed in a railway accident outside King's Cross Station on 4th February.

In 1929 he became Managing Director of The M.G. Car Co. Ltd., Abingdon, and it was through his energy and initiative that the Company scored its many brilliant successes in racing and record breaking.

It seems a tragic twist of fate that such a keen exponent of racing as "Kim" should be killed in a railway accident.

that Mr McGavin, who is devoted to his music and his work on the training ship, will materially increase this income,' he wrote. Bobbie, described in error as Kimber's godchild, had now married Major John Walkinton. 'Had the late Mr Kimber lived, it was his intention to provide financial assistance to Pauline after her marriage as occasion arose,' said Herbert.

Somewhat bizarrely, given her marriage, he stated that Kimber's intention after the war was to send his step-daughter on an extended visit to Canada, 'after which she would either have made her home with Mr and Mrs Kimber or, alternatively, would have received a first-class training in journalism at Mr Kimber's expense.'

Turning to Gillie, it was stated that she received a personal allowance which during the year preceding the death amounted to about £700. 'There is every reason to suppose that with the advent of peace Mr Kimber, engaged as he was in business connected with motoring and the internal combustion engine, would have considerably increased his earnings and that Mrs Kimber could look forward to many years of married life with a husband who would have been able to maintain her in an unusually high financial position,' wrote Herbert, claiming £20,000 in damages.

There followed a dispute over whether Kimber's earnings at Specialloid would have increased or decreased. Further to this, the LNER's Miles Beevor wasn't prepared to countenance the claims on behalf of Bobbie and Jean. 'As regards the claims of the married daughter and the step-daughter, I am not prepared to agree that either of these two ladies are legal dependants of the deceased in view of the fact that both of them have husbands to support them,' he wrote on 19 October, offering £7,000 'in full settlement of all claims which may be payable under the Fatal Accidents Acts and the Law Reform Act, subject of course to the payment of your reasonable costs.' By the end of the month he had supplemented this with a proposed 'without prejudice' payment of £750 to Jean

ABOVE: *This obituary appeared in the* The Light Car *magazine – to which Kimber had contributed right at the beginning of his professional life.*

LEFT: *The terse few lines in* The Morris Owner and Nuffield Mail *do not reflect well on the Morris organisation, which might have made a better effort to pay tribute to the founder of the M.G. marque. (Author)*

and £500 to Bobbie – whilst still contending that the two were not legally dependent on Kimber. If this offer were not accepted, the only alternative would be to go to court.

After seeking Counsel's Opinion, it was decided that the risks in going to litigation would be too great. Gillie's solicitor settled for the £8,250 offered[1], to which could be added the £12,400 she stood to inherit after tax. Whilst all this was going on, Charles Russell of Specialloid had opened a memorial fund and this had accumulated £1899, including a £100 contribution from the Nuffield Organization. According to Wilson McComb a misunderstanding resulted in the money, equivalent to £5,500 today, ending up in Lord Nuffield's general Benevolent Fund.

---

[1] Jean writes in *The Other Tack* that the railway company 'gave me and my sister £100 compensation each'. This does not seem correct, not least as Betty is at no stage mentioned in the correspondence the author has seen.

THESE TWO PAGES: *Two images of Bobbie's wedding to John Walkinton in June 1945. Her marriage meant that the LNER was only prepared to make a modest settlement in damages.*

Chapter Twenty-One: The death of Cecil Kimber

IN CLOSING

People like heroes. They like putting prominent figures on a pedestal. Daring to write critically of such a person risks an instant attack. When the author went into print suggesting that latterly the management skills of Lord Nuffield were at least a little deficient and that his wife was a disliked and baleful influence, the guns were swiftly turned on him. How dare he criticise the noble industrialist whose benefactions had brought so much good to the world?

In writing this book, the perils are the same. Cecil Kimber is venerated as the founder of the M.G. company. Yet one half of his family view him with a hostility that amounts in some instances to a seething resentment. This suggests that one should be prudent about deploying that pedestal.

One should also be wary of treating the life of a human being as one-dimensional. Observers from one or other side of the divide can be perplexed when they peek over that often very real fence between the professional and the personal, and penetrate either of those secret gardens.

The job of a biography, however, is to emerge with a broadly complete and accurate notion of the subject of the book. Cecil Kimber was not the perfect father: the words 'psychologically catastrophic' have been used by his grand-daughter. He was not – far from it, evidence suggests – the perfect husband. It would have been good to have been able to fill in the gaps in the picture, perhaps to round off the asperities. All the same it is possible to say that his enthusiasms and sense of adventure gave his children an upbringing that in some ways many would envy; also that his second marriage brought happiness to both parties.

But Cecil Kimber's place in any hall of fame is as a result of his professional activities, in which his identity was wrapped up to an extraordinary degree – perhaps to his ultimate undoing. Kimber created the M.G. sports car, nurtured the marque to global prominence in just a few years, and constructed a brand image (to use a hateful modern term) that has resisted all attempts to debase it.

It is hard to imagine Cecil Kimber regarding with equanimity the placing of his beloved octagon on the front of the products of a state-supported Chinese enterprise. But he would surely permit himself a wry smile. Of all the once-respected makes that ultimately coalesced into the doomed British Leyland, M.G. is one of only two to have survived. That resilience, and the worldwide affection with which M.G. cars are regarded, constitute an honourable achievement that merits acknowledgement.

OPPOSITE: *Kimber could feel justifiably proud of the many trophies won by the M.G. marque in all realms of motor sport.*

EPILOGUE

THE KIMBER FAMILY AFTER 1945

"Gillie was so traumatised by Kimber's death. I think it was an absolute tragedy for her when he died," says grand-daughter Easter Kirkland. Retaining The Miller's House for some years, Gillie received much support from Kimber's colleague at Specialloid, Eric Graham, whom she married in the early 1950s.

Jean's elder son Kim McGavin has fond memories of the couple. "Eric and Gillie were like film stars – a dream pair. They lived in a gorgeous old house outside Kingston and then on the Isle of Wight, and Eric had a Mercedes sports car. He was a businessman of some sort – a bit mysterious, stuff grown-ups wouldn't talk of in front of the children. I think he dealt in property. He clearly had money stashed in all sorts of different accounts. Gillie had a real talent for dressing up – pearls, make-up. Eric played the tired 'yes man' docilely feeding the ego of his partner. They had a wonderful

Gillie with her dog Whiskers. Jean's son Kim McGavin says that Gillie and new husband Eric Graham made a good couple.

ABOVE: *Eric Graham, photographed here around 1951.*

TOP: *After the death in 1950 of his wife Nell, Cecil Kimber's old friend John Howlett married Gladys Hamilton.*

OPPOSITE: *Jean with Stirling Moss and with Kimber's last VA, and her grandson Joe and daughters with the car. (Richard Monk / Malcolm Simmonds)*

sense of fun and jokiness, pulling each other's leg, pretending to be cross with each other. They'd disappear and then pop up again saying 'We've just bought half an old castle' or something like that. They kept finding obscure, quirky, oddball places. They were wonderful..."

Gillie was "just brilliant" as a step-grandmother, says McGavin. "Gillie and Eric weren't my real grandparents but they performed magnificently, as if they were the real thing. She was fantastic. Mum took to her. She was so much fun. She was funny, intelligent. She was there. She ticked all the boxes. I would have fallen for her. She was universally loved and liked."

Despite the happy times spent with Kimber, Gillie evidently felt that these years were best treated as a closed book, and she was not prepared to talk to writer and former Abingdon employee Wilson McComb when he was preparing *The Story of the M.G. Sports Car*. She died from cancer in 1980 at the age of 80.

Kimber's elder daughter Betty, known latterly as Lisa, initially remained married to Dean Delamont. Delamont did not want children, and Lisa considered a divorce on these grounds. In the end she gave birth to three children, each with a different father, before separating from Delamont at the end of the 1950s[1]. "Ideologically, politically, she didn't believe in monogamy," comments daughter Sara Delamont.

For her nephew Kim McGavin she cut a striking figure. "Lisa was a stunning woman with amazingly sleek and very long black hair. She wore stylish clothes, a strong perfume, and bright red lipstick. She was quite classy and acted the part of the designer very well – she had a bit of the glamorous about her. She was bohemian. Lisa was without doubt a funster. If she'd been born a bit later she'd have probably smoked a lot of hashish. She was more radical and better informed than my mother, who was far more conventional. The sisters were very different people. If you put them together, in their 30s or 40s, you wouldn't have known that they were sisters."

Sara Delamont remembers her mother as a spirited nonconformist. "When it snowed she wanted to go sledging. She was the only mother who climbed trees and went sledging. She was very ecological – she was an ecologist long before it was fashionable – and she was a feminist of a very strong kind. She was very firm about that. That is why I have never really understood why she married Dean Delamont when she didn't really believe in marriage. I don't know how far she was a witch, but the father of

Dean Delamont became head of the RAC Motor Sport Division and an important figure in the world of competition motoring. He died in 2003 at the age of 90.

---

[1] Delamont's name appears as father on all the children's birth certificates." I think he wanted to do the right thing. He never relinquished any responsibilities. He wanted to help the family, financially or otherwise, when there was no moral obligation. He was very kind, very honest. He was a man of high integrity, who put the interests of others first," says his grandson Dean.

Jean Kimber Cook in later life; she remained a keen sailor and latterly lived on the Isle of Wight.

my brother Jonathan was part of coven in the New Forest and into very serious high magic. Certainly she was absolutely committed to a sort of Robert Graves paganism. She was ferociously against the Christian church, which she believed was a patriarchal conspiracy to oppress women."

After living for some years in Hamble, around 1963 Lisa moved to London, briefly working as a housekeeper until she found a position with Hampstead property developers Norman Melburn and Bernard Vorhaus, two leftists who bought properties and converted them into bedsits[2]. "She would do all the plans and get them through the planning system, supervise the building work, and get them furnished. She did all the architectural drawings and all the furnishings – she thought of herself as an architect, and subscribed to *The Architects' Journal* and *The Architectural Review* until her death. She had her own company, the Belsize Contract Furnishing Company. She managed the flats and would live in them rent-free."

After many years on the fringes of the Hampstead intellectual and artistic set, Lisa returned to Hamble where she died in 1978 from intestinal cancer; she had been a very heavy smoker and her lungs were in no state for her to have the cancer operated on, says Delamont.

Kimber's other daughter, Jean, led a calmer and longer life. "For many years she worked as a school secretary – she had a talent for being secretary at little prep schools," says son Kim McGavin. "Her best job was at a small private school in Watford, which had a pretty good music department. Mother wrote a musical play, or perhaps even two or three, during her years as secretary at the school. She then had a short spell as teacher of nature studies in Hemel Hempstead, before studying sociology at evening classes and becoming a social worker."

A few years after the death of Eric McGavin in 1970, Jean married Dennis Cook, a widowed garage proprietor. Along with her meeting M.G. historian McComb, this motoring connection may well have been a contributary factor to Jean – a keen amateur historian – devoting subsequent years to researching and recording her father's life. She clearly had a fixation. "She adored her father and constantly talked him up, whereas her mother wasn't there, almost. It was as if Rene hadn't really been a strong presence in her life," says McGavin.

In her worship of Cecil Kimber she was in contrast to her sister, whose memories were in their own way equally skewed[3]. Relations between the two oscillated, but were frequently tense, especially at the end of Lisa's life, when she refused to see Jean. A regular fixture at M.G. events in her later years, Jean Kimber Cook, as she styled herself, died in November 2013 at the age of 88.

---

[2] Communist activist Melburn was a chartered surveyor and founded the Barry Amiel and Norman Melburn Trust. Bernard Vorhaus was a respected film-maker both in Britain and the United States, and nurtured the young David Lean. His son David set up early electronica band White Noise.

[3] 'When I arranged a meeting with his two daughters in the hope of learning more, it was like striking a match to find a gas-leak,' wrote Wilson McComb in a May 1988 article in *Classic Cars* magazine.

Epilogue: The Kimber family after 1945

APPENDICES

These appendices mainly comprise selected writings and talks by Cecil Kimber. The paper *The Trend of Aesthetic Design in Motor Cars* is illustrated with Kimber's own artwork and his selection of photos, with his original typed captions.

Kimber was an occasional contributor to *The Autocar* and two of his articles are reproduced here, with acknowledgement, and with thanks to Mark Tisshaw, current editor of *Autocar* magazine – the definite article having disappeared from the weekly's name at the beginning of 1962.

The content of the two *The Autocar* pieces are reprised to a large degree in the talks Kimber gave on the design of a post-war sports car and on racing, but they contain sufficient fresh material to justify their inclusion; in the case of the talk on sports cars we have however taken the decision to reproduce it only partially, omitting the second half where the repetition is almost word for word. Readers will observe the reappearance of certain Kimber hobby-horses in the material on racing.

The paper *Making Modest Production Pay in Motor-Car Manufacture* gives interesting insights into how Kimber ran the M.G. factory. The cynics might raise an eyebrow and observe that Kimber rarely made modest production pay whilst he was in full control at Abingdon, but the talk does show that Kimber was a sensible and rigorous manager.

The various papers were written for oral presentation, and have since been typed and re-typed. It is hoped that no errors or omissions are present, but this cannot be excluded; punctuation has only been altered when this has been necessary for clarity.

The final appendix recounts the history of M.G. since Kimber's death. To devote a book to Cecil Kimber without looking at his industrial legacy, and the use made of it by his successors, would have been to leave the job half-done. It is not always a happy tale, but the special atmosphere of the Abingdon factory, and the continuing appeal of the cars it produced, show that Kimber left behind him something of enduring worth.

APPENDIX 1

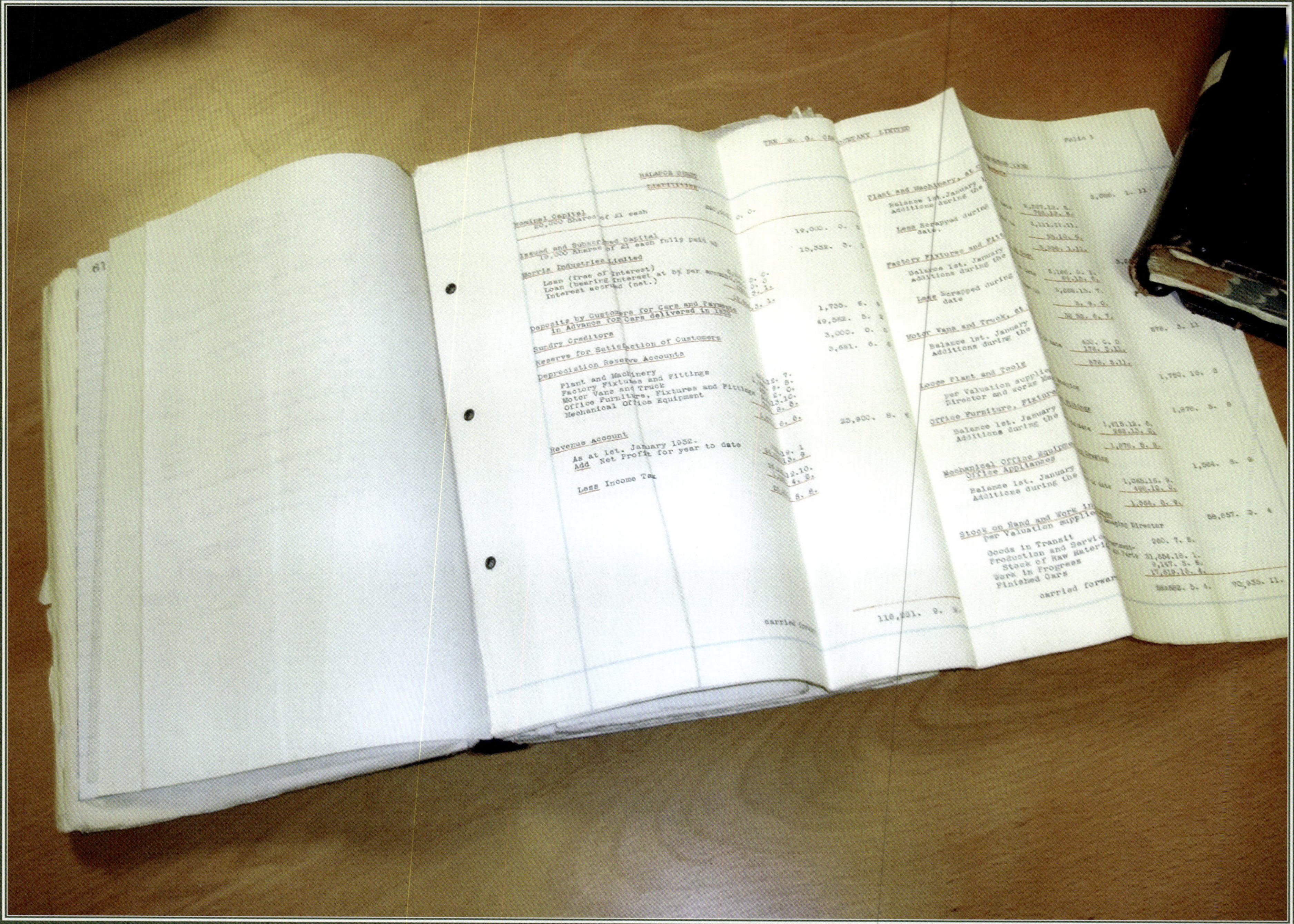

M.G. CAR COMPANY ACCOUNTS, 1930-35

These figures are those given in the volumes of M.G. boardroom minutes for the 1930-40 period, consulted at the Modern Records Centre at the University of Warwick but currently in the keeping of the British Motor Industry Heritage Trust at Gaydon.

NET PROFIT (All expenses deducted and before tax)
- 1930   £17,763 profit
- 1931   £13,046 loss
- 1932   £24,914 profit
- 1933   £5,186 loss
- 1934   £14,122 profit
- 1935   £28,156 loss (first 8 months only)

GROSS PROFIT (Profit by sales)
- 1930   £394,772
- 1931   £289,844
- 1932   £452,960
- 1933   £446,339
- 1934   £452,448
- 1935   £175,571 (first 8 months only)

COMPETITIONS & RECORD-BREAKING
- 1930   £1,011
- 1931   £4,902
- 1932   £2,789
- 1933   £5,863
- 1934   £3,505
- 1935   £4,406 (first 8 months only)

ADVERTISING
- 1930   £7,096
- 1931   £9,348
- 1932   £10,996
- 1933   £11,360
- 1934   £12,108
- 1935   £8,028 (first 8 months only)

SATISFACTION OF CUSTOMERS (warranty and out-of-warranty 'goodwill' costs)
- 1930   £6,412
- 1931   £5,020
- 1932   £7,278
- 1933   £15,276
- 1934   £8,698
- 1935   £3,371 (first 8 months only)

DEVELOPMENT OF MODELS
- 1930   £5,257
- 1931   £1,688
- 1932   £1,353
- 1933   £2,894
- 1934   £2,752
- 1935   £4,460 (first 8 months only)

ANNUAL PRODUCTION (ESTIMATED)
- 1930   1,850
- 1931   1,400
- 1932   2,400
- 1933   2,200
- 1934   2,100
- 1935   1,250 (full year)

The British Motor Industry Heritage Trust cannot supply production figures on a year-to-year basis. However, Wilson McComb's still-definitive M.G. history provides a graph, from which the above approximate figures have been extrapolated.

APPENDIX 2

'THE TREND OF AESTHETIC DESIGN IN MOTOR CARS'

A paper read to the Design & Industries Association, 14 April 1937

When the author was invited by your Society to give a paper on the 'Aesthetic Design of Motor Cars', he welcomed the opportunity of talking about a subject very near his heart. He then recollected a very masterly address on this subject given before the Institution of Automobile Engineers by his friend Mr W.O. Kennington. Reading this over again, it appeared, at first sight, that Mr Kennington had so completely covered the subject that any remarks the author might have to make would only be repetition.

However, careful reflection showed that the subject bristles with so many different aspects that its ramifications can be well-nigh endless. However, the author does feel it necessary, as far as the preliminaries are concerned, to cover somewhat the same ground, and this is where the author would like to put on record his thanks to Mr Kennington, not only for the inspiration given by his paper, but for permission to use some of his illustrations to indicate the influence of speed on progress and design.

One has only to examine nature's handiwork to observe the effect of speed on symmetry of design.

Let us start off with that quintessence of rigid immovability, a large mass of rock flung up in some prehistoric earthly upheaval, fixed and unchanged until today. **(Illustration 1)**

Then we come to living things that move. Big slow 'chunky' animals almost like lumps of rock themselves, but bearing the first signs of speed. Unlike the granite boulders, their corners are rounded off!

As we come to the faster and still faster moving animals and birds and fish, so you will observe a definite tendency to what we term today streamlining. In this respect, the fish and birds being carried in, rather than borne on, their respective elements, water and air, are able to show better streamlining form than animals which have to have appendages in the shape of legs, not only to propel them, but to support them on elements, the earth.

Illustration 1

As an example of how slow and ungainly a bird or an animal can be, out of its natural element, I should like to bring to your notice the difference between a penguin on land, a quaint ungainly creature, but when in the water an example of almost perfect streamlining and speed. An illustration of this appeared in a recent issue of Illustrated London News. *(Illustration 2)*

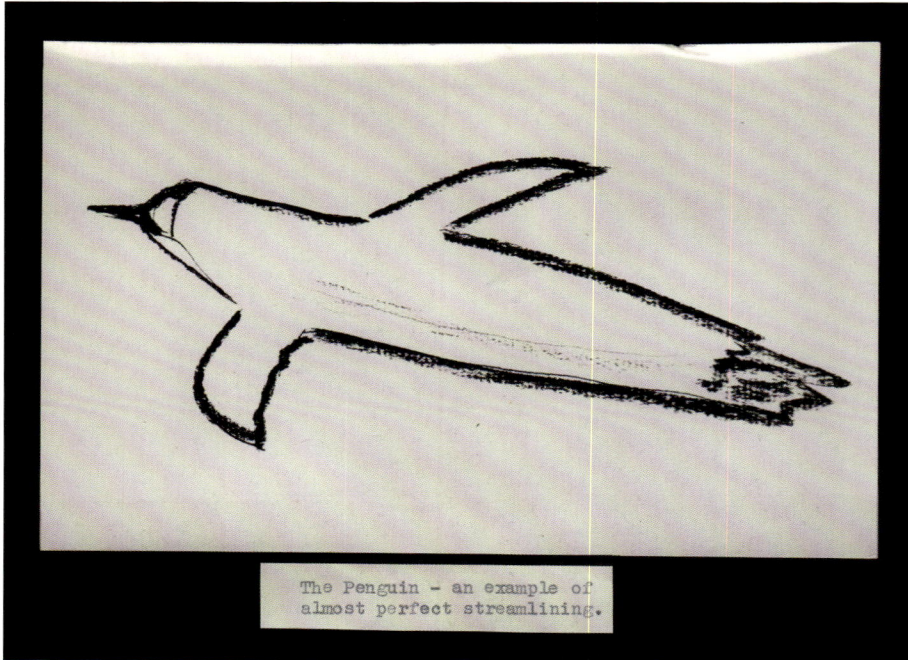

Illustration 2

If the foregoing is accepted, it will explain why man, who always copies nature, has come to associate streamlining with speed, and speed with streamlining.

As examples of man's handiwork, his earliest efforts were in the direction of fortifications, and later, castles, and as examples of massive immobility, most of them in their ruggedness, like Harlech Castle, *(Illustration 3)* emulate the granite mountains of nature. Then man, desiring transportation, designed a crude form of sleigh. Then came rude wheeled vehicles, until today, we come to man's fastest and most streamlined vehicle, the modern aeroplane. *(Illustration 4)*

Illustration 3

The author would like to mention at this point that a number of the slides that will be shown are prepared from rough charcoal sketches of his own handiwork. They are only intended to illustrate points in this paper in a graphic manner, which were not sufficiently important to justify properly finished drawings. It is hoped that the forcefulness of this means of expression will make up for the crudeness.

During this process of evolution, but only during the last thirty or forty years, there came the era of mechanically-propelled vehicles, and whilst it has taken nature hundreds of thousands of years to evolve the speed and grace of, say, the gazelle, and the swifter fish of the sea, it has only taken one man's lifetime for the evolution of the motor car from a slow, clumsy, angular, box-like affair to a thing of speed, grace and beauty. *(Illustrations 5 & 6)*

But are all motor cars things of grace and beauty? The author fears

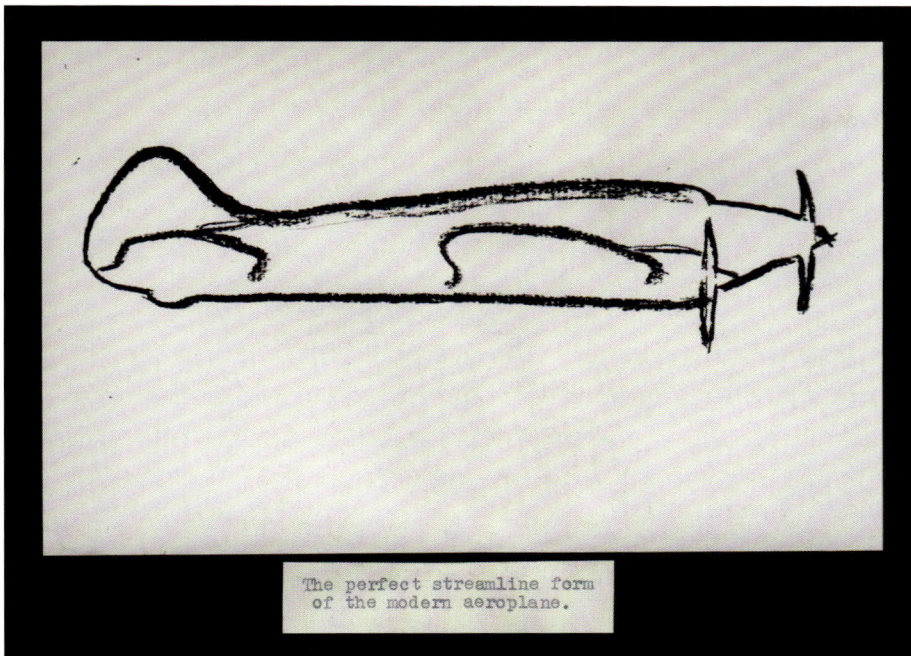

The perfect streamline form of the modern aeroplane.

Illustration 4

The evolution of the motor car from approximately 1900 – 1934.

Illustration 5

The evolution of the motor car from approximately 1900 – 1934.

Illustration 6

that this is far from the case, and it is with the idea of discussing the 'whys' and 'why nots' that we are all gathered here tonight.

As the author has mentioned previously, earthborne animals are at a disadvantage from a streamline point of view, as compared with fish and birds, which are supported in their own element. In the same way motor cars are at a disadvantage from an aesthetic streamlined point of view, as compared with yachts and aeroplanes, and when one comes seriously to analyse the situation, one of the fundamental difficulties to overcome is the question of how to treat the appendages of an earthborne machine, in other words the wheels.

The author is assuming, for the sake of this argument, that the ultimate ideal for symmetrical grace, maximum efficiency and the perfect personification of speed is a true streamline shape. The ultimate design, who knows, may be this very ideal. If so, the wheels would be entirely enclosed, perhaps two in number, and in line central to the structure, the whole machine being gyroscopically established.

Such a shape may come in future years, when cruising speeds, on special high-speed motorways, are as a matter of course 200mph or 300mph or more.

Meanwhile, we have to be practical, and design motor cars limited by the necessity of having four wheels to support whatever streamline structure we may design. Also, we have to provide for usage and convention, and the lack of length in relation to width and height, all of which makes the problem very difficult. Today the designer has to progress slowly, for if he outstrips the conventional ideas of the public, then experience has shown that commercially he is doomed to failure.

At this point it might be interesting to show some slides prepared from drawings (kindly lent to the author by Mr Kennington) showing the evolution of the motor car, and the obvious tendency to streamlined form as the speed of the cars increased year by year.

As compared with nature in the matter of evolution we, mere men, have appeared to have done wonderfully, but the author is one who considers that actually our progress is very slow indeed.

A streamlined shape is, as everyone knows, roughly that of a pear, with the blunt end pointing in the direction of travel, but more elongated. The amount of elongation depends, to some extent, on the speed.

We people who make motor cars started off by doing so with the engine in front, presumably because that was where the horse was to be found, which the engine replaced. So, practically from the very commencement of motoring, the smallest mass unit – the engine – was placed in front, then came two passengers behind that, then three passengers behind the two.

What is the result? Surely the worst possible disposition of the masses for enclosing in a streamlined shape it is possible to imagine, and that state of affairs occurs today, in spite of the fact that man's instinct is to see the motor car become more and more streamlined as the speeds of cars become higher.

Several notable examples of streamline cars have been produced, but being in advance of the conventional ideas of the public they have not been an outstanding commercial success, and in more than one instance certain firms who produced such models have reverted to the acceptable current conception of streamline beauty.

The next slide shows a photo of the well known Airflow Chrysler which, subsequent experience would indicate, was a little in advance of its time as far as public fashion is concerned. *(Illustration 7 top)*

This slide shows an English version of an Airflow body on a popular chassis, and is credited to the design of Captain Fitzmaurice. *(Illustration 7 bottom)*

Then there is the German example of streamlining, the Adler Trumpf 1.7-litre Sports Limousine, as it is termed. As you will

Illustration 7

Illustration 8

observe from the drawing, it appears to be rather well carried out in this respect. *(Illustration 8)*

This slide is of another Adler, the 2½-litre Foursome Model. Whilst not exactly designed on streamline principles, it at any rate shows the influence in that direction. Actually, judging by the drawing, it would appear to be as effectively streamlined going backwards or forwards. *(Illustration 9, following page)*

A Czechoslovakian example, shown on the next slide, is perhaps the most advanced design today. This is the eight-cylinder vee-engined Tatra, with independent springing all-round, engine at the rear, air-cooled, and altogether extremely well streamlined, as we understand the term today. The author has driven one of these cars, and was suitably impressed by its general performance.

Illustration 9

Perhaps the most notable feature was the uncanny lack of wind and engine noise at high speeds, making 70mph seem comparatively slow. It was this, more than anything else, that made one realise the possibilities of a 200mph cruising speed on special roads, as mentioned earlier in the paper. *(Illustration 10)*

The next slide will probably be something of a mystery to many of you. It is difficult to tell whether it is coming or going. It is interesting as showing a progressive yet conservative concern. The Ford company felt the public were not yet ready to accept the rear-engined streamlined car in any quantity and, it is understood, that it was from this experiment [that] the Lincoln Zephyr was produced. *(Illustration 11)*

All the cars shown in the previous six slides are reasonably well streamlined when considered in elevation but – with the possible exception of the Tatra – they all fall down badly in this respect when considered in plan.

Illustration 10

Illustration 11

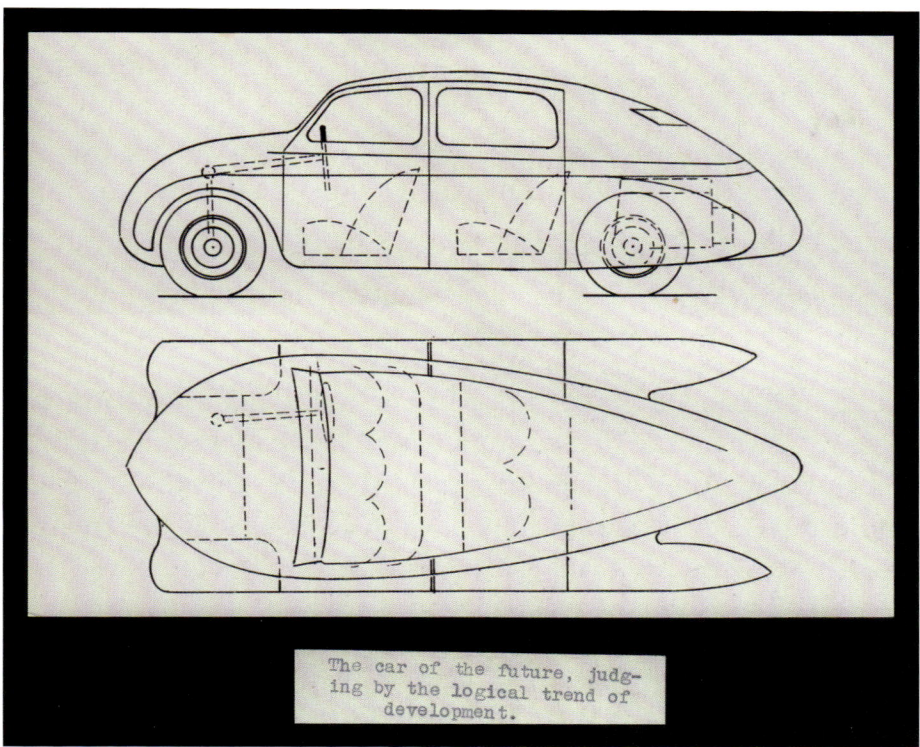

Illustration 12

It can be considered, therefore, in the author's opinion, fairly certain logically that the next line of big development will be a car designed on lines as shown on the following slide. Not only does it provide for exceptionally good streamline formation on both plan and elevation, but by tucking the engine away at the rear, the floor of the driver and passenger compartments are unencumbered. **(Illustration 12)**

How long it will be before the public are ready to assimilate such a design, it is hard to say. Ten years, at least, probably more, in the author's opinion, and there is a psychological reason for it, that may not occur to every designer. Drivers and passengers have, for so long, been used to having first the horse, and then the engine, in front, giving them, perhaps subconsciously, a comforting feeling of protection in the event of a collision, that it is going to take a long time to accustom them to the rear-engined car, which leaves occupants sitting 'so near the accident'.

To show how comparatively slow is this acceptance by the public to anything new in motor car design, a German named Jaray[1], as long ago as 1922, 1923 and 1924, obtained patents, which appeared to consist of two streamline shapes, one superimposed upon the other, to produce a complete body shape. The author believes he is right in saying that the Airflow Chrysler and rear engined eight-cylinder Tatra, and the English designs by Captain Fitzmaurice, were, and are, constructed under licence from Jaray. And here is a patented design, 15 years old, still not wholly acceptable to the public taste.

It is interesting to try and analyse out why this is so, quite apart from any possible psychological reason suggested. Surely it is because the average speed of cars is not yet sufficiently high to justify such shapes, and that the appreciation of this fact is subconscious in the minds of the motoring public!

Having dealt with this subject in a general sense, let us get down to everyday matters and review the motor car design of today.

Immediately one does this, there emerges to confront the designer – in the artistic sense – horrible limitations. Wheels, headroom, back axle, spare wheel, large luggage space, driving visibility, manufacturing costs considerations, sacrifices to accessibility, short wheelbase, ad infinitum. Shackled hand and foot, the poor artist designer is expected to produce an eyeable symmetrical-shaped body, harmonious in line, with commodious interior comfort on a mechanical structure we call a chassis which, if the body had been evolved before the chassis, we should have laughed at it. A structure that limits the height and position of our seats, determines the height of your floor, allowing to the necessary necessity of having what we engineers call a 'propshaft' and a 'diff' cluttering up the floor space.

Then there is a tendency to push the engine forward, and create an aldermanic touch to the design. Small wheels upset all sense of proportion.

---

[1] Author's note: In fact Vienna-born Jaray was of Hungarian origin.

This is the utilitarian aspect creeping in, and gaining ascendancy over aesthetic beauty. Forward engine mounting caused the protruding radiator, but this gave more body space for a given wheelbase. The earliest examples of these forward radiators were hideous, not because we were unused to the appearance but because they were carried out by engineers with nothing but utilitarian ideas in mind, who entirely disregarded all lines of symmetry and form in carrying such ideas into effect.

Then, as will be shown later in this paper, along comes the artist designer, and by degrees the new frontal aspect of the motor car is merged harmoniously into the whole.

Wings are probably the most important item as having the biggest effect on the design of the complete car from an artistic point of view. They are also the most difficult, and this problem would be easier if one did not have to legislate for the turning movement of the front wheels, or the large rise and fall of the rear. Some designers like to treat their front wings as separate units to be streamlined individually, and the Cord car is an example of this. *(Illustration 13)* Others, and these are in the majority, are tending to merge the wings into the body, but owing to the lack of proportionate length of body, this is apt to make the car look heavy and clumsy. A number of German cars have a tendency this way. A practical objection to making body panels and wings in one is the attitude of the insurance companies, who raise their rates on cars which need a complete side panel if a wing gets damaged.

Considerations of production costs have not improved wing design, and there is a natural desire to produce a complete wing from a die, with the minimum subsequent hand work, with the result that such a thing as a return curve is out of the question or a turn-under in front.

Later slides will show the difference between a cheap pressed wing that is ugly because of manufacturing costs being of primary importance, and one that has, at least, some pretence to grace of line.

Utilitarian reasons often hamper artistic line. The Buick wing cut short to allow for large forward door opening is an example. It

Illustration 13

starts off by having some pretence to streamlining, but the tail becomes somewhat of a travesty. *(Illustration 14)*

Here the author may be criticised and told a large door is more important that an artistic wing, but it is aesthetic design of cars we are considering, not the utilitarian.

This slide shows the development of radiators since approximately 1900 until a few years ago, when they started to disappear from sight under an ornamental grille. It is interesting to note how the very earliest cars made no special feature of the radiator, and it now looks as though we shall soon be back again to where we started. *(Illustration 15)*

Meanwhile, whilst we are on the subject of radiators, and as touched upon earlier in the paper, it is interesting to note the mild evolution of design since engines and radiators were moved forward. At first the complete radiator block and its integral shell were moved bodily forward, and because this was done without regard to other parts of the car, such as wings, the result looked, and was, all wrong from an aesthetic point of view. Then the artist got to work, and one saw an interesting change come over the treatment of the whole of the front end of the car that tended to make the radiator, the bonnet louvres, the wings, lamps and fairings, all part of one harmonious whole. This slide shows a radiator of an older type pushed boldly forward.

This one, the radiator as a separate entity disappears and a grille takes its place. It still retains some semblance of a radiator shell, to which the headlamps are attached. *(Illustration 16, following page)*

In the slide of the V8 Ford you see a real clean-up of the front end, in which the lines of the grille are made to harmonise with the sweep of the wings, both in frontal appearance and side elevation. The headlamps, instead of being excrescences, are merged into the fairing, and finally, there is a radical departure from the practice that has been universal almost since the beginning of cars. The radiator slats, instead of being vertical, are horizontal,

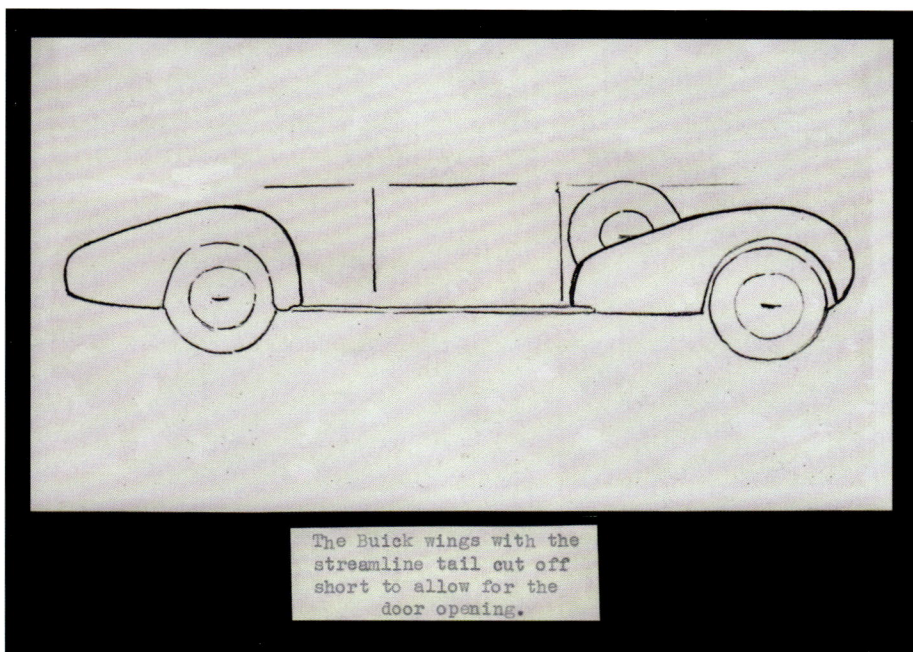

Illustration 14

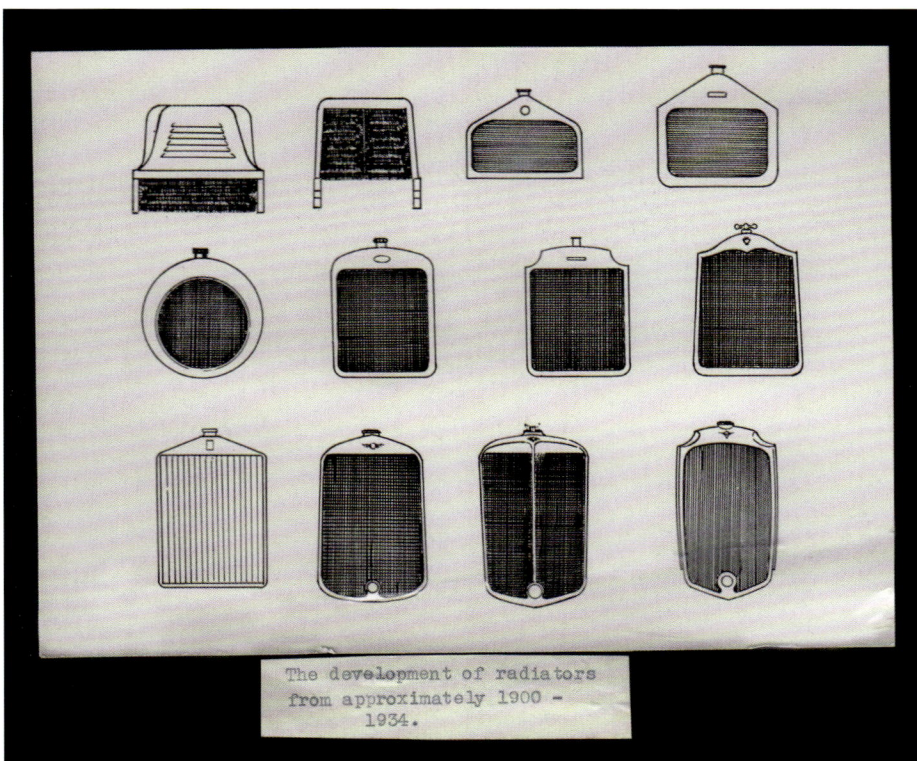

Illustration 15

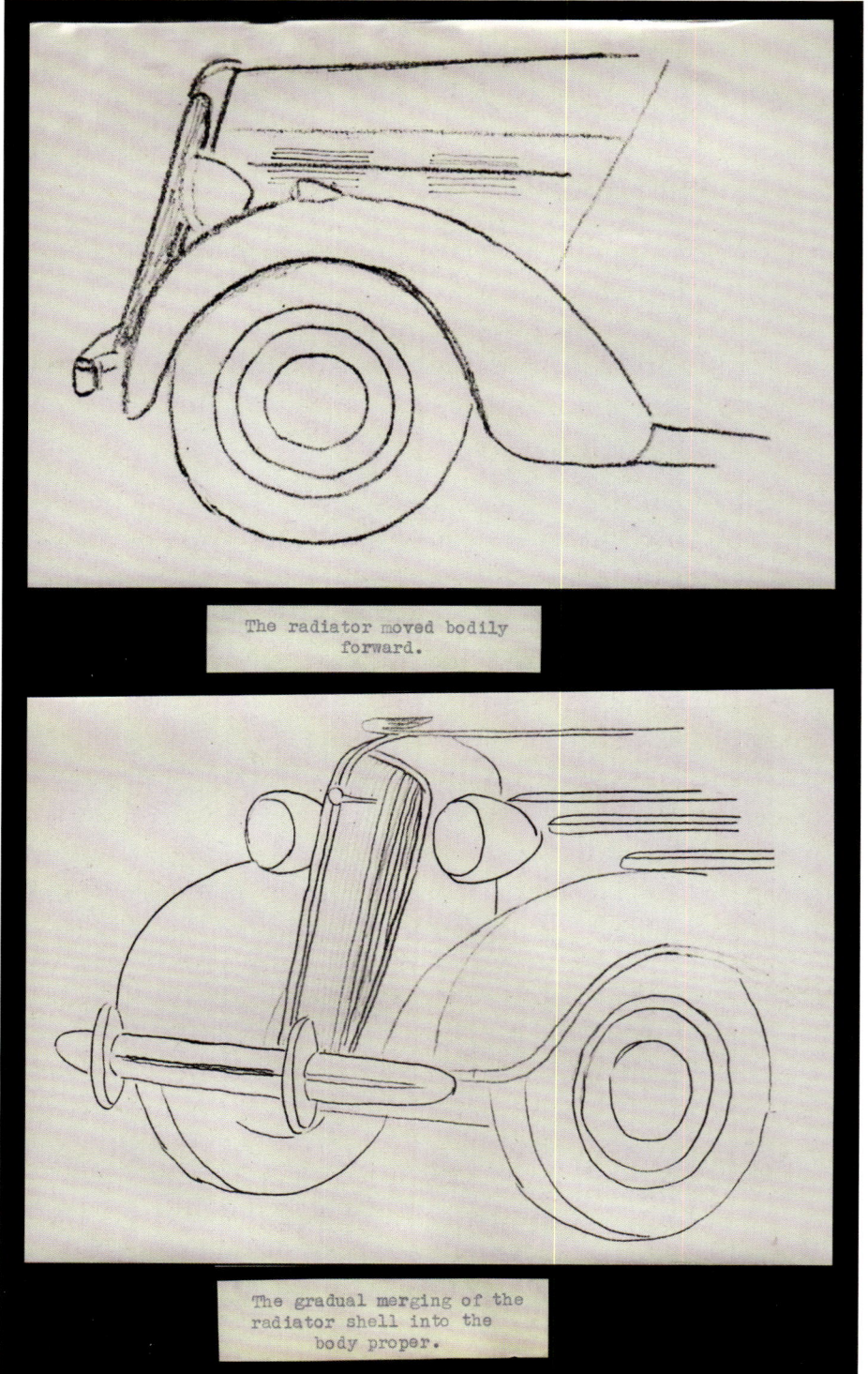

Illustration 16

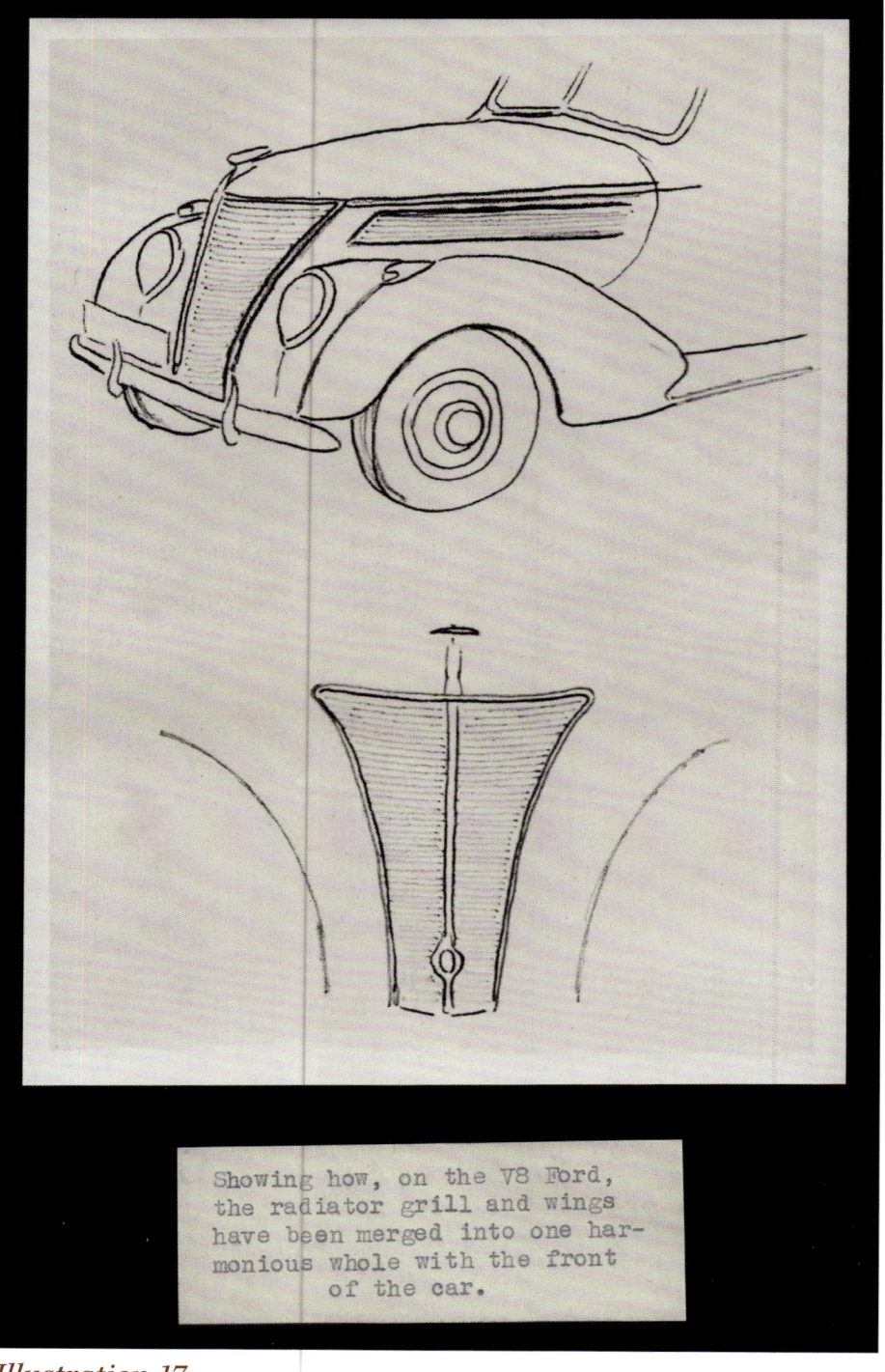

Illustration 17

Appendix 2: 'The Trend of Aesthetic Design in Motor Cars'

a feature that will be found on quite a number of new American cars. **(Illustration 17)**

One cannot help deploring the passing of the old-style radiator which, at one time, was so distinctive of the make, and had so much influence over the body design. Today the radiator grille is so much a general feature of the design of the car as a whole that no longer is one able easily to recognise makes as one meets them along the road. There are, of course, a few that still retain a certain individuality, such as Packard, Vauxhall, Rolls, Hispano and a few others.

Closely allied to the radiator comes the question of lamps. This slide, prepared from drawings kindly lent to the author by Mr Kennington, shows the same trend of streamlining grace from approximately 1900 to 1934, that has characterised the car as a whole, and even since 1934 further advances have been made. In this respect, this country has lagged behind America, due, no doubt, to the lack of competition amongst the lamp-equipment manufacturers, and one sees even the most individualistic and costly British cars fitted with, for instance, the same sidelamps as a cheap quantity-produced model by another manufacturer. Price and quantity is no doubt partly the determining factor that prevents special lamps being designed by, and for, the individual manufacturer. **(Illustration 18)**

Over a period of time a lot has been done by designers in cleaning up the externals of the motor car, and whilst a few are making determined efforts to build the lamps into the body, with the majority the lamps are still somewhat of an afterthought, and often not given the attention that is desirable. Actually the frontal appearance of the car can be marred by the spacing and arrangement of the headlamps.

Headlamps present the biggest difficulty. They must not be too large and they must not be too small. They do not want to be carried too high (as this charcoal sketch will show), or too low. It will be found in practice – according to the author's experience – that the best arrangement is for the lamps to be so arranged that

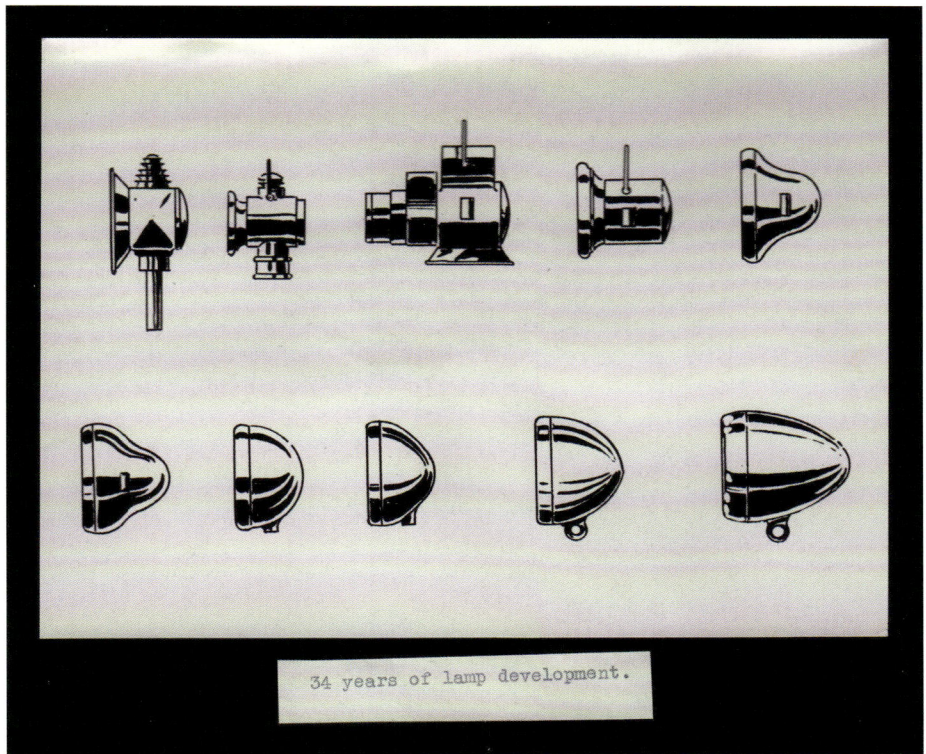

Illustration 18

an imaginary line in the shape of a bow or flattened triangle will bring the tops of the sidelamps, the headlamps and the radiator cap (or top) in line, as shown on this slide in photographic form. **(Illustration 19, following page)**

With the latest type of combined radiator, bonnet and wings, designers are forced to build in the headlamps in some way. Some Continental makers merely place them behind the radiator grille, which must materially effect their light value. Where the lamps are let flush into the body shell, this generally produces the most grotesque results, and there is a lot to be said for the Cord idea of disappearing the lamps altogether, and avoiding the awful glaring-eye appearance one sees on many foreign cars. **(Illustration 20, following page)**

Having reviewed the past, and tried to predict the future

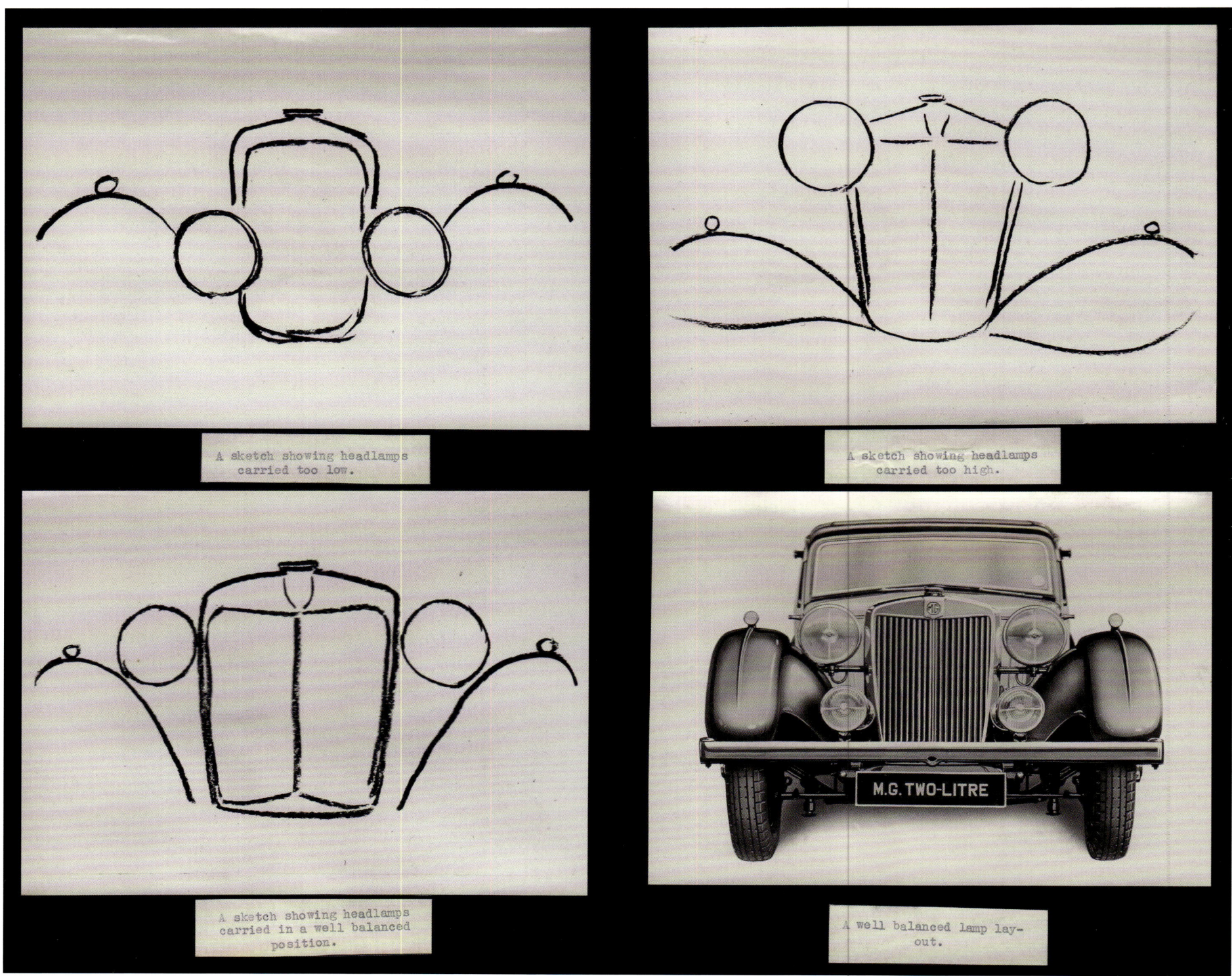

Illustration 19

Cord car showing lamps entirely enclosed when not in use.

Illustration 20

development of cars, we can now turn our attention to the present, and see what is being done with the car of today, in spite of the many limitations with which the artist-designer is faced.

One of the limitations is the size of the average person. Unfortunately, it is not the very small man who buys the very small car, or the very tall man the large car. Very often it is the other way about, and accordingly there is a minimum height from the floor of the car to the roof that has to be allowed for, however small and short the motor car.

As the ratio of length to diameter of the perfect streamline form increases in some relation to the speed, the average car has really not sufficient wheelbase to carry the length required to approximate to a streamline form in relation to its width and height, without an excessive amount of overhang at the rear. The baby car is, therefore, very badly handicapped in this respect, because it has the same minimum width and height as its larger brother, without their longer wheelbase.

Fortunately today, except in racing form, the small car is not expected to, and does not, go sufficiently fast to justify any serious attempt at streamlining, and unconsciously the public at the moment more or less accepts that.

But the large car is associated with speed, and the public are growing to expect some attempt at a streamline form, without appreciating, and caring less, about the difficulties that the present-day motor car offers in this respect. However, by careful attention to a few laws of symmetrical design, it is possible to produce some quite – to present-day eyes – beautiful results.

Aerodynamically considered, they are a joke, but they do satisfy man's sense of streamlining form in relation to speed, mentioned earlier in this page.

That sub-conscious acceptance by the public is curious. For instance, the stately limousine is readily accepted as right, with its severe architectural design, because it is visualised as a small but sumptuous drawing room, rolling slowly but majestically round the town. But if that same car were to appear at a Brooklands race meeting, no matter how fast it might go, it would look all wrong in the eyes of the public.

We, however, will concern ourselves not with the racing car or the town carriage, but the average man's car for general use. To give it stability, it must be designed in mass to appear pyramidical in form, for that is the shape that man subconsciously associates with stability, and stability means safety.

To achieve this, the lines at the front of the car must slope backward, and those at the back, forward, and the front elevation must show the sides of the body having a decided 'tumblehome'. Otherwise, the car is going to look top-heavy and therefore, in the mind of the beholder, unsafe. You will remember, perhaps, how very unsafe some of the old-fashioned cars looked through disregarding this fact. This triangulated formation of the subject, with the base at the bottom, is also considered good artistic composition. So we start off on the right basis, when we come to design our car, to give it a conception of beauty.

Reference was made to the laws of design. These are quite simple, and can be summed up by saying that all lines used must be symmetrical, harmonious and complementary. Many a good chassis has been ruined as a complete motor car, because the same engineer who designed the chassis, used his same T-square and set-square to design the body.

If you want to design an artistic body throw your T-square and set-square away, and make up your mind that, except perhaps for a few minor verticals, you will not have any straight lines in your car. Immediately you introduce any horizontal straight lines, you begin to lose the streamline effect that is to be your aim if you are going to satisfy the mind of the public which, as the author has endeavoured to show, naturally associates streamlining with the present-day car.

How often, in the past, have you not seen cars that looked faster than we know they were, just because they were designed with a clever streamline effect.

A few slides have been prepared from drawings and photographs collected by the author, which will now be shown to you, and various points of design commented upon, and perhaps criticised.

In doing this, the author is fully conscious of the risk he runs of being pulled to pieces in the discussion, which, it is hoped, will follow. However, in spite of the fact that what is Art to one in Anathema to another, there are a few fundamentals in designing modern coachwork which are bound to be acceptable to everyone. It is those simple fundamentals that are so often missed by designers, but which make all the difference between a design which the public likes, and one which they do not, although the same public are unable to analyse and realise the difference.

To illustrate the meaning, this slide shows you a mistake the author made, or allowed to go through. Observe the line at the back of the boot. There ought to be a return curve in it to harmonise with the flow of the front wing. Observe also the angle of the bottom of the side valance of the rear wing. This should follow the sweep of the bottom edge of the front wing and running-board, but it does not. It follows an ugly line entirely of its own. The law of harmonious lines has been violated. *(Illustration 21)*

How many members of the public would notice that? But since it has been altered, and a return sweep put into the tail, this particular model has been much more admired than it was before, and incidentally, won the Hastings Cup in the RAC Rally.

Earlier in the paper the author suggested that when the externals of a motor car were being designed, the T-square and the set-square should be thrown away. This slide, made from a rough charcoal sketch, is an example of an engineer's conception of a compete car, as opposed to what an artist would have made of it. Actually, it depicts a low-priced quantity-production German car, and whilst it is reasonably well-balanced by having the windscreen and rear quarter at the same but opposing angles, the hard and uncompromising horizontal lines are an offence to the eye, which unconsciously looks for graceful sweeping lines. In quantities, and produced from dies, it would have cost no more to have introduced some more graceful effects. The wings could not be improved without increasing the cost. *(Illustration 22)*

Illustration 20

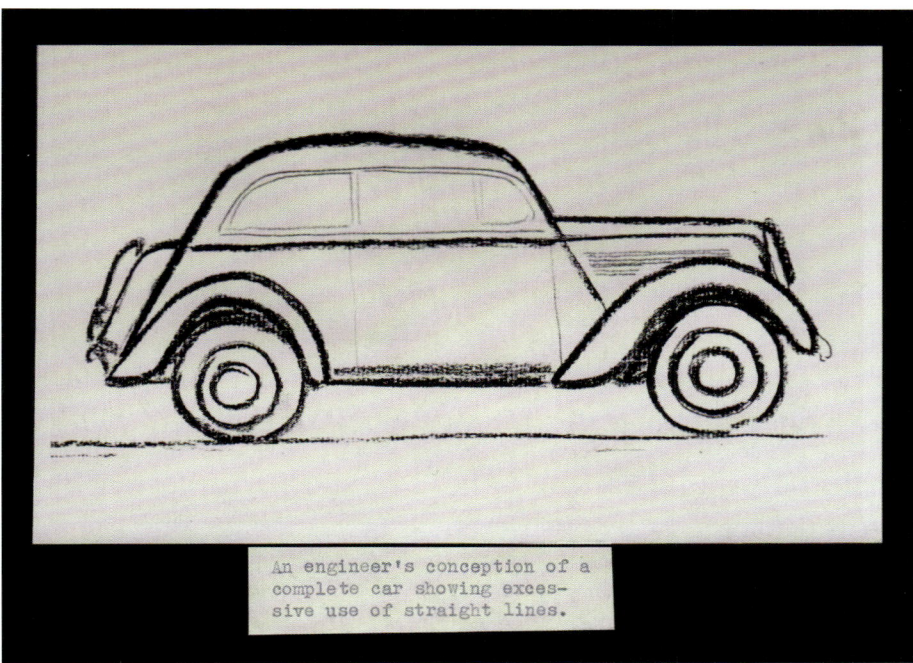

An engineer's conception of a complete car showing excessive use of straight lines.

Illustration 22

The latest type Chrysler.

Illustration 23

A present-day Chevrolet.

Like the mouth of a huge hippopotamus.

Illustration 24

Appendix 2: 'The Trend of Aesthetic Design in Motor Cars'

From an artistic point of view also, the accompanying slide of the latest-type Chrysler is not a very happy example. Its lines are nothing like so pleasing to the eye as the earlier Airflow model. There has been far too much use made of the T-square in the design, and this is accentuated by the bulbous and somewhat heavy-looking domed roof. *(Illustration 23, previous page)*

This slide, too, of the latest Chevrolet, whilst having a kinder roofline, is marred artistically by the bulbous horizontal waistline, and the hard straight edge of the running board. This slide, that looks like the mouth of a huge hippopotamus or whale, is the rear end of a specialty body on an Opel car shown at Berlin, and the somewhat gross effect is heightened by the use of a two-colour scheme. *(Illustration 24, previous page)*

The next slide shows a two-seater body on a big Mercedes, with very attractive sweeping lines, that has been entirely marred by over-ornamentation. As will be seen, it is one mass of bits and pieces of chromium plate. *(Illustration 25)*

Incidentally, it is interesting to note the effect of power and speed that is conveyed by having the radiator set well behind the front axle.

Many designers make the mistake of imagining that ornamentation is design, whereas nothing is further from the truth. It is line, and line only, that counts, and the most important is the line, or lines, formed by the highlights. Sweeping lines that merge and are complementary to one another are restful and pleasing to the eye. Lines that are meaningless, and have no relation to the whole, are not. Sometimes ornamentation, if carried out with restraint, is useful in helping to carry the eye right along the right line, in a way that unconsciously pleases, but if used without that proper degree of intelligence, unconsciously irritates.

The following slide shows the use of an imitation stretcher arm, in the one case used to carry the eye along from the top edge of the window to merge into the sweeping lines of the tail. When applied without any artistic perception, the eye follows a broken line, and is unsatisfied. *(Illustration 26)*

The next slide shows an interesting design of a sports two-seater on a 1-litre Adler Trumpf Junior, as it is called. The falling waistline is unusual, but it is one to be used with great discretion. It will be found desirable to counteract the effect that is produced, of a bonnet top line that slope downwards in a backward direction, to increase the normal height at the scuttle in relation to the

Illustration 25

radiator. In the author's opinion, this design would have been improved had the bonnet hinge been carried a shade higher and stopped at the screen pillar, allowing the top sweep of the door to suggest the continuation which, in turn, would have picked up the rim of the wheel. To bring it across the rear quarter, and the wing leading nowhere, is disconcerting. *(Illustration 27)*

The angle formed by the bottom edge of the bonnet louvres is also ugly, whilst accentuating the imitation frame member by louvering is meaningless and far from pleasing.

This slide shows two typical French examples of special coachwork design, in which sweeping lines have been so exaggerated as to be bizarre. Their fault lies, perhaps, in the fact that they are illogical. *(Illustration 28)*

It is interesting to compare the foregoing with a few examples of typical English coachwork.

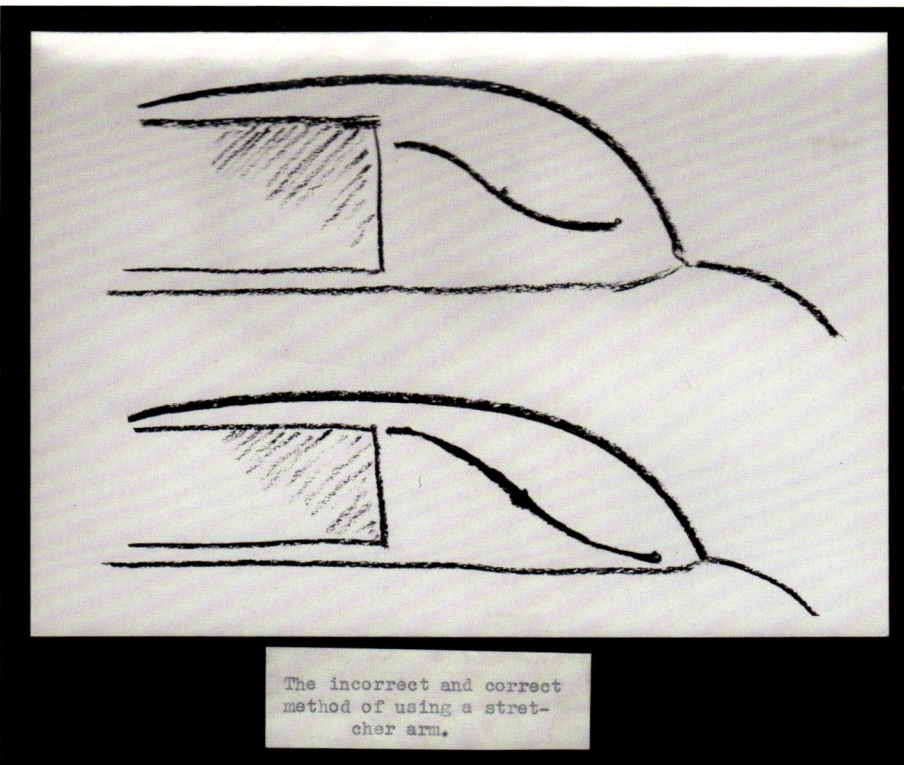

Illustration 26

Illustration 27

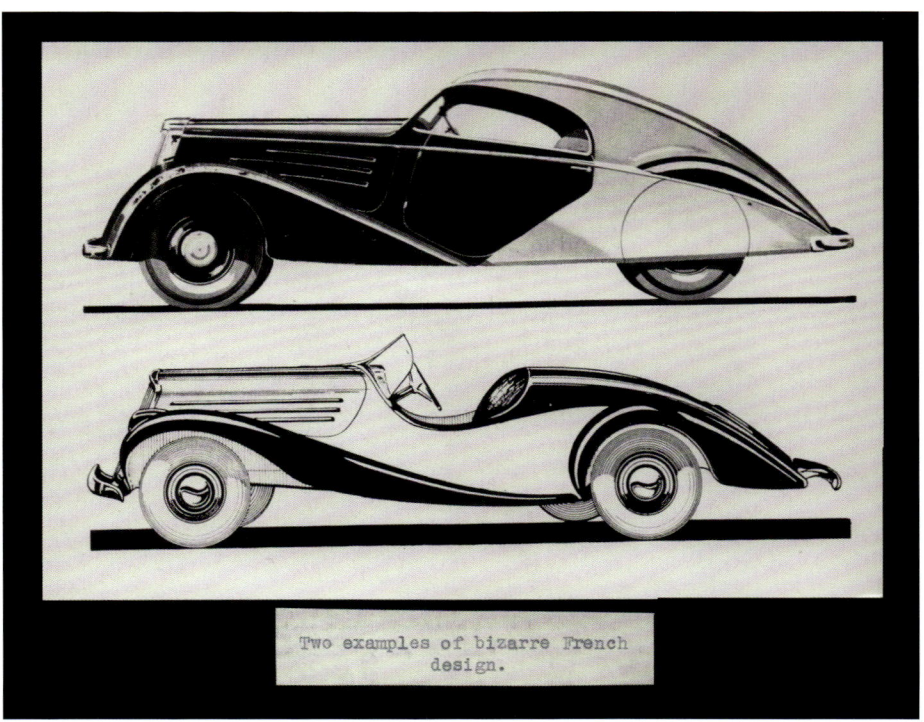

Illustration 28

Here is a photo of the 14hp Armstrong Siddeley, quiet and dignified, but sacrificed to horizontal straight lines. *(Illustration 29)*

Another example is the 4.3-litre Alvis. Quiet but faintly sweeping lines give a pleasing effect, marred perhaps by having to bow to that peculiar British liking for a boot at the rear, indication of luggage capacity. *(Illustration 30)*

This is an example of what might be termed a fashionable body of today. Actually it is a four-door saloon body on an M.G. Two-Litre. It is an example of how fashion dictates styles to a very large extent, especially if such a fashion is set by a social leader, such as the Rolls-Royce. *(Illustration 31)*

Two years ago the SS company introduced a very attractive streamlined saloon, but fashion decreeing otherwise: they and other companies are having to give the public a body in which the boot, or luggage space, is treated as a separate part of the design.

Illustration 30

Illustration 29

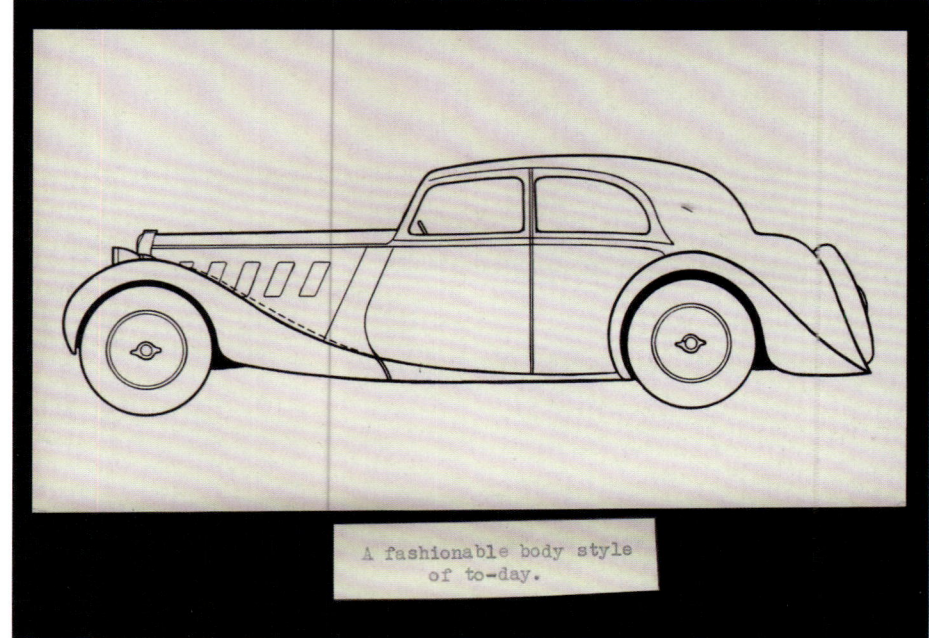

Illustration 31

Appendix 2: 'The Trend of Aesthetic Design in Motor Cars'

This slide of a drophead coupé follows very similar lines to this fashionable close-coupled saloon, and illustrates the point made earlier, showing the use of a stretcher bar – in this case not an imitation one – in carrying the eye away from the somewhat hard line of the top of the window. Incidentally, is it not possible that the close-coupled saloon did not derive its inspirations from the generally attractive drophead coupé? *(Illustration 32)*

To obtain perfect grace, sweeping lines and streamline effect, it is necessary to have a very long wheelbase, and this drawing of a really beautiful body of French design, was only possible because of the wheelbase, which in this case is about 12ft 6in. *(Illustration 33)*

Here also, in sketch form, is a beautiful body having, within the limitations of present-day progress and acceptance by the public, practically perfect lines.

Making allowances for the crudeness of the author's sketch, it

Illustration 33

Illustration 32

should be observed, first of all, how the forward edges of both the front and rear wings are so drawn that, if the line of this wing continued, it would merge gracefully into the outer circumference of the wheel. The sweep of the wing backwards, front and rear, is graceful in the extreme, whilst the sweep of the wing valance is, as will be seen, complementary to the top edge of the wings.

Then, as far as the body is concerned, starting off with a graceful but conventional type of radiator, the long bonnet lends – according to modern conception – an appearance of speed and graceful design. The shoulder-line of the bonnet is carried backwards and downwards in a graceful sweep, and this line, if continued, would naturally merge into the circumference of the rear wheel. However, it would be ugly for this line to break right into the top sweep of the rear wing. It is stopped an inch or two away from the rear wing, and swept forward and downward in a sweep that is complementary to the rear wing.

Illustration 34

The falling line of the lower edge of the window opening is designed to line up with the sweep of the rear wing, and in the same way the top edge of the window opening is complementary and would also merge into the rail of the rear wing, if carried further, whilst the top of the roof is swept backward to become a complementary curve to the rear sweep of the rear wing, to meet this at the very tail end of the wing.

This design, like practically every other motor car design, is marred by the present necessity and public insistence upon the fitting of bumpers, and this is an example of utility overcoming artistry. *(Illustration 34)*

Compared with the last design which we have effected, showing the possibilities of a long wheelbase in obtaining a beautiful effect, it is interesting to come from the sublime to the ridiculous, and observe the accompanying photograph of a short-wheelbase German car, the Steyr, fitted with a body in which a very noble attempt has been made at streamlining. The front wings and running-boards immediately nullify this effect, whilst the bonnet louvres, the traffic indicator and the recessed handle all break up a panel which, for effect, and in view of the short wheelbase, should have appeared in one unbroken sweep, whilst the angle of the windscreen is ugly, as it is not complementary to any other line on the car. The sweep of the roof and the sweep of the waist moulding is quite attractive. As far as the latter is concerned, it is interesting to note how the top edge of this moulding merges into the rear sweep of the rear wing, whilst the bottom edge of the moulding picks up the sweep of the rear wing valance. *(Illustration 35)*

Incidentally, this little car also shows the use of a two-colour scheme for reducing the apparent height.

The author discovered the usefulness of painting the car in two different colours above and below the waistline as long ago as 1925. In those days, chassis were all built very much higher, and when producing an open sports model it was desirable to obtain as long and as low an effect as possible. By painting the top of the

Illustration 35

bonnet and the top of the scuttle, and the top edge of the body and the sides of the bonnet finished in a lighter colour, carrying this lighter colour out on the wheels, having the wings in the darker colour, at once reduced the apparent height of the car by several inches.

This vogue, which the author believes to have started, rapidly spread to America, and it is only in later years, when chassis generally have been getting very much lower, that the use of upper and lower colours is dying out.

In conclusion, the author would like to show you a slide produced from a photograph of the very latest car for which he has been responsible.

This car was designed around the seating accommodation for four persons, and the first drawing was produced as long ago as September 1935. No less than four sample bodies were built before the design was finalised, and it follows out the author's ideas on design, as set out briefly in this paper. This is only a small car of 1½-litre capacity, with a 9ft 6in wheelbase, and therefore it is not possible to have the sweeping lines that one might otherwise have employed, but at any rate there are little or no straight lines in the whole design, and it follows the precepts as set out by the author on what he considers is the best possible design today for ready acceptance and approval by the public; but it is a long way from being the ideal car that logical reasoning tells us will come in the future. *(Illustration 36)*

However, as far as this car is concerned, it should be noted that the radiator is not pushed forward, the bonnet louvres are not accentuated by over-ornamentation, and are actually far less apparent than the photograph would lead you to suppose. The sweep of the front wing merges naturally into the outer circumference of the wheel forward and backward, sweeping downward to merge into the bottom edge of the tail of the body; complementary to this is the bottom edge of the front wing valance merging in with the running-board which in turn picks up the sweep of the bottom edge of the body, and the bottom edge

Illustration 36

of the valance of the rear wing. The valance of the wing proper is kept concentric with the wheel, although the photograph would lead one to suppose that this was not the case as far as the rear wheel is concerned.

The sweep of the boot follows the sweep of the roof, whilst a very faint flare is given to the rear end of the body and wings. The bottom edge of the window frame, in actual fact, picks up the shoulder line of the radiator in front, and then [falls] away to merge in with the rear wing. The top edge of the windscreen is swept, and even the top and bottom edges of the boot locker are slightly curved.

There are no mouldings whatever on this body, its attraction depending entirely upon its light lines.

Before closing, the author would like to place on record his thanks again to Mr Kennington for the loan of some of his drawings, and also to Mr Douglas Clease, of *The Automobile Engineer,* for his help in gathering certain data.

(Images in this Appendix courtesy Autocar)

CECIL KIMBER ON SPORTS CARS

CECIL KIMBER DESIGNS A CAR

Article appearing in two parts in The Autocar, *issues of 12 May 1944 and 19 May 1944*

With Spring and Easter here many sport-car enthusiasts will be wishing that another trials season had opened. Whilst many consider the classic London-Edinburgh the beginning of the sporting season, to most of us springtime in Devon and the London-Land's End run really starts the motoring year.

However, once again there was no midnight gathering at Slough, no breakfast at Taunton and no tea at Perranporth. Instead we must content ourselves and perhaps get some pleasure out of wondering what the future in this direction has in store for us.

TYPE OF EVENTS

This 'wondering' must first deal with the kind of sporting events we can reasonably expect to have after the war. Only when this is done can we logically decide just what sort of sporting motor car we shall want.

As I see it the sporting events with which we were familiar before the war is, very largely, what we can expect again. These fell, broadly, into the following categories:

a) Day and day-and-night trials of the 'stiff' variety

b) Long-distance trials over comparatively easy courses and usually winding up with a concours d'elegance and/or a gymkhana

c) Hillclimbs of the standard road variety such a Shelsley

d) Hillclimbs of the freak variety such as almost unclimbable grass gradients

e) Short sprint races and speed trials

f) Long-distance road races like the TT and Le Mans

g) High-speed touring organised by clubs or privately undertaken on the Continent

h) Finally there is the individual who merely wants to own something that looks sleek and speedy enough to draw murmurs of admiration and expressions of envy when suitably displayed in suburbia and the more fashionable watering places

It is possible that some ingenious soul will think of something new in motor sport but with the menacing hand of the law laid so heavily upon us that we are not allowed to take our motor cars more than 15 yards off the road, and hill after hill is barred to the enthuasiastic trials competitor by the local police, it is hard to visualise just what new line could be taken. Perhaps we may be allowed some special dispensation and be permitted real cross-country trials on 'Jeeps' or amphibian wagons.

TYPE OF CAR

However, whatever the future has in store for us, there is no doubt but that more than one type of car will have to be produced, both claiming the adjective 'sports'.

Apart from four-wheel-drive 'go-anywhere' vehicles principally designed for war purposes, the main differences between the various types of cars required for the different classes of sporting events, is mostly that of coachwork. Perhaps we must exclude the 'specials' produced for stunt events such as Shelsley. There, if they can survive 50 seconds of glorious life all is well. But, on the other hand, if one could produce a chassis with a power unit of such potency and reliability that it was equally capable of competing in the TT as it was of taking part in the London-Gloucester and sufficiently pleasant to drive to make a quick trip up to Scotland or a fast run to the South of France equally enjoyable, then, if one had such a chassis, would it not be just a matter of fitting suitable coachwork for the type of sporting event in which you wished to compete?

So, now we come to the question as to whether it is possible to design and produce a model that will have all the attributes for which we are looking, needing only changes in bodywork to fit it for its different functions.

To do this immediately washes out one school of thought which advocates the abolition of the chassis frame as one means of getting better power/weight ratios. Undoubtedly this offers great inducements to the designers, but – and it is a big 'but' in the sports car field – it means one model only, a saloon. That might be all right if our sporting requirements did not include (a), (c), and (d) in our list of possible events. But what of the open two-seater enthusiast or the owner who *will have* a drop-head coupé? And who in their senses would try and take some slinky enclosed model with all-enclosed wheels and a long streamlined tail through a 'Sunbac' trial?

All the foregoing is, perhaps, rather a long way of arriving at the real meat of this article: 'The Sports Car of the Immediate Post-war Future', but it is possible to arrive at the best compromise – for compromise it has to be.

All sorts of other factors come into the picture, not the least being that of first cost, and not the last, upkeep. Size also is a consideration, as this has a bearing, not only on first cost and upkeep, but also on suitability from a sporting point of view.

I think we must try and visualise this car as having to have a wide appeal to youth not blessed with too much of this world's goods. All those lads who will be coming back after the war who are used to flying Spitfires, piloting Lancasters, driving tanks and 'Jeeps' and commanding MTBs won't be satisfied with the 10hp family saloon. They'll want something with urge and life in it to provide that thrill that only comes when handling a thoroughbred.

So weighing up all these conflicting requirements, let's see where we can start!

THE ENGINE

First of all the most important item, the engine. What size shall it be?

Bearing in mind we want it to hurtle a two-seater up an impossible precipice at high speed and transport a streamlined saloon very rapidly on some fast motor road of the future and that its fuel consumption, tax and insurance have to be modest, then I think we would unhesitatingly plump for 1500cc.

Number of cylinders and type of engine is then the next consideration.

Six in line is attractive but the extra length means a longer chassis and higher cost of manufacture. Vee-eight makes a nice compact engine but is difficult to balance well and would be more costly to build. It is difficult to provide adequate big-end surfaces. It is however interesting to know that the 1500cc Mercedes Grand Prix car that was about to make its appearance when war started was of this type.

The flat-four has some advantages outweighed by greater disadvantages, particularly that of accessibility in overhead-valve form.

Radial. Not enough about this type of engine is known for car purposes and if mounted in a chassis in the conventional forward position, the high centre line of the crankshaft obviously offers difficulties of keeping the floor level low. One would also imagine that, unless fitted with some sort of impeller, carburation would be difficult at low engine speeds. This, I think, forces us to the 'four in line' as the best all-round compromise, as, with modern rubber mounting technique, it is possible to get all the smoothness that is required for really pleasant motoring.

As to bore/stroke ratios, as it is already whispered in official circles that future taxation may – and I only say may – no longer penalise short-stroke engines, we can, perhaps, hope for high crankshaft speeds with reasonable piston speeds.

The question of air or water cooling hardly wants debating as I feel sure public opinion would be in favour of the latter. It might be worth while exploring the possibilities of the 'liquid' cooling as used on certain aero engines.

VALVE OPERATION

A much more controversial point is what type of valve operation shall be employed.

Two-stroke, sleeve valve, rotary valve or poppet valve?

The ordinary plain two-stroke principle can, I think, be ruled out without further consideration but the new supercharged two-stroke sleeve-valve, with petrol injection into the induction pipe, will, I feel, well repay study for the future.

Obviously a lot of development work will have to be done and as we are thinking in terms of immediate post-war requirements we must pass this type over at the moment.

I have, personally – with no real experience to back it – a sneaking regard for the possibilities of the Aspin rotary valve design. I saw one of these engines in operation in its early life and was impressed.

However, as I have just remarked, taking into consideration that in this Sports Car of the Future we are hoping to get into production just as soon as peace conditions will permit, my bet would be for the well-tried poppet-valve engine as a commencement but not neglecting research and development on other fascinating designs such as the two mentioned. So, having decided, for many reasons, on a straight-four short-stroke, poppet-valve engine, I would start off by designing this as a racing unit and capable of standing up to high-pressure supercharging and of giving, with reliability, 180bhp to 200bhp per litre. It would have an overhead camshaft, of course, but not driven by a chain, but by shaft and bevels. It would not have valves at 90 degrees with the idea of obtaining a hemispherical head; the resultant space is no longer hemispherical but, in section, resembles an attenuated crescent moon.

The same engine with normal touring compression and fitted with a low-boost blower would provide a pleasantly potent power plant with plenty of punch at low revs and in this form would, I feel, be the most popular type and should develop about 110bhp.

Again the same engine, but unblown, with about 7½ to 1 compression ratio, would be supplied where sales resistance to supercharged engines made it desirable. This should develop about 60bhp and would be fitted with a head having slightly smaller induction passages to increase gas velocities at the lower end.

The blower mounting and drive would be designed into the engine at the beginning and not added as an afterthought. For maximum output for racing, possibly an eccentric-vane type of blower would be used but for the low-boost model, definitely a Roots type would be employed. To overcome the high cost of machining accurately this type of blower, the possibilities of making this from some form of plastic – particularly the rotor – would be explored.

By this means one basic engine would provide a racing engine, a mildly boosted super sports type and a high-efficiency unblown unit. The very fact that the basic design is capable of the highest possible power output ensures that, in its two lower-output forms, it would have the maximum of reliability and long service between overhauls.

As we must make every effort to save weight the engine block and crankcase should be of aluminium with 'wet' liners for the cylinders. This should not increase the cost to any appreciable extent and offers an easy way of replacing worn bores. The crankcase should have ample oil capacity. So much for the engine.

GEARBOX

Then comes the question of the gearbox. As price and speed in getting into production is of paramount importance, it would perhaps be wisest to use a close-ratio synchromesh four-speed box with a short stumpy gear lever carried on an extension and operated in a central position without any reaching forward. A change-speed lever carried on the steering column just under the steering wheel – a revival, as I mentioned earlier, of the practice of forty years ago – is a method of operation once more coming into favour and might be considered. If the cost was not too

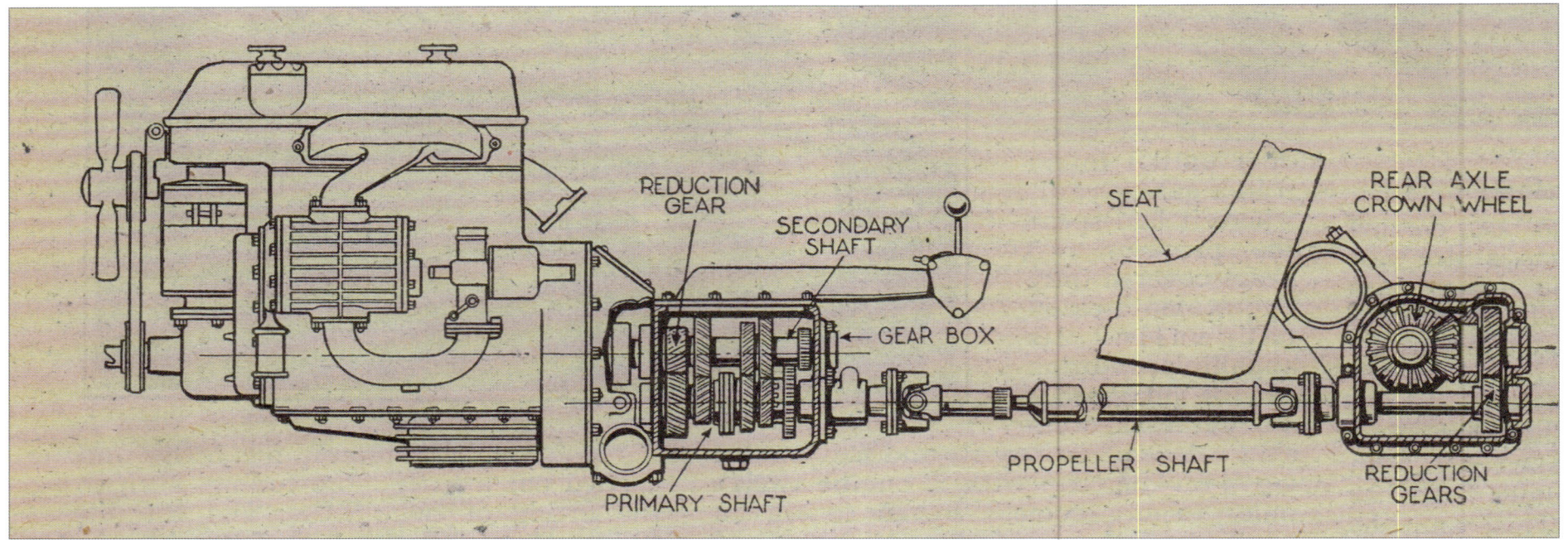

prohibitive it might be an advantage to fit this box with some form of positively-operated overdrive or a geared-up fifth gear. I would not be in favour of the complicated semi-automatic type found on some American cars.

At a later date it would be desirable to investigate other types of gearboxes and for real snap changes the Cotal electric box wants some beating but, being of the epicyclic type, it suffers from the disadvantage of rather widely-spaced ratios, judged by sports and racing standards. However, just before the war, an interesting box was taking the attention of designers. This was a synchromesh type of box in which the change was effected by the electrical operation of the synchro clutches.

Whilst dealing with gearboxes, this brings us to a consideration of the transmission. In all cases with a conventional layout and particularly the sports car with its low floor level, the housing for the propeller shaft seriously interferes with the body space, restricts the foot room and gives the body designer many headaches. Whilst the hypoid back axle, which we are likely to see in greater numbers after the war, helps the problem, the gain, in the size of car we are visualising, is only a matter of about 1½ inches and means the use of special high-pressure lubricant.

I should like to investigate the cost and possibility of a scheme I have wanted to try for years. This is to introduce a reduction gear, say two to one, at the front end of the gearbox, reducing the speed of the primary shaft by half but, more important, bringing the centre line of the primary shaft below that of the crankshaft, the amount being determined by the size of the gear-wheels used. Modern helical gears would ensure the requisite quietness. The secondary shaft of the gearbox would be arranged above the primary, contrary to usual practice. This would mean that the propeller shaft could be carried three inches or more lower than the normal position and would be revolving at half the normal speed, which again removes another bugbear of the fast car, propeller shaft whip.

Now assuming that a final reduction is desired on direct drive of 5:1, as we have already reduced the propshaft speed by half or 2.5:1 by the introduction of the reduction gears in front of the gearbox, if a further pair of gears be incorporated in the back axle casing the driven wheel being in one with the bevel pinion, this brings back the centre line of the drive to the centre line of the back axle. If the ratio of these gears is again 2:1, then instead of having to utilise a large crown wheel and a small bevel pinion to obtain the original 5:1 ratio, the crown wheel would be considerably reduced in size and the bevel pinion increased, which would result in greater efficiency, stronger construction and a smaller back axle casing. This would enable the propeller shaft to be brought under the differential and the drive to be taken up at the rear of the axle casing thus getting away from the forward nose of the differential housing and providing more seat space where these are placed just in front of the rear axle which normally is a serious handicap to the body designer.

BRAKES

Having dealt with the engine, gearbox and transmission, the question of brakes needs mention as they are of paramount importance in any fast car. My own preference is for the largest possible drums which should then be quite narrow and so less liable to distort or 'bell'. I would have them of high-duty alloy, deeply ribbed on the periphery and cast round liners of austenetic iron, the latter being, in the first place, centrifugally cast. One thing is certain, on this sports car I am endeavouring to visualise, and that is the present hand-operated parking brake that accompanies the usual hydraulic system, would not be tolerated. I would want to see a handbrake every bit as powerful as the footbrake, with a fly-off ratchet and capable of holding the car on the steepest gradients and so able to cope with 'stop and restart' tests.

After the war we are going to see a new form of automatic adjustment for the shoes, which, incidentally, must be of the 'two leading shoe' type and hydraulically operated. In my opinion, many designers make the mistake of adopting small diameter drums – possibly with the idea of avoiding flywheel spinning effect – and obtain the requisite area by making them wide. I feel that it is far better to have the smoothness and easier effort that the large diameter drum provides.

A simple way of demonstrating this point can be very easily undertaken now that most of us, in these war days, are cyclists. Turn your cycle upside down, spin the front wheel and see the ease with which one can stop the wheel by placing the finger on the rim or tyre. Now try to do the same thing by pinching the hub between finger and thumb. There is no comparison in the effort required.

WHEELS

Having dealt with brakes, the natural sequence is now to discuss the question of wheels. The die-hard enthusiast will still want his wire wheels and I must confess to a certain leaning that way myself. However, in my opinion there are so many advantages offered by the disc or pressed-steel wheel that this type needs seriously to be considered for the sports car of the future. For one thing, it allows the brake drum to be housed so snugly inside but what is more important, it brings the centre line of the brake shoe more in line with the centre line of the tyre. But, if disc wheels are fitted, they must – and this is important from a racing or sporting motorist's point of view – they must have a centre-lock attachment. Studs, nuts and a brace spanner would not be tolerated.

CHASSIS FRAME

Now we come to the consideration of the chassis frame. As already argued, because we have to cater for all types of open and closed coachwork, we are forced to provide a chassis structure capable of withstanding all torsional strains without help from the body. Also, for the projected car, we shall require two chassis lengths. A short one for racing and to accommodate two-seater sports bodies and a long one to provide for open or closed four-seater bodies.

This need present no difficulties from a production point of view as the extra length can be introduced at some point amidships which would only affect the length of the propeller shaft and the side members.

As to the question of track and wheelbase dimensions, the former, I feel, should be 4ft 3in or 4ft 4in and the length of the wheelbase governed by two major considerations. These are that the engine is carried in the frame well behind the front axle; this being for the sake of good directional stability; and that the base of the rear seats is carried in front of the rear axle.

In considering the design of this frame, I think we must use more fully, welded sheet steel of comparatively light gauge. The Budd Steel Corporation of America, before the war, were showing what could be accomplished in this direction by using spot-welded stainless-steel beam structures for high-speed rail coaches.

Also the dash and facia mounting should not be something just added but so designed and built in as to take its share of bracing the frame torsionally.

AXLES

Now comes the question of axle design. Undoubtedly independent front suspension is a 'sine qua non'. My own particular fancy, based on a fairly wide personal experience and actual trial of all kinds, is for the Delage type with the plentiful use of Silentbloc bushes. The feature of this type is the use of a long light girder on each side that holds the pivot pins at a constant angle within close limits and takes the brake torque reaction so well. I would like to see torsion bars for springs. The André-Girling follows very similar lines but uses coil springs and, as fitted to the 2½-litre Daimler, provides steering with wonderful directional stability. I attach much more importance to this latter quality than to the springing as such.

For the back axle I would like to see the differential assembly carried by the frame, driving the wheels through constant velocity universal joints, but with the rear wheels tied together with a light beam axle structure on the old de Dion principle. Again, as in the case of the front axle, I should like to see torsion bars used for the springing.

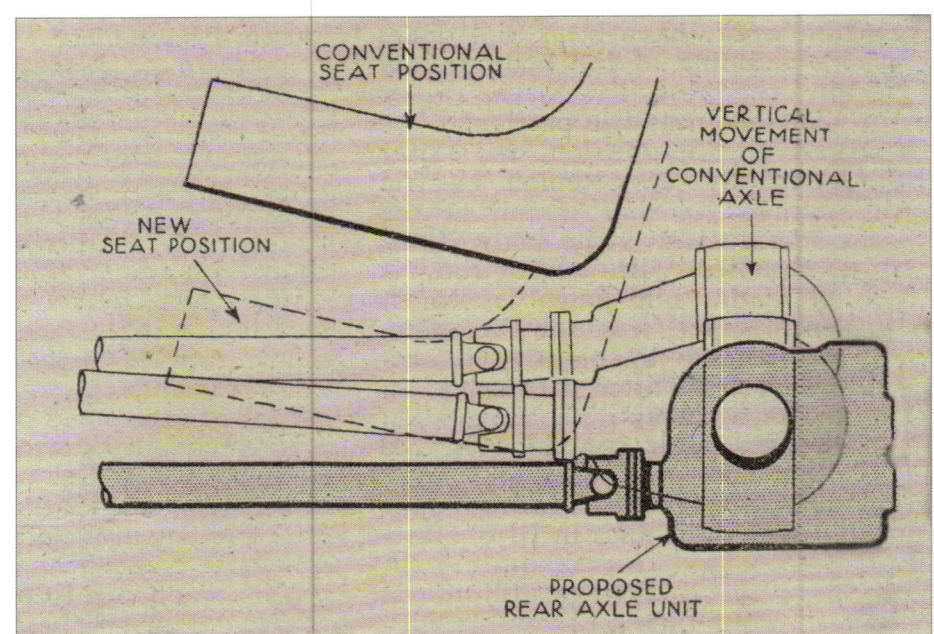

Plain swinging axles, using the amplitude required for comfort, are, in my experience, conducive to bad roadholding. The greater the amplitude the worse the roadholding and that goes, incidentally, for most springing, hence the very small axle movement one sees on the majority of racing cars. Even using comparatively small wheel movements it should be noted that the German Grand Prix cars eventually changed from the swinging type of axle to the de Dion type.

This was found to give greater road stability than having each rear wheel independently sprung in spite of the fact that the wheel movement allowed was comparatively small. With greater movement the condition is worse and that is the reason I would advocate, in this sports car we are discussing, the carrying of the differential on the frame and tying the wheels together with the de Dion type of back axle.

There are, however, two important factors to be considered before such a decision is finalised. One is noise. With the back-axle gearing carried rigidly attached to the chassis frame, it has, in the past, been found extremely difficult to keep axle noises from being transmitted to the body. Possibly rubber mounting and other forms of insulation might overcome this difficulty. The other and more important factor is that of price. Earlier on it was decided that, if it were not vital, design had to be sacrificed to cost and it might well be that the general overall comfort and roadworthiness of the car would not be sacrificed too much by the conventional type of back axle and springing.

This completes a general review of the chassis though there are a thousand and one details that could be discussed, but it is not possible to do that here. One item I should like to mention and that is the petrol tank. This must be of ample capacity and carry enough fuel for over 300 miles. Then there is the radiator. I must confess that I am old-fashioned in my ideas and deplore the growing disappearance of the radiator proper and with it the individuality of the marque. No doubt the streamline expert, when designing the enclosed coachwork, will sweep aside my desire to see my distinctive radiator design retained; but I shall go down fighting. I like the individuality of a car to be distinctly recognisable and not submerged under a bulbous exterior. From a purely commercial aspect alone, think what publicity value you lose!

COACHWORK

Now we come to the various type of coachwork with which this post-war sports car is to be offered. These, in my opinion, would comprise:

    a) Sports two-seater, open type.
    b) Sports four-seater, open type.
    c) Sports two-seater, drop-head coupé.
    d) Sports four-seater, drop-head coupé.
    e) Sports four-seater, streamline saloon.
    f) Racing body types would be special to the event.

These five body styles would be conceived as engineering structures more than individual efforts of various coachwork craftsmen. Lightness and a long life free from rattles would be the main aims. As these bodies would not be called upon to act as chassis stiffeners, they could be built lightly and every advantage

taken of aircraft technique in the fashioning of aluminium alloy structures if the price of this metal becomes commercially a proposition.

The latest type of aircraft construction, such as the Mosquito, opens up a new line of development in the use of synthetic-resin-bonded plywood that may have great possibilities for bodywork production in modest quantities. Interleaved with balsa wood, the resultant lightness, torsional strength and sound-deadening qualities of this construction would appear to be most attractive.

As regards the style of coachwork to be adopted for the various suggested modes, my ideas would be as follows:-

Sports two-seater, open type. Purely functional in style with no attempt at streamlining and suitable for traversing the stiffest trials route with minimum of damage to its externals. Small luggage space behind the seats.

Sports four-seater, open type and also the two and four-seater drop-head coupé types. As streamlined as these three body styles will permit. For use for high-speed touring only.

Sports four-seater streamline saloon. Every effort should be made in this model to produce the best streamlined form within the limits dictated by the length of the car and the necessity of providing full sitting headroom in the rear seats. As it is proposed that the body is to be primarily an engineering structure, as opposed to coachwork craftsmanship, I would advocate what is termed the pillarless saloon. The greater ease of ingress provided, if the centre pillar is omitted, has to be tried to be appreciated. There is no reason, if, as already stated, it is properly engineered, why this should not be quite satisfactory and stand up to long use without developing annoying rattles.

PRICES

Finally prices. As we cannot estimate what the ruling price of material and labour will be after the War, all we can do is to use pre-war values and on this basis I would estimate that these would range from £230 for the unblown open two-seater to £400 for the blown streamline saloon.

There, fellow sports car enthusiasts, is my recipe for the immediate post-war sports car. Nothing revolutionary but capable of being put into practical effect just as soon as peace conditions permit a resumption of our normal activities. Development during the five or so years after that will doubtless be far more exciting but that is another story.

SPORTS CARS – PAST AND FUTURE

Talk given to Derby Branch of the Institution of Automobile Engineers at Derby School of Arts, 9 October 1944

When I was invited by your Secretary Mr Towle through Mr Haggerty to give a talk to the graduates of your Section, not only did I appreciate the compliment but I looked forward to seeing and meeting again some old friends amongst the Rolls-Royce organisation. When I say that I started my career in the motor industry with the old Sheffield-Simplex company in Sheffield and that during the last war the two companies used to play golf against each other, you'll realise how far back that friendship goes. I remember that Rolls-Royce maintained the same supremacy at golf that they have maintained ever since in the motor car and aero engine fields.

Without in any way wanting to bore you with a story of my life, I thought it might interest you to hear briefly how I came eventually to build up a concern that became not entirely unknown in the sports car world.

All I had was an overpowering attraction towards motorcycles and motor cars in general. Compared with many of you here, my early engineering training was of the most sketchy nature. It must be remembered that in the early 1900s the opportunities for technical training in automobile engineering were very scant as compared with the facilities provided today. I went into my father's business of Printer's Engineers just before I turned fifteen.

Evening classes at the Manchester Technical School – taking quite the wrong subjects – helped a bit. Actually the subject that stood me in the best stead in my later business life was accountancy and to those of you with their eyes on high administrative posts in the years to come, I would strongly recommend a study of this subject that, approached in the right way, can be found most fascinating. After all, if you go into business you do it with one object and that is to make money. If you don't make money, you won't be in business, not for long, anyway, and the only way you can tell if you are making money or losing it is by means of accountancy.

During those early years, 1900 onwards, before I even owned a motorcycle, let alone a car, I would cycle miles and go to any amount of trouble just for the opportunity of seeing a solitary example of the early efforts of the automobile industry, then very much in its infancy. I used to cycle to Dunham Hill, Altrincham – a gentle slope you wouldn't notice on a modern 8hp car – to watch the few motorcycles and cars coming back to Manchester after their Sunday afternoon run. This fearsome acclivity used to test the cooling systems to the utmost and if in the course of a couple of hours I saw half a dozen, I thought my 14-mile pushbike ride well rewarded. The scarcity of motor vehicles in those days seems incredible compared with the numbers one sees on the road these days.

I well remember the thrill of seeing the first Rolls-Royce 'Silver Ghost', which was built in Trafford Park, Manchester, making its famous 10,000-mile RAC-observed trial between London and Manchester. I remember the first Motor Show in Manchester, held at the St James's Hall and at which I think the first 6hp Rover made its appearance, selling around about the £100 mark. A later show, too, at the Exhibition Grounds at Fallowfield on which previously Paulhan landed when making his historic flight from London in competition with Grahame-White.

It was during that period, about 1905, that I acquired my first motorcycle and learned to drive a car. The latter was on a 10hp Wolseley with the gear change on the steering column, where, 40 years later, we are once more seeing it. The locality being North Wales and consequently somewhat hilly, the fact that you had to climb these hills in reverse was taken quite as a matter of course. Imagine climbing, as we did once, most of the way from Beddgelert to the Pen-y-Grwyd Hotel, in reverse – and in the rain – in order to see the competitors in the Six Days Trial attack the Llanberis Pass. Rex, Quadrant, Brown, Triumph, Roe, Vindec Special, Chater-Lea and others amongst the motorcycles and Riley, Lagonda and a number of others of weird and wonderful design comprising the three-wheeled passenger contingent.

Then a motorcycle accident put me out of circulation for nearly three years and when I was able to get about again quite a lot of progress was apparent and instead of just marvelling at a motor for going at all, one started to be more interested in how they went.

Prior to that period there were really no sports cars as we know them if you except fearsome machines like the chain-driven Fiats of 120hp and other big-engined Continental cars. There were a number of French cyclecars like the Sizaire-Naudin with a huge single-cylinder engine and a maximum speed of 49mph and a weird belt-driven contraption called the Bédélia. We even suffered in those days from the pseudo sports wagon and I can remember one called the Jackson Runabout, built in my own little village at Pangbourne. This was a pathetic attempt to emulate the 120hp Fiat with its enormously high and long bonnet. The Jackson was almost as long but when you lifted the bonnet side, one could just discern at one end of a large cavern-like space a diminutive single-cylinder engine, the remainder of the space being devoted to luggage accommodation. Needless to say, the performance of this particular motor car did not live up to its appearance.

However, by about 1912, when the Manchester Motor Club and the Lancashire Automobile Club staged some exciting hillclimbs at Woodhead and Rivington Pikes, a few sports cars worthy of the name began to make their appearance. The star performer at these events was the late Mr Higginson, also noted as the inventor of the Autovac, who used to put up some lurid exhibitions on an 80hp

La Buire. Then appeared, also in Mr Higginson's hands, the Prince Henry Vauxhall, later to become the famous 30/98. A few Grand Prix type Sunbeams also used to perform but these I do not class as sports cars as they were unobtainable by the general public. Then in Manchester district appeared two of the most attractive sports cars imaginable. Even today they would be almost modern in appearance. These were Hispano-Suizas with cloverleaf three-seater bodies and of 15.9hp and 17.9hp with a bore of 80mm and a stroke of 180mm [and] four cylinders; they were fearsome brutes to start by hand.

Reverting to the Sunbeams just mentioned, these used to be driven by Chassagne and Dario Resta, both of these fine drivers being now dead, I believe. However I can still remember with what awe and reverence I once had tea with Louis Coatalen and the late Dario (Dolly) Resta.

Then with 1913 came a flock of attractive small four-cylinder cars – Singers, Calcotts, Calthorpes and the beautifully-made vee-two air-cooled Humberettes amongst a number of others. Their special competition models were always a delight to watch in the Six Day Trials. I myself bought one of the first 10hp Singers with the gearbox in the back axle. It was number 53, a very early one, and after some initial engine trouble gave me very good service for over 20,000 miles. It was far from being a sports car, though, as its maximum was only a speedometer 47mph and at that speed, with the absence of shock absorbers, it became a most frightening drive. Mr. Lionel Martin made one go quite quickly at Brooklands and the Land's End to John O'Groats record made on one of these models by a well-known competition driver of those days named Davies has never been broken. I believe the speed averaged was some 36mph.

The initial engine trouble mentioned is perhaps of sufficient interest to touch upon briefly as an indication of basically bad design. The Singer engine block was cast in pairs, the heads being integral with the cylinders. They had side valves, of course, and the valve chest for each pair of cylinders was covered by a common plate. This plate, not more than ⅜in at its thickest, was optimistically expected to hold the compression and explosion pressure held down by ¼in studs spaced at least 1½in apart. Eventually, after a long and tedious argument with the factory, the blocks were changed for ones having the then more conventional screwed valve caps.

Then came the last war and during the early stages of that I sold my little Singer at a scandalous profit and out of the proceeds bought a rather interesting machine. This was another Singer. A 14hp with side valves and a T-head which had been raced at Brooklands by a very early aviator, one Vivian Hewitt who was, incidentally, the first man to fly across the sea to Ireland after Robert Loraine, the actor, had just failed by falling in the water in sight of the Irish shore. This old Singer used to lap Brooklands, in its heyday, at 80mph and was interesting by virtue of the fact that it was an early example of a car with a four-speed box, but in this case the top gear was a geared-up indirect one. Originally fitted for Brooklands with a streamline single-seater body, when I acquired it there had been fitted one of the clover-leaf bodies off one of the Hispano-Suizas already mentioned. It made a very nice motor car to drive and for those days had quite a satisfying performance.

By this time I had joined the old Sheffield-Simplex motor car company and, as personal assistant to the Chief Engineer, got plenty of opportunities of driving their 30hp model, one of the earliest examples of a definite attempt to achieve a good power/weight ratio. It was a beautiful car to drive and had the gearbox incorporated with the torque tube. The less said about the gearchange the better.

This car was a serious attempt by the late Earl Fitzwilliam to challenge the supremacy of the Rolls-Royce car, but his unsuccessful attempt is reputed to have cost him the best part of a million pounds.

When the last war was over and came the 1919 Motor Show, a marvellous crop of weird and wonderful contraptions burst upon a car hungry public. And how they sold! I remember one concern who took, at that show, orders for more that two million pounds worth of their new model but, fortunately for their future reputation, never made more than the three prototypes.

Of the more unconventional types produced during that period, you will perhaps call to mind the Belsize-Bradshaw, the ABC with some quite good features, the Enfield-Allday Radial of which I had an opportunity of driving once, the Blériot Whippet which was an up-to-date version of the old Bédélia and might well have provided the natural step from the motorcycle-and-sidecar to the car. With its big air-cooled engine and belt drive it was quite pleasant to drive but the steering left a lot to be desired. A centre-pivoted axle and wire-and-bobbin actuation did not lend itself to safe speeding.

I have no doubt there are a number of other makes produced after the last war that I should have mentioned, but as I am living, like so many other unfortunates in this wartime, in someone else's house, I haven't the facilities for reference and have had to rely entirely on my memory for these remarks and hope therefore on this score you will show me some indulgence.

From 1920 onwards there was a rapidly awaking interest not only in cars generally, but in sports cars in particular. Sporting events flourished, the big oil and petrol interests helped in every possible way, so that it was no wonder that during that period many interesting types of sports car became available to the public. These were principally produced by this country, France and Italy but strange to say, the largest automobile-producing country in the world, America, has never brought out anything that really appeals to the enthusiast, with the possible exception of the Duesenberg.

One of the finest sports cars I had ever driven was a two-seater 1½-litre Alfa Romeo, supercharged. This was in 1928 or 1929 and whilst to some the springing might have been on the hard side, for sheer pleasure of driving, perfect controllability, brakes and steering, it was the most wonderful thing I had ever handled up to that time. I also tried the supercharged edition and that was really very good. It was in the early days of my efforts to produce a sports car worthy of the name and I must confess that that experience spurred me on in a way nothing else could have done.

I went to Oxford in 1921 to take charge of The Morris Garages. From then on I took every opportunity of driving every sort and kind of car I could get my hands on, one of the most pleasing being the 3-litre Sunbeam with ohv and brought out to compete with the 3-litre Bentley. The Sunbeam company did not go with this model which I always thought was a pity, as it was a grand car and better in my opinion than the Bentley, being very much more refined in its performance. I even had the chance, which I took, of driving back from London one of the actual Coupe de l'Auto Grand Prix Sunbeams. It had had its best days. I remember a large sports Peugeot that was quite quick and other sporting cars that the more affluent undergraduates used to run. One such was a huge 60hp Mercedes that took a strong man to start it. The owner, being a rowing Blue, was eminently suited to perform this feat.

However, enough of these old cars. Let us look instead into the future – but not too far as otherwise we might be here all night, so wide are the possibilities.

The following remarks are therefore confined to the suggested outline of a sports car that could be produced during the immediate post-war future, leaving anything untried for development during the subsequent years.

> From this point on, Kimber largely repeats his *The Autocar* article. The only new elements relate to the possibility of adopting disc brakes, a discussion of steering (to be by a high-geared rack, with damping), and a response to some queries raised by the magazine article. Notably, Kimber rejects the use of a timing chain, as likely to provoke camshaft flutter, and the use of a worm-drive axle, on the grounds of these 'coking-up' too easily.

APPENDIX 4

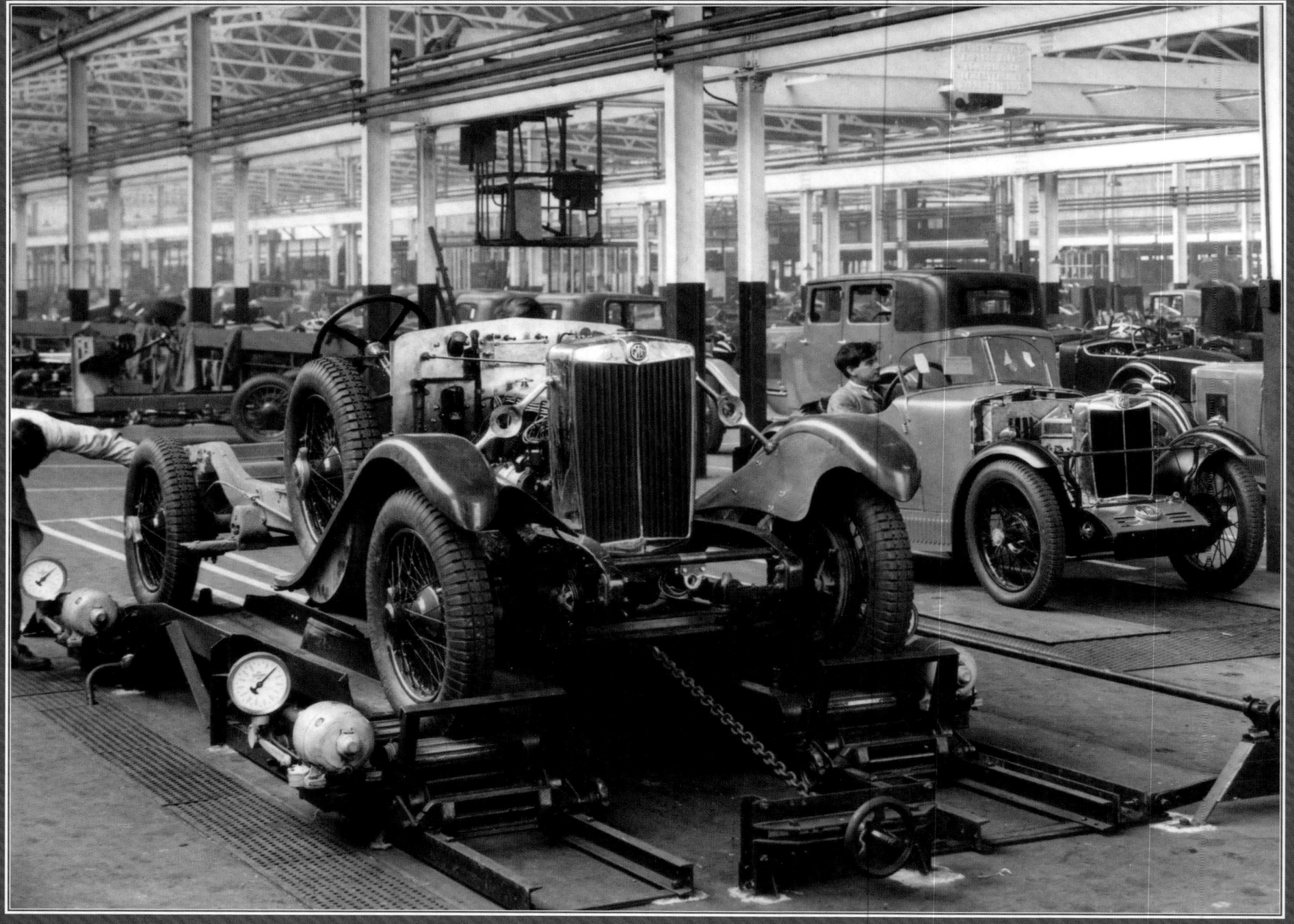

(Magna Press Library)

'MAKING MODEST PRODUCTION PAY IN MOTOR-CAR MANUFACTURE'

A paper given in March 1934 to the Institution of Automobile Engineers

Nearly 20 years ago the author stood before a similar audience to this, as the joint author of a paper on Works Organisation; it was the first experience of its kind, and his stage fright and diffidence may be imagined. Age and experience have removed the stage fright, but the diffidence has increased. The older he grows, the more he realises how very much there is to learn about running such a highly complex business as a motor car factory. He doubts whether there is another form of commercial activity that demands such close attention to detail, and contains such concentrated elements of trouble. The most insignificant detail can entirely wreck the whole production. Building cars demands intensive effort and organising ability of the very highest degree.

But members know this, and there is no need for the author to enlarge upon it. His object is to relate something of his experience in the motor trade of 'Making Modest Production Pay'. If his remarks are somewhat autobiographical, it is because he can only tell of his own experiences, which, starting in a somewhat humble way, have achieved a modest success. If such an account is of any help whatever, then he will feel that any trouble he had taken in writing this paper has been amply repaid.

Looking back over the history of making motor cars, with few exceptions the smaller manufacturer had always great difficulties in making consistent and reasonable profits, and very many found the competition from the larger concerns too much for them, and failed. The quantities were purely relative as very modest.

When the author started the concern which he now represents, the present big manufacturers were already beginning their outputs of tens of thousands of cars a year, and to have attempted to compete with them in their markets and at their prices would have been just suicidal. Ever since he started his business career he had the idea that if a firm could offer the public a product only ten per cent better than anyone else's, that firm could command a fifty per cent better price. The percentages are, of course, only figurative, and as an example of what the author means; those who remember the very early days of motorcycling, when machines were somewhat uncertain means of travel, know what a sale, and what a hold on the public, the original Triumph motorcycle had. That has been the keynote of the author's endeavour, and, in his opinion, the only possible way a small firm can exist amidst the present fierce competition in our trade.

Admittedly, he was fortunate in having behind him Lord Nuffield, then W.R. Morris. His dynamic personality – and the author means that in the fullest sense of the term – was, and has been, an ever-present inspiration. But any business of his has to be successful! Many times we have differed in some policy or other, but he has always been big enough – and that is his finest characteristic – to let the author have his way, and when he had done that, we, at the works, have moved mountains to show that we were right, and with very few exceptions we have achieved what we set out to do. Now, the most important necessity of a small firm – and the author cannot stress this too highly – is that the executive staff should be a team. Individual keenness is not enough. They must pull together, and he has always been ruthless about getting rid of any member of the staff who does not get on with his colleagues; his technical or other qualifications count for nothing compared to this. With the team spirit, enthusiasm for the factory, and its product, follows as a matter of course.

Then another item of management on which the author sets great store is putting all the higher executives, the principal department managers and the principal foremen, on a bonus on profits. In our case a certain portion of this is set aside for distribution on a percentage basis. As a result, everyone concerned realises that everything he can do to make profits for the concern, and avoid waste, will ultimately benefit him individually. The author is amazed to find instances in other firms where bonuses are paid to high officials merely on turnover, or on the number of cars produced, without the *cost* of producing that turnover being taken into account. In considering this question of making motor cars in modest numbers, and at the same time making a profit, the fact has to be faced that the product will cost more in any case. And here is where salvation comes in – the intense individualism of the Anglo-Saxon race. Mixed up with this is a certain amount of innate snobbery. Without it all efforts would be hopeless. To this end a motor car must be designed and built that is a little different from and a little better than the product of the big quantity manufacturer.

A market that is different must be found, a market that is not covered or coveted by the large concern. That is becoming difficult owing to the marvellous finish and even better performance offered by the cheapest cars. But the author believes that there will always be that market available for the car that is that ten per cent better. It is a most difficult market for which to estimate, and as cost per car is high and governed by the number of cars sold, there is little latitude for mistakes, and a certain amount of courage is necessary.

The biggest factor is, of course, overheads. It takes as much time and energy – probably more – to design and test a car of the speciality type for, say a 3,000-car output, as it does for a 30,000 output. Chassis material will undoubtedly cost more, not much perhaps, but at least a little more. Tooling per car will be higher.

Selling expenses will be heavier per unit, for it costs very little more to distribute 30,000 than it does 3,000, for the same number of distributors and dealers as the big fellow.

Advertising will also be out of all proportion, as the same page spaces in the motor press have to be taken as the large concerns, and agents expect to distribute the same amount of equally costly literature.

Olympia Show expenses are equally heavy for the small producer. If a firm caters for the sporting motorist, then the service charges per car are very much higher, and owing to the individual attention expected by the user of the car, much larger service staffs in proportion have to be maintained.

Then again, the small concern has not the advantage of a large spare parts business, which swells so comfortably the profits of the big manufacturer.

However, in spite of all these disadvantages under which the small concern labours, the author says it is possible to carve out a niche in the Empire markets, both at home and abroad, provided that the product offered has some special appeal and especially if it can be endowed with a personality that lifts it out of the ordinary rut.

Having generalised, the author would now like to tell in greater detail how our various functions of management operate. The most important is that of budgetary control. In his opinion, accountancy is not used sufficiently by the management in most of the businesses with which he has come in contact. So many seem to overlook the fundamental fact that a man is in business solely with the idea of making that business pay, and the only way in which it can be ascertained – and known from day to day – whether it is being made to pay is by means of accountancy. A vivid example of what disregard of that principle can lead to is the fate of a £1,000,000 company, with which the author was connected in a humble capacity. He well remembers his horror and amazement when one day he discovered that the managing director of that concern was totally unable to read an ordinary trading account, and did not know the debit side from the credit side. That company went into liquidation, taking with it practically all the author's hard-earned savings, and the managing director is a broken man, and looking for a job today. The author therefore urges every young member of this Institution to study the principles of accountancy hand in hand with his study of the technical and production side, as without that knowledge he will never be in a position properly to control a business organisation.

Returning to the question of budgetary control, the preparation of this is possibly the most important piece of work that the management has to do throughout the year. Courage is needed, but not rashness. The various factors that have to be reviewed are the fixed and variable overhead charges, potential sales, the selling prices, and the effect of these on sales, and the amount of profit required.

One of the difficult things that a car manufacturer has to face is the fact that his interests in a factory are diametrically opposed to the interests of the distributor or agent selling his products. This may sound strange, but is explained as follows: The manufacturer is far better off making say £15 profit on one £300 motor car than making £10 profit on two motor cars at £250, because there is less capital employed, there are fewer service charges, and less handling altogether, but the distributor and agents would obviously far sooner sell two cars at £250, because they will be easier to sell, and, what is most important, they will be getting 20 per cent on the two cars totalling £500, instead of 20 per cent on only one car totalling £300. In this respect the author considers it essential that the small manufacturer should resist the constant urge he will receive from his agents to give them cheaper and cheaper cars. Leave that to the large-quantity car manufacturer, and be content. Map out a modest programme that will assure as far as it is possible a good and reasonable return on the money laid out. To ensure this a very strict budgetary control is required.

Many large car manufacturers have been ruined by being too ambitious in their sales programme, by being led away by one good year, and imagining that because of that they are justified in planning a 50 per cent increase for the following year. In our case, assuming conditions to be normal, we plan the ensuing year's programme on what we have achieved during the previous year. We know our material costs; we estimate our labour costs fairly closely, and we plan, as far as possible, that our overheads shall be on the same scale as the previous year. With these taken as a basis we can them estimate a suitable profit per car, and fix our selling prices accordingly. This may sound unenterprising to some ears, but in the author's experience it is found that after reaching the 2,000 cars a year figure that there is very little saving in material costs, if any, in increasing the quantity by 50 per cent or even 100 per cent, as that saving only comes when the quantities go right up into the big figures of 10,000 cars a year and more. Therefore, if sales justify a mid-season increase in production, additional material purchases can be made without having lost any buying advantages. In selling a speciality car it has always to be remembered that there is only a definite size of market for it, and it is merely foolish to be unduly optimistic. Should, then, the sales exceed the previous year's figures, the estimated modest profit is converted into a really good one. Once the overheads have been absorbed, profits mount at an exhilarating rate, and the effort to beat last year's figures is well rewarded if the firm is successful.

It may be interesting to know that in our case, being primarily a design and assembly factory, the direct labour costs are very small in proportion to the total cost of the car, and because of this we do not adopt the usual procedure of spreading our overhead costs over the direct labour only, but over labour and material. This provides a much more static and truer cost figure, and any variations in labour charges do not produce costs that are out of proportion.

In our budgetary control system, each departmental manager is informed of the amount that he is permitted to spend monthly in his department on variable expenditure, and a serious view is taken if this is exceeded in any way, unless beyond the control of the manager concerned. Taking the departmental managers into the confidence of the directors in this way gives them an interest in the running of the factory, and has a very good effect psychologically.

Selling expenses are, of course, very large in proportion, and can be a very variable factor, and when it is realised that it costs roughly £160,000 in agents' discounts to sell £500,000 worth of motor cars, the author considers that the average motor car manufacturer today is having to spend far too much in addition to selling the cars to the agents, and generally assisting those agents to sell. This assistance falls particularly heavily upon the small car manufacturer, because, while, out of necessity, he cannot afford to maintain the large field staff, or the numbers of outside representatives that the larger manufacturers usually possess; at the same time he has to have a certain number, and also has to maintain a certain number of demonstration cars. In fact, if the small manufacturer is selling a car on performance, it is quite likely that his costs, as far as demonstration cars are concerned, are higher than those of the larger manufacturer, whose sales depend more on reputation, price, finish, reliability, and general coachwork appeal, and are to some extent sold straight off the showroom floor. There is one costly activity which the small manufacturer certainly cannot afford, and that it the annual agents convention indulged in by the larger manufacturers. The author imagines it is an American habit which has crept over here, but he sees no reason why the manufacturer should pay first-class travelling and hotel expenses to bring a distributor down from the Northern part of Scotland, to see new models, examples of which he may already have in his showrooms, or, at any rate, will have within a week or two of that convention. That, however, is merely a matter of personal opinion, about which the author may be entirely wrong.

Advertising can also be a bottomless sink as far as expenses are concerned, and the author does not know of anything more nebulous or more difficult to purchase with any degree of certainty than advertising space. The small manufacturer is forced to follow the lead of the large manufacturer in taking space in the semi-technical journals, but the expense of the large dailies, and also, of course, the bigger Sunday papers, is debarred. In the author's opinion, the best substitute for this is cooperation with the agents and distributors in direct mail advertising, as the amount of wastage is reduced to a minimum. Editorial publicity is of immense value if it can be obtained by genuine and honest means, but obtaining it by tricks and stunts only means that that avenue of publicity is soon closed.

The author considers it vitally necessary for the small manufacturer to have a very live publicity department, which keeps in close contact with all the agents and distributors, as well as keeping the press generally advised of any items of genuine interest. The amount of money that can be budgeted for advertising purchases is fairly easy to control, although it is sometimes not so easy to resist the blandishments of the many persuasive advertising canvassers. In our case we have found our racing and competition successes of a certain definite value, but chiefly because our product is a sports car, and any such successes have a direct bearing on the prestige of that car. The author does not think, however, that the manufacturer of what is termed the 'family' car derives any great benefit from racing, as the average man in the street knows sufficient about this today to realise the vast difference between the cars that would have to be built and raced by such firms and the standard product he eventually buys.

Experimental and development work generally is a big and very important expense that requires much forethought and planning, and must not be done in an haphazard way. It is necessary for the small manufacturer to plan two, three and even four years ahead, as it is a costly business to design and build an experimental car. The firm must not be too progressive, particularly in design, as the buying public is essentially conservative. For instance, although the author believes that the car of the future will be a true streamlined form of vehicle with the engine at the rear, the public will have to assimilate that idea gradually, but that it is coming he is sure, as is indicated by the present line of development exemplified by a certain new American model that is now on view, and also the latest German racing machine.

Works maintenance is another variable expense that can be economically carried out, and can also be very expensive. Here, again, strict budgetary control is required, and while the author insists upon the works being maintained at a very high degree of cleanliness, and does not permit such things as broken windows to remain unmended, no big expense is ever undertaken without very careful thought, very careful planning, which must definitely dovetail in with a general scheme of factory development which is decided upon for a long period ahead.

Incidentally, one great saving that we effected was to use sectional office partitions. These are three feet wide by seven feet or eight feet high, the top portions being made of glass. They are standardised and bolt readily together. In consequence, offices can be moved, enlarged, or made smaller without any wastage, and with the minimum of expense. If any work projected cannot come within the limit of the budget, then that work has to stand over until it can do so.

One item of works expense, which is practically self-supporting, is a small laundry that we run to wash the men's overalls. A condition of employment is that each man starts work every Monday morning with a clean pair of overalls, and turns in his previous pair for washing, for which purpose he has the sum of 3d deducted from his wages. Not only is this a convenience for the men, as the price charged is far less than they can have them washed for elsewhere, but the morale effect generally is good.

As an example of how every works expense is considered beforehand, the author would like to cite an instance which occurred recently. Owing to a certain amount of petty pilfering which was going on in the works, and which he imagines happens in every works, we considered the advisability of employing night watchmen. Upon going into the cost of this, it was found that two night watchmen would cost approximately £250 a year. Although we pay a good premium for insurance against fire, loss of profits by fire, theft of cars and burglary, the amount of reduction in the premium by employing watchmen was negligible, whilst it obviously would need a lot of petty pilfering to reach £250 a year, so that idea was washed out, and our overhead expenses were saved £250 a year.

The overseas market we do not look upon very seriously, simply because of the nature of our product, but in computing our prices for export, we relieve them of direct home-selling expenses, and look upon such overseas sales as being helpful in carrying a certain proportion of the general factory overheads.

Today the quantity-produced motor car, because of the vast numbers in which it is turned out, has to be, and is so accurately made, that the amount of road-testing that these cars get is negligible. In the case of the smaller car manufacturer, such as ourselves, and particularly if a product is being sold on performance, this road-testing has of necessity to be quite extensive, and we aim to do the bulk of our testing in chassis form, which means a break in the continuity of our line production, but it is an expense that has to be faced, and is, of course, not a negligible one in the labour costs incurred in producing a car.

The author considers it essential, too, for the small car manufacturer to avoid as far as possible bringing out a whole line of new models at the accepted date of September 1st or at the Motor Show. If this is done, a firm is often faced with the dilemma of having a model that has not sold very well still surplus at the end of the season, and will be compelled to continue that model, owing to commitments, for another season, or adopting the very costly method of jobbing out a batch to the second-hand car trade. This is extremely upsetting to the agents, and creates a lot dissatisfaction all round, particularly to owners of cars who may have purchased them prior to their being jobbed out, at the normal price, only to find the same model being offered at much lower prices immediately afterwards. It is far better to decide to put down a batch of so many cars of one model, and run that model until the sanction is exhausted. Towards the end of the sanction the directors can then make up their minds as to whether they are going to continue it or put in a later model, which in the meantime development has been perfecting. If only all manufacturers would do this, we would get away from the farce of yearly models produced four or five months before the end of the preceding year, and the author is quite certain the public would soon get used to the series model instead.

Incidentally, mention of the public brings up a state of affairs that is deplorable, and that is that the public to whom we sell our cars through our agents know far too much of the discount that these agents receive, and it is because the secrets of the trade have not been kept as they should have been, and as they are in other and older trades. The Guild spirit is lacking. For instance, how many people buying a 50-guinea or 100-guinea piano have any idea what discount the music dealer receives, and how many would take into consideration that discount in considering the price the dealer offers to allow for the old piano? But today the vast sums of money given to the agents by manufacturers for selling their products are handed on by those agents to the public, and today the public is buying their cars far too cheaply, and are getting far too much for their money.

The social side of a factory is one that should be encouraged, but the author does not think it should be made a fetish, and beyond reasonable help and facilities being offered by the company, the workers themselves should organise this side of their activities. It would be quite a good idea if all the various factories in the country could meet in friendly rivalry on the cricket and football fields, just as the schools do, and no doubt this does happen to a great extent in a district like Coventry, where there are a number of firms, but so far our firm has not received any invitations, although our miniature rifle shooting team would take a lot of beating.

With regard to racing, our policy has always been to let other people do this for us. So many firms in the past have built special racing cars, maintained their own racing team, all at enormous expense, and almost without exception what racing successes they have achieved have availed them nothing. In our case we have built quite a reasonable number of racing cars each year, which, incidentally, are only very slightly modified standard products, and people who wish to race those cars have to buy them. True, we afford them some measure of assistance, such as the loan of mechanics during the race, but we are definitely not believers in the building of a team of racing cars at a cost of £20,000 or £30,000 for such cars and paying the racing drivers, as we see no commercial advantage in such procedures.

The foregoing is only a series of somewhat disconnected remarks, but the author hopes they will form a basis for an interesting discussion.

APPENDIX 5

(Goldie Gardner, courtesy Mike Jones)

CECIL KIMBER ON MOTOR RACING

THE FUTURE OF MOTOR RACING

Article appearing in The Autocar, *issue of 21 January 1944*

Long before the last war when I was in my teens, the Rev B.H. Davies, writing under the pen-name of Ixion, used to contribute weekly articles to *The Motor Cycle* which were always the first read as far as I was concerned and became my outstanding memory of that journal. In later years, when Mr Davies became my friend and I became active in providing folk with sporting motor cars, it is nice to find that he still possesses that wonderful facility for writing about motoring sport in a balanced and always interesting manner. His article in today's issue of *The Autocar* fully comes up to his high standard and I would like fully to endorse everything he says so well.

At the risk of being accused of trying to gild the lily, there are a number of aspects touched on by Mr Davies in his article on 'The future of motor racing' that might, I think, be usefully amplified. Taking the same five headings as points of discussion I should like to make the following observations:

1. WORLD'S RECORDS

Supplementary to this, but of far more importance to the car manufacturer, are Class records. These Class records deserve far more attention by the general – as opposed to the technical – press, as the Land Speed Records, utilising huge aero engines, bear no real relation to motor racing or motor car development but news value is created for it for the benefit of the general public.

In connection with Class records, one anomaly requires removing and that is the rule that prevents a car in a smaller capacity category claiming records in a higher category although the speed may be greater. Major – now, by the way, Lt Col – Gardner's records on his M.G. are an example. Owing to war conditions I have not the facilities for reference but I believe that much vaunted German Mercedes and Auto Union cars hold Class records in some of the higher categories at speeds lower than Gardner's, which, to my way of thinking, is absurd.

2. TRACK EVENTS

Sheer speed as such, in my opinion, is not all necessary to provide good sport and the requisite public interest.

How many race promoters have realised that in track races in which comers, artificial or otherwise, are included – and this applies to road races as well – it is at these comers that the public always congregate thickest. There is no denying this. Then, if anyone likes to take the trouble, as I have done, to take a stop watch and time the various competitors through those corners, they will find, much doubtless to their surprise, there is very little difference in the speed at which the competing cars go through that comer. It will often be found that cars that finish low down in the final placing are quite the fastest and most exciting to watch at those comers. That fact should, therefore, rule out the need for cars costing a King's ransom to provide the necessary racing interest.

Cornering provides the real interest

Those who attended the early meetings at Donington, when a series of short handicap races were held, will remember how exciting it was to watch even elderly but potent Austin Sevens negotiating the various curves and comers.

Unfortunately a section of the technical press, with a misguided but very pro-Continental complex, have educated a large number of motor-racing fans that the only cars worth watching race are of the Grand Prix type and of Axis origin. And yet a certain type of racing that attracts the biggest crowds – and without the artificial stimulus of betting – is motorcycle dirt-track racing. The speeds are by no means high but it looks fast, the interest is maintained by short heats and it is presented in a theatrical manner. I mention this to prove my point about what can be termed the comer complex of crowds.

As to tracks, having seen the way our old favourite, Brooklands, has been hacked about for war needs, I feel its early rejuvenation is doubtful but I hope I'm wrong. The Crystal Palace provides quite a nice sporting little course and is usefully within easy reach of plenty of potential gate money. Donington appears to be the one spot where we can hope for an early reopening of racing, though the lamented death of its late owner may have some bearing on this.

3. GRAND PRIX ROAD-RACING

When this ceased to be a sport and became, instead, a means of National aggrandisement, it also became, as Mr Davies aptly puts it, a farce. However, it must not be overlooked, if the Axis powers had devoted their energy and their money to waging an economic war instead of the present bloody one, these State-aided teams of theirs would have been immense commercial value in building up international prestige in their technical motor engineering ability and would have ranked them high in the eyes of the motor-buying world, whilst their other technical engineering activities would have benefited from the reflected glory.

So let us bury and forget Grand Prix racing as practised just before the war and wait for the day, visualised by Mr Davies, when a community of nations get together and formulate a fresh series of international races on a more common-sense basis and on more level terms.

G.P. engine limit coming down

Incidentally Mr. Davies' idea that these may be run with engines possibly no larger than 1000cc was foreshadowed by the indications that the Grand Prix car, as evolved by Germany, was coming down to 1500cc. It may be news to many that the Mercedes concern had purchased from Kohlrausch, the independent German racing driver, the 750cc M.G. with which he took records at some 140mph-odd. The engine in his car was in design very similar to, and the forerunner of Major Gardner's – I give him his better known title – record-breaker. From reliable information I was able to obtain, there is no doubt the new 1500cc Mercedes Grand Prix racer was, in effect, two banks of the 750cc M.G. engine in the form of a vee-eight. It's nice to know that we can teach Germany something about racing engines.

4. LONG-DISTANCE SPORTS CAR RACES

Now we have come to a form of sport that, in my opinion, was the backbone of British motor sport. As Mr Davies says, 'Is there any race like Le Mans?' I, for one, hope that this classic will be revived but with the regulations stiffened up to prevent the entry of purely racing machines. The same applies to our own annual TT.

As far as the latter race in concerned, where our promoting club went wrong, in my opinion, was in formulating handicaps from year to year that discriminated against certain cars. This was done to attract entries that otherwise would not have come to the starting line but in doing this they killed 'the geese that laid the golden eggs'. The geese being the manufacturers. However, usually being hardheaded businessmen, they would only go on being geese for a limited time. Let me explain.

The TT was a race for cars of varying capacities as turned out as a production model by the various manufacturers. Accordingly some form of handicap speed had to be set. Instead of creating and adapting a straight-line graph from which, at a glance, one could see that from a certain capacity a certain speed was expected and that the handicap was strictly pro rata to engine size, as it should have been, quite the reverse was done.

'Cooking the handicap'

Instead each year the range of possible entries were carefully scrutinised, and if it was found, as often the case, that a certain maker might be tempted to put in a team if the handicap, from his point of view, was sufficiently attractive, the handicap graph was so 'bent' as to provide this bait. For example, let us imagine the 1000cc capacity was set to average 62mph and the 2000cc was given 70mph. One would naturally expect the 1500cc class would then be put down to 66mph, half way between the two. Not a bit of it! If the manufacturer of 1500cc machines was known, by the nature of his product, not to stand a very good chance and the organising club might thereby lose the entry, then the handicap speed for that size might be put down to, say, 63mph. Or assuming the 2000cc class is set to do 70mph and the 1500cc class 66mph, if the manufacturer of the 1000cc class was known to have a very fast model in this size and likely to make an easy win of it, then when the entry forms came out, it would be seen that the 1000cc class had to do 65mp.h to the 66mph of the 1500cc and the 2000cc still would remain also at 70mph.

I believe the reason why the motorcycle TT races have had such a long run of successes and drawn such large entries is because the manufacturers knew where they stood. There were definite engine sizes to which they had to work and every one competing in one of those engine size categories knew they had an equal chance of winning.

Relate handicaps to engine size

By all means let us have separate car races for separate classes determined by engine size if one can get sufficient entries for each category, which I doubt, but if we have to continue running varying sizes in the same race, let us, in all fairness, handicap them pro rata to engine size.

Please remember that I am referring here to long-distance races such as Le Mans or the TT. Individual handicapping will always be wanted for short sprint races with a mixed bag of drivers and cars. Personally, I doubt very much whether manufacturers are likely to interest themselves in supporting racing for some time after the war. Their energies will all be spent trying to meet the demands of a car-hungry nation.

That great sportsman Lord Wakefield did more for racing – and flying – than most people appreciate. It was far more than mere advertising. It was a fine form of patriotism and made possible sporting efforts of a national value that otherwise would not have been possible. That led the way to the various oil companies, and the accessory firms, vying with one another to pay retainers to racing drivers, bonuses to winners and subsidies to manufacturers, all made for cheaper racing in those far-off happy days before the war. All that has gone – it had disappeared before 1937 – and the amateur and the 'shamateur' and the manufacturer will find racing more expensive so that for long-distance races there does not appear to be a very bright future.

5. 'SHORTS AND 'BRIEFS'

Here I wholeheartedly concur with Mr Davies that there are hordes of young fellows – and girls – who have been debarred from fast motoring all these weary years of war, who may have tasted the joys of flying fighter planes or at least tasted the joys of living dangerously. They'll want something more than humdrum motoring in the family saloon. Many have a competition car carefully covered over and cared for, awaiting the day they come back home, fling off the dust sheets, fill up with unrationed petrol, and listen once again to a heartening burble from the exhaust.

This is the crowd for whom short races will have to be provided, and what better than a sunny afternoon at Donington with someone to do the handicapping as knowledgeable as dear old 'Ebby' used to be. Poole, Lewes and Brighton, too, but I'm not sure about Shelsley. It has become too much of a specialist's playground. This Midlands venue, however, is valuable. Not only does it provide two delightful days a year for hill-climbing enthusiasts, but also, I understand, provides a useful revenue for the promoting club, and this is a point of view that must not be lost to sight.

Events must pay

All good luck to the lads coming back from the war fronts who want to dig their 'specials' out and do a little 'dicing'. But they, and we, must not forget that the financial responsibility rests upon the promoting clubs; and their difficulty is not only to make the events sufficiently attractive for the competitors, but also sufficiently attractive to provide enough entrance-paying public to cover the organising expenses and perhaps leave a modicum over to swell the club's coffers. That is not going to be easy, and Mr Davies points a way when he suggests that municipalities will have to be induced to take a financial interest in events promoted in their district.

And, finally, there is that vast army of sports car enthusiasts whose greatest delight at week-ends is to tackle impossible cattle trails up impossible hillsides; but that is another story and, with the Editor's permission I hope to review such post-war possibilities at a later date.

RACING AND THE MOTOR MANUFACTURER
A talk delivered, seemingly before the war, to an audience it has not been possible to identify

The question as to whether racing is of benefit to the motor manufacturer is one to which there is no direct answer. It depends on the type of manufacturer and the type of racing. The Morris and Austin organisations – the largest in this country – have both been built up without any stimulus from the race track, as no one would contend for a moment that the small amount of racing which the Austin concern has done with their smallest model has had any effect at all on their bulk sales.

On the other hand, the M.G. Car Company, a concern with which the writer is associated, built up in a short space of less than ten years a prestige and worldwide renown that could not otherwise have been achieved, but in this case the type of product was entirely different from that of the large quantity manufacturer, being one that had a deliberate speed and performance appeal. Also the cars that were raced bore a very strong resemblance to the models that were sold in the ordinary way, and very many lessons that were learned in the stress of racing were embodied in the subsequent production of cars, to the ultimate benefit of the user. Brakes, steering, and engine-bearing life were perhaps principally affected and improved.

A few years ago this practice ceased, and the manufacturer who still indulged in racing not only had the expense of building and preparing the cars, paying drivers and supporting a team of highly trained mechanics and pit assistants, but after winning a race, such a manufacturer was then faced with further big expenditure in order to advertise his win. As a manufacturer can only regard racing from a commercial standpoint, many quite rightly considered that such publicity was too dearly purchased and one by one they ceased to be interested in motor racing as a means of advertisement.

This is one reason why the outlook for British motor racing is so gloomy, but there is another aspect that affected the manufacturers to a very great extent, and for this the race promoters have only themselves to blame. These promoters wanted a large field with plenty of entrance fees, and were obsessed with the idea – fostered to a very large extent by the daily press – that the general public always wanted to see the largest and fastest cars that used to compete in these races and were generally of Continental make.

The British manufacturer, making a diversity of models and concentrating largely on the small and medium-sized cars, very naturally prepared and entered these particular types. This necessitated some form of handicapping, and it says well for the small British car, and its reliability under very severe conditions, that when they won it was generally due to the lack of reliability of the larger Continental car, which so often broke up after, perhaps, leading the race for most of the time.

This handicapping by some of the race promoters would not have been too bad in providing a reasonable spectacle for the general public if they had gone about it in a fair and more logical way. The system was to divide the cars into various classes according to their engine capacity, but having done this, these handicappers did not, as they should have done, handicap pro rata to size, but would deliberately favour one particular class in order to encourage the entry of a certain manufacturer who would normally be competing in that class, but who, on a strictly pro rata handicap basis, would have no chance of winning. For example, assume that the 1500cc class in a certain race was set to lap at 70mph and the 2500cc class to lap at 80mph, and assume that both these speeds were within the capabilities of the particular cars likely to be entered in such classes, then to be logical, any car that appeared in the 2000cc class should have automatically been handicapped to lap at 75 miles an hour. However, if the only possible entrant in the 2000cc class was a certain manufacturer whose possible products were known not to be particularly fast, then, in order to encourage the entry, the race promoters and the handicappers would gaily set that particular class to do only 72mph, which gave them a distinct chance of winning, and which was naturally distinctly unfair to the manufacturer with a far more efficient 1500cc car. The more successful a manufacturer was in any particular size or class, the more the handicaps were operated against him, and this was the second, and perhaps more important, factor which has operated against the continued interest in racing by manufacturers, at any rate as far as Great Britain is concerned.

No manufacturer with shareholders could, with the serious repercussions that occurred if they were constantly unsuccessful, afford to jeopardize their firm's prestige under such conditions.

Perhaps the best attempt by any club staging a race to create fairer conditions and produce, in effect, almost a scratch race was made by the Junior Car Club, and in this particular event which they staged, a series of channels were formed at one point on the track containing corners, the larger and faster cars having to negotiate the channels with more acute corners than the smaller fry. This was fairly successful and all right as far as it went, but owing to the impossibility of providing a sufficient number of channels, a certain element of unfairness crept into the race owing to the fact that the cars of different capacities were given the same channel to go through. In theory this particular race was supposed to have all the merits of a scratch race, so that the public would know that the car first past the chequered flag was the winner, but in actual practice, when a comparatively large field had begun to string out, some cars were lapped by others, stops were made at pits, and so on, so that after a time, on a small circuit, this race was just as difficult to follow by the general public as the handicap race, in which the various classes were set off at different intervals and given credit laps, and so on.

One has to remember also that, owing to the fact that racing on the King's Highway has never been permitted in this country, the British public has never had an opportunity of seeing any real road-racing, and has not received the education in this respect that our friends across the Channel have. In consequence, motor racing of the Grand Prix variety is a closed book to the average Englishman.

Whilst this gloom was settling over the British motor industry and affecting its attitude towards road racing, a much more sinister aspect came into being in the shape of government-subsidised racing teams. Italy was the first to start this, and at one time practically swept the board at the Continental Grands Prix. It was undoubtedly done as a form of national propaganda, and there is no doubt that it obtained for her motor products a reputation that was sometimes not always deserved. Germany was quick to see the advantage of this, and went into it with typical Teutonic thoroughness. The Mercedes-Benz and the Auto Union teams were the result. The amount of money that these two teams must have cost their respective firms in designing, building, testing, and maintaining would obviously never be justified looked at as an individual commercial position. However, as an advertisement for Germany and her motor products they were undoubtedly magnificent. We, fools that we are, invited these all-conquering German teams to come and compete at our Donington road-racing circuit. The race promoters, no doubt with an eye to the gate money but with little regard for the prestige of the British manufacturer, are well known to have offered these German teams special inducements to come over, such inducements, of course, being of a financial nature.

Naturally these colossally expensive and extremely fast cars of 4½ or so litres capacity made our own 1500cc racing cars, good as they are, look silly, and what is the result? The British public obtained the impression – and who shall blame them? – that the German motor cars are invincible and that Germany obviously builds good cars. Then, when Germany begins exporting large numbers of her ordinary product, although these technically are not to be compared with a British product of the same size and price, they sell on the prestige obtained for them by the government-subsidised German racing cars, which undoubtedly are magnificent examples of engineering. This is how German racing cars assist the German motor industry, whether we, as a nation, should not take our place in Grand Prix racing, in view of the fact that our motor industry is the third-largest industry in this country, and larger than any other country in Europe. This racing can only be done nationally; there is not the incentive or the reward today for the individual manufacturer to build and race cars on his own.

MOTOR RACING

Talk for the Institute of the Motor Trade, to have been given on 16 February 1945

It was with great appreciation that I accepted your Secretary's invitation to come along and meet you fellow members because I once had the honour of being a Fellow of your Institute before I forsook the primrose path of selling and servicing cars for the thorny track of making them.

Anyway, I understand you would like me to give you a talk on motor racing which is a subject very close to my heart and about which I have acquired a little knowledge in the hard school of experience.

Unfortunately, living like so many other people in someone else's house, having let my own furnished for the duration, I have not the facilities for reference and must therefore rely entirely on my memory for what information I can give you. Having also severed my connection with the firm with which I was so closely connected throughout its racing career, I no longer have recourse to the technical data that would otherwise have been available. I hope, therefore, any shortcomings in this respect will be forgiven.

There are very few of you here this evening, I should say, that have not seen a motor race but it is astonishing how little the general public knows or cares about motor racing.

I am one of those people who say that racing improves the breed just as it does in horse racing. Furthermore, I am convinced that if it is successfully carried out abroad, it is a big factor in the capture of overseas markets. The motorcycle industry is a shining example of what can be achieved in this way. Then again, if you and the rest of the British public had been provided with the facilities for seeing and enjoying motor racing as a sport, as a nation we should be much more motor-minded today and would have been in a far better position to have repelled the German attacks in the early stages of the war.

It may interest you to know how Germany dealt with this problem of making the nation motor-minded in the pre-war years.

In the Nazi-controlled state, commercial jealousies were not allowed to interfere with the plans of the All-Highest. Two firms, Mercedes-Benz and Auto Union, were instructed to produce the latest thing in racing cars regardless of expense and to cover the latter, heavy state subsidies were made to the firms concerned.

In addition to this it may interest you to know that the Nazi government ran no less than 53 motoring schools in various parts of Germany, each of them containing anything up to 3,000 boys. These boys were drawn from the Hitler Youth movement and received one year's training in motorcycle and motor car driving under most arduous conditions, as well as being taught elementary mechanics as applied to motor vehicles. Then the more promising of these boys were kept on for a further two years and were then drafted into the various Panzer divisions.

Several times before the war, whilst I was in Berlin, I saw a number of films describing and showing the work of these schools and in particular it was interesting to note how cross-country competitive trials were staged between these various centres, trials that made our own weekend affairs tame in comparison.

It is no wonder then that the Nazis went into this war with hundreds of thousands of fully trained drivers and mechanics available to man their mechanised army.

How different have been the conditions in this country. It is only when one goes behind the scenes that it can be realised under what handicaps motor racing has operated during the last 20 or 30 years. In fact it is amazing that it has survived at all.

From the earliest years, motoring has faced nothing but restriction and frustration. What other country in the world was so grandmotherly in its attitude that, for a period, one could only use one's car provided one had a man carrying a red flag walking ahead. Then we had increasingly repressive taxation and that greatest betrayal and wholesale robbery ever perpetrated on a section of the public. I refer, of course, to the robbing of the Road Fund after the motorists of the country had been solemnly promised that if they would willingly submit to increased heavy taxation, such money would be devoted to the roads.

What short-sighted policy that was to use those millions paying the dole instead of providing employment in the building of real motorways which would have been of incalculable value to the industry and the nation as a whole. Then there has been that strange reluctance to allow little-used country roads to be closed temporarily for the holding of road races, and the abolition of organised hillclimbs on the public roads. For this latter I blame the RAC to a great extent owing to an accident to a spectator at the last hillclimb ever held at Kop Hill, Princes Risborough – I was there sitting with the one and only W.O. and the late Burgess[1], quite close to where it happened – all further events on the open road were banned. I believe I am right in saying the RAC concurred in this instead of fighting back for the sake of motoring sport which they controlled. Then prior to the present war, hill after hill used by the enthusiastic weekend trials competitor was closed by the police and even parliamentary moves had been made to forbid such trials. What short-sighted policy with a war looming ahead in which motor transport, armed and otherwise, was obviously going to play a major part.

---

[1] Author's note: This refers to Walter Owen Bentley and Frank Burgess; the latter worked with W.O. Bentley on aero-engines and on the conception of the first Bentley cars.

What a contrast to the way in which various Continental localities vied with one another to stage road-racing events of all kinds. So the British motor racing fan was forced to stage such events in the Isle of Man and Northern Ireland, both being more or less inaccessible to the great mass of the British public who otherwise would have been taking an intelligent interest in fast motor cars and been awakened to the importance of international rivalry in such sport.

Needless to say, any idea that the government should subsidise motor racing would have been laughed out of court as too ludicrous for contemplation, but what an opportunity was missed of placing the British motor industry in the forefront throughout the world. What export business would have resulted! Look at the export business the motorcycle industry enjoyed when British riders used to compete and win all the major Continental events. Great credit is due to the firms responsible, though it must be remembered that to build and prepare the necessary machines and provide suitable riders did not involve the same large financial outlay that building and racing teams of cars would mean.

Then I do not think that the manufacturers of this country were too clever. There was a time when the oil and petrol interests and the various accessory and component manufacturers subsidised race entrants, both trade and private, widely publicising the results both to their benefit and to the benefit of the car and manufacturer who was good enough and fortunate enough to win. This wide advertising made a win worthwhile. Then the big interests in the Society of Motor Manufacturers and Traders who were not interested in racing became jealous of the publicity that smaller and more energetic firms enjoyed by their initiative. In consequence all advertising by the petrol and oil companies and the accessory and component firms in connection with racing and record successes was stopped, only advertising of world's speed events with aero-engined monsters having no resemblance to any manufacturer's products being allowed. Needless to say, as soon as the contributing firms were unable to derive any benefit from the successes to which their products had contributed, the bonuses and subsidies ceased. It was quite common for a star driver to receive a retainer of £3,000 a year from one firm alone.

This communal sharing of the heavy expenses of racing was, in my opinion, all to the national good and many a British team took part in Continental events that otherwise would have been an expense too heavy to bear alone or one that commercially would not have been justified.

Then again some of the promoting clubs were very unwise in the use they made of handicapping. Admittedly handicapping is a difficult art at the best of times and it is impossible to satisfy everyone. Even so, this should be on a logical basis if cars of varying engine capacities are to compete together. Instead, a winning manufacturer one year would have the odds heavily piled up against him the next. What used to happen was this:

In the long-distance races – and I exclude the short sprint races from my criticisms – the various classes, determined by engine capacity, were given certain set speeds but these were never strictly pro rata to engine size. This was to encourage the manufacturers with the 'not so good' car to enter. For instance, if the handicap speed of the 1500cc car was, say, 65mph and the 2500cc was 75mph, instead of the two-litre class being set at the logical 70mph this particular class might be set at 67mph to encourage entries, but if a certain manufacturer had been successful in this class the previous year at 70mph and looked like being successful again, then the handicap might be raised to 72 or 73mph. I know this only too well to my cost.

That is not the way to encourage a continuance of manufacturers' interests and when the bonuses and subsidies ceased it was on the manufacturers and a very few wealthy sportsmen that the expense of racing fell.

Then, with dwindling interest on the part of the manufacturers and in spite of very gallant attempts by the ERA, motor racing, during the years prior to the war, began to decline. I believe that the promoting clubs could have very largely saved the situation or at any rate improved it if they had encouraged a non-handicap 1500cc class, but it was, in my opinion, a very grave mistake on their part when at some considerable expense to the promoting clubs, two teams of German Grand Prix racing cars were brought over to compete at Donington. This was a very great disservice to the motor industry of this country because machines of this type, built regardless of expense on lavish subsidies from their government, obviously overshadowed the smaller cars which we were producing, good as they were.

Finally, I should like to suggest that if the press, particularly the daily press, had done their share of getting the public to take an intelligent interest in motor racing there would have been far better response from the manufacturers. Instead of that, quite important motor racing events would be dismissed in a small paragraph, which event should have and would have interested tens of thousands of readers, whereas columns were devoted to minor sporting events such as public-school fencing championships and similar classes of sport which could only possibly interest a small collection of people. Needless to say, suitable publicity was given if any accidents occurred and the worse the accident the more space devoted to it, which was a very regrettable state of affairs.

The semi-technical press, whilst dealing faithfully with these various motor racing events, were very naughty in the way they extolled the Continental racing car to the disparagement of the British counterpart. Also they were apt to attach a somewhat overrated snob value to large cars, and I can well remember the time when Horton won the 500-miles BRDC race at Brooklands on an M.G. Magnette and not a single press photographer had taken a photograph of him, having concentrated their energies on drivers much higher in the social scale. The same thing happened in a later year when a hitherto unknown driver came in second in the same race in an unsupercharged M.G. Magnette of 1271cc at an average speed of over 92mph. This was really quite an outstanding performance which never got the credit it deserved. What with the attitude of the government, the manufacturers and the press, it is no wonder that motor racing began to decline and I feel that there is a very little hope of the situation getting any better in the post-war years to come.

During the immediate post-war years the large car manufacturers will be so busy endeavouring to satisfy a car-hungry public that they naturally enough are not going to be in the slightest degree interested in racing, neither can I see any early resumption of international Grand Prix racing.

However, there were a very great number of racing enthusiasts in this country, many of them with racing cars of one sort or another carefully stored away, who when they come back from the war will want to take up their favourite sport again and this they more than deserve. I therefore feel that motor racing during the few years following the war will be revived by the sheer enthusiasm of these individuals to whom I refer, and if they can count once more on Donington being re-opened as a race track, here is a venue that will provide a tremendous lot of fun to the participants and interest for the spectators.

If the somewhat false glamour surrounded the German and Italian Grand Prix cars was properly discounted, I think it will be admitted that for sheer fun and interest, nothing surpassed the early short sprint handicap races at Donington in which all sorts of weird and wonderful vehicles took part, none of them extremely fast, but all of them capable of putting up just as exciting corner work – which is what the crowd loves – as the Continental Grand Prix cars.

When the post-war car demand has been more of less met, then it is quite likely that certain firms will once more turn their attention to racing as a means of building up their prestige. In this we cannot hope to expect any possible help or encouragement from the government, but I do hope that the manufacturers, promoting clubs and the press will work along lines to encourage the sport and so build it up so that it becomes strong and healthy instead of going again into a decline.

As to my own personal connections with racing, these really started in a somewhat indirect way during the last war, because whilst I was with the Sheffield-Simplex motor company I possessed a 14hp T-headed Singer which had raced at Brooklands in the hands of one of the early aviators called Vivian Hewitt, but with what success I do not know. I believe it was capable of lapping Brooklands round about 80mph and needless to say at the time was the pride and joy of my heart. It was somewhat unique inasmuch as it was one of the only cars of its day that I ever came across that had a geared-up fourth speed and as the engines of those days were not given to revving smoothly at high speeds, to click into this high fourth gear made for quite pleasant motoring.

My first active association with racing was round about 1929 or early 1930 when I was producing the 18hp six-cylinder model known as the Mark II. I got the Morris Engines company at Coventry interested in the idea of producing one for racing purposes, and one was duly built and entered for a long-distance Brooklands race driven by Callingham of the Shell-Mex company.

The Engines company were naturally somewhat jealous of their knowledge of the engine and it was therefore left that they should be responsibie for the power unit whilst the M.G. Car Company produced the chassis. Anyway, in those days we did not pretend to have any real knowledge of racing engines, though the engine factory thought they did. The results were disappointing as the maximum speed from this engine of under 2½ litres was far short of other racing cars of similar capacity, but what we learned from this particular lesson was the necessity of having a fully balanced crankshaft. We did timidly suggest to the Engines works that this might be necessary but were told to run away and look after the chassis we were building; but the fact remained that owing to the crankshaft being unbalanced the throw-out loads at high speeds were so great that when eventually taken down after the race the crankshaft main journals were actually blued from the heat that had been generated. Needless to say, under these conditions the big-end bearings did not stand up. However, used on the road purely as a sporting car this particular engine gave every satisfaction and had an extremely long life, but it just was not capable of any sustained power output.

Round about 1928/29 someone entirely outside the influence of the Morris organisation at Cowley designed the ohv Morris Minor. I immediately saw the possibilities of this little job and designed a light fabric-covered two-seater body for it, and with a few minor modifications to the engine, produced it as the first M.G. Midget, known as the M-type. With good power/weight ratio and an 850cc engine it had exceptional acceleration performance and it was three of these models that six enthusiasts entered in the Double-Twelve Race, and with which they brought home the team prize as previously mentioned.

The general preparation work for this race, and the experience we were gaining all the time, increased our knowledge to an immense extent. We had no test shop facilities at all; not even a water brake. All our testing was done either on the track or what we termed a comparator. This consisted of two pairs of pulleys about the diameter of the road wheels, carried on a pair of shafts, one of which was extended and carried a simple air paddle as brake. The whole was let in flush with the floor, the rear wheels of the car placed on the rollers and there you were.

After this initial success the petrol and oil interests and the accessory firms began to gather round and make attractive offers which led to a series of racing successes and record-breaking that has not been equalled by any other single make of car.

One of the first lessons we had to master was how to make the big-ends stand up. The original engine had connecting rods of parallel section and it was common to find the letter 'H' of the section reproduced on the top half of the big end bearing. Splaying the connecting rod to take the big-end bolt-head helped; but there was one thing we established and that was the oil temperature in the sump must be kept below 85 degrees Celsius however hard the car might be driven round Brooklands. Very large-capacity sumps well-finned and ample pump capacity provided most of the answer.

Then I designed what became the standard Midget and Magnette frame for many years. Parallel side-members, tubular cross-members and an underslung back axle. This at once transformed the car from a roadholding point of view.

The three-speed standard gearbox was then discarded and a four-speed ENV box with remote control fitted and by degrees it became quite a motor car. As I mentioned at the beginning of my talk, I have had to rely on my memory for the various facts that I then put down on paper, but it was only recently, when I was visiting my brother and quite accidentally picked up a book on motor racing, that I found how very much my memory had been at fault. This was a book called *Combat* written by Barré Lyndon, giving in chronological sequence the history of the M.G. car.

I had to revise a lot of my notes in consequence and I thought it might make this talk more interesting if I gave you a short résumé of this history. For instance, I found that the first race ever won by an M.G. was on October 10th, 1927, a fact that I had quite overlooked. This was in Buenos Aires, when a certain Alberto Sanchez Cires won a 100-kilometre race on a new concrete track, 1½ miles to the circuit, that they had just constructed. He apparently ran away from the field to win at the modest speed of 62mph.

Over here, the first sporting event ever won by an M.G. was achieved when I won the gold cufflinks that I am now wearing by successfully getting through the 1925 London-Land's End without losing any marks, in the first M.G. that I ever built.

In the following years more similar awards were won, but what really established the M.G. in the eyes of the sporting fraternity was the way the four 8hp Midgets entered in the 1929 London-Land's End Run sailed up Beggars Roost in a procession, making faultless climbs and going on to win four gold medals. You must remember that in those days Beggars Roost failed the majority of entrants, especially in the lower-powered range. This was followed by an observed 100 ascents non-stop of this hill.

It was these successes that began to make people think about racing M.G.s and in 1930 three enthusiasts named Randall, Pollard and Edmondson entered a team in the Double-Twelve Race at Brooklands. There were seven other teams entered for the team prize which they managed to secure at something over 60mph, the individual cars being capable of lapping at over 70mph. However, their size – 847cc – was too big a handicap in the 1100cc class to win the class prize. In the same race there was also entered a Mark III 18hp M.G. known as the 'Tigress', driven by Callingham, but this retired with big-end trouble, as already mentioned.

Another entrant in the race, Captain F.H.E. Samuelson, with a wide experience of light car Continental racing, was so impressed with the capabilities of his 847cc Midget he entered it for the Le Mans 24-hour race to be held the following month. His co-driver was Murton-Neale. In spite of the handicap of only three speeds, they averaged over 60mph until they retired with a broken oil pipe following an accident when Murton-Neale was driving, when he rammed a bank. Undismayed by this failure, Samuelson entered the car for the Belgian 24-hour race which was held at Spa. Again, there was the handicap of competing in the 1100cc class.

Although he was not placed, he finished the course suffering from acute clutch slip, through oil. The real heroes of these races were the mechanics, who often worked the clock round to get cars prepared in time.

At the works we also saw the possibilities of the Midget, and set to work to build something special; this was known as EX120. It was fitted with an underslung frame which I designed and which became the standard design right up to the outbreak of war.

Anyway, one dawn, if anyone had been on the Newmarket Road they would have seen George Eyston and a party of mechanics unloading EX120 from a lorry for the purpose of secretly trying out the car to determine whether there was any chance of getting away from Austin the records they held with their supercharged model. This was late in 1930 and it was desirable to obtain this before the end of the year, otherwise the Austin record would stand until the end of 1931.

The trials at Newmarket were so promising that Eyston and his equipment went over to Montlhéry on Boxing Day, and, after some trials and tribulations, owing to the intense cold, a freezing carburettor and an icy track, on New Year's Eve the following records were taken: 50km, Austin 83.5mph, M.G. 86.38mph, whilst the 50-miles was taken at 87.11mph and the 100km at 87.3mph. A valve broke and prevented the 100-miles record being achieved. It must be remembered that M.G. took these records with an unsupercharged car, whilst the Austin had been supercharged. This led to the idea of going all out for the 100mph record with a blower added. We were spurred on by the fact that we knew Austins were after the same record, which was regarded as an important milestone of speed, and we knew Malcolm Campbell had taken an Austin out to Daytona with him with the idea of adding this achievement to his many others.

Under Eyston's guidance we fitted one of his Powerplus blowers and gave it a two-day run on our comparator at 87mph. Then, early in 1931 in bitterly cold weather, we went back to Montlhéry. Whilst there, news came through that Campbell had only achieved 94mph. The week before the effort, 'Jacko' and Kindell, the two mechanics, put in 126 hours, making last-moment alterations to combat the cold.

On February 9th, 1931, Eyston took all the records still standing to the credit of Austin; the new records were 97.07mph for 5km and also the 5-mile, the 10km and 10-mile records held by a little-known French voiturette called the 'Grazide'.

More trouble was experienced with freezing carburettors, which was got over by feeding warmed air to the carburettor from the rear of the radiator. A few days later the M.G. was wheeled out to take the 5km at 103.13mph and the 5-mile at 102.76mph, and the 10-mile at 101.87mph. Thus, the M.G. was the first 750cc car to reach 100mph but for technical reasons the mile record could not be officially taken at Montlhéry, which was a bit Gilbertian when greater distances were covered at a higher speed.

In March 1931, perhaps because it was the 13th, M.G. made an unsuccessful attempt to get the mile record, but achieved *only* 96.93mph, though this beat the Austin record.

On May 8th and 9th, 1931, the JCC Double-Twelve Race at Brooklands was again held. No fewer that 14 private owners bought M.G.s and entered the race. The result was the greatest overwhelming victory ever achieved in the history of motor racing – 1st, 2nd, 3rd, 4th, 5th, 8th and 11th was the result against the whole field, whilst they also mopped up every class prize and team prize. Then some of the same entrants went over to Dublin for the Irish International Grand Prix.

Again, a 1st, 2nd and 3rd against the whole of the field, the drivers being Black, Horton and Gardner. Speed was just under 65mph. Serious gearbox and selector trouble put other entrants out of the race.

In June came the Le Mans race again, and once more the irrepressible Samuelson entered a car as also did the Hon Mrs Chetwynd. The latter retired with a key shearing in the timing gear. Samuelson's car, again damaged by a crash, failed to complete the last lap in the time allowed under somewhat complicated rules and was disqualified in spite of being amongst the leaders. A con-rod broke on this fatal lap, though he brought the car through.

Still undaunted, Samuelson entered for the German Grand Prix at the Nürburgring, also a Czech called Urban-Emmerich. Saumelson lapped at 55mph in the rain against Caracciola's 65mph and came in 5th in the 1100cc class. Urban-Emmerich went off the course and down a precipice and was lucky to escape with his life.

Then August, still 1931, and the Ulster TT in which Black repeated his Dublin victory and won at 67.9mph. The record for the lap only, for any size of car up to then, had stood at under 67mph! There were three M.G.s in the first seven.

The racing season wound up by the BRDC's 500-Mile Race at Brooklands. This is a race in which different handicap speeds are set for various engine sizes, and to show the influence M.G. successes had on this handicapping, it is interesting to note that whilst the 1930 handicap speed for the 750cc class was 82.3mph, for 1931 it had been raised to 93.97mph – nearly a 12mph increase. In this race E.R. Hall came third, Crabtree fifth and Kindell's M.G. also got the team prize. Troubles were big-ends and blown gaskets.

Before this race happened Austin took the s/s mile and kilometre records at 74.12mph and 65.00mph and the flying mile at 100.67mph. Then, out of the blue, Viscount Ridley came down from Newcastle and calmly took the flying mile record at 104.5mph and the flying kilometre at 105.4mph, but whilst all this was going on M.G. was building a special record car known as EX127.

EX127 was meant for short-distance attempts, leaving the old EX120 for the longs. When the news leaked out, Austin went over to Montlhéry followed almost immediately by the M.G. contingent, both camps being intent on being the first to cover 100 miles in the hour.

Mrs Stewart, now Mrs Duggie Hawkes, was to drive the Austin; two attempts were made before M.G.s started, but both failed.

EX120 was ready first and thanks to all the lessons that had been learned was found capable of lapping at 106mph to 108mph. It was fitted with extra tanks for petrol, oil and water, all in the cockpit; meantime, Austin succeeded in beating Eyston's 5km record at 109mph. A third attempt at the hour record by Austin ended in failure owing to transmission trouble.

At one o'clock on September 25, 1931, Eyston set off in EX120 for this coveted hour record. Steadily, lap after lap, the little car roared round the track to achieve 101.1mph. He then went on to complete another lap, but didn't appear. His faithful mechanics jumped in a car and tore off to find out what had happened. They found the car right-side-up off the track and burning furiously. Beating their way through the smoke and flames they were astounded to find no Eyston in the car, nor could he be found anywhere around.

It appeared that Eyston had been able to decant himself from the car whilst it was still doing about 60mph and a Citroën test driver, who was also circling the track, found him, lifted him into the car and rushed him off to the hospital, where he was treated for severe burns and a broken collarbone.

Whilst he was in the hospital, trials were commenced on EX127 which were disappointing, as boiling was experienced. An aeroplane-wing-type radiator was fitted into the top of the engine cowling and on October 17, 1931, the late E.A.D. Eldridge took the 5km record at 110mph, which was the fastest speed ever recorded to date in Class H; the gasket going and the radiator tubes bursting prevented further attempts. It was found the blower was impeding the airflow [to the] radiator. A week later Viscount Ridley again appeared at Brooklands with his Ridley Special. An accident wrecked the car and seriously injured the driver, and a little later Cushman and Driscoll on the Austin took six Class H records including the six-hours and the 200-miles.

And so the ding-dong Austin/M.G. battle went on. In December 1931, again with the idea of getting the records in the 1931 period, the single-seater EX127 was sent over again to Montlhéry. Eyston was better and determined to try for the two-miles-a-minute. In spite of an ice-covered track, he raised the 5km record to 114.77mph, the 5-mile to 114.74mph, 10km to 114.72mph and the 10-miles to 114.46mph; but the 120mph eluded him.

Early in 1932 the car was prepared for 120mph at Pendine Sands in Carmarthenshire. This was attempted on February 8th after waiting days for the right condition of the sands.

The RAC timing apparatus kept breaking down and to Eyston's bitter disappointment on one run down when he was independently timed to do 123mph to 124mph it was not recorded, as although the mechanism was working the ink had run out on the recording pen. The final result was 118.39mph, though it should have been over 121mph.

In May 1932 The JCC substituted the two-day 1,000 Mile Race at Brooklands for their previous Double-Twelve event and for this a number of M.G. owners entered their cars. Rather a lot of troubles came to light in this event; during practice there was cylinder-head gasket trouble traced to green castings. In the race, big-ends, leaking petrol tanks, sheared dynamo couplings and blown gaskets made a number fall by the wayside, but Norman Black came in third at 755 which included a stop every lap on the second day for petrol. Had it not been for this he would have won easily. As it was, this was ten miles an hour faster than the 1931 Double-Twelve, still running unblown.

June 18, 1932, found Samuelson once more at Le Mans, this time partnered with Norman Black. The gasket trouble had been overcome by using solid copper ones. At half-time they were leading the race, when again an accident in which Black was involved caused a leaking petrol tank. This put the car out of the race, as no replenishments are allowed under the rules at intervals of less than twenty laps. In July, Urban-Emmerich – in spite of his accident the previous year – got us to prepare his M.G. for the German Grand Prix, whilst the late Hamilton got T & T to prepare a car for him for the same event. In practice Hamilton lapped the Ring at 61mph – remember Caracciola's 65mph the year before – and won the 800cc class at an average of 59.08mph which was faster than Dudley Froy's Riley which won the 1100cc class the year before. The big class was won by Mercedes at 74.24mph. Urban-Emmerich again ran off the road.

Back in England preparations went ahead for the 1932 Ulster TT. No Austins were entered, but this year the M.G.s were supercharged with one exception.

Hamilton started off by breaking the lap record – all classes – at 71.2 m.p.h. in practice. Then he had to change the position of the blower to standard. It had been altered by T & T. On the second day he raised the lap record to the incredible one of 74 m.p.h. Imagine a 747cc machine on that twisting, winding course, beating Freddie Dixon's best on the Riley.

A serious accident later on in practice put him out of the race.

In this race, the principal trouble was plug burning. Major Gardner was out of the race in a serious accident as was Crabtree, the lurid cornerist, with a punctured carb float.

Whitcroft was first on a Riley; Eyston second, also on a Riley, E.R. Hall third on his M.G. and Earl Howe on his Alfa fourth. 22 out of 32 retired; five crashed.

Lt. Lowe on the only unsupercharged M.G. completed the 368-odd miles non-stop, averaging over 60mph. Three years previously this would have given him victory, but in this race it only gave him tenth place. Before the TT I should have mentioned that Hamilton took the Mountain course record at Brooklands for all classes at 69.28 m.p.h.

The 1932 season wound up as usual with the BRDC's annual 500-Mile Race. Eyston's record-breaker was entered but retired with a hole in the crown of a piston. Not a Specialloid!

E.H. Hall stripped a crown wheel; Horton lapped at 108mph and won at 96.29mph. This was the occasion which I have already mentioned when poor Horton won this race practically unheralded and unsung – certainly unphotographed.

We wound up our 1932 successes by again going out to Montlhéry where Eyston was anxious to get that two-miles-a-minute with the single-seater, and the long-distance records with a perfectly standard Midget two-seater.

On December 13th, in spite of the unlucky date, he went out and took the record at 120.5mph together with five other records. Then the standard job was taken out and lapped monotonously throughout the day and night at 75mph when a broken petrol pipe caused a delay. Even so, the 24-hour record was taken at 70.61mph against the Austin's 65.5mph. Then the single-seater was taken out once more and all records were taken up to twelve hours.

By the end of 1932 every Class H record was in M.G. hands and there they have remained ever since.

This is as far as Barré Lyndon's book went, so now we will switch back to 1931, recount a little more M.G. history and then carry on from 1933 onwards, when I must again rely upon my memory.

Up to 1931 the M.G. Midgets which had been sold to the public were fitted with little semi-streamline bodies, but after attending the Ulster TT race I was struck with the very businesslike appearance of the competing cars and the obvious admiration which their appearance seemed to arouse in the hearts of all the many enthusiasts that gathered to watch the event.

When I got back to the factory I gathered my boys together and announced that we were going to produce for the next year's model a showroom edition of the typical TT machine, which was intensely practical and strictly functional. This became the very popular J2 Midget and at the same time we took the opportunity of entirely redesigning the head with the inlet on the one side and the exhaust on the other, both having a very easy sweep into the combustion chamber.

Further racing successes were achieved by this model including the winning again of the TT and all the time still more improvements were incorporated in the engine as our experience mounted.

By this time the original Morris Minor engine, which had changed over to a chain-driven camshaft, had long ago been discarded[2] and the J-type Midget engine and the F-type Magna and the K-type Magnette, the two latter being six-cylinder versions of the same engine, were entirely to M.G. design and built exclusively for them. The gradual increase in power necessitated still heavier big-ends for the connecting rods and for pure racing we finally came down to the bearing metal being run straight into the rods and did not use bearing shells.

---

2 Author's note: Kimber is muddling two things here. For the 1932 season the Wolseley Hornet forsook its shaft-driven overhead camshaft for one driven by chain; the Minor, meanwhile, had started to move away from an ohc engine with the December 1930 announcement of the famous £100 model, but would only definitively abandon the ohc unit for the 1933 model year.

All this work we put into overcoming any possibility of big-end trouble undoubtedly paid, because it became quite the last of our worries as far as racing was concerned and as an instance of how these bearings would stand up, in 1933 the Earl Howe took a team of Magnettes out to the Mille Miglia in Italy, one of the cars being driven by the late Tim Birkin and [Bernard] Rubin. With this particular car Birkin broke the Brescia-to-Bologna record, averaging 89mph, but soon afterwards had to retire through a core plug coming out in the cylinder head.

This car was then shipped back to England and without any further preparation took part in one of the Brooklands events like the Empire Trophy and though without being placed, completed the course without trouble. The same car was then in the autumn prepared for Nuvolari, who came over and won the Ulster TT on it.

From the time that car was sent out to Italy until after the TT the big-end bearings were not touched and upon examination after the TT race they were found to be in perfect condition. I put this down partly to the fact that the connecting rod in this particular engine is very rigidly held and likewise the big-ends were of sufficient size to prevent any flexing under load.

As by this time the small-engined cars with blowers and the M.G. in particular had shown up the larger cars so badly in so many races, the RAC banned superchargers for the 1934 TT. Accordingly my boys took an unblown Magnette down to Brooklands to see what they could do with it, and those of you interested in piston design will also be interested in our developments in that direction.

The results at first were most disappointing and speeds in the neighbourhood of 80mph were all that could be achieved. Then Cousins, who was a tower of strength in these matters, had a look at the pistons after running and found traces of uneven burning. As we could not alter the head shape, he had the bright idea of tilting the crown, and by a process of trial and error found a certain inclination of the crown not only gave even burning but put the speed up to over 100mph. So good was the result that Charlie Dodson won the 1934 TT on this six-cylinder Magnette unblown, and later in the annual BRDC 500-Mile Race, an entire newcomer to racing came in second at over 92mph much to our surprise, as the car had been entered purely as a demonstration of high reliability, being – apart from the pistons – an absolutely standard model anyone could buy.

Reverting to the J2 model, this was followed by the still-greater-improved model which was the P-type, Charles, our designer, who is now with the Austin Company, having applied a tremendous amount of higher mathematics to working out the cam accelerations, with the result that we could obtain very high valve speeds without flutter and with a comparatively low seated valve-spring pressure.

It is possibly interesting to note that the same crankshaft, connecting rods, pistons, valves and cylinder head were used for these racing jobs as were sold to the public and it was only when we came to record-breaking events that any departure from the standard was made. For instance, the car with which Major Gardner broke the world's record for 1100cc engines at 207mph had a modified but otherwise standard chassis with the engine set at an angle in the frame to bring the propeller shaft diagonally across to one side of the back axle, thus providing a very much lower seating position for the driver. Other than this, the springs, front axle, and steering were strictly standard.

As regards the engine, this was a standard K-type engine, but had a bronze alloy head with no gasket. The crankshaft was a special short-throw one fully counterbalanced, but connecting rods were perfectly standard as were the pistons. The inlet valve was standard but the exhaust valve was special in so far as it was sodium-cooled. Likewise the camshaft and camgear generally were standard.

It was rather interesting to note that the horsepower developed by the various record breaking engines always corresponded very closely to the speed in miles per hour achieved and that when George Eyston obtained just over 100mph the engine was giving just over 100bhp and likewise when Gardner achieved the

207mph the maximum bhp of the engine was round about 209 which incidentally I think I am right in saying is the greatest bhp per litre that has ever been achieved.

Reverting to the J-type, owing to the improvements that had been carried out to the top end with increase in power, the failings of a two-bearing crankshaft became apparent and there was a tendency for this to break. So the 'P' was designed and produced, which incorporated a centre bearing. I believe at the same time advantage was taken slightly to increase the bore. The result was a beautifully smooth little power unit with an infinite capacity for punishment.

When in 1935 the M.G. Car Company was merged into the Morris Motors group and so lost its independence, the four-cylinder P-type and the six-cylinder 'K' counterpart were discontinued.

All jigs and tools were scrapped and we had to get busy trying to make something of an entirely unsuitable pushrod job. To my mind this was nothing short of a tragedy and if anyone was to pick up those two engines and develop from the point we left off, they would have something good to start on.

Concurrently with the 'P' series we produced a pure racing job, supercharged, known as the Q-type. This was sold to the public as a regular model ready for the starting line. The K3, Magnette was equally purchasable by all and sundry, and as a model in various guises had a larger number of racing successes to its credit than any other make of car in the world. This may surprise some people, but perhaps it is not to be wondered at when it won major racing events almost without being noticed, as I mentioned earlier.

Incidentally, it was the special K3 with the diagonal shaft drive and offset differential with which Captain Eyston won a long-distance race at Brooklands – I believe it was an Empire Trophy – which was subsequently built into Major Gardner's record-breaker.

Following on the Q-type came the 'R' which was a distinct breakaway from M.G. practice as far as chassis design was concerned. This consisted of a large square-sectioned frame shaped like a tuning-fork, the engine being placed in the vee of the fork. It had torsion-bar suspension all round with double wishbones supporting each axle. What however was the biggest departure from accepted racing car practice was the amount of vertical movement allowed to the wheels. The fronts had an amplitude of about 4½ inches and the rear 5½ inches. When it is realised to obtain controllability at speed with conventional springing meant limiting axle movements to about 1½ inches in front and 2 inches at the rear with very powerful friction shock absorbers controlling the movement, you will realise how revolutionary was this design.

The outstanding feature of this car was the way in which directional stability increased as the speed went up. Anyone who has taken a small car round Brooklands at any speed will know how exciting it became when the 100mph figure had been reached and what judgement is needed coming off the Byfleet banking. With the R-type one had a really comfortable armchair ride with an intense feeling of security. My own personal experience was that very much higher speeds than the car was capable of would have been perfectly safe. Where this design failed was in road-racing, as the wheels folded over on a corner. It was precisely this shortcoming of independent suspension on all four wheels that finally brought back the Grand Prix Mercedes and Auto Union to the de Dion type of back axle in which the two rear wheels are connected with a beam axle which performs no other function than to keep the rear wheels square with the road and thus stabilise the whole chassis. This tuning-fork type of frame would be worth further development I think, as it lends itself so readily to torsion-bar suspension with the torsion bars carried lengthways on the chassis and so not limited in length. Modern aircraft welding technique could be used to advantage in a frame of this description.

Now a word about superchargers. If the plug manufacturers can, in the future, give us a plug that will stand up to full power conditions and not oil up at low speeds as I understand they will be able to do, as the result of their war experiences, then I think there is a great future for supercharging. The Aspin engine with its screened plug shows another way of overcoming this bugbear.

I myself had the most pleasure from a car I owned once. This was a K-type Magnette with normal compression ratio and a Roots-type blower giving about 6 or 8 lbs boost. The normal compression gave good performance at low engine speeds before the effect of the blower came into operation. This car, a folding-head coupé, with four up would do an actual 104mph on the road. I ran this car for nearly 50,000 miles and it quite converted me to supercharging for ordinary use. A previous experience with a 1½-litre Alfa in 1929 was equally pleasing.

For racing, however, we used the eccentric-vane type of blower using the Powerplus, the Centric and McEvoy Zoller. They absorbed more power than the Roots type, but the ultimate gain was greater.

Speaking entirely from memory I believe they absorbed something like 50bhp at full power. As to the future racing car, I would suggest this should be a 1500cc machine with eight cylinders in line, or in two banks of four. It was the latter type that the Mercedes concern was developing just before the war and it may interest you to know that in effect it was two 750cc M.G. engines on a common crank. This came about through a German racing driver named Kohlrausch who broke records on an M.G. Midget in Germany – the speed was 147mph – and whom we presented afterwards with the car as a reward. This car he subsequently sold to Mercedes for 10,000 Marks.

Reverting to this 1500cc engine, I am of opinion that the peculiar lozenge-shaped head of the M.G. with valves inclining slightly inwards had a certain hidden turbulence effect, and although a number of knowledgeable people designed spherical heads with valves at the conventional racing angle of 90 degrees, none of them were as good as the lozenge shape. Personally, I imagine that with modern high compressions obtained by excessive doming of the piston crown, the combustion space becomes in section something like an attenuated crescent moon and the advantages of the spherical shape are, to a certain extent, lost.

Needless to say, I expect the cylinder block will be an aluminum alloy with wet liners with perhaps a bronze head. For the gearbox something like the ZF with electrically-operated synchromesh gears would give instantaneous changes. The high-octane fuels that will be obtainable after the war will provide one source of increased power, but to produce a successful racing car good streamlining and intensely good roadholding qualities are just as, if not more, important.

For this future racing car I have visualised the conventional type of engine, but the new form of supercharged two-stroke with fuel injections into the induction which is now being developed by Ricardo indicates the direction in which greatly increased bhp and mep will come. Then we must not rule out entirely the petrol turbine which has made great strides during the war in connection with jet propulsion, though I think such a power unit is still many years away.

However, I feel that by this time I have gone on quite long enough, and I am sure you would like some time left in which to ask me questions about details that space has prevented my touching upon in the course of this talk. If, therefore, you have any questions to put to me I will try and do my best to answer them, but as I said before, I have to rely on my memory, and because of this I have no doubt a number of you will stump me right away.

APPENDIX 6

M.G. AFTER KIMBER

After the departure of Kimber, the Abingdon factory was administered by Harold Ryder, who had previously run Morris Radiators Branch. The construction of the Albemarle nose units had been mastered – M.G. even devising an electrics test-rig that was a first for the aircraft industry – and by the end of 1941 around 200 different contracts were keeping the expanded works a hive of activity. Among these were everything from making special Abingdon-designed variable-length hinges for storage bins to building entire Crusader tanks and repairing armoured cars.

By 1942 the M.G. works was making interchangeable power-unit modules for aircraft, having set up a flowline production process to speed manufacture of these ingenious assemblies that reduced engine-replacement times at the airfield. As part of this operation it put together over 8,600 Rolls-Royce Merlin engines for use in the Lancaster bomber and other planes. At the same time the company was deepening its expertise in military armour, building tank turrets and converting tanks to other uses such as flail minesweepers, mobile bridges and bulldozers. Making blood centrifuges was added to the list in 1943, and in 1944 the Albemarle contract was replaced by the building of wing leading and trailing edges for the Tempest fighter. Finally, as the war reached its end the M.G. workforce turned to the building of the huge Neptune amphibious carrier.

SEARCHING FOR A DIRECTION

Without Cecil Kimber, so strongly identified with the marque, what would be the destiny of M.G. in the post-war years? In terms of products, the answer was not reassuring. All the M.G. body jigs at Morris Bodies Branch had been destroyed in the 1941 Coventry blitz, Miles Thomas wrote in January 1944 to Kimpton Smallbone, by then running the Morris export department. This effectively put paid to reintroducing the VA, SA and WA, whose revival wouldn't be viable, given their relatively small sales volume and elaborate body framing. They were also essentially mid-1930s designs and relatively high-priced, two factors that would have

TOP: *Abingdon assembled 130 examples of the Neptune amphibian, developed by Morris Commercial Cars; it could do 5 knots on water and 18mph on land. (Ken Martin collection)*

ABOVE: *One of Abingdon's wartime contracts was to turn tanks into bulldozers; in all, 170 were converted. (Author's collection)*

OPPOSITE: *John Thornley's aim for 'a poor man's Aston Martin' was largely achieved with the MGB GT, which had styling honed by Italian design house Pininfarina. (BMIHT)*

Interchangeable Rolls-Royce Merlin aircraft power-unit modules on the production line at the factory; over 8,600 were assembled at Abingdon. (Author's collection)

been likely to have limited their sales in an austere post-war Britain but one that was at last poised to start making cars that were more adventurously engineered. Further to this, Riley, the newly-introduced cuckoo in the Nuffield nest, was forging ahead with the design of modern 1½-litre and 2½-litre saloons that would occupy exactly the same place in the market.

That left the T-type and a new small saloon that had been under development at Cowley since 1939 and was known internally as the M.G. Ten. Was Cecil Kimber aware of its existence? It is hard to believe he would have approved of such a car, as it was a cocktail of Morris and Wolseley parts topped by an adaptation of the Morris Eight Series E body shell, although admittedly with its own chassis, complete with independent front suspension. The result was aesthetically acceptable but lacked the élan and elegance of the pre-war M.G. saloons whose design he had guided. Powered by the same 1250cc engine as the TB, the new M.G. 1¼-litre, as it would be called, ended up being scheduled for a launch in 1946. But where – and how – it would be assembled was another matter, because the entire future of the Abingdon plant was under examination.

Miles Thomas felt that M.G. should capitalise on its wartime experience with tanks. In October 1943 he wrote to Harold Ryder, suggesting Abingdon become the home of Nuffield Mechanisations, the combine's tank, armoured-car and anti-aircraft-gun operation. Under this scheme all development and building of Army vehicles, both wheeled and tracked, would become the responsibility of Abingdon; this would be convenient, in that it was nearer to the Army testing facilities at Chobham than was the division's then home in Birmingham.

Car manufacture would be scaled back – and Abingdon would become even more of an assembly operation that it had been in pre-war years. 'The M.G. Company was visualised as taking chassis components for assembly from Cowley, their car-building activities consisting of paint, trim, and glaze body shells, mount,

A pre-production version of the M.G. 1¼-litre or Y-type. Its body was based on that of the Series E Morris Eight. (Author's collection)

The Abingdon factory was at one stage considered for the assembly of the Nuffield tractor. (Author's collection)

in January 1946 Ryder was still pitching for non-car work for Abingdon. This time he saw big: he wanted M.G. to become the production site for the future Nuffield Universal Tractor.

'Confirming my conversation with you on Wednesday last, I shall be pleased if the M.G. Car Company can be considered for the ultimate manufacture of the above,' he wrote to Thomas. 'As the M.G. Car Company have had a large experience of this type of work in the manufacture of Neptunes and tanks during the war, I feel it would be the ideal plant to undertake this work.' It wasn't to be. After various hesitations, production of the tractor would begin in 1948 at the Wolseley plant at Ward End.

CHAOS AT COWLEY

Meanwhile there was no sign for a while of the promised 1¼-litre saloon, but in 1945 Abingdon began assembly of the TC, a lightly revised version of the pre-war TB Midget. The 1¼-litre or Y-type

Second along in this row of Nuffield products is a proposed new Midget based on Morris Minor parts; it was seen as having a single-overhead-cam 1100cc engine. (BMIHT)

road-test and deliver,' Miles Thomas had summarised in his October 1943 note to Ryder. He was aware, all the same, of the risks of such a policy. 'It is imperative that sufficient manufacturing activities be maintained at the M.G. plant to emphasize the M.G. cachet,' he stressed. '[If] Abingdon is to be kept on at all as a car-producing centre – and certainly it will have to remain as a car sales and dispatching centre – I doubt whether all the floor space available will be occupied, particularly if bodies come in finished and chassis are largely constructed at Cowley'.

Ryder replied that moving Mechanisations to Abingdon from its location next to the Wolseley works wouldn't make sense, but he wasn't against 're-purposing' Abingdon. In 1944 there was talk of M.G. undertaking development of US company Clark's tow tractors and forklifts, as extensively used by the allies, and finally entered production in March 1947, ahead of its public announcement at the beginning of May. It went on to be modestly successful, but it was essentially almost as dated a car as the TC – it was old-fashioned before it even went on sale. The future of M.G. was seen as involving neither car for anything more than a holding period, however, before new and more modern vehicles arrived. Here two strands of the story coalesce: new 'badge engineered' Morris-derived M.G. models and the possibility of manufacture of these cars elsewhere than at Abingdon.

The backcloth to what happened next – and to what didn't happen – is a period of chaos, turmoil and confusedly inept management at the parent company in Cowley. The board was dominated by old faithfuls who had served Lord Nuffield since his early days in business. They were tired, unimaginative, and given no strong leadership from an ageing and demoralised Nuffield who preferred going off on long cruises to Australia to assuming the hands-on direction of his unwieldy combine.

Hugely ambitious plans for new model ranges and new engine designs were bandied around, constituting a planning soup made even more murky by engineering golden boy Alec Issigonis promoting flat-four engines and Morris Engines Branch pushing in a sterile rivalry for a new range of single-overhead-cam in-line

ABOVE: *The TC was the first M.G. into production after the war; it was a lightly modified TB, with a marginally wider body. (Author's collection)*

RIGHT: *During what might be termed 'The Great Panic of 1947' thought was given to the future Morris Minor going into production as an M.G. – built or at least finished at Abingdon. This is a mock-up of how the car might have looked. (BMIHT)*

units. Meanwhile a grumpy Lord Nuffield saw no need to replace his pre-war models with new designs.

As part of all this, there were to be M.G. versions of the proposed 1½-litre four-cylinder and 2¼-litre six-cylinder saloons – the future MO-series Oxford and MS-series Morris Six, and their Wolseley sisters – plus a new Midget probably derived from the smaller model intended to replace the Morris Eight. All M.G. models would have ohc in-line engines, and all would be in production by early 1948, according to plans laid down in 1946; indeed, there would be a Midget with a new body and a 1-litre ohc engine as early as June 1947, with a further revised 1100cc model arriving for the summer of 1948. The Y-type, meanwhile, would have a short life, and be deleted in January 1948. There was soon slippage on these dates, and eventually the programme would be severely curtailed. But the real crisis concerned the smallest model in the proposed new range – the future Morris Minor.

This was closer to production than the larger models, by some margin, but Lord Nuffield was blocking its manufacture, preferring to carry on making the Series E Eight. In desperation, at one stage Miles Thomas proposed having the car made as an M.G. as a way of breaking the logjam. Initial thoughts were that it would be assembled at Cowley, but have its final inspection at Abingdon, to give it some spurious authenticity as an M.G. product. Subsequently there was consideration of actually assembling the car at Abingdon, but the whole hare-brained scheme was soon abandoned; not long after, in November 1947, the high-level tensions at Morris ended with Thomas being forced to resign.

THE DONO PLAN – AND ITS DEMISE

This miserable period threw up one previously unthinkable notion: that an M.G. didn't necessarily have to be made in an M.G. factory. And what might apply for M.G. could equally well apply

After the dust had settled, assembly of the RM-series Rileys moved to Abingdon. This is the bigger 2½-litre RMB model. (Author's collection)

to the other lesser marques in the Nuffield Organization portfolio. One Morris high-up was already articulating such thoughts, and in October 1948 he laid out a root-and-branch restructuring of the business. This was George Dono, MD of the Nuffield Metal Products pressings and body operation – and his plan had Abingdon in its crosswires.

A recent recruit to the Morris board, Dono could see the folly of the group's numerous and widely dispersed plants. He was particularly appalled by how Wolseley was preparing to go into production with the 4/50 and 6/80, near-identical cars to the Morris Oxford and Six that would be made in much greater quantities at Cowley. Just transporting a body made at Pressed Steel in Oxford up to the Wolseley factory in Birmingham would add nearly a pound per car to manufacturing costs, he calculated. 'At the present time between 60 per cent and 75 per cent of our customers are abroad,' he was recorded as saying. 'I find it impossible to believe that they care whether the car is made in Birmingham, Oxford, or (for that matter) Aberdeen!'

Dono's idea was that there would be three divisions. These would be Cars, centred at Cowley; Engine and General Machining mainly in Birmingham; and Sheet-metal, split between Llanelli for radiators and Birmingham for presswork. As a footnote, amongst the intended casualties was to be Morris Radiators Branch in Oxford, the home of M.G. in the 1925-27 period; in fact the plant survived the axe and continued in operation until 2001, outliving the original Morris works at Cowley. Under the Dono plan, which at least partially came about, Wolseley manufacture did indeed move to Cowley, with Ward End becoming a new Tractors and Transmissions Branch. Another key element was to end car manufacture at Riley in Coventry and M.G. in Abingdon. 'After the Wolseley production has been absorbed, Riley and M.G. should follow,' Dono was minuted as saying. In other words, the cars of Nuffield's small-volume specialist marques would in the future be made at Cowley.

In some ways this made absolute commercial sense. Modern cars and their components, made using modern production processes, in rationalised high-volume modern factories: this was the way forward. But even after new Vice-Chairman Reggie Hanks had instigated a management purge and brought in fresh blood[1], the Morris directors lacked the bravery to implement the Dono plan in full. Insofar as M.G. and Riley were concerned, perhaps they were right: the wood-framed M.G. T-types and RM-series Rileys would have been difficult to integrate smoothly into a factory churning out vast numbers of pressed-steel monocoque Morrises and Wolseleys.

Ultimately, in December 1948, a halfway-house decision was made: M.G. and Riley would be brought together in one operation – at the Riley factory. 'This will create a tidy bloc comprising our two "specialist" cars with Bodies Branch on their door-step. All three factories will be under common management,' it was minuted. This never happened. Less than two months after the M.G. transfer to Coventry had been mooted, it was decided instead that Riley production would be transferred to Abingdon.

That the board changed its mind about the proposed move may have been down to lobbying by M.G. management. "We read about [it] in the *Daily Graphic*, I think," future M.G. boss John Thornley recalled in a 1989 interview. "The centre page of the paper had a little column of news snippets, and halfway down was 'M.G. Car Company to move to Coventry'. Well, that kicked the hive in the biggest possible way, and a deputation waited on the Vice-Chairman of the Nuffield Organization, Reggie Hanks, and persuaded him to change his mind."

The minutes of the boardroom meeting of 19 January 1949 unsurprisingly tell a different story. There was apparently not enough space at the Riley plant for both M.G. and Riley production, but the works would be perfectly suited to being a

---

[1] "Rome is burning," Hanks told Nuffield. Getting rid of the aged courtiers of the old régime did much to sanitise the poisonous atmosphere at Cowley, and the Nuffield Organization visibly rebounded, with new products and a new sense of purpose.

satellite factory for Morris Engines Branch; as for Morris Bodies Branch, that could possibly switch to the Cowley region, to be near the new M.G./Riley operation. In the end, Bodies Branch stayed where it was, merrily churning out archaic wood-framed Morris Minor Traveller bodies until 1971, but Riley production did indeed move in 1949 to Abingdon. The 2½-litre was made at the M.G. works until 1953, after which it gave way to the ungainly and troublesome Pathfinder, and the 1½-litre continued until 1955.

THE ARRIVAL OF THE BRITISH MOTOR CORPORATION

So it was that the M.G. business at last emerged from ten years of turmoil. Design was still centred on Cowley – even if the next Midget, the TD, would be a largely Abingdon-led project – and there would ultimately be a Cowley-conceived modern saloon, the Z-type Magnette, to replace the Y-type. This was to share its monocoque body with a closely-related Wolseley model, something it is hard to imagine Kimber accepting and which after the car's 1953 announcement provoked fiery outbursts in the correspondence columns of *Motor Sport* magazine.

In fact the Magnette was a thoroughly good car and occupied a unique position, as the only modestly-priced mid-sized sports saloon in the British market. But the holy waters of marque purity had been adulterated with the notion that an M.G. could be regarded as such even if essentially the same car was available under another identity, just by changing the radiator grille and a few other details. This became known as 'badge engineering' and was to destroy Riley and compromise the M.G. image.

The Z-type Magnette, designed by Gerald Palmer, shared its basic body with a Wolseley, to the outrage of marque purists. This is a ZA, recognisable by the 'hockey stick' side mouldings. The ZA and subsequent ZB were assembled at Abingdon. (Steve Favell)

The TF held the fort for Abingdon whilst the MGA was held in abeyance; it was a clever facelift of the TD that had replaced the TC in 1949. (Author's collection)

During the development period of the Magnette the merger between the Morris and Austin companies had taken place, creating the British Motor Corporation. The first consequence was that Abingdon's new saloon was launched with an Austin engine under the bonnet. The second consequence was more serious: plans for a new M.G. sports car were put on ice.

In the first half of 1951, when the Austin and Morris businesses had not yet merged, Abingdon had built a racer for privateer George Phillips to enter in that year's Le Mans 24-hour race. The car, known as EX172, was built on an M.G. TD chassis and had an attractive all-enclosed body. After Le Mans it was decided to adapt this design, with a new chassis, as the basis of a new M.G. to replace the TD. A blueprint for a revised body – basically that of the future MGA – had been laid down by February 1952, the same month that the Austin-Morris fusion became an administrative reality.

At the 1952 Motor Show, however, BMC chief Leonard Lord agreed to collaborate with Donald Healey on the manufacture of his new Austin-based sports car, unveiled at the show. Overnight it became the Austin-Healey 100, and in 1953 assembly began at Longbridge, using body/chassis units supplied by Jensen Motors of West Bromwich. The industrial logic behind this was questionable, given that in M.G. the company already had a maker of sports cars under its corporate umbrella. By now M.G. had built a prototype of its proposed new sports car, and reasonably enough had expected this to be approved for production. But the project, coded EX175, was not sanctioned, and Abingdon fell back on a facelift of the TD to create the TF of 1953.

GLORY DAYS: ABINGDON FINDS ITS SPOT IN THE SUN

It soon became clear, however, that the TF was living on borrowed time, faced with faster and more modern sports cars – not just the Austin-Healey 100, but also the Triumph TR2. Despite this, it contrived to outsell the Austin-Healey, supply of which could not keep up with demand. It thus looked as if there might be room in the market after all for a production version of EX175. Accordingly, in June 1954 what would become the MGA was authorized for manufacture, with a design office being re-opened at Abingdon.

The MGA went on to be a success, with 101,081 being made

ABOVE: *The six-cylinder Austin-Healey was assembled at Abingdon from 1957; this 100-Six has the 'works' hardtop. (Author's collection)*

LEFT: *M.G. entered the modern era with the MGA, the first new model to be designed at Abingdon since the mid 1930s. There was also a coupé version. (Author's collection)*

between 1955 and 1962. In 1956 the roadster was joined by a fixed-head coupé and in 1958 the MGA Twin-Cam was announced; with an engine specific to M.G., this created much excitement, but there were so many in-service problems that the model ended up being dropped in 1960. Then, in a rare burst of industrial common sense, BMC decided to move assembly of the Austin-Healey from Longbridge to Abingdon and to make the M.G. works the combine's dedicated sports-car factory. Body/chassis units continued to be built and painted by Jensen, who now would carry out more work on the cars than previously, supplying the shells fully trimmed and with the electrical equipment and steering in place; all Abingdon had to do was to fit the engine and gearbox and the front and rear axle assemblies. As a consequence of all this, assembly of the Riley One-point-Five at Abingdon was stopped virtually as soon as it had started, and transferred to Longbridge, and the building

TOP: *The Austin-Healey Sprite in its MkII form; in this photo can be seen Bruce McLaren by the car, with John Cooper leaning over the single-seater behind. (Author's collection)*

ABOVE: *The installation of the BMC Competitions Department at Abingdon further enhanced the prestige of the M.G. factory. (Author's collection)*

of the Pathfinder's successor, the Riley Two-point-Six, moved to Cowley. Abingdon's association with the Riley marque was over.

Meanwhile Donald Healey had been working on a new cheap sports car. John Thornley had studied making a model smaller than the MGA and had come to the conclusion that such a vehicle would not be commercially viable. But Healey and Len Lord pushed ahead, despite Thornley's continuing doubts about the rigour of BMC's Austin-based accounting procedures, and in 1958 production of the 'Frogeye' Austin-Healey Sprite was confided to Abingdon. Variants of the Sprite would be manufactured at Abingdon until 1979, with a total of 354,164 of all types being produced.

With components for these cars being transported around the Midlands from BMC's various manufacturing units, the economics were less than ideal. For the big Austin-Healey they were the worst of all. Costs of production unearthed by the author reveal that in 1963-64 the Austin-Healey 3000 cost £658.59 to manufacture, when an MGB roadster cost £425.16. Even allowing for the extra cost of the 3000's six-cylinder engine and accompanying gearbox, the difference is staggering. But Abingdon had been transformed into a bustling specialist works, and from 1955 was in addition home to the BMC Competitions Department. Newly established at the end of 1954, this would oversee the return of M.G. to factory-backed motor sport, including three sorties to Le Mans with the MGB, but would achieve its greatest fame with the rallying Minis and Austin-Healeys.

The final cuckoo in the Abingdon nest was the Morris Minor. Between 1960 and 1964 a total of 20,014 Minors were built at the M.G. works – Travellers, vans and a handful of pick-ups. This helped keep the factory turning at a time when sales of the mainstay sports cars had dipped sharply. "We judged the relative cost of stitching the things together against those produced at Cowley. The figures were shoved under the carpet very sharply, because they showed Cowley up in a very bad light," recalled John Thornley. "What was more interesting still was that we hadn't been doing it long before distributors were saying 'Yes, I'll have five more Travellers, but I want them to be from Abingdon'..."

With half a million examples built, the monocoque-construction MGB of 1962-80 was a resounding success for John Thornley and the Abingdon team. (Author)

With excellent labour relations and high audited quality levels, the M.G. plant at Abingdon came to prove that there were virtues in small size and in being a semi-independent unit within a large conglomerate. But the ride to get to that point had been a bumpy one. The next challenge came with the need to replace the MGA. Thornley realised that long-term economics demanded a move to monocoque construction. To make the initial investment easier to swallow, he agreed a deal with Pressed Steel whereby the tooling costs would be lower but M.G. would pay a commission on each shell. With broad-shouldered good looks and straightforward mechanicals, the 'B' was an instant success. In 1965 the fastback coupé MGB GT arrived, offering what was at the time a unique recipe amongst British-built cars: a compact sports coupé in the mould of Italy's Alfa Romeo and Lancia models.

MISJUDGEMENTS AND MISMANAGEMENT

The MGB was a certified winner, and the Austin-Healey Sprite had spawned an M.G. derivative, the Midget. But if these two cars added lustre to the M.G. name, this risked being tarnished by BMC's further descent into 'badge engineering'. In 1959 the Z-type Magnette was replaced by a new model that was one of a series of five Farina-styled saloons that differed one from the other only in chromework, radiator grilles and interior presentation. This stodgy machine convinced nobody, and sales were poor.

BMC then repeated the trick with the 1100. Here it was more fortunate. Sticking an M.G. radiator on a gussied-up Morris 1100 might have seemed cynical, but it was an adequately successful marketing exercise. With the 1100/1300 range, higher-priced badge-engineered variants accounted for 12.3 per cent of output, of which the Cowley-built M.G. 1100/1300 alone represented 7.3 per cent of the total – a decent although hardly spectacular 157,409 cars. In contrast, Wolseley and Riley derivatives together accounted for just 3.1 per cent of the mix. Conclusion: the M.G. badge had some clout, so perhaps BMC shouldn't be criticised too hard for capitalising on this.

But this was peripheral to the survival of M.G. and its Abingdon factory. The problem was that the MGB would need replacing, most likely by the early 1970s, and the tooling costs were likely to be a major deterrent, given its relatively limited production. There was also the question of replacing the Sprite/Midget and the big Austin-Healey. For what were fringe products for the massive BMC conglomerate, this was a challenge. All that would emerge was a supposed replacement for the 'Big Healey' in the shape of the MGC. This was on the surface a thoroughly sensible move, given the limited and shrinking sales of the Healey. But the 'C' was too similar in looks and presentation to its smaller-engined sister, had an uninspiring engine shared with the Austin 3-litre, and was slated in the press for its leaden handling. It had none of the charisma of the Austin-Healey 3000. After two years it was withdrawn, with just 8,999 having been made.

Advertising the second-generation of post-war Magnette by evoking the K3 took some neck, when the car was an Austin Cambridge in a party frock, assembled at the Morris works in Cowley. (Author's collection)

ABOVE LEFT: *A derivative of the advanced front-wheel-drive Austin/Morris 1100 series, the M.G. 1100 was another 'badge engineering' special, but it sold well – unlike the 'Farina' Magnette. (Author's collection)*

ABOVE RIGHT: *An MGB with a 2912cc six-cylinder engine, the MGC made sense on paper, but the reality was disappointing; as a replacement for the much-loved and charismatic Austin-Healey 3000 it did not convince. (BMIHT)*

TOP: *Based on Mini underpinnings, ADO34 had Pininfarina lines and a very rigid body shell; for some while it seemed to be slated for production. (Author's collection)*

ABOVE: *A mock-up of the coupé version of 'Fireball'. The body was built around a substantial centre tunnel and the engine was intended to be the Rolls-Royce unit found in the Vanden Plas Princess 4-Litre R – another BMC clunker. (Author's collection)*

OPPOSITE: *Again a Pininfarina creation, EX234 was a slightly bigger car than ADO34; the power unit, however, remained a BMC A-series. (Author)*

This was all that BMC was able to manage in the five years since the launch of the MGB. This was a reflection on the rot at the heart of the company. During the 1960s BMC gave the impression of being at the top of the game, riding a wave of success with the Mini and the 1100. In fact it was in a state of decadence and decay, wretchedly run by Chairman George Harriman and Technical Director Alec Issigonis, a duo who managed by hunch and on the basis of decisions arrived at after well-oiled luncheons in the directors dining room. BMC was making too many unrelated cars, in outdated and strike-prone factories. It had a mess of poorly-selling mid-range models, while Ford was making hay with its popular and cheap-to-make Cortina. The advanced engineering of the Mini and 1100 was bringing in far too little money. Worse, its limited engineering resources relative to those of its rivals were being dissipated in ill-considered and often capricious projects of limited value to the financial bottom line; most never made production.

This sorry state of affairs had an ultimately fatal impact on the M.G. business. Under the direction of Issigonis three separate designs for sports cars were initiated. Not one of them became a production reality. Project ADO34 was for a Mini-based front-wheel-drive replacement for the Sprite/Midget, Project EX234 was for a slightly larger rear-wheel-drive car, and the final design – ironically nicknamed 'Fireball' after a TV series of the time – was for a large 4-litre sports car to rival the E-type Jaguar. All would have had Hydrolastic suspension – adding to their manufacturing costs – and at least the first two would have carried the M.G. badge. Even if these ventures individually took up relatively little time and money, they nonetheless collectively prevented BMC focusing on what was really needed for Abingdon: an updated or new model to replace the MGB.

SINKING BENEATH THE WAVES

Instead, BMC was overtaken by events. In 1968 it was merged with Leyland. The chief concern of the resultant British Leyland Motor Corporation was to develop successful and profitable mid-range saloons; a new sports car could wait. Meanwhile Abingdon's modest engineering resources became totally occupied by adapting the Sprite/Midget and MGB to ever more stringent US safety and emissions regulations. This depressing process resulted in the cars being sapped of their power (at least in US form) and being given heavy and ungainly urethane-covered black bumpers.

British Leyland did not want to abandon the largely US-based sports car market. Work was already underway on a new Triumph model. Alongside this a project was initiated to create a mid-engined replacement for the Sprite/Midget, and this evolved into a bigger mid-engined car to take over from the MGB. Abingdon began engineering work, and built a development 'mule' MGB GT with a mid-mounted Austin Maxi engine and

ABOVE: *Disfigured by urethane bumpers and sapped of power to meet emissions requirements, the MGB continued to sell adequately well in the United States; catalogue photography, as here, was always of high quality. (Author's collection)*

RIGHT: *Artwork for ADO21 at the stage when it was envisaged as a replacement for the Sprite/Midget and the Triumph Spitfire; with vision and determination it could have been a British riposte to Fiat's X1/9. (Author's collection)*

de Dion rear suspension. But ADO21 was soon cancelled in favour of a conventional front-engined rear-wheel-drive corporate sports car. Based on a willfully misleading analysis of the key US market it was decided that the new car would be sold principally as a Triumph, although an M.G. version might conceivably follow. The car would be made in a new purpose-built facility at Speke on Merseyside. This would be the combine's dedicated sports car factory, with an intended output of an unrealistically high 84,000 cars per annum, once all the planned variants were in production. Effectively this spelt the end of Abingdon, at least as a manufacturing unit, but this was never made explicit[2].

All this was dependent on the success of the new car, launched in 1975 as the Triumph TR7. The new sports car was controversially styled, only available as a fixed-head coupé, and was poorly assembled and catastrophically unreliable. The MGB was always going to be discontinued when the TR7 had found its feet. This never happened, despite the arrival of convertible and V8 versions, and despite two moves to different factories in a bid to reduce the losses made in manufacturing the car.

So much investment had been poured into this legendary lemon that BL felt it had to continue in the hope that sales would pick up – at which point the MGB could be axed. That was always the intention, and in the abstract the idea was reasonable enough. The MGB was technically obsolete, to the point where among enthusiasts it had become a laughing stock. Despite this, in

---

[2] In its peak year of 1970-71 Abingdon completed over 57,000 vehicles, up from 10,000 or so in 1949-50. This was despite the very basic unautomated assembly processes. There had been plans for a new plant to be built on land acquired from the Pavlova company, but these were abandoned in the wake of the creation of British Leyland.

ABOVE: *The Abingdon factory was starved of investment, but remained an efficient and harmonious workplace, with high audited quality levels. (BMIHT)*

TOP LEFT: *This artwork shows how ADO21 ended up as a larger car – which put it in competition with what would become the Triumph TR7. (Author's collection)*

LEFT: *The last-of-line Midget was the 1500, again with those 'rubber' bumpers and now with a Triumph engine under the bonnet. More were built than any other of the Sprite/Midget series. (Author's collection)*

Appendix 6: M.G. After Kimber

the United States it finished up outselling the Triumph. But the economics were stacked against it, as its key components, once shared with mass-produced mainstream models, gradually became unique to it and thus endowed with a higher unit cost. With or without the TR7, the MGB was doomed, but the death was a lingering one; there were even notions that its life could be prolonged by fitting BL's new O-series engine[3].

Ultimately a crumbling BL, struggling to survive, embarked on a massive retrenchment exercise in 1979 and in September that year it announced the closure of the Abingdon factory and with it the end of MGB manufacture; the Midget was already in the process of being phased out. Attempts by a consortium led by Aston Martin to take over making the MGB, with or without the factory, came to nothing. Indeed, their main effect was to prevent Abingdon surviving as a pre-assembly facility for the Triumph Acclaim, the Honda-derived small saloon that was to enter production at Cowley in 1982. In October 1980 the last MGB left the lines and the Abingdon factory was closed.

FROM BADGE-ENGINEERING TO THE MGF

The M.G. story didn't stop there, however. The capital enjoyed by the name saw its revival on 'badge-engineered' versions of the Metro, Maestro and Montego. Present on the market between 1982 and 1991, these were the best that could be hoped for whilst a state-owned BL was trying to pull itself back to health. Happily the cars were competent enough not to tarnish the reputation of the marque. They also sold relatively well. The octagon-badged Metro accounted for 8.93 per cent of total 1980-90 Metro production, while 7.9 per cent of Maestros carried the M.G. name, and 7.3 per cent of Montegos. To put those figures in perspective, the revered Cooper and Cooper S variants of the Mini took an appreciably more modest 5.9 per cent of 1963-67 Mini MkI production.

In 1988 the BL business, by then renamed Rover Group, was acquired by British Aerospace. The alliance with Honda had resulted in increasingly well-regarded models, and with a newfound sense of optimism it was decided to re-enter the sports car market. The car would have to use the maximum of existing mass-production components, and have a design that stood apart from the competition. To prime the market for the return of an open two-seater M.G. an extraordinary initiative was taken: the MGB returned to production in 1993 as a restyled limited-production luxury V8, fishing in the same pool as TVR and the lower-priced Porsches. Bringing back the MGB a dozen years after it had ceased production was made possible by the availability of brand-new MGB body shells made on the original tooling by British Motor Heritage, as a service to Britain's thriving classic-car scene. Just 1996 examples of the RV8 were made, in a small factory unit at Cowley: the UK market wasn't convinced, and it

ABOVE: *The octagon badge subsequently found its way onto the Maestro – this is a 2-litre version – and its saloon derivative, the Montego; sales were respectable. (Author's collection)*

OPPOSITE: *The unprecedented revival of the MGB with the announcement in 1992 of the RV8 provoked much debate in the press, but relatively few sales were made in the United Kingdom. (Magic Car Pics)*

---

[3] The design of this engine, which was basically a re-hashed overhead-cam version of the old B-series, had been finalised in September 1972. That by the time of the MGB's demise BL had proved incapable of installing it in a production MGB speaks long on the company's managerial and engineering abilities.

was only Japanese interest that saved the project, with 1,581 cars going to Japan.

The intended new sports car emerged in 1995 as the MGF, a mid-engined open two-seater based around the corporate K-series engine, a Honda-derived gearbox, and the suspension and subframes of the Metro. Manufactured at Longbridge, the 'F' was an immediate success; its overall sales were limited, however, by it not being engineered to be sold in the United States.

LAST WALTZ: MG ROVER AND ITS 'ZEDS'

By this time BL was owned by BMW, who had taken over the company in 1994. When BMW pulled out in 2000, the game was over. The best that could ever have been hoped for by the new owners, the so-called Phoenix Consortium, was a soft landing by moving towards selling what remained of the old British Leyland to anyone prepared to buy it.

Renamed MG Rover, the new entity brought in M.G. versions of all the Rover models it inherited. The MGF was replaced by the TF,

TOP LEFT: *The marque's real re-launch, with the arrival of a two-seater open sports car, came with the MGF of 1995, a cleverly-engineered mid-engined design put together on a slender budget. (Author's collection)*

ABOVE: *Advertising of the M.G. models sold by MG Rover was in-your-face. There was also a motor sports programme, including forays to Le Mans with a re-badged Lola. (Author's collection)*

with the styling lightly modified and the Hydragas suspension replaced by conventional steel springs. With the help of outside engineering resources the Rover 75 was converted to rear-wheel drive and a V8 engine, resulting in the ZT-260 as an upmarket sister to lesser front-drive ZTs. Accompanied by some memorably crass advertising, the Rover-derived ZR, ZS and ZT were promoted as boy-racer sporting derivatives for the sub-BMW market. There was even an attempt to get into the Porsche 911 market with a re-bodied Qvale Mangusta, a vanity project of stupendous futility that resulted in just three XPower SVs having been sold to the public by the time MG Rover collapsed at the beginning of 2005.

It is tempting to judge the final British-built cars to carry the M.G. name as an exercise in last-gasp cynicism – or, being more generous, as an ill-judged failure to recall the perils of the 'badge engineering' policies of BMC days. In fact there was no choice. Although the 75 is regularly described these days as the best Rover ever produced, the signs were that Rovers weren't what the British public wanted, at least in any great numbers. In such a situation, the Phoenix team had two choices: carry on flogging an ailing Rover horse or inject a new dynamism into the product by exploiting the only other extant name available to them.

The rightness of the decision was proven when under MG Rover the trend for Rover-badged cars continued downwards. Sales of the new M.G. models weren't spectacular: in fact those of the ZS and ZT were pretty slender. But they shored up the bottom line, for a limited investment; indeed, as MG Rover crumbled to marketplace dust in 2004, output of the best-selling model, the ZR, inched ahead of that of its Rover 25 sibling. Without exploiting the M.G. marque the company would have sunk even faster. Those 'Zeds' were all that Phoenix could ever have conjured out of a very empty hat, and they played their only card as well as they could, underpinning the MG Rover company identity with a three-car M.G. range. It wasn't smoke and mirrors: the cars were well received. It's just that it was never a winning hand.

The M.G. name was purchased by China's Nanjing Automobile as part of its 2005 acquisition of MG Rover, after the company went into administration. Nanjing merged with state-owned Chinese giant SAIC in 2007. For a brief period the mid-engined TF was made in China, and approximately 900 were assembled at Longbridge, from Chinese parts, in the 2008-2009 period; there was also a Chinese-made version of the ZT. Today everything from pick-up trucks to electric SUVs carry the M.G. octagon on their nose, with the vehicles made in China, India and Thailand.

The SV was a re-bodied Qvale Mangusta, and a pointless diversion whilst MG Rover was spiralling down the plughole. (Author's collection)

POSTSCRIPT: WHEN SHOULD THE M.G. CENTENARY BE CELEBRATED?

If you look at the golden side-stripes on the 1975 limited-edition 'Jubilee' MGB GT, it pronounces 1925 to be the year the M.G. marque was born. Indeed, a whole publicity campaign was built around this date. According to the M.G. company, however, writing in pre-war times when memories were fresher, the first M.G. saw the light of day in 1923. Or 1924. Or indeed in 1925. It couldn't make up its mind. If the manufacturer of the cars, during the lifetime of the man who created the make, couldn't decide on a date, what hope do historians have, a century (or so) later?

The grenade thrown into the water is 'Old Number One'. The moment you give a car such a name, it is automatically perceived as being the first of the line. Part of the problem is that for many years there were people at Abingdon who believed – heaven knows why – that the car had been built in 1923, and who went into print to this effect. Duly the tale spread to the press, who uncritically repeated it. But even when the factory dated construction of the car to its correct year of 1925, they continued to refer to it as 'the first M.G. to be made'.

So on occasion did Cecil Kimber. 'To Wilf, my first passenger in my first M.G,' he inscribed a copy of Barré Lyndon's *Combat* given as a present to his navigator in the car, Wilfrid Mathews. But then Kimber also wrote on another occasion that after winning his 'Gold' on the 1925 Land's End Trial in 'Old Number One' he took a pair of cufflinks instead of the medal – whereas these cufflinks were in fact in lieu of the gold medal that he won on the 1923 event, in a Morris Garages Chummy[1].

Proof that Kimber's memory was playing him up, here is the gold match case – not a set of cufflinks – that he accepted instead of a medal after winning a 'Gold' on the 1925 Land's End Trial. This is an important detail in nailing the myths that continue to percolate around 'Old Number One'.

---

[1] This was in the talk on racing that Kimber was scheduled to give on 16 February 1945 to a branch of the Institute of the Motor Trade; see Appendix 5. In the typescript Kimber wrote that 'the first sporting event ever won by an M.G. was achieved when I won the gold cufflinks I am now wearing by successfully getting through the 1925 London-Land's End without losing any marks, in the first M.G. I ever built'.

This 1930s M.G. publication managed to get the date of 'Old Number One' wrong.

Faulty memory? Subtle warping of history to tell a good story? Flattery of old friend Mathews? It doesn't really matter. The main point is that 'Old Number One' wasn't a production model, and spawned no series-made derivatives. It was a dead-end, not a vital step on the creation of the marque. Its main importance is that it has survived, today incorrectly painted in a 'look-at-me' red, to become a potent if misused marketing tool. In the words of Cecil Cousins, "it wasn't Number One, it was a one-off bastard".

Perhaps the last observation on the matter should be left to Wilson McComb: 'To this day there are some who, despite all evidence to the contrary, still insist that the 1925 Land's End car *must* be the first M.G. Their ability to believe what they want to believe, come what may, would almost compel respect if it were not so ridiculous,' he writes in *M.G. by McComb*. So we'll eliminate 'Old Number One' from this enquiry.

The next candidate raised its head in the February 1938 issue of *The Sports Car* when the M.G. house magazine noted that a Brian H. Morgan had been in touch, asking if his M.G. Super Sports, sold new in July 1925, was the first of the line. No, said the magazine: 'the first M.G. was sold to a Mr Jack Gardiner in 1924'. When recording his reminiscences for Lytton Jarman, Gardiner said that he regarded his car as the first of the line. He has a point.

But let's put to one side for a moment the Gardiner car. Stand back, and there is a clear lineage of cars, Bullnose and Flatnose, all carrying the same name and which continue with this nomenclature until late 1927. This lineage begins with the six Raworth two-seaters, the first of which were built and sold in 1923. These cars did not lead to a continuing production run of identical models.

Such a production run was however initiated after the construction of the Gardiner four-seat tourer, with subsequent cars, or at least the most common open two-seaters and four-seaters, closely following its style of coachwork. In setting the template for all future M.G. Super Sports, the Gardiner car does indeed have a claim to being the first of the line, and thus to that line starting in

The Gardiner four-seat tourer has some claim to being the first production M.G. – but the argument is not watertight. This is a similar but slightly later car with Gardiner at the wheel. (Magna Press Library)

1924. As the car was a one-off commission, perhaps that accolade should in fact go to the first of the series to be produced after the Gardiner car, a tourer that was registered MF 8068 in May 1924 and was built for racing motorcyclist Billy Cooper. Either way, the date remains the same.

But to plump for the date of 1924 it is necessary to ask how the Gardiner and Cooper cars and the M.G. Super Sports Morrises that followed them differed from the Raworth cars. The answer is that they differed only in the style of their coachwork, although in all cases this was characterised by a three-pane windscreen with triangular glass side-pieces. All had chassis modifications to lower the suspension, and a steering column altered in rake[2]. The Raworth sextet had a special carburettor according to Cousins, the implication is that the Gardiner car had some improvements to the engine, and later cars equally had modified engines.

So if the 1924-27 cars – tourers, two-seaters and Salonettes in the main – are considered as M.G.s then so must the genetically

---

[2] There is a slight ambiguity about the Gardiner car. According to Gardiner the steering was raked. Barraclough and Jennings say it was not. It seems likely it was raked to a lesser degree than on later cars, but raked all the same. Whether the angle of the steering column should disqualify the car from being considered as an M.G. seems questionable.

similar Raworths of 1923 which were advertised under the same name, as the M.G. Super Sports Morris. It is noteworthy that Cecil Cousins, one of those who built these cars, and who stayed with the company until 1967, regarded the six cars with this sports bodywork as the first products which could be considered MGs: 'These were really the first M.G. Sports,' he told Lytton Jarman.

But if one accepts that sporting coachwork, minimal chassis modifications and a lightly tuned engine suffice to make an M.G. out of a Morris, where does that leave those Morrises – and indeed Morris-Léon-Bollées – given special coachwork but none of those mechnical modifications, and also given the M.G. name by the enterprise that created them?

In pondering that question one should bear in mind that in the 1920s there was a love of using initials to designate a product. The practice wasn't new to the 1920s, and would continue afterwards, but it was certainly a feature of commercial life at the time. It was a neat way of creating a brand identity that was easy to assimilate. So it was that any product of The Morris Garages carried the M.G. identity – down to an M.G. patent brake-drum drawer.

It is more to the point that up until 1927 the name Morris was consistently associated with the M.G. Super Sports models and then suddenly, for the 1928 model year, this ceased. The cars were renamed the M.G. 14/40 MkIV and carried a Morris Garages ID plate with an M.G. car number. Much ink was spilt on emphasising that these Morris-derived cars were in fact not lightly modified Morrises with a smart sporting body but M.G. cars in their own right. There was also – and this is not unimportant – a new limited company behind the cars, a change consecrated in early 1928 by the formation of the M.G. Car Company.

But if renaming the 14/28hp M.G. Super Sports Morris as the M.G. 14/40 MkIV might be regarded as a marketing sleight of hand, the end of 1927 marked something much more significant. For the first time the cars were registered as M.G.s and not as Morrises. In administrative terms, then, the first M.G. car dates from 1927. But these cars are the same – give or take a few trinkets – as those previously registered as Morrises, and which have a lineage going back to those Raworth two-seaters of 1923.

If we take a genealogical approach we can therefore say – using our words carefully – that the M.G. marque can trace its origins back to…not 1925…not 1924…but 1923. Whether that makes the first Raworth the first M.G. or whether the first M.G. is the first car to be registered as such, late in 1927, is something readers can decide for themselves.

The six Raworth-bodied two-seaters – this is the Arkell car – have genetics on their side. (Early M.G. Society)

ACKNOWLEDGEMENTS

This book would not have been possible without the kindness of members of the Kimber family, who welcomed me into their homes, fed and sometimes lodged me, and provided testimony, documentation and access to photographic material. Special thanks go to Kim McGavin, Joe McGavin, Pete McGavin, Sara Delamont and Edward and Easter Kirkland; thanks also to Dean Delamont and Elwyn John Kimber (formerly Jonathan Delamont) for their assistance.

The bulk of the photos in this book come from the collections of the above. For other images I am grateful to the following: Jon Day at the National Motor Museum, Elin Bornemann at the Abingdon County Hall Museum, Sarah-Jane Wilson at BMIHT, Kevin Wood and Zoë Schafer at Motorsport Images, Andrew Webb at the IWM, Ken Martin of the Morris Register, Kate Clendenning at RM Sotheby's, Alastair Clements at *Classic & Sports Car*, Andy Knott and Pete Neal at the M.G. Car Club, Richard Monk at the MGOC, Chris Keevill of the Early M.G. Society, Richard Dredge at Magic Car Pics, Peter Seymour, Mike Allison, Karl Ludvigsen and Trevor Lloyd. Particular thanks go to Mike Jones for making available a large amount of material relating to Goldie Gardner, and to Malcolm Green of Magna Press for so generously – and swiftly – providing many images. For their work printing and scanning photos, thanks go to Jean-Louis Nespoulous and Nelly Blaya.

Documentary research has been made more agreeable by the warm welcome received at the Bodleian Library (thank you to Amy Ebrey), the Oxfordshire History Centre in Oxford and the British Library in London, and from Patrick Collins at the National Motor Museum at Beaulieu and Trevor Dunmore at the RAC Club.

Advice on medical matters has been provided by my old friend Dr Ian Brown, guidance on sailing by Bobbie and Jean-Louis Grenier, and identification of motorcycles from James Hewing of the National Motorcycle Museum and James Robinson of *The Classic MotorCycle* magazine. For insights into Cecil Kimber's musical tastes I am grateful to Peter Cook of the M.G. Car Club, while for last-moment Oxford research the team at the Oxfordshire Local History Association came to the rescue.

Thanks for their support and help also goes to Howard Quayle and Pete Neal at the M.G. Car Club, Chris Keevill, Keith Herkes and Geoff Radford of the Early M.G. Society, David Knowles, Phil Jennings, Jonathan Wood, Russell Hayes, Cathelijne Spoelstra, John Lakey, Mike Allison and David Burgess-Wise, and to friends Alex and Nelly for keeping me smiling. Finally, my heartfelt gratitude to Jodi Ellis for the patience, understanding and skill she has expended on the design of this book.

BIBLIOGRAPHY

This list is not exhaustive, but identifies the key secondary sources.

Allison, Mike and Browning, Peter: *The Works MGs* (Haynes)

Barraclough, R.I. and Jennings, P.L.: *Oxford to Abingdon* (Myrtle Publishing)

Clausager, Anders Ditlev: *MG Saloon Cars* (Bay View Books)

Gardner, A.T.G.: *Magic MPH* (Motor Racing Publications)

Haining, Peter: *The MG Log* (Souvenir Press / Greenwich Editions)

Howlett, John: *The Guv'nor* (Howlett)

Hywel, William: *Modest Millionaire – The biography of Captain Vivian Hewitt* (Gwasg Gee)

Jennings, P.L.: *Early M.G.* (Jennings)

Knudson, Richard (ed): *The Cecil Kimber Centenary Book* (New England M.G. T Register)

Lyndon, Barré: *Circuit Dust* (John Miles)

Lyndon, Barré: *Combat – a Motor Racing History* (Heinemann)

McComb, Wilson: *MG by McComb* (Osprey)

Pressnell, Jon: *Morris – The Cars and the Company* (Haynes)

Thomas, Sir Miles: *Out on a Wing* (Michael Joseph)

Thornley, John: *Maintaining the Breed* (MRP)

Wentworth Day, James: *Kaye Don – The Man* (Hutchinson)

Wood, Jonathan: *MG from A to Z* (MRP)

INDEX

Abbey Coachworks 210, 213-214
ABC 471
ABC aero-engines 47
Abingdon Sailing Club 317
AC Cars 47, 50-52
Adler 245
    2½-litre 444
    Trumpf 442-443, 454-455
Alfa Romeo 196, 224, 256, 509
    1½-litre 471, 495
    8C-2300 231
Allingham, Henry 235-236, 239, 243-244
Allison, Mike 135, 211, 236, 264, 269, 391
Alpine Trial 213, 224
Aluminium-Français Grégoire 415
Alvis 110, 239, 397-398
    12/50 92
    4.3-litre 456
André-Girling suspension 405, 466, 478

Andrews and Brunner 9, 74, 55, 120, 253, 387-390, 395
Angus-Sanderson 54-56
Anstey, Bill 389
Appleby, Barry 236, 280, 368-369
Appleby, Ernest 151, 236, 280, 305, 308, 369
Architects' Journal (The) 433
Architectural Review (The) 433
Arkell, Oliver 81, 86, 523
Armstead, Edward 77
Armstrong Siddeley 14hp 456
Armstrong Whitworth 403
    Albemarle bomber 381, 387, 393, 497
Arrol-Johnston 63
Aspin engine 463, 495
Aston Martin 516
Asturias, Prince of the 89
Austin 72-75, 259-260, 482, 491, 493, 506
    3-litre 510
    Maxi 513
    Seven 78, 134-135, 182, 202, 251, 263, 479, 489-491
Austin-Healey
    100 506-507
    3000 508, 510
    Sprite 508, 513, 515
Auto Union 140, 256-257, 335, 343, 479, 483, 494
Autocar (The) 127, 135, 137-138, 148, 151, 157, 159, 163, 177, 178, 182, 183, 191, 193, 212, 223, 235, 236, 239, 245, 247, 255, 267, 269, 275-276, 279-280, 289, 297, 305, 331, 373, 405, 416, 421, 422, 424, 435, 471
Automobile Engineer (The) 459
Autovac 469

Bailey, W.B. 166
Barnes, Stanley 203, 374
Barraclough and Jennings 9, 81, 92, 95, 131, 522
Barson, Bill 116
Barton, Frank 59, 101
Bastock, Jack 302
Beaverbrook, Lord 380, 392-393
Bédélia 469-470
Beevor, Miles 426-427
Beiderbecker, Bix 358
Bell Hotel, Tewkesbury 398

Bell, Adrian 358
Belsize / Belsize-Bradshaw 63, 471
Belsize Contract Furnishing Company 433
Bennett, Sam 149-151, 247
Bentley 329
    3-litre 471
    3½-litre 276
    8-litre 47
Bentley, W.O. 485
Bicycling News 15
Birkin, Sir Henry 216-219, 411, 493
Black, Captain Sir John 406-407, 411-412, 421
Black, Norman 181, 265, 490-491
Blériot aircraft 46
Blériot Whippet 471
BMC 68, 72-75, 361, 506-513, 519
    1100/1300 511, 513
    Fireball 513
    Mini 116, 513, 516
BMC Competitions Department 508
BMW 518
BOAC 392
Boden, Oliver 297, 391
Bolster, John 113, 194-195, 216
Boniface Sheepskin Company 167
Booth, Albert & Co 166
Boston Deep Sea Fishing Company 422
Bournemouth Daily Echo 304-305
Breeden, Carl 77
Briault, D.L. 260

British Aerospace 516
British Leyland Motor Corporation (BLMC or BL) 429, 513-518
British Motor Corporation see BMC
British Motor Heritage 516
Brixton Bicycling Club 17
Brooke, Rupert 358
Brooklands 45-47, 50, 79, 140, 157, 164, 177-178, 182, 202, 213, 223, 224, 237, 242, 255, 255, 257, 260, 263, 270, 284, 323, 470, 479, 486-494
Brooklands Gazette (The) 91
Brown motorcycle 469
Brown, David 412
Brown, Reg 90
Browning, Peter 405
Bruce, J.M. 50-52
Brunell, Bill 204
Brunell, Kitty 204
Budd Steel Corporation 68, 414, 466
Bugatti 159
Bugatti, Ettore 255
Buick 446-447, 473
Buist (Newcastle-on-Tyne) 79
Bull, Wallace 17
BUPA 72
Burgess-Wise, David 211
Burgess, Frank 493
Butler, Dr Harrison 316, 328

Calcott 470
Callingham, Leslie 140, 487, 489
Calthorpe 470
Campbell, Donald 330
Campbell, Sir Malcolm 263, 266-267, 330, 331, 347-351, 489
Cannell, John 398
Cannell, William 391
Caracciola, Rudolf 490-491
Carbodies 78-79, 90-92, 98, 109, 110, 115, 135, 156, 159, 184, 193, 235-236, 244, 289
Charles, Hubert Noel (H.N.) 114-115, 135, 148-149, 160, 164, 171-172, 183, 196, 216, 239, 245, 246, 250, 252, 259, 261, 266-267, 269, 395, 493
Charlesworth 278, 284, 397-398

Charlie's Aunt 304
Charnock, Harry 77, 117, 121
Chassagne 470
Chater-Lea motorcycle 469
Chetwynd, Hon Mrs 490
Chevrolet 453-454
Chiesman, Russel 79, 81, 86, 131, 139, 280, 305, 307
Chrysler 453-454
    Airflow 442-435, 454
Churchill, Sir Winston 380
Circuit Dust 225
Citroën 414, 491
    DS 405
    Traction Avant 245, 414
Citroën, André 414
Civilian Repair Organisation (CRO) 392-393
Clark tractors and forklifts 500
Clark, Ned 19, 22, 25
Classic Cars 433
Claudel-Hobson 403
Clausager, Anders Ditlev 276
Clease, Douglas 459
Coatalen, Louis 470
Cobb, John 234, 335, 347-348
Colegrove, Ted 164, 183
Combat 79, 106, 114-115, 225, 488, 492, 520
Connolly, Harold 133, 160, 189, 202-203, 277-279, 332, 403, 406
Cook, Dennis 433
Cook, Jean Kimber see Kimber, Jean
Cooper, Billy 522
Cooper, George 148, 246
Cooper, John 508
Coppa Acerbo 242
Cord 446, 449, 451
Corduroy 358
Corsica Coachworks 209, 226-227
Cousins, Cecil 9, 79, 84-85, 87, 95-96, 99, 107, 114-117, 131, 134-135, 164, 190, 493, 521-522
Cowper, 'Captain' 293
Crabtree (first name unknown) 490, 492
Craigantlet hillclimb 182, 411
Crawfords 328

'Cream Crackers' 301-303
Cromwell, Oliver 11
Crosby, Frederick Gordon 163
Crossley 47
Crown and Thistle, Abingdon 306, 325, 327
Crusader tank 381, 505
Crystal Palace 479-480
Curtiss aircraft 46
Cushman, Leon 491

Daily Express 280, 421
Daily Graphic 504
Daily Mail 87
Daily Telegraph (The) 421, 423
Daimler 75, 95
Daks 328

ABOVE: *Kimber's card-index of addresses.*

OPPOSITE BOTTOM LEFT: *A rather charming pocket barometer.*

OPPOSITE TOP RIGHT: *One of Kimber's earlier cameras.*

Daniels, Jack 116, 148, 246
Daniels, Stewart 276
Davidson, Ronald 102, 105
Davies, Rev B.H. ('Ixion') 479-481
Davis, S.C.H. (Sammy) 267
De Clifford, Lord Edward 216
Delage 466
Delamont, Dean 304-305, 310, 313, 330, 374, 384-385
Delamont, Jonathan (E.J. Kimber) 14, 316, 433
Delamont, Sara 43, 172, 206-207, 211, 305, 310, 357-358, 385, 432-433
Denly, Bert 202, 233
Derrington, Vic 226
Dewar, Muriel (Gillie) 206-207, 288, 305, 310, 318-320, 325-328, 330, 350, 353-359, 365, 371, 376, 381-384, 393, 397-402, 406-409, 421, 427, 431-432
Dewar, Owen 206
Dewar, Pauline (Bobbie) 9, 206-207, 288, 304-305, 308, 325, 327-328, 330-331, 350, 353, 356-357, 365, 374, 376-378, 384, 397-398, 401, 407, 421, 425-427
Dewhurst, Frank 47
Dixon, Freddie 491
Dodge 75
    Victory Six 71
Dodson, Charlie 242, 493
Don, Kaye 239, 264-267
Donington 255, 479, 481, 483, 486-487
Dono, George 389, 504

Douglas motorcycles 63, 75
Downer (first name unknown) 316
Dresden Unversity 13
Driscoll, L.P. (Pat) 260, 491
Druck, Charles 240
Duesenberg 471
Dugdale, John 9, 194, 231, 255, 257, 288-290, 305, 331, 334
Dulwich College 13

Early M.G. 117, 121
'Ebby' (A.V. Ebblewhite) 481
Eberan von Eberhorst, Robert 343
Edgar, Alfred 79
Edge, S.F. 47
Edmondson, Bill 489
Edwards, Wendy 144
Eldridge, E.A.D. 491
Emergency Services Organisation 380
Enever, Syd 148, 334, 340-341, 361, 363
Enfield-Allday Radial 471
ERA 255, 486
Eustace Watkins 243
Eustace, Albert 109, 116
Evans, Doreen 240, 281
Ewing, Norman 203, 277
Eyston, George 181-182, 202, 209, 214-219, 233, 239-240, 242, 250, 259, 302, 331, 343, 347, 489-493

Fairwind 316, 321, 328, 336, 365, 374
Falcon 290-293, 321
Ferguson R4 418
Ferguson, Harry 395, 398, 402-405, 411-419
Ferguson, Victor 411
Fiat X1/9 514
Fisher and Ludlow 68
Fitzmaurice, Captain 442-435
Fitzwilliam, Earl 47, 470
Flat Out 182, 214
Ford 412-414
    Anglia/Popular/Prefect 413
    Cortina 513
    Model T 65
    V8 447-448

Ford, Henry 412
Fordson tractor 411-412
Fraser, Robert Atkin 166
French Grand Prix 242
Froy, Dudley 491

Gardiner, Jack 79, 90-92, 521-522
Gardner, Goldie 200, 203-205, 231, 239, 241, 268, 301, 322-323, 325, 327, 331-335, 340-351, 359-365, 379, 422, 479-480, 490, 492-504
Garner Booth / Garnar-Scotblair 167
Gentleman's Magazine (The) 12
George Hotel, Silsoe 409
George, Prince 221
Gibbs Nan/Ann 290-293
Gibbs, Bill 140, 175, 200, 202, 205, 245, 272, 290-293
Gibson (first name unknown) 148
Gilchrist 102
Gloster Aircraft 330, 398
Glyn, Elinor 105
Gouvy (first name unknown) 287
Graham, Eric 330, 398, 431-432
Grahame-White 469
Graves-Morris, Cecil 206
Graves, Robert 433
'Grazide' 489
Grégoire, Jean-Albert 414-415
Grosse Bergpreis von Deutschland hillclimb 224
Guy's Hospital 72
Hall, Eddie 179, 202, 223-224, 239, 260, 490, 492

Hall, Joan 239
Hamilton, Claud Reginald Matheson 206
Hamilton, Gladys 206-207, 305, 318-320, 325-327, 350, 376, 381, 383, 394
Hamilton, Hugh 200, 202-203, 216-219, 224-225, 267-268, 411, 491-492
Handasyde, George Harris 50
Hanks, Reginald (Reggie) 75, 140, 389, 504
Harpenden Co-ed School 272
Harriman, George 513
Harry Ferguson Research 418
Hastings, Harold 6, 406-409
Hawker Siddeley 398
Hawker Hurricane 415
   Tempest 505
Healey, Donald 403-406, 506, 508
Healeys and Austin-Healeys 405
Heidelberg University 13
Hendy, Frank 316
Hennessey, Patrick 412
Herbert, L.F. 425-426
Herring, Harry 135
Hesse, Prince Richard of 344-345
Hewitt, Vivian 45-47, 50, 134, 470
Hicks, Jack 160
Higginson, Joseph 469-470
Hillman 75
Hispano-Suiza 42, 45, 134, 415, 449, 470
Hitler, Adolf 340, 362
Hobbs, Wilfred 148, 151
Hollick and Pratt 78, 82, 92
Honda 516, 518
Horsch, Dr 308
Horton, Ronnie 202, 322, 333, 335, 486, 490, 492
Hotchkiss 68, 130
Hotson, Mark 266
Hounslow, Alec 226
Howe, Earl 216-219, 222, 225, 237, 492-493
Howes (first name unknown) 116
Howlett, John 380-383, 387, 393-395
Hudson 75
Hughes & Kimber 12-13, 17
Hughes, Clarey 90-91

Hughes, Richard 12
Hughes, Sarah 12
Hühnlein, Adolf 344-345
Humber 63, 75
Humberette 470
Hunt, Aimée 41-42
Hunt, Charles 40-42, 45
Hunt, Irene (Rene) see Kimber, Rene
Hupmobile 63

ICI 14
Illustrated London News 440
'Imshi' 89
Indianapolis 255
Institute of the Motor Trade 528
Institution of Automobile Engineers 27, 37, 47, 55, 115, 245, 256, 281, 297-300, 399, 405, 439
Irish International Grand Prix 182, 490
Isis (The) 78, 87, 193-194
Issigonis, Sir Alec 116, 409, 501, 513
Iver Grammar School 13

Jackson Runabout 469
Jackson, Reg 134-135, 181, 203, 236, 264, 269, 330, 341, 363, 395, 489
Jackson, Robin 236-237, 341
Jaguar E-type 513
   XK engine 361
Jamieson, Murray 260, 263
Jaray, Paul 334, 445
Jarman, Lytton 9, 84, 107, 116, 135, 190, 521-522
Jarvis of Wimbledon 182, 240
Jeep 413-414
Jeffress, Randolph 203
Jennings, P.L. 9, 92, 95
Jensen 198, 202, 506
Jones, Bobby 92

K-series engine 518
Kaiser, Henry 414-416
Kaye Don - The Man 266-267
Keller, J.H. 278, 329
Kendall, Denis 414-418
Kennington W.O. 439, 449, 459

ABOVE: *Kimber's motoring coat, on display at the MGCC offices in Abingdon.*

OPPOSITE TOP LEFT: *A silver ink well presented to Kimber after the first M.G. sortie to Le Mans in 1930.*

OPPOSITE RIGHT BOTTOM: *This bronze celebrating Eyston's 113.38mph at Pendine in 1932 was one of Kimber's desk ornaments.*

Kent, Duke of 411
Kesselberg hillclimb 252
Kesterton, Les 341
Kimber & Bull 17
Kimber Brothers 17, 27
Kimber, Betty (Lisa) 53, 56-57, 80, 94, 102, 127, 140, 168-169, 171, 174-175, 207, 211, 226, 241, 249, 272-273, 292, 295, 304-306, 310-316, 321, 327, 336-337, 350, 354-358, 365, 374, 384-385, 402, 425, 427, 432-433
Kimber, Edward 11-13, 17
Kimber, Fanny 13-15, 23, 26, 33
Kimber, Henry 13-17, 39
Kimber, Isaac 11-12
Kimber, Jean *passim*
Kimber, Phyllis 18, 23, 25, 33
Kimber, Rene 39-49, 53, 56-57, 78, 80-81, 94, 97, 105, 114, 128-129, 131, 140-141, 144, 160, 168-169, 172-173, 195, 202-211, 241, 249, 272-275, 280, 288, 290, 295, 304-316, 325, 393, 433
Kimber, Richard 11
Kimber, Richard Godsell 12
Kimber, Sydney 15, 385, 402-403, 406
Kimber, Vernon 13, 19, 29, 38-39, 43, 52, 55-56, 106, 290, 293, 304
Kimber, Walter 17

Kindell, Fred 160, 489-490
Kingerlee, Carl 140, 175, 209, 295, 374, 387-388
Kingerlee, Eileen 209, 295
Kingerlee, Felice 295
Kirk, Cecil 421
Kirkland, Easter 206, 353
Knudsen, Richard (Dick) 9, 85
Kohlrausch, Bobby 250-252, 260, 305, 331, 480, 495
Kop Hill hillclimb 485
Ku Klux Klan 32

La Buire 470
Lacey, Clive 374, 400
Lagonda 469
Lancashire Automobile Club 47
Lancashire Motor Club 469
Lancaster bomber 497
Lancia 509
    Augusta 198
Land Rover 413
Land's End Trial 79, 81, 86, 100-102, 128, 131, 139-140, 157, 374, 461, 470, 488, 520-521
Langley, Archie 302
Lanstad, Hans 290, 293

Lauder, Harry 358
Lawrence, T.I. & Co 13
Laystall 195
Le Mans 157, 160, 216, 242, 250, 481, 489-491, 506, 508
Lea-Francis 406
League of Industry 71
Lean, David 433
Lee, Ted 82, 85-86
Leeds High School for Girls 42
Leek, Sybil 312, 316
Light Car and Cycle Car (The) 38, 66, 160, 426
Lincoln Zephyr 444
Linfield, H.S. 422
London & North Eastern Railway (LNER) 424-427
London and Suburban Meat Stores 47
London Magazine (The) 11
London School of Economics 163
Lord, Leonard (Len) 70-71, 75, 233, 245, 252, 264, 269-271, 275, 297, 391, 417-418, 506, 508
Lorraine, Alsace 272
Lowndes, Jack 101, 148
Lucas, Oliver 77, 347
Lund, Edward 6, 393
Lurani, Johnny 209, 211-219, 242
Lyndon, Barré 79, 106, 114-115, 225, 488, 492, 520
Lyons, Sir William 187, 276, 278, 300
Lytton, Sir Henry 169

Macclesfield, Earl of 66
MacDermid, 'Mac' 302
Magic MPH 331
Maillard-Brune, Philippe 240
Making Modest Production Pay in Motor-Car Manufacture 47, 55, 115, 256, 435
Man, Isle of 242, 255, 264-267
Manchester Guardian (The) 47, 423
Manchester High School for Girls 43
Manchester Motor Club 47, 469
Manchester Royal Infirmary 31
Manchester Technical School 28, 469
Manchester University 43
March, Earl of (Duke of Richmond) 140, 171, 173, 178, 416-418
Martin, Helmuth Paul 50

Martin, Lionel 470
Martinsyde 47, 50-52, 81
Maserati 196, 255, 267
Mathews, Florence 109
Mathews, Wilfrid (Wilf) 100, 102, 109, 528-529
Matilda tank 380-381
Matthewman, Sidney and Elizabeth 14
Matthewman, Fanny see Kimber, Fanny
McComb, Wilson 9, 12-13, 15, 38-39, 52, 77, 88, 114, 130-131, 171, 182, 189, 202-203, 211, 226, 233, 246, 252, 267, 304, 330, 358, 380, 395, 403, 427, 432-433, 521
McConnell, Hugh 216-219
McEvoy, Michael 239, 260, 360
McGavin, Eric 374, 402, 408, 425-426, 433
McGavin, Kim 371, 374, 431-433
McGavin, Peter 306
McGuire, William Anthony 94
McLaren, Bruce 508
Mechins 55
Melburn, Norman 433
Mercedes-Benz 257, 331, 335, 338, 343, 362, 454, 479-480, 483, 491, 494-495
Mercury 402, 425
M.G. Car Club 107, 160-163, 166, 182, 189, 195-196, 202, 212, 273, 275, 276, 278, 358, 365, 375
M.G. Magazine (The) 209, 222, 224, 226, 265
M.G. models
    18/80 71, 127-136, 139, 154-164, 182, 212, 487, 489
    1100/1300 510-511
    Maestro/Montego 516
    Magna F-type 182-189, 196, 198, 204, 212-215, 492
    Magna L-type 187, 199, 209-210, 212-215, 224, 228-229, 233-234, 244
    Magnette K-type 197-200, 203, 209, 213-219, 223-227, 230, 233-234, 239-240, 242, 244, 247, 251-252, 260, 263, 301, 411, 486, 492, 494-495, 510
    Magnette N-type 199, 213, 233, 236, 239, 242-244, 247, 275-276, 297, 301-302, 493
    Magnette Z-type 505-506, 510
    Magnette (Farina) 510
    Metro 516
    MGA 506-507
    MGB 497, 508-509, 513-516, 520
    MGC 510-511
    MGF and TF 518-519
    Midget M-type 134-140, 142-143, 147, 157-161, 164, 173, 182-183, 185, 189, 237, 488
    Midget C-type (Montlhéry or MkII) 177-183, 186-187, 202-203, 216, 411
    Midget D-type 173, 183, 186-187
    Midget J-type 189-195, 212, 224-225, 233, 235-236, 247, 251-252, 302, 411, 492, 494
    Midget P-type 233, 235-236, 238-240, 247, 275-276, 302-303, 493-494
    Midget Q-type 236-239, 255, 257, 259, 494
    Midget T-type 189, 235, 288-290, 301-303, 322, 359, 361, 366-367, 373, 473, 498-501, 514-507
    Midget (1961-1979) 510, 513, 515
    R-type 252, 255, 257-264, 269-270, 276, 494
    RV8 516-518
    SA (Two-Litre) 276-287, 295, 299, 301, 322, 326-329, 338-339, 359, 366-367, 397-398, 456, 497
    Super Sports (and 14/40) 77, 81-111, 117-123, 363, 521-523
    VA (1½-litre) 297, 300-310, 314-315, 318, 322, 359, 366-367, 371, 373, 378, 421, 424, 459, 497
    WA 278, 301, 328-330, 338-339, 359, 366-367, 379, 398, 497
    X Power SV 519
    Y-type 498-502
    Z-series 518-519
M.G. prototypes, experimental cars and record-breakers
    ADO21 513-515
    ADO34 511, 513
    EX120 181-182, 489-490
    EX127 182, 202, 233, 250, 331, 490-491, 495
    EX135 198, 239, 324-325, 331-335, 340-342, 349, 351, 361-364
    EX150 245, 264, 275-276
    EX172 506-507
    EX179 182
    EX181 182
    EX234 513
MG Rover 518-519
MG Saloon Cars 276
Mille Miglia 209, 214, 216-222, 224, 237-239, 242, 255, 331, 405, 493
Milnes family 42

Monk family 151, 249, 288, 373
Monte Carlo Rally 154, 181-182
Montlhéry 202, 216, 233, 255, 322, 489-492
Moore, John 421
Morris 482, 498, 506
    25hp 276
    Eight 71-73, 498, 502, 505
    Fifteen-Six 72-73
    F-type six-cylinder 94-95, 130
    Isis 71
    Minor (pre-war) 71, 116, 134-135, 137, 183, 189, 275, 488, 492
    Minor (post-war) 500-501, 505, 508
    Oxford and Cowley 64-67, 77-100, 134
    Oxford (post-war) 502
    Oxford Six 390

ABOVE: *Kimber's octagonal cufflinks and collar studs.*

OPPOSITE: *The inscribed silver cigarette cases Kimber and Gillie gave each other.*

Morris, continued
- Six 71, 131, 134
- Six (post-war) 361, 502
- Ten 289, 390
- Twelve 297

Morris Bodies Branch 92, 193, 236, 244, 302, 389, 497
Morris Commercial Cars 56, 134, 151, 245, 246, 391, 497
Morris Engines Ltd (Morris Engines Branch) 56, 68, 70, 102, 157, 275, 487
Morris Garages, The 50, 56, 59, 63-64, 75, 77-101, 120-121, 135, 246, 471, 522
Morris Industries Exports 246
Morris Industries Ltd 68, 117, 323
Morris Motors (1926) Ltd 68, 114, 245-246, 270
Morris Owner (The) 68, 186, 191, 234, 264, 422-423, 426
Morris Radiators Branch 106, 114, 504
Morris-Léon-Bollée 112-113, 140, 522
Morris, Frederick 63
Morris, George 156
Morris, Lillian (Lady Nuffield) 113, 388-389, 393
Morris, Sir William (Lord Nuffield) 9, 53-56, 59-75, 77, 86, 92, 109, 112-117, 127, 134, 148, 151-152, 154-155, 163, 172, 178, 202, 216, 218, 221, 224, 233, 237-239, 245, 246, 252-257, 267-268, 271, 276, 281, 297, 310, 331, 334-335, 367, 370-371, 387-395, 403, 411-412, 473, 501-502
Mosley, Sir Oswald 218
Motor (The) 55, 98, 102, 136, 140, 151, 185, 196, 216, 245, 251-252, 255-257, 270, 276, 281, 297, 300, 303, 310, 323, 327, 331, 334-335, 338, 346-348, 364, 367, 371, 373, 387-395, 424
Motor Cycle Club 101
Motor Cycle (The) 29, 479
Motor Enthusiasts Club (Birmingham) 56
Motor Sport 91, 182, 202, 218, 259, 513
Mulliners (Birmingham) 275-277
Munro, Bill 91
Murton-Neale, Robert 160, 489
Mussolini, Benito 331

Nanjing Automobile 519
Neptune amphibian 497, 500
Nichols, Charles 297
North American MMM Register 149

Norton motorcycle 35
Nuffield Foundation 63
Nuffield, Lord see Morris, Sir William
Nuffield Mechanisations 499-500
Nuffield Metal Products 504
Nuffield Organization 72, 140, 391-393, 427, 504
Nuffield Trophy 268
Nuffield Universal Tractor 500
Nürburgring 490
Nuvolari, Tazio 211, 224-226, 257, 411

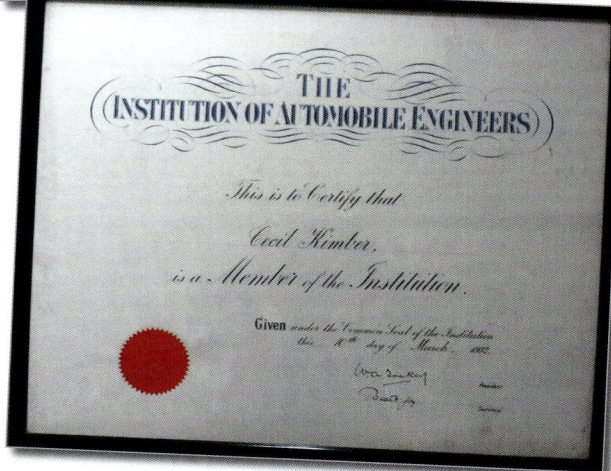

ABOVE: *Two of Kimber's certificates of association.*

OPPOSITE: *One of two of Kimber's tobacco cabinets on display at the MGCC offices.*

O-series engine 516
Opel 253, 453-454
Out on a Wing 130-131, 297, 393, 395
Oxford Automobile & Cycle Agency 59, 62
Oxford Garage (The) 63
Oxford High School for Girls 310, 381
Oxford Journal Illustrated 114
Oxford Motor Club 100
Oxford Times (The) 115, 266
Oxford University 72, 211

Packard 449
Palmes, Jimmy 181-182, 240
Panhard 415
Park Ward 289
Parker, Harold 140
Parkside Garage 79
Paterson, Oscar 200
Paul, Cyril 203
Paulhan, Louis 469
Pavlova Leather Company 147-148, 166-167, 381, 514
Pavlova, Anna 166
Peat Marwick 163
Pen-y-Grwyd Hotel 37, 469
Pendine Sands 202, 491
Pendrell, Arthur George 131
Penn-Hughes, Clifton 219, 242
Perkins 421
Phillips, George 506
Phoenix Consortium 518
Pilcher, Reverend 60
Pininfarina 497
Pittard 167
Plymouth Brethren 305
Pollard, Arthur 489
Pomeroy, Laurence 239, 260, 338, 342, 344
Porsche 270, 519
Porsche, Ferdinand 257
Portwine, John 47, 51
Powerplus supercharger 240
Pratt, Lancelot 78, 82
Pressed Steel 68, 71, 414, 504, 509
Preston, Kiki 221

Price Waterhouse 151
Propert, George 134, 164, 181, 203, 305
Punch 94

Quadrant motorcycle 469
Qvale Mangusta 527

RAC 304, 398, 408, 432, 491, 493
RAC Rally 452
Railton, Reid 331-335
Rally cyclecar 186
Ramsbottom, John 385
Randall, Cecil 497
Raworth, Charles 81-89, 109, 522-523
Reed, John Henry 116
Reeves, A.W. 47
Reinbolt & Christé 278, 301, 329
Remembering Kim 353, 374
Renault 73
Resta, Dario 470
Rex motorcycle 28-33, 469
Reynolds, John 398
Ridley, Viscount 490-491
Riley 72, 197, 270, 276, 338, 405-406, 469, 491-492, 504-505, 510
   1½-litre and 2½-litre (RM) 498, 502-505
   One-point-Five 507
   Pathfinder 513, 508
   Two-point-Six 508
Roberts, Morley 14
Robson, Graham 148, 246
Roe motorcycle 469
Roesch, Georges 346
Rolls-Royce 381, 449, 470, 473,
   Merlin/Griffon engine 381, 497-498
   Silver Ghost 469
Rootes Group 403
Rootes, Sir Reginald 74
Rootes, Sir William (Billy) 74
Rostock University 12
Rothschild, Victor 164
Rover 516
   2000 405

25 519
6hp 469
75 519
Rowse, Arthur 390-391
Royal Air Force 11
Royal Aircraft Factory SE5a aircraft 52
Royal Enfield motorcycle 63
Royal Geographical Society 12
Rubin, Bernard 216-219, 493
Russell, Charles 427
Ryder, Harold 497, 499-500

Safety Fast 107, 117, 121, 148-149
Safety Fast in the Making 299
SAIC 519
Sallon, Ralph 234
Sampson, Maurice 159
Samuelson, Sir Francis 154-155, 160, 489-491
Sanchez Cires, Alberto 488
Savernake Glove Company 167
Savoy Hotel 47
Scott motorcycles 75
Sea Witch 402, 425
Seaward, Harry 389-390
Selby, T.G.V. 216
Seymour, Peter 77
Sheffield-Simplex 47, 50-52, 470, 487
Shell-Mex 140, 495
Shelsley Walsh 179, 260, 461
Simpson, Jim 149, 211-212
Simpsons 328
Singer 63
   10hp 37-38, 470
   15.9hp 37, 42, 44-47, 50-52, 470, 487
   Nine Le Mans 250
'Six-Cylinder Love' 94
Sizaire-Naudin 469
Skinner, Barbara 240
Slade School of Fine Art 14
Slingsley, Bill 360
Smallbone, Kimpton 297, 389-391, 395, 497
Smith, Geoffrey 398
Smith, Rowland 414

Smith, W. (H.) 12
Smiths 297
Society of Motor Manufacturers and Traders 485
Spa 24-hour race 489
Specialloid 398-407, 416-417, 421, 426-427, 431, 492
Sporting Life 216
Sports Car (The) 92, 222, 259-260, 269-270, 300, 346, 360, 375, 521
SS Cars 187, 276, 278, 338, 366-367, 406, 456
   SS Jaguar 278-279, 297, 301, 328-330, 366-367
St Andrews Steam Fishing Company 422
St Anne's College, Oxford 310
St James's Secretarial College 398
St John's College, Oxford 381-382
Standard 63, 278, 406
Staniland, Chris 178
Stanley-Turner, Dorothy 195
Stanley-Turner, Dr Henry 94
Stevens, Frank 135
Stevenson, John 94
Stevenson, Kathy/Kattney 81, 94, 144, 174

Stewart, Gwenda (Mrs Douglas Hawkes) 490
Steyr 458
Stockport Grammar and Free School 17
SU Carburettor Company 240, 246, 341
Sun motorcycle 50
Sunbeam 75, 264
    3-litre 471
    Grand Prix 470-471
Sunbeam motorcycle 63, 90
Sunbeam-Talbot 406
Sunday Express 239
Supermarine Spitfire 392, 415
Sutton, Billy 29, 32-33
System 114

T&T (Thomson & Taylor) 491
Tate, John 166
Tatra 443-444
Taw and Torridge Sailing Club 140
Tayler, Frankie 264-267
The Descendants of Richard Kimber 11-13
The Evolution of a Yachtsman 19, 22-23, 140, 171-172
The Future of Motor Racing 331
The Guv'nor 381, 387, 393-394
The Long Rifle 358
The Luck of the Game 182
The MG Log 15, 50, 276-277, 288, 359, 393
The Other Tack 50, 105, 127, 151, 171-172, 211, 206, 209, 293, 353, 384, 395, 402, 427
The Trend of Aesthetic Design in Motor Cars 297-300, 435
Thomas, Sir Miles 68, 74, 130-131, 193, 245, 253, 264, 269-271, 297, 390-393, 497-502
Thornley, John 6, 148-149, 160, 163. 185, 191-193, 246, 269-270, 290, 322, 375, 391-392, 409, 497, 504, 508
'Three Musketeers' 302-303
Tickford 278, 281-282, 289, 297, 305, 367
Times, The 266, 423
Tobin, Edward 120, 350
Tongue, Reggie 193-194
Toulmin, Maurice 302
Tourist Trophy (TT) 181-182, 190, 200-205, 224-225, 239, 242, 255, 411, 480-481, 490-493
Tractors and Transmissions Branch 504

Trinity College, Cambridge 240
Triple-M Yearbook 149, 211
Triumph 338, 403-406, 515
    1800 Roadster 406
    Acclaim 516
    Dolomite 406
    Gloria 250, 276
    Spitfire 514
    TR2 507
    TR7 514-516
Triumph motorcycle 29, 63, 425, 469
Tubbs, D.B. 276
Tuck, George 6, 153, 203, 277-279
Turner, Graham 390
Turner, Harry 102
TVR 516
Tylor, J. & Sons Ltd 55

Uhlik 192
Ulster Automobile Club 411
United Alkalis 14
University College Hospital 425
University Motors 143, 199, 330
Urban-Emmerich, Hugo 490-491

Van den Plas 192
Vanden Plas Princess 4-litre R 513
Vauxhall 449
    30/98 90, 470
    Prince Henry 470
Vickers-Armstrong Light Tank 380
Vindec Special motorcycle 469
Vindilis 328
Viner, Tom 211
Vogue 207
Voisin 95
Volkswagen 73, 359-360, 362
Vorhaus, Bernard 433
Vorhaus, David 433

Wakefield, Lord 489
Wales, Prince of (Duke of Windsor) 221, 411-412
Walkerley, Rodney 139, 255

Walkinton, John 207, 304-305, 356, 365, 374, 381, 426-427
Walsh, Andrew 148
Walton, Izaak 358
Ward, Thomas 403-405
Warrington and District Motor Cycle Club 29
Watt, James 405
Weller, John 47, 51
Wellworthy 380-381
Wentworth Day, James 266-267
Whitcroft, Cyril 500
White and Poppe 66
White Noise 433
Whittingham & Mitchel 236, 243-244
Who's Who in the Motor Industry 50
Who's Who in the Motor Trade 47, 50
Wilkins, Gordon 360
Wilks brothers 412
Wilmot-Breeden Ltd 77
Wisdom, Elsie 182, 205, 223
Wisdom, Tommy 202, 216, 409
Wister, Owen 358
Wolseley 63, 70, 113, 130, 134, 196, 245, 263, 275-276, 278, 367, 391, 498, 500, 504-505, 510
    12/48 297
    21/60 77
    6/80 361
    Hornet and Hornet Special 183, 185, 187, 196, 198-199, 243, 251, 492
    Super-Six (18/80) 276, 278, 280
    Ten 288-289, 469
    Twenty-Five (25hp) 276, 329
Wolseley Aero Engines Ltd 246, 297
Wood, Jonathan 82, 85-86, 167
Woodhouse, Jack 360, 363
Woollard, Frank 52-56, 68, 77, 131, 389-390
Wrigley, E.G. 50-56, 131
WRM Motors Ltd 66

Yachting World 316, 402, 421

Cecil Kimber's roll-top desk – see page 185 – is perhaps the prize item of Kimber memorabilia on display at Kimber House, the Abingdon headquarters of the M.G. Car Club.

Design:	Jodi Ellis Graphics
Printer:	Interpress Ltd, Hungary
Page Size:	290 mm x 254 mm
Text paper:	150gsm Magno Gloss
End paper:	140gsm Woodfree Offset
Dust jacket:	170gsm Glossy Artpaper
Casing:	Foil stamping on front and spine, on black Geltex, over 3 mm board
Chapter Heads:	36pt Bodega Sans Medium
Sub Heads:	22pt Bodega Sans Medium
Main Body Text:	13pt Kepler Standard Regular
Captions:	13pt Kepler Italic Caption